Understanding Research in Education

An Introductory Guide to Critical Reading

Edward M. Wolpert

Ball State University

D1708487

KENDALL/HUNT PUBLISHING COMPANY
Dubuque, Iowa, USA • Toronto, Ontario, Canada

Cover photo by Strix Pix,
David S. Strickler.

Copyright © 1981 by Kendall/Hunt Publishing Company

Library of Congress Catalog Card Number: 81-81350

ISBN 0-8403-2448-0

Printed in the United States of America

B   402448   01

To
Carolyn, Jim, and Linda

Contents

Preface

This is a book about research for consumers of research—educational research and research in related social sciences such as psychology, sociology, nursing. It is intended for both undergraduate and graduate students alike, whose purposes would be served by its unique treatment. In addition, it should be valuable to active professionals in these fields who need a review or new approach to the learning of this material.

There exists an immense body of research in the field of education and more is being added each day. The quality of this research varies widely, and accordingly one cannot merely read a study passively and then blithely accept its findings as a true indication of a social phenomenon. Most texts on the subject of educational research present the reader with the techniques and approaches used in the field, but the needs of a large portion of readers of such texts are not met by this type of a presentation. I have made a very fundamental distinction between two types of people who need to know about research. Some people, *producers* of research, will, in their professional lives, actually engage in research activities. They will formulate hypotheses, collect data, analyze data, and present findings to their professions. In order to be successful as research *producers,* they need to be expert in research methodology—the specific techniques used in research. These producers must have the type of understanding of the methodology of research to enable themselves to *apply* research techniques to become good producers of research. There are many excellent textbooks which address themselves to the needs of these research producers. This book is not really for them.

However, most people engaged in meaningful careers in education and related areas will in all probability never actually *produce* any research of note other than action type research or informal formative evaluations. Neither their professional responsibilities nor their innate proclivities will impel them to do more than this. On the other hand, they will be coming in contact with research in their respective professional journals. Indeed, a large part of their in-service professional growth will be determined by their ability to find, read, understand, evaluate, and utilize the research they encounter. They will be *consumers* of research rather than producers, and it is for these consumers that this book has been written.

What This Book Is Not—and What It Is

This book *is not* a "statistics" book, nor a "research methods" book, nor a "research techniques handbook." It is *not* meant to replace a text in a statistics class, nor is it designed to guide a person through the act of developing a proposal and executing a research study (although the information contained herein would provide excellent background and understanding of this activity).

This book *is* an introductory guide to the critical reading of educational research. It is introductory in that it provides basic, important information to research consumers but is not a treatise on the subject—there is more that could be written on any of the topics presented. It is aimed at practitioners in education and related fields, pre-service and in-service, who must focus on understanding and evaluating the conclusions derived from research studies rather than be expert in the techniques needed for conducting the research studies which yield these conclusions.

In order to understand research and critically evaluate it, it is necessary to know why, by whom, and how research studies are conducted. The focus of this book is on such matters. I have made no attempt to present information to readers which would discuss how to use specific procedures since the intended readers are not necessarily potential producers of research. Rather the portions of the text which deal with specific research procedures seek to develop an understanding of the procedures—what they are, why and when are they used, how to read and interpret them, what do they mean. With this and other information contained in the text readers will be able to read *critically* within the limits of their background and experience the research they encounter. I must emphasize the word *critically* in the last sentence. A mere reading with a surface understanding of a research study is not a highly desirable activity for a professional. If research is to be acted upon it should be believable—and in order to be deemed believable it must be read *critically* and found to be acceptable. Thus the ultimate objective of this book is the reader's consideration of the veracity of the findings of a given piece of research.

At the heart of any evaluation of a piece of research is the relationship of a study itself to the conclusions derived from it. Often this is stated as a question: *Are the conclusions from the study justified by the data?* Unfortunately, in answering this question the term *data* is frequently defined naively as the numbers or words which are analyzed for the purpose of answering the research question. With this definition of *data,* the determination of whether the conclusions are justified by the data is made by examining the consonance of the data with the conclusions. The starting point for this examination is with the body of data itself. It is my belief that such a practice does a disservice to the pursuit of truth.

The actual data which exist as part of a research study are but the result of many technical decisions which preceded their being—decisions such as research approach, design, instrumentation and analysis—as well as theory, context, and the characteristics of the researcher. These matters go well beyond the numbers and words which are subjected to analysis. They deal with the development of the data in the particular context of a given research study. In view of this ambiguity of the meaning of the word *data,* this book takes the point of view that the question *should not* be stated "Are the conclusions of the study justified by the *data,*" but rather *should be* stated, "Are the conclusions from the study justified by the *study itself.*" This question gets to the essence of critical reading of research and the development of background information to answer this question is what this book is all about.

There is an important sub-question which should be asked when evaluating a research study: are the conclusions from this study consistent with the conclusions from other studies? The answer to this question addresses the issue posed by a research question larger than that posed by any individual study but of which any individual study is a part. It is an important question the consideration of which presupposes on the part of the reader a background of theory and research in the area in which a given study is conducted. I have specifically not included material on this issue because I have found no satisfactory way in which this can be handled given the limitations of the scope of the book and its intended readership.

The Content of the Book

Part one introduces the reader to the idea of research: what it is and where to find it. Part two extends this information by considering the research process from the point of view of the researcher, and by presenting some basic concepts upon which are based many specific procedures used by researchers. Part three deals with the designs and methods used in experimental and descriptive methodologies. Parts four and five present material on how data are developed and analyzed. Emphasis is placed on knowing the scope of the available techniques and understanding the rationale for the techniques employed.

This book was developed with readers in mind. Its presentation style is characterized by numerous examples from the field of education as well as other fields. Its tone tends to be informal: this is not meant to belittle the importance of the subject, but rather to reflect the author's philosophy that anything worth doing is worth doing enjoyably. At the end of each chapter, will be found an annotated bibliography which will direct the readers to additional sources of information if they desire them. Preceding each part of the book is an "Author's Comment" which serves as a general introduction and overview of the forthcoming chapters. I take the liberty of expressing a few informal comments which I might make to the readers if I were to see them in person.

Instructors of courses in which this book may be used should be aware of three decisions I made regarding certain aspects of its content. First, in all cases of examples presented in this book, I have used hypothetical data in order to keep the presentation simple, brief, and direct. Hopefully, the data used are not too divergent from the data which might occur from a realization of the study they exemplify. Secondly, I have aimed this book at relatively unsophisticated potential consumers of research. These people could be at a bachelors or masters level or even beyond. I do not believe that there is a genuine dichotomy between the various degree levels which exists over educational institutions and over generations. To my way of thinking, an uninformed consumer is just that—regardless of the letters which will or do follow his or her name. And third, I have tried to deal openly and honestly with the weaknesses of educational research, especially its methodological limitations and the socio/political context in which it is conducted. One reviewer of an early draft of this book opined that to bring up "professional issues" to a neophyte was probably premature. Presumably, such people are at too tender a stage in their intellectual development to handle such a trauma. However, I find it inconceivable to expect anyone at any level of cognitive sophistication to read critically a given piece of research without attending to these professional issues. Their effect on research endeavors are profound and to ignore them is ill advised. Accordingly I have presented a frank discussion of these matters throughout the text whenever appropriate.

Readers of this book are encouraged to approach learning its content with rigor and with confidence. Albert Einstein has commented that the whole of science is nothing more than a refinement of everyday thinking. In the same spirit, I believe that understanding educational research is an extension of the use of common sense. Informed readers whose common sense has been thus extended will be more critical readers of the research they encounter in their fields and ultimately they will be more effective professionals. It is toward the accomplishment of this goal that this book has been conceived and written.

I am grateful to many people who have influenced the actualization of this book. My teachers have been many: those with whom I have had personal contact and those whose thoughts have come to me through their writings. The influence of my students at Ball State University as indicated by their expressed and unexpressed questions has been great. To all these people go my thanks.

Thanks also to my brother, Dr. Stephen M. Wolpert, and to my Ball State colleagues, Professors Larry Henriksen, Van Nelson and Jerry Ulman for their review of selected portions of the original manuscript. Thanks, too, to Mrs. Edie Ferrill, reference Librarian at the University of Arizona, for her assistance in writing Chapter 2. Each of the five anonymous reviewers of the first draft original manuscript contributed significantly to this book although in ways that would probably surprise them. Mrs. Diana Duncan and Mrs. Tasha Worden provided excellent typewritten copies from my barely decipherable longhand. Any errors in content, coverage or clarity are mine.

Muncie, Indiana   Edward M. Wolpert
December, 1980

Part One
Introduction to Research

Author's comment:

These two chapters were written to give you an idea of what educational research is all about and where and how you might locate it. In the first chapter I have tried to provide an overall view of educational research in the context of general scientific inquiry. In all research endeavors there is a wide range in quality—educational research is no exception. I have tried to bring out this point with some examples and some contrasts between good and poor research.

Most readers of this text will have experienced some training in scientific methods as part of their high school or college education; I suspect that lab work in chemistry or biology would be most typical. In the last section of Chapter 1, I have contrasted research procedures in the natural sciences with procedures used in the social sciences in order to point out many of the difficulties encountered in social science research. Hopefully, this will sensitize you to many of the issues brought out in later portions of the text.

Chapter 2 is a nitty gritty exposition of how to locate research. There was a time (and not so long ago) when the task of locating research was considered one of the most onerous, time-consuming, and boring chores known to man. Eye strain, back fatigue, cramped fingers and paper cuts typified the physiological status of a person engaged in research retrieval. Fortunately, the present day facilities and materials available to us for manual and computer assisted searching have relieved us of most of the burdensome aspects of this task. Thus, it was with great relish that I approached the writing of this chapter hoping that its content, spiced with examples, would enable you to learn how to locate research quickly and efficiently and then get on to the fun of reading it critically. The bulk of the material on indexing systems is focussed on using the ERIC collection, since most readers of this text will find it the most appropriate source. However, I have included many other indexing systems too, because, although there is a considerable overlap among them a truly comprehensive literature search might have to consider several other sources besides ERIC.

Chapter 1

Introduction to Research

Knowledge is power. The more a person knows the better that person's ability to predict future occurrences, solve problems and make decisions. Acquiring knowledge of the quality which can be relied on is a formidable task and one worthy of our attention.

Now, there are various ways of "knowing." There is tradition—"Of course this is right. We've always done it this way." There is knowing from personal experience or from intuition—"I know this because . . . well—because I know it." These various ways of knowing, sometimes effective—sometimes not, suffer from some very distinct weaknesses. They lack objectivity, formality and generalizability; they are tainted by the biases of the "knower." This problem existed for centuries and the weaknesses associated with this style of knowing led to the development of a scientific method in the seventeenth century. In essence, a scientific method involves the systematic gathering of evidence in order to test hypotheses and thus produce knowledge.

You will note the specific use of the indefinite article rather than the definite article when reference is made to scientific methods: *a* scientific method, not *the* scientific method. This is not a stylistic variation, but rather a reflection of the belief that there is no *one* scientific method—there is no *one* way of finding truth. This book takes the point of view that there is a scientific way of going about a search for truth, and this way may manifest itself in many different specific methods, the appropriate choice of which depends upon the needs of the specific situations. The opposing point of view which is quite narrow in focus seems inappropriate for consumers of research.

Generally in a scientific method a problem is first perceived and defined. Then hypotheses are developed to help explain or further understand the problem, and finally evidence is gathered and analyzed in order to confirm or reject each hypothesis. It is the focus on *evidence* that typifies a scientific method from a non-scientific one. The development of scientific methods represented a great leap toward the acquisition of reliable knowledge.

Educational research seeks to develop reliable knowledge through the application of scientific methods to its problems. But the efforts we find as we peruse the journals are sometimes lacking in credibility. We sometimes see conclusions reached which are based upon a low quality of evidence, or a high quantity of inference or a naive assessment of human motivation and still other deleterious phenomena. Consider the following examples:

Example 1

A Study of Teaching Methods

Fred Dolton seeks to discover the effect on achievement of the ABC text-based mathematics program used alone compared to the same text-based program supplemented by the XYZ programmed instruction. Achievement will be measured by the results of a standardized mathematics achievement test. Fred selects six eighth grade mathematics classes to participate in the study. He, himself, teaches three classes using the text-plus-programmed instructional format; a colleague of his teaches the other three classes using the text-only format. The study takes place over a period of eight months. During this time, all six classes are provided instruction five times per week, although the three text-plus-programmed classes often run over their normally alloted forty minutes per day because of the extra work they do in programmed instruction. At the end of the eight months, the achievement tests are administered, scored, and analyzed. The findings indicate that the text-plus-programmed classes scored substantially higher on the achievement test than did the text-only classes, and furthermore, that it is highly unlikely that these findings could have happened by chance. Fred concludes that "when a mathematics textbook is supplemented with programmed instruction, the achievement of students is higher than if they had used only the textbook."

How believable is Fred's conclusion? Do his findings justify his conclusions? Could any of the procedures used in his study have influenced the findings? Let's examine these issues a bit. But first let's assume that Fred has told us everything we should know about his study and that there are no arithmetic errors in his computations and analyses. Now, is Fred justified in his conclusion? He stated that "when a mathematics textbook is supplemented with programmed instruction, the achievement of students is higher than if they had used only the textbook." Note the general nature of his conclusion: "when *a* mathematics textbook" . . . can he logically generalize from *the* ABC mathematics textbook to *any* mathematics textbook on the basis of his study? One would think not. Similarly can he generalize from *the* XYZ programmed materials to *any* programmed materials? Again one would think not. If he had conducted a study in which a representative selection of available texts and programmed materials were employed, his general statement could be accepted more readily, but based upon the actual study that transpired his generalized conclusion is unjustified. It is possible that the ABC text and the XYZ programmed materials were in some way special—individually or in combination with one another, and accordingly are not representative of all such materials.

Fred reports that he himself taught the text-plus-programmed classes and a colleague taught the text-only classes. Could it be that his reasons for conducting the study in the first place were a predisposition in favor of the text-plus-programmed method? And if so, could he have become ego-involved in the outcome of the study? And if so could he have engaged in superior teaching so his classes would learn well while at the same time assign a less competent teacher to teach the other classes so as to increase the spread between the achievement of the two sets of classes? Knowing what we do about human nature such motives and actions are possible, indeed plausible.

Finally, Fred tells us that the text-plus-programmed classes often exceed their normally allotted forty minutes per day of instruction. In other words, these classes had more instructional time than the text-only classes. Could the higher achievement of the text-plus-programmed classes be attributable to more instructional time rather than the addition of programmed materials to the text? If the text-only classes had spent a similar amount of additional time say, reviewing their text materials, would they have had the same level of achievement as the text-plus-programmed classes? It is possible, even plausible, that they would have. Fred's study does not allow us to make that comparison, though.

In view of these bona fide concerns of ours and considering the possibility of other perhaps even more serious problems, it is difficult to accept with confidence the results of this study. The entire question could have been investigated much more rigorously which would have resulted in a study whose findings would have been less suspect.

Example 2

An Attitude Survey

The Thomasville School Corporation plans to institute a program of mainstreaming orthopedically handicapped (OH) children into its regular elementary school classrooms. Susan Lund, the staff researcher, decides to survey the elementary school teachers to determine if they are ready to receive these special students. She devises five questions to determine the teachers' attitudes toward OH children: 1. Do you believe in the American ideal of equal education for all children? 2. Does anyone in your family have a handicap? 3. If so, how do you feel about them? 4. How do you feel toward orthopedically handicapped children? 5. Would you be willing to share your love and ability with these deserving youngsters? Ms. Lund mimeographs these questions leaving enough space after each for a one or two word response, and mails them to each of the 150 elementary teachers in the corporation. Included with the questions are instructions to answer the questions and return to her via the stamped, self-addressed envelope enclosed. It is early August, three weeks before school resumes, and right in the middle of contract negotiations between the teachers' organization and the school board.

Two weeks after the mailing, Susan has received forty-two responses which represent 28% of number sent out. She reads each response, tallies them and reports the following to the school board:

*** Ninety-eight percent of the teachers believe in equal education for all children.

*** Fourteen percent of the teachers have someone in their family who is handicapped. Of these fourteen percent, all feel sympathetically toward the handicapped person.

*** Ninety-eight percent of the teachers have positive feelings toward orthopedically handicapped children.

*** Ninety-six percent of the teachers want to teach orthopedically handicapped children.

These data show that the teachers of the Thomasville School Corporation have a positive attitude toward orthopedically handicapped children and are desirous of having them in their classroom. It is recommended that these children be mainstreamed into the regular elementary classrooms at the earliest possible time.

We must ask ourselves: How credible are Susan's conclusions? How appropriate is her recommendation? Could any of the procedures used in her study have biased the findings? Again, let's examine these issues. Susan states that "these data show that the teachers of the Thomasville School Corporations have. . . ." Is this indeed the case? She sent out 150 letters and received 42 back, thus only 28% of the teachers responded. Do we have any reason to believe that the attitude of these 28% are representative of the attitudes of all 150 teachers? Why didn't the other 108 teachers respond? Were they on vacation? Were they too busy? Did they all receive the letters? Perhaps the context of the situation had something to do with the low response rate. Could the fact that the teachers' organization was then negotiating with the school board have influenced some teachers not to respond ("We'll cooperate with them when they cooperate with us")? These and other considerations create doubts in our minds as to whether the feelings of those teachers who returned the questions are representative of the feelings of all teachers in the school corporation.

And even if this issue of representativeness were resolved satisfactorily, we are left with a host of procedural issues which cast doubt upon the credibility of the study. For example, let's examine the actual questions to which the teachers were asked to respond. Did you notice the way they were stacked? Question 1 refers to "the American ideal of equal education." To respond negatively to such a question might indicate a lack of patriotism or perhaps even racism. Question 5 asks the teachers if they would "be willing to share your love and ability with these deserving youngsters." Who else but a heartless cad could respond negatively to such a query? Then there are ambiguities as well. Question 2 asks teachers if anyone in their family has a "handicap." There is no definition provided to inform the teachers as to what constitutes a handicap. Some teachers may understand the term to mean only physical handicaps while other teachers think in terms of psychological handicaps as well. Several of these questions might be answered, "Yes. But . . ." however the short space in which the respondents were to write their answers may have precluded the possibility of a fuller answer which might have revealed a more accurate assessment of the teachers' attitudes. In short, the strategy Susan used was to ask loaded questions in such a way as to elicit short but not necessarily accurate responses, and arrange the questions in such a way as to induce a positive response in the last question.

Considering the problems concerning the 1) representativeness of the responding teachers 2) the questions themselves, and 3) the socio/political context in which the entire survey was conducted, it is difficult to have much confidence in the findings of this study. Furthermore, the recommendation of the study assumes that a positive attitude of the part of the receiving teachers is the only significant element in predicting the success of the mainstreaming program. This seems highly unlikely. So what we see here is a poorly designed study with uninterpretable data which is used to overgeneralize and which in turn leads to a baseless, uninformed, and naive recommendation for action.

In the two examples the names and the contexts were changed to protect the guilty, but the issues and problems are real and are taken from actual cases of educational research. These examples show how "researchers" can sometimes use the most superficial aspects of a scientific method in order to make a conclusion to which they hope someone will pay attention. Such research is research in name only. It uses what appears to be research techniques in gathering evidence but in reality it just goes through the motions of scientific inquiry by providing style without substance. This is why we need to read research critically—not merely reading the summary, conclusions, implications, and recommendations of a study, but rather reading the procedures as well, following the logic, understanding what the researcher is doing and why, and finally understanding the socio/political context in which the research was conducted. By engaging in such a critical reading of research we can uncover problems which might have effected the findings. Thus we can evaluate the findings more rationally.

Good vs. Poor Research

It would be instructive at this time to consider some of the characteristics of good research in contrast to what is often found in low quality research efforts.

1. *Good research generates evidence from the best possible sources.* Research questions can be answered by using many various techniques and sources of information. Good research uses the most appropriate techniques and sources which can yield the most pertinent information to use in answering a research question. Poor research often uses the most convenient or economical techniques and sources. For example, attitudinal information on highly sensitive issues such as politics, religion, or sex, is often best gathered by in-depth techniques used by skilled interviewers. However, mailed questionnaires are a much more economical way of getting this type of information, and accordingly this technique is frequently used instead. As another example, college students are often used as subjects of studies. There is nothing wrong with this except when the researcher seeks to generalize the findings to a larger adult population. In this case it would have been better to use members of the larger adult population who, although less convenient than a captive audience of college students, are more closely associated with the research question being investigated.

2. *Good research is systematic,* that is, the procedures for gathering evidence are carefully formulated. Competent researchers think through the procedures they will use. They try to identify biases which would detract from the quality of the evidence they seek to gather, and having

identified the biases they plan to eliminate them or if this not possible, to control them. Good research is planned carefully. Poor research on the other hand is characterized by a lack of system and planning. For instance, in Example 1 above in which a text-only method was compared to a text-plus-programmed method, a major criticism of the study was that the text-plus-programmed classes spent more instructional time in mathematics than did the text-only classes. The increased instructional time rather than the method of presentation might have accounted for the difference in achievement between the two sets of classes. The researcher could have anticipated the advantage the extra instructional time would have given the text-plus-programmed classes. Then he could have provided a method for equalizing the instructional time.

3. *Good research uses measurements or descriptions that are both appropriate and precise.* Competent researchers seek out measuring instruments which yield exactly the kind of measurement needed to answer the research question. Moreover, they employ these instruments in such a way as to maximize the precision of the measurements. Poor research is often characterized by the use of measuring instruments which possess low or unknown quality. For instance, in Example 2 above in which the attitudes of teachers toward mainstreaming were described, several of the individual questions were loaded, the sequence was stacked, and the content was not appropriate to the research question. An example of imprecision in description can be seen in the same example. In the answer format, not enough space was allowed for a complete response. The format provided encouraged Yes or No answers yet the answers might have really been "Yes, but . . ." or "No, but. . . ." Thus, the answers received were lacking in precision; the teachers were not revealing precisely what their attitudes were.

4. *Good research is objective.* The biases of the researcher are identified and controlled. Competent researchers will remove themselves from any situation in which their biases could color their efforts or judgments; they know that their expectations, desires, and values could subtly effect a study in some way even if they themselves are conscious of the problem of objectivity. Poor research often presents situations where the researchers themselves have their egos on the line. For instance, in example 1 above, the researcher himself taught the classes which were to receive the text-plus-programmed instruction and he himself assigned the specific teacher who was to teach the classes with the other method. These decisions are tainted by subjectivity; he should not have taught the classes, and some objective method—an unbiased selection method perhaps—should have been used to determine which teachers were to teach which classes.

5. *Good research is rigorous and unhurried.* All procedures, measurements/descriptions, and analyses are thought through, tested and employed carefully and thoroughly. Competent researchers are in no hurry to determine the findings and draw their conclusions. They know that if a procedure in a study is weak, then no matter what the findings, the credibility of the study will be attenuated. Haste makes waste. Poor research sometimes seems to have been conceived in a flash of ignorance and executed without due regard for the realities of the situations. For instance, in Example 2 above, the attitude survey, the researcher's questions should have been scrutinized carefully to note the stacking. The opinions of outsiders should have been solicited in order to evaluate the appropriateness of the questions to the research question. And finally, the questions should have been field tested with some of the teachers in order to ferret out any ambiguities or other mechanical or interpretive problems. The researcher's decision to send the questions to the teachers before checking out the whole system was at best premature. As a consequence, this hurried-up procedure contributed to a weakening of the study's credibility.

6. *Good research is reported in its totality.* Consumers of research, whether they be other researchers, professionals, lay people or whatever, need to be informed of all pertinent facts so

6

they can evaluate the findings in light of what transpired in the study. Competent researchers recognize this and make every effort to reveal the *whole truth,* not just those elements which reflect favorably upon themselves or the study. Poor research is often characterized by an incomplete style of reporting which leaves the reader wondering what really went on. In example 1 above we might wonder why the ABC mathematics text was chosen to be used with the XYZ programmed materials. Was it chosen because it is better or worse than most, or was it typical, or was it chosen at random? The researcher never told us. In example 2 above, it was never mentioned why the researcher sought to undertake the study in the first place. Was it idle curiosity? Did the school board ask her? Did the teacher's organization ask her? Was it required by law? She never told us, and her motivation might have affected the outcome of the study.

The body of educational research which is available for our perusal is large. It contains a wide variety of research studies and it includes some studies of the highest quality as well as some studies of extremely low quality. The two studies used as examples in the discussion above are obviously of low quality; they contain numerous weaknesses which contribute to their lack of credibility. Most studies do not have as many or as glaring weaknesses as these do. Yet, all it takes is just one weakness to engender a reasonable suspicion as to the veracity of the findings of a study, so our efforts to uncover potential problems must be diligent.

Research endeavors in education vary as to type, and there are specific problems which are associated with the various types. As consumers of research findings we need to know what type of research a given researcher is attempting to perform. By being aware of what the researcher was trying to do we can focus our attention on evaluating what actually was done. So, let's examine the various types of research we will be encountering.

Types of Research

Research may be typed according to its purpose. *Pure research* (also called *basic research*) is aimed at the development of theories. It seeks to discover broad generalizations or principles usually without regard to their application. This type of research can take place in a laboratory or in the solitude of a small cubicle. *Applied research* focuses on the development of a real solution to a real problem. It tests theories in the real world. It actualizes pure research through invention and engineering. The contrast between these two types of research is exemplified by the following pairs of pure and applied research: a) Einstein's theory of the interconversion of mass to energy ($E=mc^2$) vs. the development of the atomic bomb. b) Discoveries concerning electricity by Ampere, Galvani, and Volta vs. Edison's invention of the incandescent lightbulb. c) Maxwell's equations of electromagnetism vs. Marconi's development of the intercontinental radio. d) The analysis of cross relationships among variables to determine the thought processes involved in reading vs. the study of the effects of a specific method of teaching reading on children's achievement.

It should be noted that there is not an absolutely precise dichotomy between pure and applied research. Although it would seem that the theory of pure research should precede the practice of applied research this is not always the case; sometimes the reverse is true. In medicine for example, sometimes a drug is found to cure a given disease; then researchers set out to determine why. Thus applied research can contribute to the development of a theory as well as be directed by it. Indeed, sometimes an applied study can uncover information which is not explained by a theory; this necessitates a revision of the theory. Unsuccessful attempts at applying a wrong theory for example, could force its revision.

However, it is important for us to try to distinguish between these two types because in judging the findings of a study we must be aware of its intent. For example, if a study is clearly a case of pure research such as a factor-analytic study of the reading process, its findings may reasonably imply further research, pure or applied. Implications which suggest specific classroom reading methods are at best premature. Such implications are better left to those suggested by applied studies. Also, acceptable levels of statistical significance should be determined by the nature of the research. This will be discussed in detail in subsequent chapters.

In education there is a third type of research called *action research* which is aimed at studying a specific, local problem in order to apply the findings immediately. These studies are usually modest in scope, moderate in rigor, and overall less formal in nature than pure or applied research. An example of this would be a fifth grade teacher experimenting with a new method of teaching spelling in order to see if the pupils improve their spelling.

Research may be further typed as to the chronological direction in which its purpose is oriented. Experimental research investigates "what might be." Descriptive research looks at "what is," and historical research is concerned with "what was."

Experimental Research

Experimental research asks the question, "What happens when . . . ?" Researchers organize procedures for gathering data which would enable them to answer such a question. This is done by setting up an experimental situation in which all possible influences are controlled or accounted for. Then one possible influence, an experimental condition, is varied in such a way that its effect can be measured. Based upon the measurement of the effects of the experimental condition, the researcher can state, "I did this, and that happened."

For example, a researcher might want to investigate the effect of a film presentation vs. a text presentation on social studies achievement. The researcher would devise a situation in which two groups of students who were as identical as possible in every respect were presented a social studies curriculum which was identical in every respect except that one group had a film presentation and the other group had a text presentation. The presentation of content—film or text—is the experimental condition which is allowed to vary. Since the groups were alike in all aspects except the experimental condition, if a difference were to be found between the achievement of the two groups, the difference could be logically attributed to the experimental condition. This experimental procedure is based on a principal called the law of the single variable. The logic of this principle is understandably appealing and is the basis for many procedures used in experimental research.

As another example, some researchers might want to investigate the extent to which a child's self concept might be influenced by the teacher's expectancy of his achievement. A class of thirty children might be identified and their self concepts measured. Then ten children might be randomly selected to receive the experimental condition. The experimental condition involves a researcher telling the teacher that these ten children are extremely bright and capable and should be encouraged to do superior work; this information although not true develops an expectancy and a suggested behavior pattern on the part of the teacher. Six months later, the self concepts of all thirty children are again measured. The average self concept of the ten children who received the experimental condition is compared to the average self concept of the other twenty children. If the self concepts of the ten children are noticably different than those of the other children then the difference could be logically attributed to the experimental condition.

The purpose of most experimental research is to allow an inference of *causality,* that is, to show that one phenomenon caused another. In order to show that it was one specific phenomenon which was the causal agent rather than another, experimental situations called *designs* are very carefully devised. The various designs used in experimental research are discussed in detail in Chapter 5 of this book.

Descriptive Research

Descriptive research differs from experimental research in that the researcher investigates the status of a phenomenon: what it is and/or to what it is related. The researcher does not intrude upon a situation and manipulate a phenomenon. Rather, the researcher observes and measures the phenomenon as an outsider looking in.

Descriptive research is sometimes assigned an inferior status by some researchers (often by those who are enthusiastic proponents of experimental research). This is unfortunate because descriptive research serves several important functions. For one thing it can provide useful information which allows a person to make intelligent decisions. For example, a study of the demographics of a school district—number of children in a family, in-migration, out-migration, and similar types of data—would allow the planning committee of a school board to arrange for the anticipated space requirements of the school corporations.

As another example, a curriculum coordinator might want to plan an effective in-service program for her corporation's teachers. She might conduct a survey to determine what the teachers perceive as their greatest needs and base the in-service program on the findings. Or she, in conjunction with other research workers, could systematically observe classrooms and use the perceptions of the observers as the basis for the in-service. In either of these examples, the information developed by the research if duly considered would probably yield a higher quality decision than a decision based upon ignorance.

A second purpose of a descriptive research is the development of hypotheses which can be tested through experimental designs. For example, a descriptive study can uncover the fact that children who lack ingredient X in their diet tend to be more lethargic than their peers whose diet contains this ingredient. This observation can lead to the development of a hypothesis stating that the lack of ingredient X causes lethargy among children. This hypothesis may have been *developed* by this descriptive study, but was not *tested* by it; the rigorous testing of hypotheses dealing with causality can only be accomplished through experimental studies or in some cases other descriptive methods.* The point is that the causal hypothesis to be tested may never have been developed if a descriptive study had not suggested it.

As another example, a descriptive study might show that in those cultures in which a large proportion of men are kindergarten and primary grade teachers the boys tend to be better students. From this finding it could be hypothesized that the presence of men teachers in the early years of school causes boys to be better students. To test this hypothesis, an experimental study could be conducted in which the achievement of boys who had men teachers was compared to the achievement of boys who had women teachers. Third, descriptive research may provide a substitute for experimental research in situations where economic, logistic, or ethical considerations make an experimental study impossible. For example, suppose a descriptive study discovers that certain substances found in air pollutants in industrial areas are present in the environments of persons who contract a certain form of cancer. That is, the presence of the pollutant is associated with the

---

*This point will be developed further in Chapter 6 and 7.

presence of the cancer. A logical question is "Does the pollutant cause cancer?" To answer that question, it would seem that an experimental study is called for, but ethical considerations preclude the conducting of such a study: you can not just take people and subject them to a treatment which might have disastrous effects upon their health. Experimental studies with laboratory animals are possible but this type of study assumes that animals have a close enough resemblance to humans to substitute for them; this presents problems when we seek to extend the findings to humans. Also, years of accumulative pollutants in a person's body may have to be simulated by massive doses of the pollutant in a shorter time—this also presents problems in interpretation of the findings. Thus causality becomes difficult to infer, unless you are willing to accept all assumptions of the comparability of 1) animals to humans and 2) small doses over a long time to large doses over a short time. If in this pollution/cancer case, a cessation of pollution were to occur at a given site because of say, legislation limiting the emissions from industrial plants and a decreased incidence of cancer were then observed, an inference of causality might be justified. And if a similar decreased incidence of cancer were to be found at other sites in which pollution had ceased, and at other times, the inference of causality would be even higher. In situations such as this descriptive studies are often the only way to deal with the issue of causality and avoid problems with generalizations based upon debatable assumptions.

Historical research

Historical research is another type of research in education, but appears with less frequency than experimental and descriptive research. It gathers data concerning past events from historical sources. It seeks to describe the past in such a way as to shed light upon our understanding of the present. Researchers engaged in these efforts work at the pleasure of the available data; they have little say over many of the issues which the experimental or descriptive researcher could control. A historical researcher uses as data sources 1) artifacts, eye-witness testimony, original documents, etc. referred to as *primary sources* and 2) textbooks, second hand accounts, etc. referred to as *secondary sources.* These sources are evaluated by the researcher in terms of their authenticity (external criticism) and usefulness in answering a question (internal criticism).

An example of historical research would be a study of methods of teaching mathematics in the United States of America. A researcher might locate a variety of primary and secondary sources: the actual books used for mathematics instruction, curriculum guides, the writings of educators concerned with mathematics, accounts of learning mathematics (found in literature, textbooks, testimony of senior citizens), and other sources as well. With all these data sources and with an understanding of the historical context in which they existed, a researcher could piece together a chronology of attitudes, events, and outcomes which would give a reader a broad perspective on mathematics instruction today. Then, when we hear the "Back to Basics" slogan we can investigate whether we were ever there.

Historical research can present us with valuable information to help us understand the present. Indeed its methodology is often the only way such information can be made available to us. However, the techniques of historical research will not be dealt with in this text. This is not meant to denigrate the efforts of historical researchers nor to imply an insignificance to their findings, but rather to reflect the realities of the needs of those for whom this book is written. The realities are that the techniques used by historical research are typically not expressed in highly specialized terminology or mathematically based analytical models which would require extensive explanations as is the case with experimental and descriptive research. In addition, almost all the research with which most readers of this text will be coming in contact is experimental and descriptive.

When we do come across an occasional historical study if it is reasonably well written we should be able to read it critically by following its logic and evidence and evaluating its conclusions based upon the quality of its logic and evidence.

Evaluation

Evaluation is a special case of descriptive research. It focuses on a specific situation—a program, a person or perhaps an event. It uses many of the same techniques as descriptive, experimental, and historical research but has two major distinctions: 1) rather than being broad in concept and scope so as to be able to generalize to other situations, it focuses specifically upon a particular, individual existing situation. 2) it is action-oriented, that is, the results are organized and presented in such a way that decision makers will be able to use the findings to help them choose from the alternative options available to them.

For example, some researchers might want to evaluate an in-service training program for school administrators in order to improve it so it would be more effective for another group of administrators. They might assess the competencies of the administrators before and after the training sessions in order to find out where the least growth occurred. They might interview some participants to determine their reactions to the program: they might do some checking to find out what previous training the administrators had. Using this information as well as other information, the researchers could recommend changes in the program to improve its quality.

As another example, a group of secondary school English teachers might want to evaluate a new literature text in order to decide whether or not to purchase it for their students in the next academic year. They might examine its content, style, organization, durability, and still other aspects, and on the basis of their findings decide to purchase it or not to purchase it.

Well conceptualized, systematic and meaningful evaluations are appearing with increasing frequency in educational research. Our understanding of this type of research requires us to be knowledgeable about experimental and descriptive research techniques. But there are other seemingly non-research considerations which are important for us to know too, as we shall see in subsequent discussions.

We have noted earlier that there is a considerable range in the quality of the educational research with which we will come in contact. However, there seems to be much less variation in the quality of research done in the physical sciences, such as chemistry, geology, or biology. We might reasonably ask why this should be. For example, why are similar experiments in say, chemistry usually repeatable, that is, yielding similar or identical results, while in education this is usually not the case? What problems do educational researchers have that physical science researchers do not have? It is worthwhile to examine these issues briefly in order to gain a perspective on educational research as a scientific endeavor.

Social Sciences vs. Physical Sciences

Educational research includes studies done in a variety of specific disciplines such as psychology, sociology, medicine as well as studies done within the confines of the educational enterprise. The corpus of research we encounter may be best described as social science research since it has as its common element an emphasis on people rather than other forms of life or inert matter. And when we compare research in the social sciences with research in the physical sciences we are struck with the fact that research in the physical sciences has had a profound effect on the history of the world. Social science research has had a much lesser effect on humanity although the problems it addresses are of equal or greater importance. Why this disparity? There are two major reasons.

First, the physical sciences have a longer tradition of scientific inquiry than do the social sciences. Atomic theory goes back to the fourth century B.C.; the identification of "elements" fire, earth, air and water closely follow chronologically. These concepts were revived and revised in the 17th and 18th centuries. The alchemy of the year one developed into the chemistry of the middle ages. And finally, when structured scientific inquiry was applied to these sciences in the Renaissance, they advanced rapidly and have not yet peaked. In contrast, the history of research in the social sciences is measured in decades rather than centuries or millennia. For example, the first efforts in education go back to the end of the nineteenth century. Many of the frequently used statistical tests were developed in the 1920's and 1930's. Major fundings for large projects began in the sixties. Thus, social science research is just beginning, relatively speaking. The physical sciences have been at it for much longer; it would be expected that their accomplishments be far ahead of those of the social sciences.

But more importantly, there is a major and fundamental difference between the physical and social sciences which has an immense effect upon the advancement of each. This crucial difference is the nature of the objects of the research. The physical sciences deal with *matter,* organic or inorganic, which has certain properties which typically vary very little from sample to sample. They also deal with living things, plant and animal life which similarly varies very little from sample to sample. For example, anthracite coal is classified into three subgroups, each of which is defined in terms of moisture content, volatile matter, and fixed carbon content. The variation of samples of say, meta-anthracite is between 98%–100% dry fixed carbon. In the animal kingdom, pigeons (Columbidae) for example, comprise about 290 species; within each species is similarly very little variation.

In contrast the social sciences deal with human beings of which there are several billion inhabiting this planet, and as a result of genetics and environment *every single one is different from the rest.* The closest we come to uniformity is with monozygotic twins, but even in this case the different environments in which each lives renders them different from each other.

There are some general, identifiable social similarities among all people, and certain subgroups of peoples (races, for example) have identifiable unique qualities, but within any group there is extensive variety. It is this fact of the variety of subjects upon whom our research efforts are based that leads to the major problems in social science research.

The variety among people is caused by the complexity of the makeup of a person. There is an infinity of attributes which comprise the totality of a human being. Those attributes are induced both genetically and environmentally and occur in differing degrees in different people. For this reason, it is very risky to generalize with confidence from one person to another. Human beings lack the uniformity to allow for the development of social "laws" in the same way that natural "laws" are developed. For example, if some chemists are seeking to test an additive which they believe will raise the boiling point of water, they might start with the established fact that water at sea level will boil at 212° Farenheit. The specific samples of water they might use in their experiments might vary somewhat depending upon the impurities in the samples and this variation may have a slight effect on what temperature is needed to make a given sample boil. But the variations are quite small, and when the various samples of water are brought to approximately the same temperature they boil: same cause, same effect.

In contrast, suppose some psychologists seek to test out a treatment designed to raise the threshold of anger among high school male students. The immediate problem they face is identifying what is the threshold of anger in high school male students. The variation among these students can be expected to be very large: some students seem never to get angry while others seem always to be angry. Now, they might approach this on a group basis, that is, combine individual students into groups thus spreading around the variation among students into groups which would have similar amounts of variation and a computable average threshold of anger. Then they could proceed with the treatment and measure the effect of the treatment on the group. The problem would come when they seek to apply the findings to an individual, or to a group with somewhat different characteristics. For instance, the treatment might work on a student with a low threshold of anger but not on a student with a high threshold. A sample of water -H_2O- is comprised of many molecules each containing two atoms of hydrogen and one atom of oxygen. If you've seen one H_2O molecule you've seen 'em all. But such is not the case with our sample of students. This then is one of the chief problems in social science research—the variability of the objects of research.

Another problem concerns the definition of the attributes with which we are dealing. To continue with our examples, in the physical sciences temperature may be defined in terms of molecular motion: higher temperatures of substances are shown by an increase in the molecular motion of those substances. A boiling point may be defined as the temperature necessary to generate bubbles of vapor from a liquid. We raise the temperature of a liquid to a certain point and it boils. But with the threshold of anger we encounter problems in defining exactly what we mean. We need to have an operational definition so we would know when someone has arrived at the threshold. Even more basic than that, we need to have an operational definition of anger so we know when someone is indeed angry. Part of the problem is that different people show anger in different ways. Some shout, some stamp their feet, some throw a fit, some just sit quietly and inwardly fume—they may not show anger but they may be just as angry as those who do, as evidenced by higher blood pressure, or peptic ulcers discovered at a later date.

This lack of definition leads to yet another problem: that of *measurement*. Physical scientists can take a direct measurement of the temperature of water by using a simple measuring instrument: a thermometer. They can observe the water, paying attention to when it begins boiling and note the reading on the thermometer when that time comes. The reading is a direct, non-inferential measurement of temperature. In contrast, what instruments do the social scientists have to measure anger? The determination of when a person is angry is not measureable directly, but rather must be inferred by whatever observable manifestations of which they may be aware. And as noted above, different people will manifest anger in different ways.

Still another problem concerns the effect of the environment on the measurements we take. For example, a given sample of water will boil at the same temperature on Monday as on Tuesday when the environmental factors (air pressure and humidity, for example) are held constant. But the environment in which human subjects exist is extremely complex and unwieldy: a social event, a change in the weather, getting up on the wrong side of the bed—these environmental factors may influence the measurement of threshold of anger to the extent that Monday's threshold is different from Tuesday's and the researchers may not know how it is different.

A final problem concerns the reactive nature of an experiment on the subjects. A sample of water is incapable of thought. It cannot know when heat is being applied, and even if it did it could not do anything about it. On the other hand, when engaged in a research project, human subjects may react to the procedures and they may do this in many different ways. Some may become hostile and uncooperative; others may become flattered by the attention and seek to please the researchers. Whichever is the case, the human subjects are reacting to the procedures and as such are somewhat different than they would be otherwise. So when researchers seek to generalize the findings of an experimental study to a larger population which was not subjected to the research procedures, the generalization may not be valid.

What we see here is that by comparison to the physical sciences, social science research is fraught with difficult problems. The subjects addressed by social science research vary widely. The attributes studied are quite complex and are often interactive with other attributes. As a consequence, research studies in the social sciences are often non-repeatable: same procedures, different findings.

Variance among subjects, interaction of attributes, inadequate definitions of attributes, inferentially based measurements, interaction of subjects with procedures—what a mess. At this point, one is tempted to throw up one's hands in frustration and shout, "What's the use: Why bother conducting research in social sciences?" Actually, the picture is not quite as gloomy as it would appear from the previous discussion. Rarely do all these problems present themselves in the same research study; more typically one or two problems are found. But more importantly, researchers in social sciences are aware of the problems and have developed procedures which help attenuate the potential deleterious effects of these problems. The procedures do not solve the problems directly but rather control them through careful planning and statistical treatments. For example, the use of a control group allows relative judgments to be made, the concept of measurement error allows us to know the confidence limits of a given measurement. The point is that *good research* recognizes problems, seeks to control them, reports fully and accurately, and generalizes carefully and conservatively. Research characterized by such qualities is useful in understanding social phenomena. It may never approach the accuracy of research in the physical sciences, nor will it result in any immutable laws of nature, but it can provide a basis for a reasonably intelligent understanding of people and how and why they function. The alternative to good research is to revert to ignorance, superstition, and so-called traditional wisdom. Such a course of action, a know-nothing approach, would set back social progress decades if not centuries. Civilization does not need another Dark Age.

As discussed earlier, the quality of educational research varies widely. Some studies are exemplary and as such may represent quite significant advances in knowledge; other studies are so poorly planned and executed as to be worthless, and there are many studies between these extremes. The fact that a study is published in a journal does not guarantee its quality, nor does the fact that the researcher is well known guarantee the quality of his or her work. We have already discussed the idea that *good* research is useful to us. Yet there are no governmental agencies which label studies as being "grade A" or "prime" or "fancy" as the Department of Agriculture does with foods. Nor is there any objective non-governmental organization to rate research as being "acceptable," "not acceptable," or a "Best Buy," as Consumers Union does with consumer goods. How then do the readers of research—the consumers of research—decide upon what studies are good enough to represent advances in knowledge? Simple: each person reads, and thinks, and decides. It's every person for himself. How then does a person read research? It has its own form and language—it has its own way of presenting itself. What does the reader of research need to know in order to read research critically and intelligently? Well, that is what this book is all about.

Parts Two through Five of this book contain information which should enable the reader to read research effectively. The specific formats and language used in research—the designs, data, and analytical techniques—are presented and explained in sufficient detail for readers to understand most research they will come across. As the text progresses, there will be discussions of significant issues and problems which could influence a given research study. To focus the reader's attention on these problems, critical questions will be interspersed in the text, set off from the rest of the text by indentation and capital letters as illustrated by the following:

CRITICAL QUESTIONS INTERSPERSED IN THE TEXT WILL FOCUS THE ATTENTION OF THE READER

These questions will be compiled into a research evaluation instrument which will be presented in an appendix. With the background information about research which is presented in this text, and with the specific focus provided by these critical questions, the reader will then need to exercise common sense and good judgment in deciding whether a given study is of sufficient quality to be taken seriously. No book can teach this. It will have to come from within each individual reader.

Summary

The purpose of research is to generate knowledge—reliable knowledge—which can be used as the basis for understanding phenomena and ultimately for making decisions. From the various ways of knowing, scientific methods evolved as the best procedures for generating reliable knowledge. Scientific methods rely heavily on evidence rather than intuition or reliance on authority. In the educational research literature, the quality of the research endeavors consumers will encounter is varied. Often we find the results of poorly executed or inadequately planned research passed off as Truth. An informed critical reading of such research endeavors will allow consumers of research to evaluate its results rationally rather than blindly accepting them as statements with inherent veracity.

Good research differs from poor research in several ways. It generates evidence from the best possible sources rather than from the most convenient and/or inexpensive sources. Its procedures for gathering evidence are systematic rather than haphazard. The measurements used by good research are appropriate to the research question and have sufficient precision to be relied upon. Good research recognizes biases and seeks to control them: this yields a level of objectivity necessary for accuracy. It is well planned, carefully executed and unhurried, and finally it is reported in its totality so the research consumer has all the needed information upon which to base a judgment.

Consumers need to know the different types of research encountered in the literature so they can judge what researchers did in light of what the researchers were attempting to do. One dimension of research is its purpose. Pure research efforts seek to develop theories, whereas applied research efforts focus upon solutions in the real world. Another dimension of research is the chronological direction of its findings. Experimental research is future oriented: what would happen if. Descriptive research is present oriented: what is happening. Historical research is past oriented: what happened. Evaluation is described as a special case of descriptive research.

Compared to research in the physical sciences, educational research efforts encounter many difficult methodological problems. The root cause for most of these problems is the fact that human beings who by nature vary substantially from one another are often the subjects from whom measurements are taken.

Further Readings for Chapter I

Baumrin, Bernard (ed.). Philosophy of Science Volume 2. New York: Interscience, 1963.
    The five papers in part one of this book deal with scientific exploration, prediction and theories. The authors are philosophers and although the reading gets a bit thick at times, their views are helpful in developing a perspective on science.

Dubin, Robert, Theory Building. (revised edition). New York: Free Press, 1978.
    If you really want to go deeply into the role of theory in social science research, this text provides a full treatment.

Feigl, Herbert and Brodbeck, May. *Readings in the Philosophy of Science*. New York: Appleton-Century-Crofts, 1953.
    This is a very inclusive book of readings in the philosophy of science. Sections one and three may be of special interest to the reader of this text.

Hopkins, Charles D. *Educational Research: A Structure for Inquiry,* Columbus, Ohio: Merrill, 1976.
    Chapters one and two of this text are especially relevant to the content of this chapter you have read.

Kaplan, Abraham. *In Pursuit of Wisdom, The Scope of Philosophy*. Beverly Hills: Glenco Press, 1977.
    An excellent treatment of theories of knowledge and the philosophy of science is presented in chapters 4 and 5 of this text. It is unusually readable for a philosophy book and is highly recommended.

Chapter 2

Locating Research

Every field of endeavor has a literature. By literature is meant original research, reviews of research, thought pieces based on research, explications of theories, critiques of theories and/or research, book reviews, biographies, bibliographies, and even financial statements of major organizations in the field. The research-based literature is merely a part of the total literature in the field.

At the outset, a distinction should be made between the various types of research-based literature. *Original research* includes studies which generate their own data for analysis or use existing data on which is performed a new or different analysis than had been performed previously. The purpose of this book is to assist you in reading such original research. *Reviews of research* are articles which select research studies already accomplished in order to summarize, compare, contrast, critique or any combination of these purposes. Usually reviews are organized around a specific topic or theme, and can acquaint the reader with a large body of research in an encapsulated form. *Thought pieces,* sometimes called *perspectives* or *opinion pieces* are often based upon research but rather than merely listing the research they attempt to synthesize it into a theory or otherwise show its meaningfulness and usefulness. As was mentioned before, the focus of the content of this book is upon reading original research critically and carefully; this is important because although reviews and thought pieces are valuable to the literature, they can be no better than the research upon which they are based, except to the extent that they clarify or otherwise improve one's understanding of the research.

Much research is published in the journals of a given field or of several fields if the research is important and multidisciplinary in nature. There exists a "publication lag" in many fields, that is, it takes a while—perhaps months, perhaps years—between the time a study is completed or accepted for publication and the time it actually appears in print. Once it is in print it will be indexed by one or more indexing systems thus rendering information of its existence to those who do not subscribe to the particular journal in which it was published. Then the journal can be consulted and the study read. Unpublished research, too, is often available to read in abstract form but acquisition of the complete study is often not as easy as is the case with published studies.

The *Educational Resources Information Center* (ERIC) is a primary tool for locating research in the field of education; its distribution lag is only a few months. The various clearinghouses of the ERIC system solicit research reports from many sources. These studies are then selected, assorted, indexed and made available to librarians on film. Access to this collection is obtained through the index called *Resources in Education* (RIE). Another branch of the ERIC system is called the *Current Index to Journals in Education* (CIJE), and indexes studies appearing in professional journals.

Summaries of research presented in abstract form are found in *Sociological Abstracts, Psychological Abstracts,* and *Dissertation Abstracts.* These publications give the reader an idea as to what studies have been done and what their findings were. But to get to the original sources takes some further doing. If the study was a dissertation then it may be available in microfilm or hard cover from University Microfilms in Ann Arbor, Michigan, or it may be able to be borrowed from the library of the degree-granting institution through the inter-library loan system. For other research, the complete study is often available from its author upon request.

Strategies for Locating Research

There are several strategies available for locating research. The particular one to use depends upon how much information the reader has and what the purpose of the search is.

1. If you know the author or the title of a study and, furthermore, know the journal volume and number, then you can go directly to the journal to find the study. Journals are often listed in the *card catalog* or a *current listing of periodicals* depending on the organization of the particular library.

2. If you know the author or the subject, but do not know the journal, then you can use one of the indexing systems described in the next section. These systems will guide you to the desired journals.

3. If you know even only one significant word from the title of the study or if you know of another writer who cited the study you can use the Social Science Citation Index (SSCI) to find out the author, title and journal of the study.

4. If you are not looking for a particular study, but rather seek to locate studies on a given topic, then you can enter the most appropriate indexing system under its subject headings and find specific studies listed there. This can be done manually using the indexing systems in print form, or it can be done using a computer-assisted search.

Indexing Systems

The social sciences* are fortunate to have several well-organized systems for locating research. In this section will be presented fourteen systems which vary in inclusiveness, complexity of organization, thoroughness of indexing, and overall sophistication of usage. Each of them serves the needs of a group of users who have specific search requirements and have only certain information to initiate a search. Those systems which include the term "index" in their titles contain entries which are for the most part limited to bibliographical information. Those systems which have the term "abstracts" in their titles contain entries which are summaries of the content of the original source in addition to bibliographical information.

There is so much overlap in the social sciences that the indexing systems can not be divided into discrete subjects, yet each system has its own particular focus. Accordingly, the fourteen systems described below are presented in the generalized order of education, psychology, sociology, and nursing.

*For the purpose of a literature search the term "educational research" must be broadened to *social science* research. The latter term includes educational research but also includes those research studies in related social sciences which have an application in the field of education.

Education Index (EI)

The Education Index (EI) is published monthly by the H. W. Wilson Co. with periodic and annual cumulations. EI indexes articles from over 200 periodicals, yearbooks, and proceedings in the field of education.

Articles are indexed by author and subject together, and entries guide the researcher directly to the original periodical source. Figure 2.1 shows an excerpt from the EI. No annotations are listed with the titles. This presents problems sometimes when a title does not accurately reflect the content of the article. Another problem with the EI indexing system is that the 200 periodicals indexed include non-research oriented publications such as *Instructor* and *Grade Teacher*. Publications such as these have merit and value for classroom practitioners but do not have the research orientation necessary for scholarly endeavors. The subject headings used by EI are similar to those used in most library card catalogs. Typically a broad heading is followed by several subdivisions.

LIQUIDS
  Qualitative observations concerning packing densities for liquids, solutions, and random assemblies of spheres. W. C. Duer and others. bibl J Chem Educ 54:139-42 Mr '77
    See also
  Hydrodynamics
  Solution (chemistry)
  Surface tension
LIQUOR problem
    See also
  Alcohol and youth
  Alcoholism
LISITRANO, Larry F.
  Three-dimensional design: the environment. Sch Arts 76:26-8 Ap '77
LISKA, Jo. See Cronkhite, G. jt. auth.
LISPING
  Listeners' impressions of speakers with lateral lisps. E. M. Silverman. bibl J Speech & Hearing Dis 41:547-52 N '76
LISSANDRELLO, Eugene
  Let there be light and color. Sch Arts 76:66-7 O '76
LISTENING
  Hey, did you really hear that kid? C. M. Galloway and T. Whitfield. Instructor 86:84-6 O '76
    See also
  Attention

Teaching
Evaluation
Pre-, post- and follow-up testing of teacher effectiveness training. D. T. Pedrini and others. Education 96:240-4 Spr '76

Colleges and universities
Remediation in college. B. S. Walter. Acad Therapy 11:335-8 Spr '76

Elementary schools
Cognitive approach to teaching listening. D. J. Tutolo. il Lang Arts 54:262-5 Mr '77
Listening while reading: a four year study. H. Schneeberg. bibl il Read Teach 30:629-35 Mr '77
Oral reading: misused? J. G. Hosey. il El Sch J 77:218-20 Ja '77

Special schools and classes
Auditory-vocal activation: a tool for teaching children with a specific language disability. L. Kaliski. il J Learn Dis 10:210-18 Ap '77

Teaching aids and devices
Pupil as a listener. M. Ediger. Read Improv 13:249 Wint '76

Figure 2.1. Sample entries in *Education Index*. (Source: *Education Index*, Vol. 27, New York: H. W. Wilson Co., 1977, p. 447.)

Educational Resources Information Center (ERIC)

The *Educational Resources Information Center* (ERIC) is a national system which disseminates literature in the field of education. ERIC has two complementary indexing systems described below:

1. The *Current Index to Journals in Education* (CIJE) is published monthly with a cumulative edition appearing annually by CCM Information Corporation. CIJE indexes over 700 education and educationally related journals. As such it is an excellent source of research studies. It contains a) a section of main listings each with an annotation and a direct reference to the journal of origin; b) an index of subjects; c) an index of authors; and d) an index showing the table of contents of each of the journals indexed. Figure 2.2 shows an excerpt from the subject

Science Curriculum Improvement Study
Validity and Reliability of the SCIS Test for the
Organisms Unit, *Journal of Research in Science
Teaching* v13 n3, pp243-247, May 76
EJ 141 805

Science Departments
Fragmentation of Physiology: Possible Academic
Consequences, *Physiologist* v19 n1, pp35-39,
Feb 76
EJ 136 863

Science Education
NSF and Science Education--Who, Why, and
How Did It Work Out?, *Journal of General
Education* v27 n3, pp188-98, F 75 EJ 132 096
Science Curricula and Attitudes to Science: A
Review, *Australian Science Teacher Journal*
v21 n2, pp23-40, Aug 75   EJ 133 202
Mixed Ability Teaching, *Education in Science*
n65, pp19, Nov 75   EJ 133 224
Biological Congress in Sweden, *Education in
Science* n65, pp20-22, Nov 75   EJ 133 225
Computers and Science Education, *Education in
Science* n65, pp25-26, Nov 75   EJ 133 226
Discrepancies in Measuring Adoption of New
Curriculum Projects, *Education in Science* n65,
pp26-28, Nov 75   EJ 133 227
Notes on Researching the Process of Scientific
Classification with Both Adolescent and Adult
Populations, *School Science and Mathematics*
v76 n1, pp50-56, Jan 76   EJ 133 235
A Strategy for Disseminating Elementary Science
Curricula, *School Science and Mathematics*
v76 n1, pp57-62, Jan 76   EJ 133 236
The Science-Education Doctorate: Competencies
and Roles, *Journal of Research in Science
Teaching* v12 n4, pp399-405, Oct 75
EJ 133 314
Observational Skills of Children in Montessori
and Science-A Process Approach Classes,
Journal of Research in Science Teaching v12
n4, pp407-413, Oct 75   EJ 133 315
Relationship of Formal Reasoning to Achieve-
ment, Aptitudes, and Attitudes in Preservice
Teachers, *Journal of Research in Science
Teaching* v12 n4, pp423-431, Oct 75

EJ 133 227   SE 515 454
Discrepancies in Measuring Adoption of New
Curriculum Projects Nicodemus, R. B., *Education in Science* n65. pp26-28, Nov 75
*Adoption, *Curriculum, *Science Education,
*Surveys,   Curriculum   Development,
[*England]
Reports on two questionnaires designed to
measure the adoption of twelve new science
curriculum projects. Points out discrepancies in
the results of the surveys in the areas of
percentage of adoption, use by teachers with
different subject area specializations, and position
of the teacher doing the reporting. (GS)

EJ 133 228   SE 515 541
Teaching the Concept of Speed Boulanger, F.
David, *School Science and Mathematics*, v76 n1,
pp3-8, Jan 76
*Conceptual Schemes, *Elementary School
Science, *Intellectual Development, *Motion,
Elementary Education, Instructional Materials,
Learning Theories, Science Education, Science
Activities. [*Piaget (Jean)]
Presents a series of activities intended to enable
teachers to determine if children are ready to be
introduced to the concept of speed. Reviews
Piaget's theories and the empirical evidence on
which the sequence is based. (Author/CP)

EJ 133 229   SE 515 542
**The Scientific Attitudes of Tenth-Grade Students
in Israel, as Measured by the Scientific Attitude
Inventory** Novick, Shimshon; Duvdvani, Dina,
School Science and Mathematics, v76 n1, pp9-14,
Jan 76
*Educational Research, *Secondary School
Science, *Scientific Attitudes, *Surveys, Inter-
national Education, Science Education, Second-
ary Education, Scientists, [*Israel, Research
Reports]
Examines the scientific attitudes of a stratified
sample of 684 tenth-grade students in Israeli
schools. Compares these scores with those
generated by a similar study in the United States.
(CP)

Figure 2.2. Excerpt from subject index of *CIJE*.
(Source: *Current Index to Journals in Education*,
Vol. 8, New York: Macmillan Information, A
Division of Macmillan Publishing Co., Inc.,
July–December 1976, p. 973.)

Figure 2.3. Excerpt from main entry section of
CIJE. (Source: *Current Index to Journals in
Education*. Vol. 8, New York: Macmillan
Information, A Division of Macmillan Publishing
Co., Inc., July–December 1976, p. 60.)

index. Figure 2.3 shows an excerpt from the main entry section. Each main listing is assigned an ERIC Journal (EJ) accession number which makes the indexing system compatible with the ERIC retrieval system explained below.

2. *Resources in Education* (RIE) is published monthly with an annual cumulative edition by the National Institute of Education. RIE, which before 1974 was called *Research in Education,* indexes research reports which are not published or otherwise widely disseminated. This would include research presented at scholarly gatherings, government reports, curriculum guides, etc. Contained in each issue of RIE is a) a listing of each document with a resume (abstract) of the document. An ERIC document (ED) number is assigned to each listing and is used for accession purposes; b) a subject index; c) an author index; d) an institution index; and e) other items to assist the researcher in using the ERIC system. Figure 2.4 shows an excerpt from the subject index. Figure 2.5 shows an excerpt from the document listings. The document listings refer the user to the ERIC document itself which is available in hard copy or microfiche. Most libraries

Mental Health Programs
A Comprehensive Mental Health Program at Shennan Indian High School.
ED 138 408
Diverting Youthful Offenders Through Law Enforcement-Social Service Collaboration.
ED 140 182
Ethnicity and Service Delivery.
ED 139 877
Evaluation of the Impact of Community Mental Health Center Consultation Services on School Systems. Volume 1. Executive Summary.
ED 134 873//
Evaluation of the Impact of Community Mental Health Center Consultation Services on School Systems. Vol. 2, Final Report: The Dynamics of School Consultation.
ED 134 874//
Humanistic Approaches in the Delivery of Community Mental Health Services.
ED 137 675
An Invisible Crisis: The Burden of Family Coping With the Mentally Ill as an Unintended Consequence of Deinstitutionalization.
ED 136 133
A Psychosocial Data System for Children's Community Mental Health Services.
ED 134 879
Self-Control Skills Training: A Manual for Personal Development and Self-Help.
ED 138 879//
Social Inventions: Saskatchewan NewStart.
ED 134 914
Transcultural Psychiatry: An Hispanic Perspective. Spanish Speaking Mental Health Research Center Monograph Number Four.
ED 139 585

Mental Illness
Ethnicity, Social Class and Mental Illness. Working Paper Series Number 17.
ED 138 665
An Invisible Crisis: The Burden of Family Coping With the Mentally Ill as an Unintended Consequence of Deinstitutionalization.
ED 136 133

Figure 2.4. Excerpt from subject index of *RIE.* (Source: *Resources in Education,* Vol. 12, New York: Macmillan Information, A Division of Macmillan Publishing Co., Inc., 1977, p. 313.)

have the documents available in fiche since it is much more convenient to store. (Microfiche is a photographic process that can reduce up to 76 pages onto a 4 x 6 film sheet. Thus an entire book can be reduced to a few film sheets.) The entries in ERIC may be accessed manually or through a computer.

ED 134 874   CG 011 045

Evaluation of the Impact of Community Mental Health Center Consultation Services on School Systems. Vol. 2, Final Report: The Dynamics of School Consultation.

Spons Agency—National Inst. of Mental Health (DHEW), Rockville, Md.

Report No—MH-PPE-72-14-6; PB-225-774

Pub Date Oct 73

Note—183p.; For related document, see CG 011 044 ; Study developed by Behavior Science Corporation, Los Angeles

Available from—National Technical Information Service, 5285 Port Royal Road, Springfield, Virginia 22151 (HC $5.25, MF $1.45, order number PB-225 774)

Document Not Available from EDRS.

Descriptors—*Community Consultant Programs, Consultants, *Consultation Programs, *Mental Health Programs, Program Descriptions, *Program Effectiveness, Program Evaluation, *Public School Systems, Student Personnel Services

There were four relevant objectives of this study: (1) describe the extent and nature of school case-oriented and program consultation as currently practiced, and to evaluate its impact; (2) evaluate the congruence of the local consultee's and consultant's expectations of consultation and the degree to which their expectations are attained; (3) describe and analyze the problems that are experienced by the consultees and consultants in developing school consultation programs; and (4) obtain information about the evaluation and feedback system in operation for school consultation and any data available on outcomes. (Author)

ED 134 875   CG 011 046

Mental Health Consultation to the Schools: Directions for the Future.

Spons Agency—National Inst. of Mental Health (DHEW), Rockville, Md.

Report No—MH-PPE-72-14-C; PB-225-775

Pub Date May 73

Contract—HSM-42-72-110

Note—143p.; Proceedings of a Conference on School Consultation (San Diego, California, March 15-16, 1973)

Available from—National Technical Information Service, 5285 Port Royal Road, Springfield, Virginia 22151 (HC $4.50, MF $1.45, order number PB-225 775)

Document Not Available from EDRS.

Descriptors—*Community Consultant Programs, Conference Reports, Consultants, *Consultation Programs, *Mental Health, Professional Services, *Program Development, *Program Effectiveness, Psychological Services, *Public School Systems

These are the speeches and the results of the Conference on School Consultation. The conference had four primary purposes: (1) provide an opportunity for mental health professionals to

Figure 2.5. Excerpt from document listing of *RIE*. (Source: *Resources in Education,* Vol. 12. New York: Macmillan Information, A Division of Macmillan Publishing Co., Inc., 1977, p. 40.)

Using the ERIC Thesaurus

The key to the efficient use of the ERIC system is the proper use of the ERIC Thesaurus (ET), now in its seventh edition. The documents in the ERIC system are organized and indexed in a highly systematic manner. Like any highly organized system, ERIC has its own language, knowledge of which affords the user easy access to its contents. The descriptive words under which the documents are indexed are called *descriptors*. These descriptors are quite narrow and specific in their meaning unlike the broad subject areas found in EI. In the ET the descriptors are organized in four different displays, each with its special characteristics. These displays comprise the body of the thesaurus.

1. *Descriptors* (Alphabetical Display)

This is the first and main section of the Thesaurus, and the descriptors are listed alphabetically in bold print capitals. Figure 2.6 shows an excerpt from this display. Accompanying each term

```
DIALECTS                    Jul. 1966
          CIJE: 194    RIE: 270
NT   Nonstandard Dialects
     Regional Dialects
     Social Dialects
BT   Languages
     Language Variation
RT   American English
     Cebuano
     Dialect Studies
     Diglossia
     Foochow
     Idioms
     Language
     Language Classification
     Language Standardization
     Language Usage
     Linguistics
     Mutual Intelligibility
     Native Speakers
     Sociolinguistics

DIALECT STUDIES             Jul. 1966
          CIJE: 177    RIE: 298
BT   Language Research
     Sociolinguistics
RT   Dialects
     Diglossia
     Etymology
     Language Variation

DIALOGUE                    May 1969
          CIJE: 164    RIE: 64
BT   Literary Conventions
RT   Analytical Criticism
     Film Criticism
     Formal Criticism
     Literary Genres
     Literature
     Local Color Writing
     Realism
     Scripts
```

Figure 2.6. Excerpt from alphabetical display of ERIC Thesaurus. (Source: *ERIC Thesaurus of Eric Descriptors*, 1977. New York: Macmillan Information, A Division of Macmillan Publishing Co., Inc., p. 56.)

in this alphabetic display are one or more notations to assist the user in understanding the fullness of the term.

a. SN—Scope note

A scope note is a brief statement indicating to the user the scope of the term. This statement serves to define, clarify or restrict the term. For example:

SOCIAL DIALECTS
SN Special varieties within a language,
defined by the social environment of its
speakers.

b. UF—Used for. Any term following this is a term subsumed by the descriptor.

The user must enter the ERIC system with the descriptor itself and not with any term following UF.

The term following a UF notation is also listed alphabetically in this display, but it will be followed by a USE notation which directs the user to the descriptor. For example,

PARENT PARTICIPATION
UF Parent Involvement

Parent Involvement
USE PARENT PARTICIPATION

if you wanted to find research dealing with parent involvement and looked this up in ET, you would be referred to the term Parent Participation through the USE notation. If you had gone directly to the Parent Participation entry the UF notation would indicate that that term subsumes parent involvement. In either case, however, Parent Participation is the term to be used in accessing the ERIC system.

c. NT—Narrower Term
BT—Broader Term

The terms following NT and BT are descriptors themselves and show a hierarchal relationship among the terms. A narrow term is included in the class represented by the main entry descriptor. For example:

PERCEPTION
NT Auditory Perception
Cultural Awareness

Auditory perception and Cultural Awareness are included in the term Perception.

A broad term is the reciprocal of NT notation and thus includes the NT. For example:

AUDITORY PERCEPTION
BT Perception

This shows that Auditory Perception is included in Perception.

d. RT—Related Term

Terms following an RT notation have a close conceptual relationship to the main entry descriptor but are not part of a direct hierarchy as are the NT and BT notations. These RT terms provide leads for developing other entry points to ERIC. In addition they tend to clarify the scope or meaning of the term. For example:

24

VALUES
RT Affective behavior
   Altruism
   Beliefs
   Credibility

All the terms following the RT notation are aspects of the descriptor VALUES.

In choosing descriptors, one should select the most specific descriptor available. Broader descriptors may not include citations which are narrower in their subject coverage.

e. Add date—The date on which the descriptor was added to the Thesaurus. This information allows the user to know the currency of use of the descriptor. One will note that most of the descriptors have been in use since the inception of ERIC in 1966.

f. Postings—These are frequency counts indicating the number of documents which are indexed under that descriptor. Separate counts are maintained for CIJE and RIE. These postings enable a user to know how much literature is available under that heading—how much "action" it generates.

g. Parenthetical qualifiers—These are expressions in parentheses which follow a descriptor. They serve to clarify homographs and are considered an integral part of the descriptor. For example:

DEMONSTRATIONS (CIVIL)
DEMONSTRATIONS (EDUCATIONAL)

The parenthetical words distinguish between the two meanings of the term *Demonstrations*.

2. *Rotated Descriptor Display*

This is an alphabetical index to all significant words which *form* descriptors. Figure 2.7 shows an excerpt from this display. This display is useful to determine all usages of a particular word

```
                          DIABETES
                          DIACHRONIC LINGUISTICS
                          DIACRITICAL MARKING
                 CLINICAL DIAGNOSIS
              EDUCATIONAL DIAGNOSIS
                  READING DIAGNOSIS
                          DIAGNOSTIC TEACHING
                          DIAGNOSTIC TESTS
                 SENTENCE DIAGRAMING
                          DIAGRAMS
                          DIAL ACCESS INFORMATION SYSTEMS
                          DIALECT STUDIES
                          DIALECTS
                    BLACK DIALECTS
              NONSTANDARD DIALECTS
                 REGIONAL DIALECTS
                   SOCIAL DIALECTS
                          DIALOGUE
                          DIARIES
                          DICTION
                          DICTIONARIES
                          DICTIONARY CATALOGS
                          DIDACTICISM
            TOOL AND DIE MAKERS
```

Figure 2.7. Excerpt from rotated descriptor display of ERIC Thesaurus. (Source: *ERIC Thesaurus of Eric Descriptors,* 1977, New York: Macmillan Information, A Division of Macmillan Publishing Co., Inc., p. 56.)

in a descriptor comprised of more than one word. Also it may inform the user as to a particular descriptor not encountered elsewhere. For example, suppose a user wants to find documents dealing with the speech of inner-city students. He may look in the Alphabetical display under DIALECT and find information as indicated in figure 2.6. He may then choose the NT NONSTANDARD DIALECTS and find information as indicated in figure 2.8. This would refer him to the NT BLACK DIALECTS found in figure 2.9. All these entries are in the Alphabetical display.

A faster way would be to look in the Rotated Description Display under DIALECT as shown in figure 2.7. This shows at a glance all uses of the word "dialects" in the ERIC descriptors,

NONRESIDENT STUDENTS Jul. 1966
      CIJE: 23   RIE: 48
UF Out Of State Students
BT College Students
RT Admission Criteria
     Residence Requirements

Nonreversal Shift
USE SHIFT STUDIES

NONSTANDARD DIALECTS
              Jul. 1966
      CIJE: 272   RIE: 465
NT Black Dialects
BT Dialects
RT Diglossia
     Regional Dialects
     Social Dialects
     Sociolinguistics
     Standard Spoken Usage
     Tenl
     Urban Language

Nonteaching Duties
USE NONINSTRUCTIONAL
      RESPONSIBILITY

NONTRADITIONAL STUDENTS
             Jun. 1977
      CIJE: 0   RIE: 0
SN Adults beyond traditional college age (beyond the middle twenties), ethnic minorities, women with dependent children, low achievers, and other special groups who have historically been underrepresented in higher education
BT College Students
RT Educationally
      Disadvantaged
     Higher Education
     Open Enrollment

BLACK CULTURE   Jul. 1977
      CIJE: 379   RIE: 320
UF Black Subculture
     Negro Culture (1966 1977)
BT Culture
RT African Culture
     African History
     Black History
     Black Institutions
     Black Literature
     Black Role
     Blacks
     Black Studies

BLACK DIALECTS   Jul. 1977
      CIJE: 235   RIE: 340
UF Negro Dialects (1966 1977)
BT Nonstandard Dialects
RT Blacks

BLACK EDUCATION   Jul. 1977
      CIJE: 369   RIE: 380
UF Negro Education (1966 1977)
BT Education
RT Black Colleges
     Blacks
     Black Students
     Black Studies
     Black Teachers
     School Segregation

Figure 2.8. Excerpt from alphabetic display of ERIC Thesaurus. (Source: *ERIC Thesaurus of Eric Descriptors,* 1977. New York: Macmillan Information, A Division of Macmillan Publishing Co., Inc., p. 142.)

Figure 2.9. Excerpt from alphabetic display of ERIC Thesaurus. (Source: *ERIC Thesaurus of Eric Descriptors,* 1977. New York: Macmillan Information, A Division of Macmillan Publishing Co., Inc., p. 21.)

regardless of what word order position it is in. The user then is immediately informed of the existence of the descriptor BLACK DIALECTS.

3. *Two-Way Hierarchal Display*

This display shows at a glance the broader and narrower terms associated with each descriptor. Each entry in this display is listed in alphabetical order. A hierarchy of broad terms is listed above it; a hierarchy of narrow terms is listed below it. The relationship among the terms in each hierarchy is indicated spatially by the indentation of the terms caused by colons or periods which precede the terms. Figure 2.10 shows a sample from this display. This display allows the user to see where in a hierarchy of terms a specific descriptor lies. Then he may narrow or broaden at will.

4. *Descriptor Group Display*

Each descriptor in the ERIC system is grouped into one of 52 Descriptor Groups. These are broad categories and serve as a table of contents for the entire Thesaurus. This display is useful for a user to survey quickly all possible descriptors in a category and select the most promising ones to be looked at in one of the alphabetical displays. Figure 2.11 shows a sample from this display.

```
LANGUAGE
 .ARTIFICIAL LANGUAGES
 .BRAILLE
 .CHILD LANGUAGE                               :ABILITY
 .EXPRESSIVE LANGUAGE              LANGUAGE ABILITY
 .FIGURATIVE LANGUAGE              .LANGUAGE PROFICIENCY
 ..ALLEGORY                       .LANGUAGE SKILLS
 ..AMBIGUITY                      ..AUDIOLINGUAL SKILLS
 ..ANTITHESIS                     ...LISTENING SKILLS
 ..IMAGERY                        ...SPEECH SKILLS
 ..IRONY                          ..COMMUNICATIVE COMPETENCE
 ..METAPHORS                           (LANGUAGES)
 ..PUNS                           ..HANDWRITING SKILLS
 ..SYMBOLS (LITERARY)             ..LANGUAGE FLUENCY
 .LANGUAGE OF INSTRUCTION         ..LINGUISTIC COMPETENCE
 .LANGUAGES FOR SPECIAL PURPOSES  ..READING SKILLS
 ..ENGLISH FOR SPECIAL PURPOSES   ...READING COMPREHENSION
 .LANGUAGE UNIVERSALS             ..VOCABULARY SKILLS
 .OFFICIAL LANGUAGES              ..WRITING SKILLS
 .PROGRAMING LANGUAGES            ...COMPOSITION SKILLS (LITERARY)
 .RECEPTIVE LANGUAGE              .READING ABILITY
 .SECOND LANGUAGES                ..READING RATE
 ..ENGLISH (SECOND LANGUAGE)      ..READING SKILLS
 ...ENGLISH FOR SPECIAL PURPOSES  ...READING COMPREHENSION
 .SIGN LANGUAGE                   .VERBAL ABILITY
 .SYMBOLIC LANGUAGE
 .TONE LANGUAGES
 .UNCOMMONLY TAUGHT LANGUAGES      ::INSTRUCTIONAL MEDIA
 .UNWRITTEN LANGUAGE              :AUDIOVISUAL AIDS
 .URBAN LANGUAGE                  LANGUAGE AIDS
 .WRITTEN LANGUAGE                .LANGUAGE RECORDS (PHONOGRAPH)
```

Figure 2.10. Excerpt from two-way hierarchal display of ERIC Thesaurus. (Source: *ERIC Thesaurus of Eric Descriptors*, 1977. New York: Macmillan Information, A Division of Macmillan Publishing Co., Inc., p. 354.)

Teacher Alienation
Timeout
Verbal Operant Conditioning
Verbal Stimuli
Withdrawal Tendencies (Psychology)

430 RACE RELATIONS
Anti Semitism
Black Power
Classroom Integration
College Integration
College Segregation
Defacto Segregation
Dejure Segregation
Faculty Integration
Grade A Year Integration
Integration Effects
Integration Litigation
Integration Methods
Integration Plans
Integration Readiness
Integration Studies
Legal Segregation
Neighborhood Integration
Personnel Integration
Race
Race Influences
Race Relations
Racial Balance
Racial Characteristics
Racial Composition
Racial Differences
Racial Discrimination
Racial Distribution
Racial Factors
Racial Integration
Racial Recognition
Racial Segregation
Racism
School Integration
School Segregation
Teacher Integration
Token Integration
Voluntary Integration

440 READING
Adult Literacy
Adult Reading Programs
Applied Reading
Basic Reading
Beginning Reading
Content Reading
Corrective Reading
Critical Reading
Decoding (Reading)
Developmental Reading
Directed Reading Activity
Dyslexia
Early Reading
Elective Reading
Factual Reading
Functional Illiteracy
Functional Reading

Reading Improvement
Reading Level
Reading Material Selection
Reading Materials
Reading Programs
Reading Rate
Recreational Reading
Remedial Reading Programs
Sequential Reading Programs
Sight Vocabulary
Silent Reading
Speed Reading
Story Reading
Supplementary Reading Materials

450 RESEARCH
Action Research
Advanced Systems
Agricultural Research Projects
American Studies
Architectural Research
Area Studies
Asian Studies
Attrition (Research Studies)
Behavioral Science Research
Case Studies
Case Studies (Education)
Classroom Research
Cohort Analysis
Control Groups
Creativity Research
Cross Sectional Studies
Curriculum Research
Data Collection
Deaf Research
Dropout Research
Economic Research
Educational Experiments
Educational Research
Environmental Research
Exceptional Child Research
Experimental Groups
Experimental Programs
Experimenter Characteristics
Facility Case Studies
Factor Structure
Feasibility Studies
Field Studies
Institutional Research
Interest Research
Language Research
Library Research
Lunar Research
Media Research
Medical Research
Methods Research
Middle Eastern Studies
Pilot Projects
Poverty Research
Reading Research
Research
Research Coordinating Units
Research Criteria

Figure 2.11. Excerpt from descriptor group display of ERIC Thesaurus. (Source: *ERIC Thesaurus of Eric Descriptors,* 1977. New York: Macmillan Information, A Division of Macmillan Publishing Co., Inc., p. 442.)

Abstracts of Research and Related Materials in Vocational and Technical Education
(ARM) and *Abstracts of Instructional Materials in Vocational and Technical Education* (AIM) (AIM/ARM)

These abstracts are published by the ERIC Clearinghouse on Vocational and Technical Education. AIM/ARM contains abstracts of some materials already indexed in ERIC, but in addition it contains other resource information as well, such as reports from State Departments of Education, unpublished or uncirculated research papers, and a variety of other fugitive documents. The scope of the content of AIM/ARM is divided into ten broad areas. Access to the abstracts may be had through any of five indexes: subject, author, vocational and supporting services, document number, and conversion of document number. AIM/ARM's data base may also be accessed through computer searching.

Dissertation Abstracts International (DAI)

Dissertation Abstracts International (DAI) is published monthly by University Microfilms Inc., and includes abstracts of most doctoral dissertations written at North American colleges and universities. A cumulative index is published annually. A comprehensive index of abstracts from 1861–1972 and for succeeding years is also available. Since 1977, DAI has also abstracted dissertations from European institutions (the abstracts appear in English translations, but not the titles). The content is divided into three main groupings: (A) Humanities and Social Sciences; (B) Sciences and Engineering; and (C) all European dissertations. Within group A, which is the main concern of the readers in this text, the content is divided into five broad areas: Communication and the Arts, Education, Language/Literature/Linguistics, Philosophy/Religion/Theology, and Social Sciences.

Access to abstracts in specific volumes can be made through 1) the broad subject headings of the table of contents; 2) a "keyword from title" index (used since 1970); or 3) an author index. The annual cumulative indexes provide access to the abstracts through a subject index using *keywords* and an author index. Figure 2.12 shows a sample abstract from DAI. Figures 2.13 and 2.14 show subject and author index entries respectively for that abstract.

A COMPARATIVE STUDY OF THE WISC–REVISED, THE SPANISH WISC (ESCALA DE INTELIGENCIA WECHSLER PARA NINOS), PPVT (ENGLISH VERSION), PPVT (SPANISH VERSION), AND THE CMMS ON MEXICAN–AMERICAN CHILDREN

GUZMAN, Maria Del Carmen, Ph.D.
Texas Woman's University, 1976

The purpose of the study was to determine the relationship among the IQ's on the Columbia Mental Maturity Scale (CMMS), the Peabody Picture Vocabulary Test (PPVT–English version), the Peabody Picture Vocabulary Test (PPVT–Spanish version), the Wechsler Intelligence Scale for Children-Revised (WISC–R), and the Spanish version of the WISC (Escala de inteligencia Wechsler para ninos) on Mexican-American children.

A random sample of 52 pupils from both public and parochial schools in Corpus Christi, Texas, were selected to participate in the study. The subjects, 26 boys and 26 girls, met the following criteria: 1) Mexican-American descent, 2) bilingual, 3) nine-years-old, 4) enrolled in regular fourth grade classes, and 5) low socio-economic background.

For establishing bilingualism, the Dos Amigos Verbal Lan-

Figure 2.12. Excerpt from an abstract from DAI. (Source: *Dissertation Abstracts International,* Vol. 37. Ann Arbor, Michigan: University Microfilms International, 1977, p. 4280–A.)

PPVT
A COMPARATIVE STUDY OF THE WISC-REVISED, THE
SPANISH WISC (ESCALA DE INTELIGENCIA WECHSLER
PARA NINOS), PPVT (ENGLISH VERSION), PPVT
(SPANISH VERSION), AND THE CMMS ON MEXICAN-
AMERICAN CHILDREN.— GUZMAN, MARIA DEL CARMEN
(PH.D. 1976 TEXAS WOMAN'S UNIVERSITY) 151p.
37/07-A, p.4280 DCJ77–00742

GUZMAN, MARIA DEL CARMEN
A COMPARATIVE STUDY OF THE WISC-REVISED, THE
SPANISH WISC (ESCALA DE INTELIGENCIA WECHSLER
PARA NINOS), PPVT (ENGLISH VERSION), PPVT
(SPANISH VERSION), AND THE CMMS ON MEXICAN-
AMERICAN CHILDREN. (EDUCATION, SPECIAL) (PH.D.
1976 TEXAS WOMAN'S UNIVERSITY) 151p. 37/07
A, p. 4280 DCJ77–00742

Figure 2.13. Sample entry from subject index of DAI. (Source: *Comprehensive Dissertation Index Five-Year Cumulation 1973–1977*, Vol. 10. Ann Arbor, Michigan: University Microfilms International 1979, p. 87.)

Figure 2.14. Sample entry from author index of DAI. (Source: *Comprehensive Dissertation Index Five-Year Cumulation 1973–1977*, Vol. 17. Ann Arbor, Michigan: University Microfilms International, 1979, p. 903.)

Psychological Abstracts (PA)

Psychological Abstracts is published monthly by the American Psychological Association. PA abstracts articles from over 900 journals, and includes abstracts of technical reports, monographs and other documents as well. The scope of PA's content is divided into 16 major classifications such as experimental psychology—human, personality, and developmental psychology. The abstracts in each volume are sequenced in numerical order, each volume starting with 1. Figure 2.15 shows a sample of an abstract. Access to the abstracts can be achieved through the *Author Index* (figure 2.16) or through the *Brief Subject Index* (figure 2.17), both of which indexes appear in each copy of PA. In both indexes the user is directed to the serial identification number which can be used to locate the abstract. Figures 2.16 and 2.17 show the author and subject entries respectively for the main entry shown in figure 2.15. Every six months the indexes are cumulated; at that time descriptive phrases are added to the index terms providing more detailed subject access.

The Brief Subject Index found in each copy of PA is extracted from the longer 4,000 term Thesaurus published by PA and is useful for common, straightforward searches of familiar titles. For more difficult searches, however, the *PA Thesaurus* should be consulted. The book is the recognized authoritative source for all terms related to psychological concepts. The PA Thesaurus contains three sections:

1. Relationship section—(Figures 2.18 and 2.19) This section is consulted when the user needs to determine the preferred term from a variety of near-synonymous terms. Through the descriptions "Used for," "Broader," and "Narrower," users can select the term which most closely approximates their search interests.
2. Hierarchal section—(Figure 2.20) This section is consulted when a user needs to note the relationship of a possible preferred term to all related terms.
3. Alphabetic section—(Figure 2.21) This section is consulted when the user needs to make a rapid selection of a term for a search.

Using any of these approaches, when the users have identified the term with which they seek to locate entries, they may then consult the desired volume of PA and initiate the search. Access to entries in PA may also be had through use of a computer assisted search using commercial vendors or directly with the American Psychological Association's PsycINFO data base. All PA volumes since 1967 are available on magnetic tapes.

8531. **Miller, Jane N. & Engin, Ann W.** (Mishawaka Schools Personnel Services, IN) **Tomorrow's counselor: Competent or unemployed?** *Personnel & Guidance Journal,* 1976(Jan), Vol 54(5), 262–266. —The premise that certification standards are based on competencies requires a determination and an evaluation of the competencies. Problems of training and retraining are discussed, and a possible evaluation session is described. —*G. S. Speer.*

Figure 2.15. Sample abstract from PA. (Source: *Psychological Abstracts,* Vol. 59. Washington, D.C., The American Psychological Association, Inc., 1978, p. 890.)

Miller, Dulcy B., 8418
Miller, Gary J., 7792
Miller, Gerald, 7879
Miller, Henry K., 8239
Miller, Jane N., 8531
Miller, Janice H., 8419
Miller, Jeffrey O., 7156
Miller, Kenneth E., 9007
Miller, Louise M., 8971
Miller, Malcolm, 7961
Miller, Nancy, 8104
Miller, Thomas W., 8240
Miller, Tiiu-Imbi, 7833

Figure 2.16. Excerpt from author index of PA. (Source: *Psychological Abstracts,* Vol. 59. Washington, D.C.: The American Psychological Association, Inc., 1978, p. xxxv.)

Counselor Characteristics 8208, 8222, 8225, 8229, 8233, 8239, 8334, 8413, 8432, 8434, 8499, 8508, 8531, 8539, 8545, 8555, 8592, 8904, 8905, 8919
Counselor Client Interaction [See Psychotherapeutic Processes]
Counselor Education 8499, 8519, 8528, 8531, 8540, 8544, 8545, 8550; 8555
Counselor Effectiveness [See Counselor Characteristics]
Counselor Personality [See Counselor Characteristics]
Counselor Role 8542, 8544
Counselor Trainees 8499, 8508, 8519, 8539, 8545, 8546, 8552, 8555

Figure 2.17. Excerpt from brief subject index of PA. (Source: *Psychological Abstracts,* Vol. 59. Washington, D.C.: The American Psychological Association, Inc., 1978, p. vii.)

Clinical Judgment (Psychodiagnosis)
    Use   Psychodiagnosis
Clinical Methods Training
    Used for   Training (Clinical Methods)
    Narrower   Clinical Psychology Grad Training
        Clinical Psychology Internship
        Community Mental Health Training
        Counselor Education
        Mental Health Inservice Training
        Psychiatric Training
        Psychoanalytic Training
        Psychotherapy Training
    Related   Education/
        Microcounseling
        Practicum Supervision
Clinical Psychologists
    Broader   Mental Health Personnel
        Psychologists
    Related   Clinicians
        Hypnotherapists
        Psychotherapists

Figure 2.18. Excerpt from relationship section of PA Thesaurus. (Source: *Thesaurus of Psychological Index Terms,* 1977 Edition. Washington, D.C.: American Psychological Association, 1977, p. 36.)

Counselor Client Interaction
    Use   Psychotherapeutic Processes
Counselor Education
    Broader   Clinical Methods Training
    Related   Education/
        Microcounseling
        Practicum Supervision
Counselor Effectiveness
    Use   Counselor Characteristics

Figure 2.19. Excerpt from relationship section of PA Thesaurus. (Source: *Thesaurus of Psychological Index Terms,* 1977 Edition. Washington, D.C.: American Psychological Association, 1977, p. 44.)

Learning And Thinking And Conditioning
Classical Conditioning
  Conditioned Responses
    Conditioned Emotional Responses
    Conditioned Suppression
  Conditioned Stimulus
  Unconditioned Responses
  Unconditioned Stimulus
Comprehension
  Listening Comprehension
  Number Comprehension
  Reading Comprehension
  Sentence Comprehension
Concept Learning
  Nonreversal Shift Learning
  Reversal Shift Learning
Deprivation
  REM Dream Deprivation
  Sleep Deprivation
  Stimulus Deprivation
    Food Deprivation
    Sensory Deprivation
    Social Deprivation
      Social Isolation
Feedback
  Biofeedback
  Delayed Feedback
    Delayed Auditory Feedback
  Knowledge Of Results
  Sensory Feedback
    Auditory Feedback
      Delayed Auditory Feedback
    Visual Feedback
Games
  Chess
  Entrapment Games
  Non Zero Sum Games
  Prisoners Dilemma Game
  Simulation Games
Incidental Learning
  Latent Learning
Interference (Learning)
  Proactive Inhibition
  Retroactive Inhibition
Learning Schedules
  Distributed Practice
  Massed Practice
Masking
  Auditory Masking
  Visual Masking
Mathematics (Concepts)
  Algorithms

Cortisone
Costs And Cost Analysis
Counseling Psychology
Counseling/
Counselor Attitudes
Counselor Characteristics
Counselor Education
Counselor Role
Counselor Trainees
Counselors
Counterconditioning
Countertransference
Countries
Courage
Cousins
Crabs
Crafts

Figure 2.20. Excerpt from hierarchal section of PA Thesaurus. (Source: *Thesaurus of Psychological Index Terms,* 1974 Edition. Washington, D.C.: American Psychological Association, 1974, p. 322.)

Figure 2.21. Excerpt from alphabetic section of PA Thesaurus. (Source: *Thesaurus of Psychological Index Terms,* 1974 Edition. Washington, D.C.: American Psychological Association, 1974, p. 281.)

The Social Science Index (SSI) and The Humanities Index (HI)

Each of these indexes is a separate new index which supersedes the combined *Social Science and Humanities Index* as of 1974 when that index ceased to be published. They are published by the H. W. Wilson Company. Each indexes more than 250 appropriate journals and presents subject and author listings together. The format of HI is similar to that of the Education Index described earlier. Figure 2.22 shows a sample page from SSI; Figure 2.23 shows a sample page from HI.

Thorson, James A.
Variations in death anxiety related to college students' sex, major field of study, and certain personality traits. Psychol Rept 40:857-8 Je pt 1 '77

Thorson, Stuart J.
Axiomatic theories of preference-based choice behavior: an overview. bibl Am Behav Sci 20:65-92 S '76

Thorsrud, Einar
Democracy at work: Norwegian experiences with nonbureaucratic forms of organization. J App Behav Sci 13 no3:410-21 '77

From ship deck to shop floor: autonomous work group experiments. il Scand R 65:21-6 Je '77

Thorward, Thomas E.
Philippine internship program. Pub Mgt 59:11-13 Ja '77

Thought and language
Building a tree structure: the development of hierarchical complexity and interrupted strategies in children's construction activity. P. M. Greenfield and L. Schneider. bibl il Develop Psychol 13:299-313 Jl '77

Discriminant analysis of psychological judgments of literal and figurative meaningfulness and anomaly. R. G. Malgady. J Psychol 95:217-21 Mr '77

Frontal lobe system maturational lag in juvenile delinquents shown in narratives test. A. A. Ponitus and K. F. Ruttiger. bibl Adolescence 11:509-18 Wint '76

Instantiation of general terms. R. C. Anderson and others. bibl J Verb Learn 15:667-79 D '76

Language as an attribute of memory. P. D. McCormack. bibl Can J Psychol 30:238-48 D '76

Language in child and chimp? J. Limber. bibl Am Psychol 32:280-95 Ap '77

Linguistic representation of a macroenvironment under three communication conditions. E. M. Edelman and others. bibl Environ Behav 9:417-32 S '77

Mystical experience as related to present and anticipated future church participation. R. W. Hood, jr. bibl Psychol Rept 39:1127-36 D pt2 '76

Personal and common components of cognitive dictionaries. L. J. Moran. bibl Psychol Rept 40:795-806 Je pt 1 '77

Thinking with restricted language: a personal construct investigation of pre-lingually profoundly deaf apprentices. A. Gordon. bibl Brit J Psychol 68:253-5 My '77

Verbal planning functions in children's speech. B. MacWhinney and H. Osser. bibl Child Develop 48:978-85 S '77

Vygotsky's contributions to a dialectical materialist psychology. R. Bickley. Sci & Soc 41:191-207 Summ '77
See also
Communicative disorders

SEWAGE disposal
See also
Refuse and refuse disposal

SEWARD, John H.
Veracruz massacre of 1879. Americas 32:585-96 Ap '76

SEWARD, Thomas A.
Peculiar Leonese dialectal forms *dulda, portalgo, selmana,* etc: a problem in diachronic phonology. Hispan R 44:163-9 Spr '76

SEWERAGE
See also
Storm sewers

SEWING
See also
Quilting

SEX
Overview of female sexuality. S. D. Hubbard. Humanist 36:9+ N '76
See also
Bisexuality
Homosexuality
Sex customs
Women and men

SEX (in religion, folklore, etc)
Bawdy monologues and rhymed recitations. G. Legman. Southern Folklore Q 40:59-123 Mr/Je '76

Carsalesmanese. R. J. Desmond. ETC 33:77-9 Mr '76

Earthquake erotica: some bawdy lore from the Los Angeles catastrophe of 1971. C. C. Doyle. Western Folklore 35:73-4 Ja '76

Figure 2.22. Excerpt from SSI. (Source: *Social Sciences Index,* Vol. 4. New York: H. W. Wilson Company, 1978, p. 976.)

Figure 2.23. Excerpt from HI. (Source: *Humanities Index,* Vol. 3. New York: H. W. Wilson Company, 1977, p. 673.)

Sociological Abstracts (SA)

Sociological Abstracts (SA) is published by the American Sociological Association five times per year with a cumulative annual index. Several hundred domestic and foreign journals are reviewed, but not every issue of every journal is abstracted; each issue of SA will specify the scope of the abstracting for that issue. The abstracts in SA also include those of papers presented at major gatherings of sociologists, which may later appear in the published proceedings of the sponsoring society.

The content of SA is divided into 31 subject headings such as mass phenomena, sociology of the arts, and sociology of health and medicine. The abstracts of published articles are assigned a serial number and are listed alphabetically by author's name under each heading. Figure 2.24 shows a sample abstract. Abstracts of unpublished papers are separate from the published ones listed under the particular meeting at which they were presented. Access to all abstracts may be had through the cumulative indexes which include both author and subject approaches. Both indexes provide a serial accession number which would direct the user to the abstract. Figures 2.25 and 2.26 show entries from the author and subject index respectively for the abstract appearing in figure 2.24.

76H8630
  Blasi, Anthony J. (DePauw U, Greencastle IN 46135), **Vocations and Perceptions,** *Sociological Analysis,* 1975, 36, 1, Spr, 67–72.
¶ The study of sacerdotal vocations is considered from the vantage point of social role-taking theory & role-model theory. 2 hypotheses are proposed: (1) the propensity toward selecting the clerical occupation is higher among R's who perceive priests being positively evaluated than among R's who perceive them being negatively evaluated, & (2) R's who see themselves similar to priests & who see priests positively evaluated have higher clergy occupation choice scores than other R's. [?] data collected from a sample of adolescent M's in a Ru section of central US support the hypotheses. The results are interpreted as illustrative of a 'pedestal effect', whereby respect for priests is seen to encourage vocations, but too much such respect has counterproductive consequences. 2 Tables. AA

Figure 2.24. Sample abstract from SA. (Source: *Sociological Abstracts,* Vol. 24. San Diego: Sociological Abstracts, Inc., 1976, p. 371.)

Birch, David L., 76I1061
Birch, H. G., 76H8939
Birdil, H. S., 76H9135
Birenbaum, Arnold, 76H8628
Birksted, Ian K., 76I1113
Birnbaum, Norman, 76I0536
Bishop, Charles A., 76I0737
Bishop, F. Marian, 76H8810

Figure 2.25. Sample entries from author index of SA. (Source: *Sociological Abstracts,* Vol. 24. San Diego: Sociological Abstracts, Inc., 1976, p. 1432.)

Nurse –s, –ing
  attitudes of nursing home administrators; 76H7991
  attitudes toward male nurses; 76I2181
  changes in nursing homes; 76H8030
  charges for & payment of nursing home services; 76H8028
  chronic illness in nursing home residents; 76H7998
  medical care for the elderly; 76I0279
  night workers; problems; hospitals; review; 76I1913
  number of employees in nursing homes; 76H8029
  professional identity of nurse practitioners; 76H8628
  rehabilitation & recreation services in nursing homes; 76H8031
  social position of African nurses; 76H7523

Figure 2.26. Sample entries from subject index of SA. (Source: *Sociological Abstracts,* Vol. 24. San Diego: Sociological Abstracts, Inc., 1976, p. 1383.)

Reproduction of complete unpublished papers is available in hard cover or microfiche format if the author of the paper had previously authorized such reproduction. If the authorization is lacking, then a copy of the paper can usually be secured directly from the author. Because of the inconsistency of the indexing of its journal sources, SA lacks appeal for highly rigorous searching. It is used more frequently by sociologists as a document to be perused in order to develop a current awareness of the field.

Social Sciences Citation Index (SSCI)

A unique and very valuable indexing system for all the social sciences is the *Social Sciences Citation Index* (SSCI). It is published by the Institute for Scientific Information, Inc. tri-annually with the final issue cumulating the entire year. The entries in SSCI represent the complete indexing of over 1,000 journals in all aspects of social science, plus selective indexing of over 2,000 additional sources. Foreign as well as domestic sources are indexed. SSCI started publication in 1972, has worked forward and backward, and now includes the year 1969 to the present.

An issue of SSCI contains four component parts:

1. *Citation Index* (figure 2.27). The entries in the citation index list a) authors whose paper(s) have been cited by others; b) the specific paper(s) of his or hers which has been cited; and c) the author and title of the paper in which the citation appeared. For example, Figure 2.27 shows that an article by K. S. Goodman which appeared in *Elementary English*, Volume 42, page 639 in 1965, was cited by G. H. Maring in *Reading Teacher,* Volume 31, page 887 in 1978, and by another person as well. Following this are other papers by Goodman with the citers mentioned similarly.

2. *Source Index* (figure 2.28). The entries in the source index are the sources of the citations appearing in the citation index. For example, Figure 28 shows the entry for the source of the citation of the Goodman paper in the previous example (figure 2.27). This tells us that Maring's paper which cited Goodman is entitled "Matching Remediation to Miscues." Maring is associated with Washington State University—Center for Reading in Pullman, Washington. There were twelve citations in this paper including Goodman, and they are shown here.

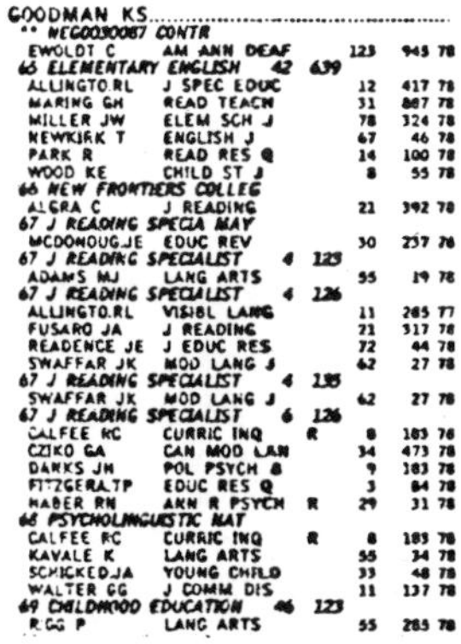
GOODMAN KS
** NEG0030087 CONTR
EWOLDT C AM ANN DEAF 123 945 78
65 ELEMENTARY ENGLISH 42 639
ALLINGTO RL J SPEC EDUC 12 417 78
MARING GH READ TEACH 31 887 78
MILLER JW ELEM SCH J 78 324 78
NEWKIRK T ENGLISH J 67 46 78
PARK R READ RES Q 14 100 78
WOOD KE CHILD ST J 8 55 78
66 NEW FRONTIERS COLLEG
ALGRA C J READING 21 392 78
67 J READING SPECIA MAY
MCDONOUG JE EDUC REV 30 237 78
67 J READING SPECIALIST 4 123
ADAMS MJ LANG ARTS 55 19 78
67 J READING SPECIALIST 4 126
ALLINGTO RL VISIBL LANG 11 285 77
FUSARO JA J READING 21 317 78
READENCE JE J EDUC RES 72 44 78
SWAFFAR JK MOD LANG J 62 27 78
67 J READING SPECIALIST 4 135
SWAFFAR JK MOD LANG J 62 27 78
67 J READING SPECIALIST 6 126
CALFEE RC CURRIC INQ R 8 183 78
CZIKO GA CAN MOD LAN 34 473 78
DARKS JH POL PSYCH B 9 383 78
FITZGERA TP EDUC RES Q 3 84 78
HABER RN ANN R PSYCH R 29 31 78
68 PSYCHOLINGUISTIC NAT
CALFEE RC CURRIC INQ R 8 183 78
KAVALE K LANG ARTS 55 34 78
SCHICKED JA YOUNG CHILD 33 48 78
WALTER GG J COMM DIS 11 137 78
69 CHILDHOOD EDUCATION 46 123
RIGG P LANG ARTS 55 285 78

Figure 2.27. Excerpt from citation index of SSCI. (Source: *Social Sciences Citation Index,* Vol. 3. Philadelphia: Institute for Scientific Information, 1978, p. 7504.)

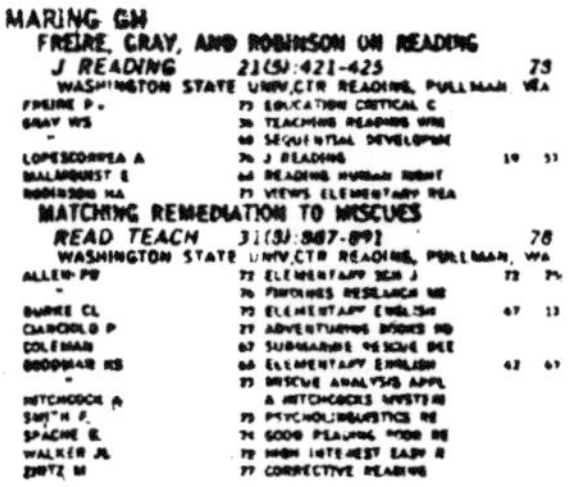
MARING GH
FREIRE, GRAY, AND ROBINSON ON READING
J READING 21(5):421-425 78
WASHINGTON STATE UNIV,CTR READING, PULLMAN, WA
MATCHING REMEDIATION TO MISCUES
READ TEACH 31(8):887-891 78
WASHINGTON STATE UNIV,CTR READING, PULLMAN, WA

Figure 2.28. Excerpt from source index of SSCI. (Source: *Social Sciences Citation Index,* Part 4, Source Index. Philadelphia: Institute for Scientific Information, 1978, p. 6288.)

3. *Permuterm Subject Index* (PSI). SSCI has a subject index called a *Permuterm Subject Index* (PSI). This is a "natural language" indexing system which pairs every significant word from the title of a paper with every other significant word. For example, figure 2.29 shows an entry in the PSI for the term MISCUES. You will recall that this word appeared in the title of Maring's paper in the previous example. Here we are told of the existence of a paper by G. H. Maring which has the term MISCUES in its title along with the term MATCHING. The term MISCUES also appears with the word REMEDIATION in the same paper.

4. *Corporate Index* (figure 2.30). The entries in the corporate index are an alphabetic listing of the organizations and/or institutions with which the source authors are affiliated. For example, figure 2.30 tells us that G. H. Maring from Washington State University, Center for Reading, Pullman, Washington wrote an article in *Reading Teacher,* Volume 31, page 887 in 1978.

The real value of the unique features of SSCI may be appreciated by considering its major uses:

1. Citation search: If the users know the author of a key paper on a subject and desire to know how that paper has influenced others, they can look in the citation index and follow through to the source index, if desired. For example, the 1965 paper by Goodman was cited twice in this indexing period.

2. Subject search: If the users know a significant word from a title of a paper, they can locate a reference for the word in the PSI. This identifies the author an entry for whom can then be located in the source index. For example, if all the users know is the term "miscues," they can check the PSI to see who has used this term in the indexing period.

3. Author: If the users want to know if a particular author has published anything during the indexing period, they can check the source index for possible entries. For example, if the users know that G. H. Maring wrote a paper of interest, they can check the source index for the bibliographical information.

4. Organization: If the users know the name of an organization or institution from which some papers of interest might emanate, they can consult the entries in the corporate index which lists the papers published during the indexing period. For example, if the users know that someone at Washington State University—Center for Reading published a paper of interest, then they could check the corporate entry to find the specific citation.

MISCUE
ANALYSIS - -•HOOD J
- -•NEWMAN H
- -•STANSELL JC
- -•WEBER RM+
COMPLETE - NEWMAN H
FINDINGS - - WEBER RM+
GOOD - - - - NEWMAN H
ORAL - - - - "
PRACTICAL - HOOD J
READING - - NEWMAN H
RESEARCH - - WEBER RM+
TEACHERS - - HOOD J
VIEWS - - - STANSELL JC

MISCUES
MATCHING - -•MARING GH
REMEDIATION

Figure 2.29. Excerpt from Permuterm Subject Index of SSCI. (Source: *Social Sciences Citation Index,* Part 5, Permuterm Subject Index, A to Z. Philadelphia: Institute for Scientific Information, 1978, p. 2528.)

WILLARD W HUMAN ORG 36 352 77
YOUNG D WEED SCI 26 209 78
WASHINGTON STATE UNIV,PULLMAN,WA 99164, USA
WARD DA J DRUG ISS 8 373 78
WASHINGTON STATE UNIV,PUYALLUP,WA 98371, USA
SCHRAGER LS WHARTON MAG L 3 69 78
WASHINGTON STATE UNIV,ANTHROPOL LAB, PULLMAN,WA 99168, USA
FLENNIKEN JJ AM ANTIQUIT 43 473 78
WASHINGTON STATE UNIV,COLL BUSINESS & ECON,PULLMAN,WA 99163, USA
MENASCO MB J MARKET C N 15 650 78
WASHINGTON STATE UNIV,COLL ECON & BUSINESS,PULLMAN,WA 99163, USA
BREEN DA TRANSP J 18 19 78
WASHINGTON STATE UNIV,COLL VET MED, PULLMAN,WA 99163, USA
LEATHERS CW J AM VET ME 173 1218 78
WASHINGTON STATE UNIV,CRIMINAL JUSTICE RES CTR,PULLMAN,WA 99163, USA

Figure 2.30. Excerpt from corporate index of SSCI. (Source: *Social Sciences Citation Index,* Corporate Index, A to Hung, Vol. 3. Philadelphia: Institute for Scientific Information, 1978, p. 941.)

Thus we see that with a very small amount of original information the desired references may easily be located. There are other uses of SSCI as well. An evaluator might want to know how much is being published in the social science area at a given institution. An author might want to know if anyone is reading his or her stuff. A researcher might want to know who else is working in his or her field of research. The possibilities for using SSCI are endless.

National Technical Information Service (NTIS)

The National Technical Information Service (NTIS) is a branch of the U. S. Department of Commerce, and is a central source for the publication of government sponsored research. It publishes its *Announcements and Index* biweekly and a cumulative index annually. The scope of the content of NTIS is contained in 22 broad fields which include a wide range of human endeavor; Field 5, Behavioral and Social Sciences, would be of most interest to the readers of this book. The main entries in NTIS are abstracts of longer reports which can be ordered from NTIS in paper copy or microfiche format and which are available in many large libraries. Figure 2.31 shows a sample main entry.

Main entries can be accessed manually through five types of index entries, the choice of which to be used depending upon the information the user has. The following are the index entries for the sample entry in figure 2.31:

1. Personal author (figure 2.32)—These entries are sequenced alphabetically for personal author.

2. Corporate author (figure 2.33)—These entries are sequenced alphabetically by name of corporate author.

PB-288 364/3GA   PC A19/MF A01
Horace H. Rackman School of Graduate Studies, Ann Arbor, MI.
Underemployment of Ph.D.s. Volume I and II.
Final rept. 1 Sep 76-28 Feb 78,
Theodore J. Settle. 25 Apr 78, 428p DLETA-91-26-76-66-1
Grant DL-91-26-76-66

Descriptors: *Employment, *Professional personnel, Attitudes, Job satisfaction, Education, Universities, Manpower utilization, Unemployment, Placement, Statistical analysis, Surveys, Theses. Identifiers: *Underemployed, Doctoral degrees.

The purpose of this study was to examine the increasing gap between the educational preparation and skills of Ph.D.s against position requirements for placement, i.e., the underemployment of Ph.D.s. A survey was sent to 1968-69 and 1974-75 Ph.D. graduates of eight departments in six universities. The major conclusions based on the data analyses are: (1) Underemployment is a subjective rather than an objective phenomenon. (2) The least underemployed graduates studied Economics or Sociology (most: English or History), graduated in 1968-69, and were close to a faculty member who took a special interest in their professional career.

SETSER, D. W.
Experimental Investigation of the Chemistry of Excited States of Rare Gases. Annual Technical Progress Report, October 15, 1976--October 14, 1977.
COO-2807-11   7D

Experimental Investigation of the Chemistry of Excited States of Rare Gases. Second Quarterly Progress Report, January 15, 1978--April 15, 1978.
COO-2807-13   7D

SETTLE, THEODORE J.
Underemployment of Ph.D.s. Volume I and II.
PB-288 364/3GA   5I

SEVERSON, S. D.
Economic Evaluation of Fabric Filtration Versus Electrostatic Precipitation for Ultrahigh Particulate Collection Efficiency. Final Report.
EPRI-FP-775   13B

Figure 2.31. Sample main entry from NTIS. (Source: *National Technical Information Service,* Vol. 79. Washington, D.C.: U.S. Department of Commerce, NTISUB/E/001–005, 1979, p. 39.)

Figure 2.32. Sample from personal author index of NTIS. (Source: *National Technical Information Service,* Vol. 79. Washington, D.C.: U.S. Department of Commerce, NTISUB/E/005, 1979, p. PA–49.)

3. Subject (figures 2.34 and 2.35)—These entries are sequenced by keywords (descriptors). Note that the main entry in our example has two asterisked descriptors: *employment* and *professional personnel*. Figures 34 and 35 show the entry referred by both the descriptors.

4. Contract grant number (figure 2.36)—These entries are sequenced in alphanumeric order of contract grant number.

5. Accession/Report number (figure 2.37)—These entries are sequenced by the NTIS order number.

Main entries may also be accessed by a computer assisted search through commercial vendors (to be explained below) or through direct contact with NTIS via its Hot Line. NTIS also publishes

HONEYWELL, INC., ST. PAUL, MN. SYSTEMS AND RESEARCH CENTER.
Application of Wind Power Systems to the Service Area of the Minnesota Power and Light Company. Final Report, July 1975–August 1976.
COO-2618-1   10B

HORACE H. RACKMAN SCHOOL OF GRADUATE STUDIES, ANN ARBOR, MI.
Underemployment of Ph.D.s. Volume I and II. *(DLETA-91-26-76-66-1)*
PB-288 364/3GA   5I

HOUSTON UNIV., TX. DEPT. OF PHYSICS.
Microstructural Studies of Hydrogen and Deuterium in BCC Refractory Metals. Progress Report, 1 June 1977–31 May 1978.
ORO-5111-2   11F

Figure 2.33. Excerpt from corporate author index of NTIS. (Source: *National Technical Information Service,* Vol. 79. Washington, D.C.: U.S. Department of Commerce, NTISUB/E/ 001–005, 1979, p. CA–16.)

EMPLOYMENT
Job Bank Frequently Listed Openings (JOB-FLO), 1978 (11 regions).
NTISUB/E/262   5I
Job Bank Frequently Listed Openings (JOB-FLO), 1978 (11 regions and national summary Reports).
NTISUB/E/275   5I

Underemployment of Ph.D.s. Volume I and II.
PB-288 364/3GA   5I

WIN Clients in Suspense. Special Mail Surveys of Sponsors of Work Incentive (WIN) Programs.
PB-288 594/5GA   5I

WIN Clients Deregistered for Other Reasons. Special Mail Surveys of Sponsors of Work Incentive (WIN) Programs.
PB-288 595/2GA   5K

Figure 2.34. Excerpt from subject index of NTIS. (Source: *National Technical Information Service,* Vol. 79. Washington, D.C.: U.S. Department of Commerce, NTISUB/E/001–005, 1979, p. SU25.)

PROFESSIONAL PERSONNEL
Underemployment of Ph.D.s. Volume I and II.
PB-288 364/3GA   5I

PROFESSIONAL TRAINING
The Educational Information Consultant. Skills in Disseminating Educational Information. Training Manual.
ED-149 725   5I

Figure 2.35. Excerpt from subject index of NTIS. (Source: *National Technical Information Service,* Vol. 79. Washington, D.C.: U.S. Department of Commerce, NTISUB/E/001–005, 1979, p. SU–64.)

DL-91-26-76-66
Horace H. Rackman School of Graduate Studies, Ann Arbor, MI.
PB-288 364/3GA   5I

DL-91-36-74-09
Columbia Univ., New York.
PB-288 178/7GA   5C

Figure 2.36. Excerpt from contract grant number index of NTIS. (Source: *National Technical Information Service,* Vol. 79. Washington, D.C.: U.S. Department of Commerce, NTISUB/E/ 001–005, 1979, p. CN–3.)

PB-288 364/3GA
Underemployment of Ph.D.s. Volume I and II.
PB-288 364/3GA   5I   PC A19/MF A01

PB-288 365/0GA
A Rational Approach to Damage Mitigation in Existing Structures Exposed to Earthquakes.
PB-288 365/0GA   13M PC A05/MF A01

Figure 2.37. Excerpt from accession/report number index of NTIS. (Source: *National Technical Information Service,* Vol. 79. Washington, D.C.: U.S. Department of Commerce, NTISUB/E/001–005, 1979, p. AR–49.)

bibliographies which are prepared in anticipation of users' needs. The entries in field 5 of NTIS sometimes duplicate those of other governmental indexing systems such as ERIC. Yet on occasion the only indexing of a fugitive document may be through NTIS, so an absolutely thorough search might require its usage.

Index Medicus (IM)

Index Medicus (IM) is published by the National Library of Medicine on a monthly basis; a cumulative index is published annually. It indexes more than 2,000 serial journals and selected monographs including many from foreign sources. A unique feature of IM is its publication of "medical reviews"—previously accomplished through surveys of recent bio-medical literature. Through use of one of these medical reviews, a user can immediately possess an up-to-date list of entries on an available subject.

The inclusion of IM in this book which is devoted to educational research may seem incongruous at first thought, but the field of medicine is sufficiently broad to include more than just its biological and chemical aspects. The social aspects of medicine, as well, are included in its contents: psychiatry and psychology, anthropology, education, sociology, social phenomena, humanities and health care.

Access to the entries in IM may be gained through the author section or subject section. The author section may be entered through the last name of the senior author of the entry. However, access to the subject section usually requires use of a thesaurus-type companion volume called *Medical Subject Headings* (MeSH). A careful use of MeSH is necessary to determine the specific terms needed for access to a subject.

There are two listings of subject headings in MeSH: *alphabetic* and *categorized*:

1. In the alphabetic listing, all terms are presented in alphabetical order and are cross referenced. Figure 2.38 shows a page from the alphabetic listing. The larger, bold face capitalized terms are access terms (comparable to descriptors in ERIC) under which entries are found. The smaller capitalized terms included in the alphabetic listing are not access terms but are cross referenced to access terms. For example, the term INADEQUATE PERSONALITY is not an access term but we are directed to "see under" PERSONALITY DISORDERS. We follow this cross reference to the page shown on Figure 2.39, where we find the access term PERSONALITY

PERSONALITY DISORDERS
F3.709.597
XU AS IF PERSONALITY
XU CYCLOTHYMIC PERSONALITY
XU IMPULSE-RIDDEN PERSONALITY
XU INADEQUATE PERSONALITY
XU OBSESSIVE-COMPULSIVE PERSONALITY
XU PASSIVE-AGGRESSIVE PERSONALITY
XU PASSIVE-DEPENDENT PERSONALITY
XU TENSION-DISCHARGE DISORDERS
XR ANOMIE

PERSONALITY, HYSTERICAL see HYSTERICAL PERSONALITY

IMPULSIVE BEHAVIOR
F1.145.527   F3.126.517

IMURAN see AZATHIOPRINE

INADEQUATE PERSONALITY see under PERSONALITY DISORDERS

INBORN ERRORS OF METABOLISM see METABOLISM, INBORN ERRORS

Figure 2.38. Excerpt from alphabetical listing of MeSH subject headings. (Source: *Cumulated Index Medicus,* Vol. 18. Bethesda, Maryland: National Library of Medicine, DHEW Publication No. (NIH) 78–259, January–December 1977, p. 181.)

Figure 2.39. Excerpt from categorized listing of MeSH subject headings. (Source: *Cumulated Index Medicus,* Vol. 18. Bethesda, Maryland: National Library of Medicine, DHEW Publication No. (NIH) 78–259, January–December 1977, p. 610.)

DISORDERS followed by those other non-access terms it subsumes. A non-access term may be followed by "see," "see under," or "see related." The access term will show this cross referencing by preceding the listing of the non-access terms it subsumes with X (if cross referenced from "see"), XU (if cross-referenced from "see under") or XR (if cross-referenced from "see related"). By this means, when an access term is located the user can note at a glance which terms are related to it and the nature of the relationship.

2. The categorized lists (sometimes called "tree lists" because they branch) of MeSH represent another means of access to entries via subject headings. Figure 2.40 shows a page from the table of contents of a MeSH volume. Listed under the heading CATEGORIZED LISTS OF MEDICAL SUBJECT HEADINGS are the 14 broad areas of subjects. From this, the user is directed to the desired categorized list as shown in figure 2.41, where is found a listing of each access term in a spatial arrangement showing its relationship to other related terms. For example, if we were interested in entries dealing with the *development of personality* we could: 1) look at the broad areas on figure 2.40; 2) identify area F—(Psychiatry and Psychology) as a tentative area; 3) check the categorical lists for personality as shown in figure 2.41; 4) locate PERSONALITY DEVELOPMENT as an access term; and 5) locate the term in the IM itself, as shown in Figure 2.42. There we find two entries.

This brief explanation will serve as an introduction to the IM and its effective usage. Details concerning fine points of indexing and explanations of all symbols will be found in the IM itself.

International Nursing Index (INI)

The *International Nursing Index* (INI) is published quarterly by the American Journal of Nursing Company in cooperation with the National Library of Medicine and has a cumulative index published annually. More than 200 domestic and foreign journals in nursing are indexed as well as all nursing articles in the non-nursing journals indexed by Index Medicus.

Access to entries may be had through a subject listing (figure 2.43) or a name listing (figure 2.44). In the subject listing, a given article may be indexed under several subjects headings, thus reducing the cross referencing typical of other indexing systems. A nursing thesaurus appears in each annual issue. The terminology in this thesaurus is an extension of the MeSH used in the Index Medicus described previously. Figure 2.45 shows a sample from this thesaurus.

Cumulative Index to Nursing and Allied Health Literature (CINAHL)

The Cumulative Index to Nursing and Allied Health Literature (CINAHL) is published by the Seventh-Day Adventist Hospital Association bi-monthly with a cumulative annual issue. Originally published as the *Cumulative Index to Nursing Literature,* it expanded its coverage to include allied health journals in 1977, thus rendering the new, present title. CINAHL indexes some 250 journals: all periodicals in nursing and major periodicals in the allied health professions such as laboratory technology, medical records, and social service in health care. The entries include research and non-research sources. To assist those users searching specifically for research entries, the words "research," "research med," or "research nursing" appear following the title and/or author of each entry.

The entries may be accessed through a subject index (figure 2.46) or an author index (figure 2.47). An appendix includes entries for audiovisual materials, book reviews and pamphlets. Each annual edition contains a list of subject headings and cross references used.

CONTENTS

Figure 2.40. Excerpt from table of contents of MeSH volume. (Source: *Cumulated Index Medicus,* Vol. 18. Bethesda, Maryland: National Library of Medicine, DHEW Publication No. (NIH) 78–259, January–December, 1977, p. 3.)

PERSONALITY	F1.752	
AUTHORITARIANISM	F1.752.98	
CHARACTER	F1.752.190	
CREATIVENESS	F1.752.264	F2.463.785.
DEPENDENCY (PSYCHOLOGY) •	F1.752.330	
EMPATHY	F1.752.355	
INDIVIDUALITY	F1.752.488	
INTELLIGENCE	F1.752.543	
LEADERSHIP	F1.752.609	
MACHIAVELLIANISM •	F1.752.650	
PERSONALITY DEVELOPMENT	F1.752.747	
EGO	F1.752.747.189	F2.739.794.
REALITY TESTING •	F1.752.747.189.508	F2.739.794.
EXTRAVERSION (PSYCHOLOGY)	F1.752.747.246	F2.739.794.
ID	F1.752.747.347	F2.739.794.

Figure 2.41. Excerpt from a categorized list in MeSH. (Source: *Cumulated Index Medicus,* Vol. 18. Bethesda, Maryland: National Library of Medicine, DHEW Publication No. (NIH) 78–259, January–December, 1977, p. 46)

PERSONALITY ASSESSMENT

Implications of the personality assessment system for marital counseling: a pilot study. Saunders DR, et al. **Psychol Rep** 1980 Feb;46(1):151-60

PERSONALITY DEVELOPMENT

see related
CHILD DEVELOPMENT
GROWTH
SOCIALIZATION
Adolescent and family abandonment: a family systems approach to treatment. Reposa RE.
Int J Group Psychother 1979 Jul;29(3):359–68
The value of reconstruction in adult psychoanalysis. Blum HP. **Int J Psychoanal** 1980;61(1):39–52
The value of reconstruction in adult psychoanalysis. Brenman E. **Int J Psychoanal** 1980;61(1):53–60
[Television and aggression] Nitsch K. **Med Welt** 1980 Jan 25;31(4):III   **(Ger)**

Figure 2.42. Sample entries in IM. (Source: *Index Medicus,* Vol. 21. Bethesda, Maryland: National Library of Medicine, NIH Publication No. 80–252, August, 1980, p. 610.)

MENSTRUATION, LUTEAL PHASE see under MENSTRUATION

MENSTRUATION, RETROGRADE see under MENSTRUATION DISORDERS

MENTAL DEFICIENCY see MENTAL RETARDATION

MENTAL DISORDERS

Health in 1980-1990. Major health problems. Three challenges to health: cancer, cardiovascular diseases, and mental illness. Selby P. **Australas Nurses J** 5(3):7-10, SEP 76
Response to critique on 'An epidemiological study of psychiatric symptom pattern change: pilot study findings'. Nakagawa H, et al. **Commun Nurs Res** 5:36-7, Nov 72
An epidemiological study of psychiatric symptom pattern change: pilot study findings. Nakagawa H, et al. **Commun Nurs Res** 5:9-27, Nov 72
Critique of 'An epidemiological study of psychiatric symptom pattern change: pilot study findings'. Roberts DE. **Commun Nurs Res** 5:28-35, Nov 72
Locked doors in the management of disturbed psychiatric patients. Cobb JP, et al. **J Adv Nurs** 1(6):469-80, Nov 76
Changes in attitudes about mental illness among nursing students following a psychiatric affiliation. Creech SK. **J Psychiatr Nurs** 15(6):9-14, Jun 77
A scale for the measurement of attitudes to mental illness. Jegede RO. **J Psychol** 93(Pt 2):269-72, Jul 76
Psyciatric patients and the public in this country. Opondo WW. **Kenya Nurs J** 5(1):41, Jun 76
Women, psychiatric disorder and social class. Brown GW, et al. **Midwife Health Visit Community Nurse** 13(2):37-45, Feb 77

Figure 2.43. Sample entries in subject listing of INI. (Source: *International Nursing Index,* Vol. 12. New York: American Journal of Nursing Co., 1977, p. 169.)

Reimann R: Drei Jahre Bildungszentrum Essen des DBfK. Teil II: Das Bildungsangebot für zukunftorientierte Krankenpflege Krankenpflege 31(5):160–1, May 77 (Ger)
Reimnitz CA: Major time wasters in a large long-term care facility. J Long Term Care Adm 4(4):29–36, 1976
Rein I: Medical and nursing students: concepts of self and ideal self, typical and ideal work partner. J Pers Assess 41(4):368–74, Aug 77
Reinberg A see Smolensky MH
Reinecke RD, Coleman N, Kelly J: An eye mobile screening unit. Sight Sav Rev 46(4):147–53, Winter 76–77
Reinhart E: Independent study: an option in continuing education. J Contin Educ Nurs 8(1):38–42, Jan-Feb 77
Reinherz H, Griffin CL: Identifying children at risk: a first step to prevention. Health Educ 8(4):14–6, Jul-Aug 77
Reinhoud LJ, de Jager–v.d. Kam J: Opleidingen 'en' gezondheidszorg Tijdschr Ziekenverpl 30(9):435–6, 26 Apr 77 (Dut)
Reinskou I see Bratteli E
Reisner V: V lázni ano domini 1550 Zdrav Prac 27(1):55–6, Jan 77 (Cze)
Reitov J: Undervisning af hospitalindlagte børn og unge ved somatiske sygehuse: sygeplejersken får vaerdifuld viden for diagnose og terapi Sygeplejersken 76(35):14–8, 8 Sep 76 (Dan)

Figure 2.44. Excerpt from name listing in INI. (Source: *International Nursing Index,* Vol. 12. New York: American Journal of Nursing Co., 1977, p. 371.)

HOUSEKEEPING

(The care and management of property.)

see also
Hospital Housekeeping

Human Relations see Father-Child Relations; Interpersonal Relations; Interprofessional Relations; Mother-Child Relations; Nurse-Patient Relations; Parent-Child Relations; Physician-Patient Relations; Professional-Family Relations; Professional-Patient Relations; Sibling Relations

HUMAN RIGHTS

(The rights of the individual to cultural, social, economic and educational opportunities as provided by society, e.g. right to work, right to education and right to social security.)

See also Civil Rights
Ethics
Women's Rights

HYGIENE

IDENTITY CRISIS

(Chaotic concept of self wherein one's role in life appears to be an insoluble dilemma; often expressed by isolation, withdrawal, rebellion and extremism.)

Image (Nurses and Nursing) see Nurses; Nursing; Psychology, Social; Self-Concept

Immigration see Emigration and Immigration

Inactive Nurses see Nurses, subheading "supply and distribution"; Health Manpower

Indexing see Abstracting and Indexing

Indigent Care see Medical Assistance; Medical Indigency

Figure 2.45. Excerpt from thesaurus in INI. (Source: *International Nursing Index,* Vol. 12. New York: American Journal of Nursing Co., 1977, p. 9.)

MOTOR SKILLS--IN INFANCY AND CHILDHOOD

Behavioral and nystagmus response of a hyperkinetic child to vestibular stimulation (Bhatara V et al) AJOT 32:311-6, May/Jun 78

Measurement for curriculum building for multiply handicapped children (Whitney PL) PHYS THER 58:415-20, Apr 78

MOTOR SKILLS--INFANCY AND CHILDHOOD--EVALUATION

Stimulating developmentally delayed infants: evaluation of a short term project (Wolpert R et al) (research, med) PHYSIOTHER CAN 30:76-82, Mar/Apr 78

MOTOR VEHICLES

Assessing the driving potential of the handicapped (Gurgold GD et al) AJOT 32:41-6, Jan 78

WOLLAM GL, GIFFORD RW Jr: Four basic problems in controlling hypertension. CONSULTANT 18:25-30, Aug 78

WOLPERT R, GOUSE-SHEESE J, LEUCHTER SL ET AL: Stimulating developmentally delayed infants: evaluation of a short term project (research, med) PHYSIOTHER CAN 30:76-82, Mar/Apr 78

WOLSTENHOLME WA, GERBER JN: GC/MS with complete microprocessor control. AM LAB 9:69-70+, Feb 77

WONG S: Nurse-teacher behaviours in the clinical field: apparent effect on nursing students' learning (research, nurs) J ADV NURS 3:369-72, Jul 78

Figure 2.46. Excerpt form subject index of CINAHL. (Source: *Cumulative Index to Nursing and Allied Health Literature,* Vol. 23. Glendale, California: The Seventh-Day Adventist Hospital Association, 1979, p. 323.)

Figure 2.47. Excerpt from author index of CINAHL. (Source: *Cumulative Index to Nursing and Allied Health Literature,* Vol. 23. Glendale, California: The Seventh-Day Adventist Hospital Association, 1979, p. 749.)

Computer Assisted (on-line) Literature Searches

The indexing systems described in the previous section exist in print form and may be used for a manual search. However, the contents of many indexing systems have been transferred to magnetic tape which allows a computer to do the bulk of the work in a search. Virtually all academic and special libraries have the capability to undertake a *computer assisted search* (CAS) and they usually make their services available to all users on a fee basis.

There are several advantages to utilizing a CAS. One is *speed:* out of the thousands and thousands of entries, those particular studies which are appropriate for your purposes are selected in a matter of minutes. The same search performed manually might take days or weeks. Another advantage is *flexibility:* the search can be done using individual index terms or using groups of terms. Furthermore, the scope of the search can be broadened or narrowed at any time according to the needs of the user. The third advantage to a CAS is *coverage:* there are more points of access to the entries using a CAS than can be used manually and often the information on the computer is more up to date. In addition, there are some indexing systems which do not appear in print but only on computer tape, thus rendering them completely inaccessible to the manual user. An example cited below will demonstrate these advantages.

In order to understand more fully the operation of a CAS, let us briefly examine how the system operates. An organization collects entries which may (or may not) appear in print form. For example, the American Psychological Association receives abstracts of papers which are collected in *Psychological Abstracts*. In order to be compatible with computer capabilities, the entries are transferred from print form to magnetic tape. This collection of entries is referred to as a *data base*. The tape is then sold or leased to one or more *vendors* that make the data base along with other data bases available for searching. At present, the three major vendors are *Lockheed Missiles and Space Company,* whose data base system is called DIALOG and *Systems Development Corporation* (SDC), whose system is called ORBIT, and *Bibliographic Retrieval Services* (BRS). These vendors are privately owned companies that market their services to libraries and other institutions.

Now when you, the *user,* decide to employ a CAS, you need to think through exactly what you are looking for and contact a librarian who acts as the *searcher* and who will assist you in preparing for the *search*. A vendor whose data bases are appropriate for your search will be selected, and the search will be initiated.* The searcher telephones the vendor from a terminal and then relays the directions to the computer via a telecommunications system. Messages are typed at the computer terminal's console. This is the *on-line* phase of the CAS, so called because the searcher is in direct interactive contact with the computer. After giving instructions to the computer, the searcher may wish to find out how many entries on the topic are available. The computer will relay this information back to the searcher through the terminal: it will appear in printed form. Then the searcher can decide how many entries are desired and when they are needed. If the searcher desires, the entries can be printed at the terminal immediately. This is referred to as *on-line printing*. If there is no rush, the entries can be printed at the computer site at a time when the computer is under-utilized, and then the entries can be mailed to the searcher or user within a week. This is known as *off-line printing,* and the cost is far less than on-line.

The costs of a CAS vary among data bases and among vendors. On-line costs are computed by the hour or fraction thereof: in the social sciences the on-line costs range from $25 to $120 per hour. The off-line costs are based on the number of entries printed: the range is from 8¢ to 25¢ per entry. Typical costs for a moderate search using off-line printing range between $10 and $30 depending on how extensive the search is.

Preparing for a Search

In preparing for a CAS, there are three preliminary questions a user needs to ask of himself or herself:

1. Do you need a CAS? Although there is a glamour and an aura of science, thoroughness and objectivity associated with the use of the computer, you may not really need it. For example, if your topic is very specific and you are interested only in finding a few studies then you may be able to accomplish your search manually in less time than it would take you to prepare for and execute an on-line search.

2. Is your topic suitable for a CAS? A topic should be fairly narrowly defined. For example, "open education programs" is probably too broad; "IGE programs in elementary schools" would be better. The reason for this requirement is that with a topic that is too broad the number of entries available may be overwhelming, thus rendering the search expensive and useless. Also, a topic should have two or more elements which need to be coordinated: this is very difficult to handle manually, but it is easy for a computer. For example, a good topic for a CAS might be "compensatory programs in mathematics for rural pupils." The computer would search for entries which contained *each* of the three elements: 1) compensatory programs (or synonyms thereof); 2) mathematics (or synonyms thereof); 3) rural pupils (or synonyms thereof). If your topic had only one element it might be done easily by hand.

*Of the indexing systems described in the previous section of this chapter, the following are available for computer searching: ERIC (both CIJE and RIE), DAI, PA, SA, SSCI, NTIS, and IM.

Topics which have elements that may be described with many synonyms are very difficult to search manually. For example, entries on the topic "black English" might appear as black dialect, Negro speech, non-standard dialect, black English vernacular, Afro-American dialect, social dialects, etc. A CAS can handle these almost-synonyms very effectively. It is of importance to note that some data bases are not readily available in printed form. Your library may not subscribe to them, and the only way you can gain easy access to the data base is through the vendor's library of data bases.

3. How much can you afford? This cold, hard fact of life needs to be considered before executing a search. A general idea of the charges can be made by inspection of the vendor's prices and by the experience of the searcher. While the searcher is on-line the number of entries for the topic can be ascertained and an estimate of the cost can be projected.

If you need a CAS (or don't need it but want it anyway), and if your topic is suitable and if you are willing to pay the charges for this service, then you need to prepare for a consultation with the *searcher* who will perform the search for you. In essence you will need to think through your problem to the point where you are capable of being helped.

The strategy for preparing a topic for a CAS is a five step procedure. In order to put some meat on the strategy's skeleton let us employ as an example a user, Tom Stevens, who needs a search of the literature concerning "the use of drugs with hyped-up kids."

Step One: Identify concepts. A problem must be thought through to the point where it can be distilled to its essence. Our user wants to know something about "using drugs on hyped-up kids." He needs to be worked with to ascertain with more precision exactly what he wants. One way of doing this is to require him to write two or three reasonably short sentences to state his problem. Each sentence has the effect of identifying a concept and isolating it in verbal form. Our user may have given us these two sentences: "Drugs are used on some hyped-up children. Does this get them to learn better?" Within these two sentences are three conceptual elements: 1) drugs; 2) hyped-up children; 3) learning. Having determined these concepts, we can begin transforming them for a CAS.

Step Two: Selection of data base(s). Before transforming the concepts to words (or perhaps simultaneously with this) we need to determine which are the most appropriate data bases for these concepts. This is important because each data base has its own special vocabulary through which access to its entries is possible, as we shall see below. For our user, the ERIC system seems best (most inclusive and cheapest) but we may want to search Psychological Abstracts (PA) as well.*

Step Three: Determine established vocabulary. Access to entries in data bases is made through words rather than concepts. Moreover the words must be acceptable for a particular data base. You will recall from earlier in this chapter that the ERIC system has its own thesaurus of descriptors. This thesaurus needs to be consulted to identify the specific descriptors to be used in searching for the concepts desired. For *learning* we may use LEARNING, LEARNING DIFFICULTIES, LEARNING DISABILITIES, BEHAVIOR CHANGE, STUDY HABITS and CHANGE STRATEGIES. For *hyped-up kids* we may use HYPERACTIVITY. For *drugs* we may use STIMULANTS, DRUG THERAPY, "RITALIN." You will note the term *ritalin* appears here in quotes. This emphasizes that it is not an ERIC descriptor but rather a "natural language" term. The computer can be directed to search for this phrase through the titles and abstracts of the entries in the ERIC system, rather than merely in each entry's list of descriptors.

---

*A complete up-to-date listing of available data bases is published by the vendors. A reference librarian in an academic library would probably have this information.

In preparing for the possible use of PA as a data base we can identify a similar list of terms. But we find that PA requires the concept of "behavior change" to be stated as BEHAVIOR MODIFICATION or CLASSROOM MODIFICATION, and "hyperactivity" needs to be expressed as HYPERKENESIS.

Step Four: Judge adequacy of terminology. At this point we need to step back from our list of terms and judge whether the terms we have selected are inclusive enough to yield the scope of entries we desire. Also we need to ask ourselves if there is any other natural language term which should be used in the search. A natural language term is a very effective device for a CAS; it can pin-point a very specific idea. Some natural language terms are used so frequently in the literature that they come to be added to the system as descriptors. For example, MISCUE ANALYSIS refers to a technique for analyzing oral reading behavior which was developed in 1965. After a number of research studies using the technique were published the term became sufficiently important to be used for identification purposes. The term entered the ERIC Thesaurus as a descriptor in 1974.

Step Five: Develop a search strategy. The concepts have been identified and the appropriate terminology selected. Now the terminology needs to be structured to make the computer search efficient and effective. First, we arrange the terms into groupings called *sets* and then put them in a logical order. For our problem the sets are as follows:

1.	2.	3.
HYPERACTIVITY	STIMULANTS	LEARNING
	DRUG THERAPY	LEARNING DIFFICULTIES
	"RITALIN"	LEARNING DISABILITIES

4.

BEHAVIOR CHANGE
BEHAVIOR HABITS
CHANGE STRATEGIES

Set one is comprised of the single term HYPERACTIVITY. This term stands alone because it represents the thrust of the whole question—the *symptom* we are focusing on. Set two contains near-synonyms for the *treatment* of the symptom. Set three contains near-synonyms for the potential *effect* of the treatment on the symptom. Set four is similar to set three but does not specify learning as the potential effect, but rather it uses broader terms which are potential effects.

We could, at this point, direct the computer to search for entries under any single term (as would be done in a manual search) or single set of terms (which could be done by several manual searches). But here is where a computer is really valuable: we can utilize a Boolean strategy to direct the computer to search for various combinations of sets and thus locate entries which have precisely the qualities we seek. In our search we may analyze our sets and direct the computer to search for studies which are described by the terms:

HYPERACTIVITY	*and*	STIMULANTS	*and*	LEARNING
		or		or
		DRUG THERAPY		LEARNING DIFFICULTIES
		or		or
		"RITALIN"		LEARNING DISABILITIES

or   BEHAVIOR CHANGE
        or
        STUDY HABITS
        or
        CHANGE STRATEGIES

This strategy may be summarized as follows:

Search for sets 1 and 2 and either 3 or 4.

This would yield entries for a) 1, 2 and 3; or b) 1, 2, and 4. The result of such a search would locate only those studies which had all three qualities. This strategy may be shown graphically by Figure 2.48. Let circle 1 represent all entries described with the term HYPERACTIVITY. Let circle 2 represent all studies described by the terms STIMULANTS or DRUG THERAPY or "RITALIN." Let circle 3 represent all studies described by the terms LEARNING, LEARNING DIFFICULTIES, LEARNING DISABILITIES. Now when the circles are placed in such a position that they overlap, the portion in which all three circles overlap represents the entries which have all three qualities we seek. These are our target entries and they can be found very quickly with a computer.

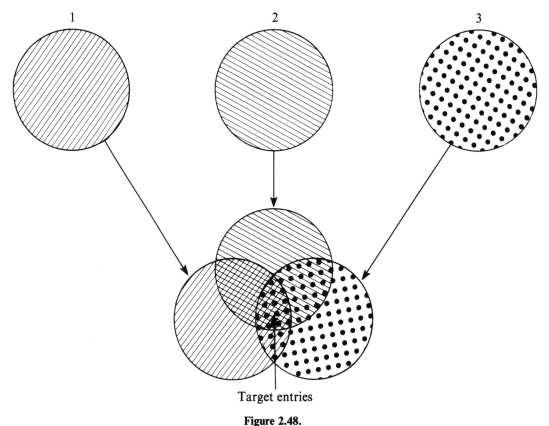

Target entries

Figure 2.48.

It turns out that our strategy was effective. Our 1, 2, and 3 configuration yielded 45 entries; our 1, 2, and 4 configuration yielded 40 entries. Although we can expect some overlap between the two configurations, we request an off-line printing of the full bibliographical information and abstracts on all 85 entries. The cost for this search:

Computer time	$2.88
Telecommunications	.58
Printing (off-line)	8.50
Total	11.96

We could have searched more broadly by using only two sets of terms. The results would have been as follows:

Sets 1 and 2 yield 140 entries.
Sets 1 and 3 yield 130 entries.
Sets 1 and 4 yield 84 entries.

Or we could have searched more narrowly with the following result:

Sets 1 and 2 and 3 and 4 yield 11 entries.

If we had determined our vocabulary and set up our strategy so poorly that we searched only under set 3 we would have located 5,985 entries.

The example about hyperactivity used in this description was a relatively simple one; many other problems present formidable challenges. But typically the greatest problems are in the early stages of the CAS. Some reflection on the matter will lead to the conclusion that a computer is a fantastic technological device. It can do repetitive tasks like searching with amazing speed and accuracy, but it can only do what it is told to do. The author has specifically used the term Computer *Assisted* Search rather than Computer Search because it reflects the relationship between the user, searcher and computer better. It is a partnership with the user and searcher doing lots of planning to develop instructions so that the computer in turn can do its job. Preparation and planning are the keys to effective CAS usage.

The use of CAS has enabled scholars to access easily and inexpensively large amounts of research. If access were restricted to manual searching many searches could never have taken place because of the time needed for such projects. We are fortunate to be engaging in scholarly activities at a time when computer assistance is available. And this is only the beginning. New data bases are continually being added to computer libraries, and retrieval procedures become increasingly convenient. In ten years CAS may be so sophisticated that we will then wonder how on earth we were able to manage our business with such crude and rudimentary procedures as exist now. In CAS, the best is yet to be!

Summary

The literature of any field includes a variety of types of writing in that field including research. Various portions of the literature can be identified and made available to a consumer through retrieval systems provided by indexing services. There are fourteen prominent indexing services in the social sciences whose entries may be accessed through author, subject, title, citation, organization or contract number, depending upon the particular system. In the field of educational research, the primary tool for locating research is the ERIC system. The use of the ERIC thesaurus will permit very effective utilization of the system. Most indexing systems may be searched manually or with computer assistance. A computer assisted search enables a user to search a body of literature quite thoroughly and quickly and at moderate cost.

Further Readings for Chapter 2

The field of information retrieval has grown so large so fast that as of this writing there are no up-to-date print sources to which the reader of this text can be directed for further information. If the reader plans to conduct a manual search, then the indexing system which is most likely to contain the desired references should be consulted. A more detailed explanation of its contents than offered in this text will be found there. If the reader plans to do a Computer Assisted Search, then a conversation with a good reference librarian should prove productive. This librarian should have 1) the latest catalogs of the major vendors which show the scope of available data bases, and 2) knowledge of current procedures and costs. Any information of this type which would appear in this text would be hopelessly outdated by the time the reader would come in contact with it.

Part Two
The Framework of Research

Author's comment:

Before we get into the specific techniques used in education research, there are a few basic things of which you should be aware. One important understanding you should have is what research looks like from the researchers' point of view. In Chapter 3 I have tried to take you through a research study from inception to presentation from the research producer's viewpoint. Researchers have to make many decisions as they plan and execute a study: the reasons behind their decisions may surprise you. I have tried to bring out several key issues by using examples from other fields of endeavor: economics, medicine and nutrition for example. I hope to show how universal these issues are in the total scope of research, in order that educational research may be seen in perspective.

Chapter 4 lays some basic groundwork for understanding the techniques used by researchers which are described in subsequent chapters. You will be introduced to some new concepts and terms which are used to describe them. Although the going may seem a little tough at times, hang in there. Once you understand this material the remaining chapters will be that much more meaningful.

Chapter 3

The Research Process

In the first chapter of this book, we discussed in general terms the types of research found in education, and some of the problems endemic in these endeavors. With this background and perspective we are ready to develop a somewhat deeper understanding and appreciation of the research process. So let us examine in this chapter the various steps which culminate in the presentation of the finished research studies we will encounter in the literature. We will do this often from the point of view of the researcher and as a consequence we will gain an idea of why researchers make the decisions they do.

Before our examination of the research process, we need to consider some aspects of the researchers themselves—their motivations, their qualifications and their biases. All those of us who walk the earth have both strengths and weaknesses. As we critically read research, it is important for us to determine as best we can the strengths and weaknesses of those who produce the research we encounter. When we know where they are coming from, we may judge better where they are going.

All research efforts begin with a desire to do research; without such a desire, of course, nothing would get started. All right—what motivates people to do research? As is the case in most other human endeavors, motivation can be described as being intrinsic or extrinsic.

There are people in the field of education and the related social sciences who have a keen desire to explore the unknown. They have a bent toward inquiry, which is often a distinct facet of their personality dating back to early experiences in their lives. These are people who are not satisfied with the present state of knowledge; the use of the term "tradition" as a reason for doing something often offends them. When confronted with a given situation, they think, "Why," or "Why not?" They challenge so-called conventional wisdom. Or they pick up on ambiguities or loose ends they perceive. For these people, research is a mode of thinking—a way of life. These researchers possess intrinsic motivation and their efforts are typically labors of love. Often, it shows in the quality of their work and their persistence in ferreting out truth through ongoing research efforts.

The world is so constructed that there are persons who do not possess an instrinsic motivation to pursue truth through research but nevertheless are enticed to produce research by means of extrinsic rewards. Now, as every salaried employee is aware, there is nothing intrinsically wrong with extrinsic motivation. But sometimes it results in research being done in a half-hearted, perfunctory manner. It is a fact of life that much research is done at universities where a publish or perish policy prevails. Also, virtually every recipient of a doctoral degree in any of the social sciences needs to accomplish a piece of research as a degree requirement, whether that candidate is interested in research or not.

So, what we see here in the field of research is a situation in which research is initiated for a variety of reasons. But, we must understand that the motivation for the initiation of a research project is not necessarily an indication of its quality; some doctoral dissertations are valuable contributions to knowledge and some impressively funded and staffed studies are worthless. The point is that there exists a wide range in the quality of research, *some* of which range is attributable to the motivation of the researchers.

We may attribute another portion of the range of the quality of educational research to the qualifications and biases of the researchers who produce the studies. It is difficult for us to determine the motivation of researchers, but we can attempt a judgement as to whether they were the right people for the job, that is, whether they were sufficiently qualified and unbiased to conduct a given study.

How Qualified and Unbiased Is the Researcher

A person who undertakes a research study should be both qualified to conduct it, and unbiased towards its potential findings. Both these attributes should be present; one without the other is not sufficient. In order to be a qualified researcher, a person normally needs to have had graduate level training in the technique of research. But the mere fact that a person has engaged in such training is no guarantee of his or her qualifications. As was noted earlier, virtually all doctoral level programs in the social sciences include a research component, but completion of the degree requirement does not mean the recipient is qualified—passing grades of B's and C's do not necessarily a good researcher make nor for that matter do A's. The literature in educational research includes more than a few poorly executed studies accomplished by seemingly qualified researchers with advanced degrees. And those are the ones that got published! Nor is the university or institution with which a researcher is associated a guarantee of quality. We see from time to time researchers with impeccable credentials turning out worthless and/or misleading research. However, the fact that researchers are experienced in the techniques they have used and are thought well of by their peers may give us some, but not complete confidence.

But the more important issue about the researchers is their biases. We must ask ourselves how independent are the researchers? How free of financial aid are they? When the person who pays the researchers' salary has a vested interest in the findings coming out a certain way, the researchers' independence may be compromised. It is not surprising, for example, that the scientists doing cancer research for the tobacco industry have not found a causal link between cancer and smoking. We must also ask ourselves how independent are the researchers of the restraining influences of their profession. It takes a courageous person to go against the mainstream thinking of a profession. Ignaz Semmelweis, a nineteenth century medical doctor, made few friends among his fellow physicians by discovering that physicians themselves were a major cause of spreading infection because they didn't wash their hands before treating patients.

Further restraints upon the independence of researchers may be due to the effect of their prior research efforts. Repeated investigations by a group of researchers of a given phenomenon may yield consistent results over a long period of time. When these researchers have devoted their lives to work which has demonstrated that A = B, and then they conduct a study which shows that A ≠ B, but rather A = C, will those researchers have the courage to state it, and by so doing attenuate if not negate the importance of their life's work? Closely associated with this problem is the restraining influence of researchers' training on their independence. A researcher may be trained to believe that only one research paradigm is considered an acceptable format in which meaningful research can be conducted.

When assessing an evaluation study the question of bias is of paramount importance. If the relationship between the evaluator and the subject or object of the evaluation is not known we need to be *extremely* suspicious of the findings of the evaluation study, especially if the findings were positive. This will be discussed in great detail in a later chapter.

The personalities of scholars and researchers and the societal contexts in which they operate may from time to time influence the course of their thinking; indeed the influence may be directly on the accuracy of data presented in a study. Fraud is not unknown in science. Witness the findings of "scientists" in Nazi Germany regarding notions of racial inferiority and superiority. But sometimes the biases are quite subtle and reflect little-known information about researchers. For example, John Maynard Keynes, the noted British economist of this century espoused economic theories which result in deficit spending by governments in order to stimulate free economies. When criticized for this idea—"in the long run a government's debts need to be paid, and we are burdening our children and grandchildren with this debt"—he is said to have responded, "In the long run, we'll all be dead," thus justifying his suggested economic policies. A seemingly minor but perhaps highly significant point which is frequently overlooked in evaluating his theories is that Keynes himself married at age 42 and never had any children. He needed not concern himself with the debt obligation of his grandchildren because he would have none. It is interesting to speculate how his economic theories might have been different if his marital situation had been different.

In educational research, the work of Cyril Burt represents a situation worthy of note. Burt, an eminent British psychologist did pioneer work in the area of human intelligence, especially the degree to which heredity and environment affect measured intelligence. His efforts exerted a profound influence upon the English educational system, and provided a data base for some of the writings of psychologist Arthur Jensen and sociologist Christopher Jencks. After Burt died in 1971, his research was critically scrutinized by his colleagues. From their analyses, it appears that Burt falsified a significant portion of his data.

A recent book by Hearnshaw, a colleague of the late Cyril Burt, devotes an entire chapter to Burt's human characteristics and personality development.* Burt is portrayed as a man with many positive personal qualities: a disinterest in wealth or position, a sense of humor, an "unworldliness." Yet, he is also described as a loner, a jealous man, a product of an education which induced feelings of superiority and elitism. He was overly sensitive to criticism, suspicious of rivals and possessed of an exaggerated egotism. These attributes, according to Hearnshaw, were the result of behavior patterns developed in his childhood as well as the result of several professional setbacks which occurred in the last decades of his career. Hearnshaw summarizes:

> It would seem, then, that we are justified in concluding that Burt suffered, in the final phase of his life, from a marginally paranoid condition. . . . This, we suggest, is the basic explanation of the deceptions and subterfuges which marred his work in its later stages. In the end he chose to cheat rather than see his opponents triumph.

That Cyril Burt, or any researcher for that matter, had feet of clay should not come as a surprise to any astute observer of life on this planet. The disappointment is that some of those persons responsible for making decisions based on Burt's data accepted the veracity of his data, apparently without question or corroborating evidence. It is with the utilization of research findings that real

*Hearnshaw, L. S. *Cyril Burt, Psychologist* Syracuse, N.Y. Cornell University Press, 1979. (Chapter 13)

damage may be done—the consumers of Burt's data were perhaps not sufficiently critical of his work.

It is extremely difficult for us as research consumers to be sufficiently informed to make a judgement about the qualifications and biases (actualized or potential) of the researchers with whose work we come in contact. Indeed many highly sophisticated consumers have been fooled more than once. This entire discusssion of bias is presented to alert the research consumer to its existence and to temper any enthusiasm based upon a particular research finding with the idea that the finding might, just might be pure nonsense.

With our understanding of what the researchers bring to their task, we are ready to examine the process by which an idea becomes a completed research study. The process is comprised of three consecutive phases: 1) the *planning* phase during which time major strategic and tactical decisions are made 2) the *execution* phase in which the data are generated, analyzed and interpreted and 3) the *presentation* phase at which time the study is put into its final written form. In some studies, however, these phases are not consecutive but rather concurrent. For example, in some case studies major strategic and tactical decisions are made during the execution phase of the study because they are dependent upon events which transpire during the execution phase.

Phase I—PLANNING

The planning of a study goes through several stages before it is complete. The process may be visualized as a funnel with the wide part at the top gradually tapering to the thin neck at the bottom. This represents the identification of a broad area of endeavor and its gradual refinement into hypotheses which may be tested with research procedures.

Researchers first identify a broad area in which they have an interest. This interest could be the result of an ongoing investigation started much earlier, or it could be new interest inspired by someone else's research, or (typically nowadays) the interest could be the result of the presence of extensive funding opportunities—this is particularly the case when researchers are associated with an organization which relies on external funding to assist in financing its operations.

In the latter two instances in which the research area may be quite new to the researchers, their next task is to read widely in the area. They usually start with general sources such as reviews and summaries and work deeper toward original sources. During this time, they are gaining a perspective of the field and thinking of possible topics. The more experienced the researchers, the more possible topics become apparent. This is because their experience allows them to see possibilities that a neophyte researcher would overlook. Their goal is to select and refine a topic in such a way that the topic will be 1) significant in terms of its potential contribution to the field, 2) reasonable with regard to scope, 3) amenable to solution through research processes and 4) if being funded by external sources, within the guidelines of the funding agency.

Prior Research

Whether the researchers are extending their prior work in a given area or developing ideas in a new area, they need to show that the research problem is related to some existing corpus of knowledge.

HOW WELL DOES THE RESEARCH PROBLEM FIT INTO A CONTEXT OF THEORY, PRACTICE OR OTHER RESEARCH?

Research is not conducted in a vacuum. Rather it exists in a context of a world, real or imagined, which context elicits a research problem. The problem does not come from nowhere, but is directed by a need in a theory's development, or a knowledge gap in the development of an inclusive body of information. The research problem is developed in such a way that it can be seen to fit into a larger enterprise. Without this larger context within which a study may be viewed, the meaningfulness of its findings can not be appreciated.

In addition to being a part of a larger context, the research problem should represent an extension of this context.

HOW WELL DOES THE RESEARCH PROBLEM FLOW FROM THE EXISTING LITERATURE IN THE FIELD?

No research problem is altogether new: everything comes from somewhere and research is no exception. Researchers review the literature pertaining to the research question so as to enable their anticipated study to capitalize on the strengths and weaknesses of prior research efforts. This has the additional effect of enabling their study to flow from the generalized findings of the studies they review. They attend to the procedures and methodologies of prior work in the area as well as noting the findings.

The Research Strategy

At this point researchers come to a major crossroad in their deliberations. They need to select an overall approach or *strategy* to guide the research effort.

HOW CONSONANT IS THE RESEARCH STRATEGY WITH THE RESEARCH PROBLEM?

The selection of a particular strategy will determine the procedures to be utilized in a study which in turn will determine the resources needed (personnel, materials, computer time, etc.) to actualize the study. For example, some researchers might seek to investigate childrens' problem solving ability. One strategy might involve administering to a group of children a pencil-and-paper problem solving test. Another strategy might be to deal with children individually and confront each with a problem; an examiner would then make careful observations of each child's approach to solving the problems and engage in introspective interviewing by asking each child to tell why he or she did whatever had transpired. A third strategy might be to reanalyze some older, existing data dealing with childrens' problem solving by using newer, more sophisticated analytical techniques which were not in existence at the time the old data were generated. There are of course many other strategies available to the researchers. The first strategy involving pencil and paper tests would probably utilize the least amount of financial and personnel resources. The second strategy would cost little for materials but much for personnel. The third strategy would require some organization, clerical assistance and probably some computer time.

In many instances, researchers need to work backwards from a budget to a strategy. This is especially true when funds are limited by a decision from a funding agency. In this type of situation, researchers are provided a given sum of money which in effect sets the parameters for their strategy. They are obliged to keep their expenditures within the assigned budget and accordingly select procedures which they can afford. The selection of certain procedures is really an operationalization of an overall strategy. This is a major source of concern for researchers: having a large enough budget to utilize the best strategy for a given research problem. Our concern, though, as consumers of research is to evaluate the strategy that was employed with regard to its consonance with the research problem. Ultimately it is we who are left with the decision as to whether to accept the finding of a given study as being credible, and the research strategy employed is a crucial consideration. For example, it is hardly credible to accept the findings of a study which investigated inferential thinking in ten year olds when the only subjects in the study were college students. These are two different types of subjects probably with two different ways of thinking. Similarly, researchers would be asking a lot of us to accept the findings of a study investigating racial prejudice when the data used in the study were developed by telephone interviews with randomly dialed adults. People generally do not respond well to strangers on the telephone when matters of some delicacy or sensitivity are at issue.

It should be noted that budgetary restraints are usually beyond the control of the researchers who perform the studies. And when we judge the findings of a study to be lacking in credibility we are not necessarily casting aspersions on the researchers themselves who may have done the very best with what they had to work with. Rather our concern is with the findings: did the strategy which was used have sufficient rigor and appropriateness to the research problem to justify *any* findings which could emanate from the study. Or were there other, better strategies which could have been employed?

Assumptions

Inherent in any research study are certain assumptions about the subjects, the measurements, the procedures, or any other aspects of the study. If the assumptions are reasonable, we can have more confidence in the findings than if the assumptions are specious.

HOW REASONABLE ARE THE ASSUMPTIONS—EXPLICIT AND IMPLICIT—UPON WHICH THE STUDY IS BASED?

The quality of any research study rests heavily upon the assumptions which underlie it. Explicit assumptions are identified and stated openly, usually at the beginning of a research report. This is considered a good practice because it shows the researchers' awareness of the soft spots in their methodology. But the mere fact that an assumption is stated explicitly does not absolve us from the responsibility of evaluating its potentially harmful effects. Researchers can not get off the hook that easily. For example, they can state explicitly the assumption that in an experimental study using elementary school pupils, the treatment group did not interact with the pupils in the nontreatment group. Indeed the procedures might have included a speech delivered by the teachers of the treatment group pupils to the effect that they were not to talk with these other pupils. However, in view of what we know about pupils, schools, and teachers' instructions, we must ask ourselves if it is indeed a *reasonable* assumption that the pupils indeed did not talk to one another. Merely stating the assumption explicitly does not *ipso facto* make the assumption reasonable. And of course this is even of greater significance when the assumption is implicit. For example, an implicit assumption in the valid use of a standardized achievement examination is the fact that the pupils taking the test are familiar with the test taking procedure and are trying to do well. For pupils who had not previously demonstrated any degree of test wisdom and who furthermore never showed any interest in scoring well on school achievement tests, such an assumption is not reasonable. There are other assumptions to be considered as well, such as the assumptions necessary for using certain analytical procedures. These will be dealt with in later chapters.

The assumptions in a study should be stated and discussed openly. If they are not, we may conclude that: 1) the researchers are unaware of them or 2) that they do not believe them to be important or 3) that they would rather not think of them. In any case, the omission of the assumptions keeps useful information away from the reader.

Operational Definitions

When an idea is coverted to an action it often loses something in the translation. A philosophical statement, a phrase, a word—these may mean different things to different people depending on how they are translated into a specific action. In research, each term that is used needs to be defined as a specific action; such a definition is referred to as an *operational* definition because the term takes on a specific meaning when it is viewed in the operation of a study.

HOW REASONABLE ARE THE OPERATIONAL DEFINITIONS OF THE TERMS?

Knowing precisely what researchers mean by a word or phrase is essential to understanding what they are doing. Most words in the English language derive their meanings in large part from their particular use in a given context. But in research, sometimes the context is not developed enough to reveal the exact intended meaning for a given usage of a word, especially if a word could be defined in loose, general terms. An *operational definition* is a highly descriptive and specific statement of the meaning of a given word in a given context. A dictionary definition of "intelligence", for example, might read "the capacity to apprehend facts and propositions and their relations and to reason about them"—this is a generally accepted definition which is useful in most situations. But in a research study, an operational definition is needed so the reader knows exactly what the writer means by the term and can thus judge the degree to which the operational definition fits within the parameters of the generally accepted dictionary definition. An operational definition of "intelligence" might be: "verbal intelligence as measured by the Peabody Picture Vocabulary Test." Or it might be: "academic intelligence as judged by classroom teachers." Without the specificity of an operational definition, the reader can not judge the meaningfulness and generalizability of a study's findings.

After having reviewed prior research efforts on the general topic of interest, developed an overall research strategy, made reasonable assumptions and operationalized the concepts involved, researchers then endeavor to reduce their research question to one or more hypotheses which they will test. The hypothesis is the heart of any research study. It effects all aspects of the research study; it determines the parameters of the previous research to be included in the written report and strongly influences the method, design and analysis requirements of the study. It is, in effect, an operational statement of the purpose of the study and it represents the one aspect of a study with which all other aspects must be consonant. Accordingly, the construction of the hypotheses is one of the researchers' most crucial tasks and they deal with this very carefully.

At this point, when the hypothesis has been developed and the specific research procedures have been decided upon we may say that the planning phase has been completed. Before moving along to the next phase in the research process it would be helpful to us as research consumers to have some background information to assist us in evaluating research strategies and procedures. In a well planned research project the strategy and procedures will be consonant with the hypothesis as discussed above. Yet, within the boundaries imposed by the hypothesis there is room for a certain amount of choice. When we note the procedures which were indeed selected for use in a study we may ask ourselves why these, and not other alternate procedures were selected. The reasons *may* be influenced by the personality of the researchers and the socio/political context in which the research is being conducted. We have already discussed the restraining influences of a smaller than desired budget; if they don't have enough money to do a study the way they would really like, they have to settle for the best alternative. Also, we discussed in Chapter One some ethical considerations involved in research; an experimental study might be clearly the most appropriate strategy for a particular research question, but the researchers can not ethically subject people to the necessary experimental condition. There are other issues as well that from time to time enter into the thinking of researchers as they make decisions about strategy and procedures. Let us examine some prominent examples.

The members of *any* profession tend to be prisoners of their training. They are taught that there are certain acceptable ways of doing things and if they do them that way they will be regarded as competent by their colleagues. And if they deviate from generally accepted methods they risk the scorn and ridicule of their peers and in some professions even perhaps a malpractice suit. Whether these generally accepted methods are good or not is a matter of personal judgement—everyone has to judge for himself or herself. But the effect of this is to reduce the strategic and operational alternatives available to the professionals. For example, medical doctors typically are trained to operate in a diagnostic-prescriptive format. A patient exhibits symptoms of a malady, they prescribe drugs to cure the malady or at least relieve the symptoms. They rarely if ever have any training in nutrition. If they did, they might operate from a preventative medical format rather than a diagnostic-prescriptive format, that is, they would focus their efforts on preventing disease through nutrition and exercise rather than waiting until a disease surfaces and then treating it with chemicals. Thus they can be prisoners of their training. In educational research, too, some researchers appear to be prisoners of their training. For example, a researcher whose training was restricted to experimental studies characterized by tightly controlled procedures, precise behavioral measures yielding quantitative data, and sophisticated analytical procedures, may not be willing to accept the value of descriptive studies especially when causality is at issue. Similarly, researchers who are trained to isolate a specific case, probe deeply and at length into this case, and report findings in a descriptive narrative may not be inclined to accept the value of experimental research. They, too, may be prisoners of their training.

Related to this issue of training is the technical expertise of the researchers themselves. Interestingly, this works both ways. On the one hand there is a tendency among some researchers to investigate problems whose solutions require just a few particular analytical techniques in which those researchers have demonstrated competence. The present author has known researchers who purposely limited their endeavors to projects which required a minimum of statistical analysis because they lacked ability to do anything complex. On the other hand, some researchers use procedures which require the particular ultra-sophisticated analytical techniques in which they happen to be skilled. One graduate student known to a colleague of the present author when queried as to what topic she would like to write a dissertation on, replied, "I don't care, as long as it uses analysis of covariance." Obviously, this is not an appropriate basis for a decision of this sort. The analytical technique should fit the data which in turn should fit the research problem being investigated.

Sometimes a given research strategy is adopted because its alternative could lead to findings implying actions which cannot be actualized. Again using medicine as our first example, cancer research has focused on finding a cure for cancer so that when a person has cancer a treatment can be administered. Unfortunately, this research strategy has not been very successful—and this after billions of dollars of expenditures and countless person-hours of effort. One other strategy available in cancer research is to try to find the causes. But the problem here is that if the causes were indeed located could be anything be done about it? Suppose for example it were found that the preservatives in foods were causing cancer. The elimination of preservatives might require a complete overhaul of our national food distribution system. Some food, perhaps, could not be distributed at all. The resultant economic upheavals might be too unacceptable politically to be allowed to occur. In addition, people might not want to accept the necessary changes in their dietary habits. So if causes were found, conceivably it might not do any good in reducing cancer because the changes needed to eliminate the causes might never occur. Similarly, in educational research, we see Ritalin being tested as an agent for the control of hyperactive children. This is one strategy available to deal with this problem of hyperactivity. Another strategy might be to determine the causes of hyperactivity—diet, family life, genetics are a few possibilities. But even if the cause or causes could be ascertained, could anything be done about it?

Thus we note that the basis for decisions concerning research strategy and procedures may be influenced by many factors somewhat removed from the actual research process itself. In any event, decisions are made as to what kind of data is to be sought, and how, when, and by whom it is to be gathered. This leads to the next phase of the research process—the execution of the plans formulated.

Phase II—EXECUTION

In this phase of the research process, the strategy and procedures planned in the prior phase are implemented. First data are generated. The data may be derived from scores of tests, frequencies of behaviors, observations or any of a variety of other sources. Secondly, the data are analyzed. Data in their raw form are rarely useful to researchers. The data need to be reorganized, summarized, compared to other data, or in some other way manipulated and treated so as to be the most helpful in testing the hypothesis which guides the entire study. Thirdly, the results of the data analysis are interpreted. That is, the results will be applied to the hypothesis to determine whether or not the hypothesis should be retained. Then the meaning of this fact, its application and implications is conceived.

The generation, analysis, and interpretation of data are often quite technical matters and there are many questions we as researcher consumers will need to pose. The specific questions to be considered will appear within the subsequent chapters of this book which deal specifically with these technical issues.

Phase III—PRESENTATION

Research is performed in order to find answers to questions. Having found answers the researchers are obliged to share their findings with the profession. This may be via the spoken word or the written word or both.

When research is presented via the spoken word, this usually takes place at an annual meeting, a scholarly gathering of a learned society, otherwise known as a convention. Here researchers present their findings to colleagues who share their interests. When we say that this presentation is made through the "spoken word" this is only partially true. Typically, the research is organized in the form of a research paper which has been carefully written. The researchers bring their papers to the session, pass them out to the audience and then "present" them usually not by reading them but by talking around them.

You may ask, why if the paper is to be presented orally do researchers need to write formal papers, especially since they are not going to read them *verbatim*? There are two reasons for this. First, there is a huge difference between spoken language and written language. People may talk all they want, using words loosely and get away with it. Time passes and the sounds of language fade. But in written language, they must force themselves to be precise, coherent, and organized, because the written word unlike its spoken counterpart remains with us, staring back at us from the printed page for years and years. As they search for precision and coherence, researchers sharpen their focus, qualify their statements and in general produce more solid pieces of thinking than if they had left their thoughts in the shifting sands of spoken language.

A second reason is also related to differences between written and spoken language. When researchers present their papers, their sessions may be attended by only a few people, although many more may be interested in it. At most conventions several presentation sessions take place concurrently; moreover, registrants at the conventions who might be interested often are engaged in other activities taking place at the time the paper is being presented. So, in order to make their studies available to many, researchers write it up and send copies to colleagues who request reprints. Also, they may expect to have their papers solicited by an ERIC clearinghouse for inclusion in the ERIC document collection.

In addition to or instead of presenting a study at a convention, a researcher may choose to submit a paper for publication in an appropriate journal. There is at least one suitable journal for just about every conceivable research study. Most of the better journals are known as "referee" journals—an editorial board screens papers and recommends for publication only those they believe to be most suitable. If a paper is submitted but is not accepted for publication, a researcher may choose to send it to other journals. Or it may be rewritten for resubmission to the original journal. Or it may be left in its present form but resubmitted to the same journal at a later date when the journal may have a different editorial board.

If the paper does appear in print somewhere, it will be indexed in the Education Index and Current Index to Journals in Education as well as in other appropriate index services. It may appear in a book of readings in the general subject area. It may be cited in textbooks and other journal articles. Through one of these sources educators and other parties who are interested in the study will find it and hopefully will use the results of the study to their advantage.

When we encounter research in a printed format there are several questions we need to ask about the actual formal written presentation of a study. The format in which a research study is presented is of great importance to us. The scope, clarity and inclusiveness of the report may determine in large part how useful the efforts of the researcher will be to us.

HOW INTELLIGIBLE IS THE RESEARCH REPORT?

Readers of research have the right to expect a research report to be readable. The presentation of a report should be clear, concise, organized and written with the readers in mind. The title should be an accurate description of the study, headings for main sections should let the readers know where they are; charts, graphs, tables, and figures should be used when appropriate to enhance the readability. The style of writing should be straightforward, without any unduly long sentences or unnecessary jargon; examples should be presented when needed for understanding complex material. In evaluating the intelligibility of a research report, consider the journal in which it was found and the intended audience for that journal. The writer of a given research report needs to consider the audience, but also has the right to expect the audience to bring a generalized knowledge of research to the reading task.

HOW SUCCINCT AND UNAMBIGUOUS IS THE STATEMENT OF THE RESEARCH PROBLEM?

The heart of any research study is the statement of the research problem upon which the entire study is based. Depending upon the author's style, the research problem could take the form of a question (research hypothesis) or a statement (null hypothesis).* In either case it should be stated very directly, and fairly close to the beginning of the study. It can call attention to itself by having its own heading or by being introduced by a phrase such as "The purpose of this study. . . ." It should be succinct, that is, it should present itself in a minimum of words which represent the thrust of the study's intent. It should be clear and unambiguous by avoiding jargon on one hand, and words with multiple meanings on the other.

HOW FULLY REPORTED ARE THE PROCEDURES EMPLOYED IN THE STUDY?

As consumers of research findings, we need to know what actually transpired during the course of a study. If we do not know, we are not in a position to evaluate each procedure. Thus, it is incumbent upon researchers to disclose fully the specific procedures used in a study. For example, if a given study used interviews to generate data, we need to know how well trained the interviewers were, how long were the interviews, did the interviewer take notes or use audio tape, was the interview conducted face-to-face or via telephone and other similar questions. As another example, if a study generated data from high school students we need to know how many students were selected to participate in the study, how many actually did participate, of those who participated what proportion of all high school students they represent, how were they chosen to participate, etc. If a test was administered, we need to know which specific test was administered, when, by whom, in what context etc. Without this specific information, we are unable to evaluate what occurred.

An interesting example of the effect of a lack of procedural specificity in the field of bio-chemistry is seen in a recent book by an exiled Russian scientist.** In the late 1960's, there appeared in Russian scientific journals reports of experiments in "artificial" contamination of some natural environments produced by radioactive isotopes. The author noted that the procedures reported in these experiments were quite vague and from a careful analysis of what procedures *were* reported and *were not* reported, he concluded that the contamination was not "artificially" induced for the experiments, but rather actually in existence before the so-called experiments took place. (In effect, this fact made these studies descriptive, not experimental). From this he surmised that a nuclear explosion had occurred in the Ural mountains in the 1950's and that the radioactive contamination mentioned in the "experiments" was a result of this, rather than having been artificially induced. In educational research, consumers of research have a right to expect full disclosure of procedures in order to evaluate the significance of the results of a study. If the procedures are not fully reported, then we must assume that what was not reported was not done, or was done so poorly as to have been an embarrassment to the researcher and was omitted consciously.

---

*This will be discussed in Chapter 4.
**Medvedev, Zhores A., *Nuclear Disaster in the Urals,* New York, Norton, 1979.

We may ask ourselves just how specific a description of procedures should researchers be expected to provide. In general, the level of specificity required should enable us to understand and visualize what happened to the extent that we could duplicate the study ourselves. In other words, when they present us with the cake, they should give us the recipe, too.

Summary

Research activities are initiated for a variety of reasons; some of the range in the quality of research is attributable to the motivation of the researchers. The qualifications, biases, and personalities of the researchers have a profound effect on their accomplishments.

Research may be viewed as a three stage process: *planning, execution,* and *presentation.* In the *planning* phase, major decisions regarding strategy and tactics are made. A broad area of endeavor is identified and gradually narrowed down into one or more hypotheses. Decisions are made as to the particular research strategy to be utilized. This decision tempered with budgetary restrictions suggests specific procedures. Assumptions are made, definitions are operationalized, and specific plans are laid. Researchers have many actions available to them as they seek answers to the research questions they pose. Their decisions as to the selection of specific options may be influenced by their personality, training, and the socio-political context in which their research is taking place.

In the *execution* phase, the data are generated, analyzed and interpreted. In the *presentation* phase the entire study is put into written form and made public through presentation at a scholarly gathering or publication in print or film format. The presentation should be intelligible and fully reported.

The following questions need to be asked by consumers of research when they encounter research:

HOW QUALIFIED AND UNBIASED ARE THE RESEARCHERS?

HOW WELL DOES THE RESEARCH PROBLEM FIT INTO A CONTEXT OF THEORY, PRACTICE, OR OTHER RESEARCH?

HOW CONSONANT IS THE RESEARCH STRATEGY WITH THE RESEARCH PROBLEM?

HOW REASONABLE ARE THE ASSUMPTIONS—EXPLICIT AND IMPLICIT—UPON WHICH THE STUDY IS BASED?

HOW REASONABLE ARE THE OPERATIONAL DEFINITIONS OF THE TERMS?

HOW INTELLIGIBLE IS THE RESEARCH REPORT?

HOW SUCCINCT AND UNAMBIGUOUS IS THE STATEMENT OF THE RESEARCH PROBLEM?

HOW FULLY REPORTED ARE THE PROCEDURES EMPLOYED IN THE STUDY?

Further Readings for Chapter 3

Barber, Theodore X. *Pitfalls in Human Research Ten Pivotal Points*. New York: Pergamon Press 1976.
    This is a fairly complete treatment of some very important problems encountered in experimental research. It shows how misleading results and conclusions can be caused by the personal and professional characteristics of the researchers themselves. Highly recommended.

Finn, Charles E. *Scholars, Dollars, and Bureaucrats*. Washington, D.C.: The Brookings Institute, 1978.
    Chapter five of this book presents some interesting information concerning the role of the federal government in the research endeavors of colleges and universities.

Hopkins, Charles, D., *Educational Research: A Structure for Inquiry*. Columbus, Ohio: Merrill, 1976.
    This text provides a structured introduction to educational research.

Kaplan, Abraham. *The Conduct of Inquiry, Methodology for Behavioral Science*. San Francisco: Chandler, 1964.
    A philosophical treatment of the research process is contained in the Kaplan text. There is some repetition of the material from his book suggested at the end of chapter one; much of this book is aimed specifically at the process of behavioral research.

Tuckman, Bruce W. *Conducting Educational* Research. New York: Harcourt Brace Jovanovich, 1972.
    Tuckman's text is a very good one. It emphasizes the techniques of design and analysis rather than the philosophical rationale.

Van Dalen, Deobold B. *Understanding Educational Research: An Introduction*. New York: McGraw-Hill, 1973.
    Van Dalen's book is an excellent treatment of the educational research process. Of special interest are his appendices showing various examples of research thinking and writing.

Chapter 4
Basic Concepts Used in Research

Educational research, or any research for that matter, is an enterprise which uses specialized techniques which are referred to with a specialized vocabulary. These techniques and vocabulary can only be understood when the underlying concepts are clearly comprehended by the reader. In this chapter we will deal with several key concepts upon which many specific research techniques are based.* The concepts to be considered are: 1) variables—the measures of attributes which are the focus of researchers' attention 2) sampling—the techniques for selecting the subjects or objects researchers measure 3) hypotheses—tentative answers to research questions investigated by a study 4) the basis for inferential statistics and decision making—this includes a discussion of the normal curve, levels of significance and errors in decision making.

Variables

When a study is being planned, researchers identify important elements of the study by labeling them as *variables*. In its generalized meaning, a variable is anything that is subject to variation, that is, anything that is changeable: the weather, the time of day, an attitude, the skills of a group of people. In its specific research meaning, a variable refers to a characteristic of a group of subjects or objects, or of a situation, which may differ. For example, among subjects a variable might be their attitude toward school bussing; in a group of people we could expect to find differences in this attitude. Among objects, say, library books, a variable might be a measure of their readability, how difficult they are to read; we could expect to find differences in readability among them. In a situation, such as a research framework a variable might be whether or not a given group of subjects received a treatment; we could expect that in some research studies different groups got different treatments and perhaps some groups got no treatment. In these examples we have identified just one variable to develop the explanation. In reality there are many, many variables of interest existing within a given group of subjects, objects, or other aspects of a research framework. For example, in addition to varying in terms of readability, library books also vary in terms of size, shape, color, cost, inclusion of graphic material, print style, subject matter, authors, sexist dialogue, writing styles, etc.

In educational research, researchers identify certain variables they seek to study; they label these variables and label other variables which might influence them. The labels assigned to the

*This entire chapter and those subsequent chapters which deal with data analysis are presented in the context of a "traditional" statistical approach. An alternative methodology may be found in the *Bayesian* approach which uses such concepts of conditional probability and maximum rationalization to test hypotheses. It is well beyond the scope of this book to offer even the briefest of expositions of Bayesian statistics. And in addition, since virtually all extant research in education uses traditional procedures, a discussion of Bayesian statistics is specifically omitted from this presentation.

variables reflect their function in a research endeavor. Interestingly, the actual name or label given to a variable is a variable itself—different researchers will refer to a given type of variable by different names. The most frequently encountered names will be presented here.

Variables in Experimental Research

In experimental research there are several types of variables identified by researchers. Suppose for example, researchers are investigating the effect of manipulative materials on mathematical computation. They devise an experimental situation in which two comparable groups of subjects are identified: one group of subjects gets to use the materials and another group does not. Then they measure each group's mathematical computation proficiency. There are several types of variables present in this study.

1. *Independent variable*: In our example, this variable is whether or not a group got to use the materials: one group did, one group did not. It is the understanding of the effect of this variable which is the major focus of the study. This is also called a *treatment* variable since it defines the treatment aspect of the study. Occasionally, this variable is referred to as a *predictor* variable, since one can use information about the variable to predict an outcome.

2. *Dependent variable*: In our example, this variable is a measure of mathematical computation proficiency, perhaps a mathematics test score, or an instructor's judgment of ability. The differential effect, if any, of the independent variable, the use or non-use of materials, is reflected in the dependent variable. Thus the actual scores of the subjects are thought to *depend* upon the treatment, hence the name *dependent variable*. Sometimes this variable is called a *criterion* variable because the scores or judgments serve as criteria by which the effect of the treatment (independent variable) is assessed. It is the dependent variable which is subjected to rigorous analysis to determine the effect of the independent variable.

3. *Extraneous variables*: These are variables which may be known or unknown, important or unimportant, but which in any case vary freely and may have an effect upon the dependent variable. For example, the time of day for instruction, the ability of the teachers involved, the mathematical background of the subjects, might affect the mathematical computation proficiency scores of the subjects, the dependent variable. If any of these or other variables are not controlled, they may have an effect upon the dependent variable which might be confused with the effect of the independent variable. All studies except those conducted in the most rigorously controlled laboratory settings with inanimate or non-human animate subjects or materials have a large number of extraneous variables. The degree to which these extraneous variables are accounted for satisfactorily will in large part dictate the confidence one may have in the findings of a given study. This will be discussed in great detail in the subsequent chapters.

4. *Moderator variables*: Sometimes there are other, secondary, independent variables which are not the major focus of the study but which add to the importance and interpretation of its findings. These are called *moderator variables*. In our mathematics example, suppose the subjects in both groups possessed varying degrees of mathematics aptitude and could be divided into subgroups within each treatment/no treatment group: high aptitude or low aptitude. The researchers might be interested in knowing whether the independent variable, the materials, had a differing effect on high or low aptitude subjects. This variable, mathematics aptitude, is a *moderator variable*. And suppose our researchers also were interested in knowing if the independent variable had a differing effect on boys and girls. Then sex too would be a moderator variable. A study may have one or more moderator variables or it may have none.

5. *Control variables*: An experimental research environment is a highly complex affair. There is an infinity of variables within subjects, objects, and the research situation. In order to keep a research situation manageable, researchers seek to eliminate or effectively neutralize certain variables which might influence the dependent variable. These variables are referred to as *control variables*; they are actually *non-variables* or *constants* since they no longer vary after having been neutralized. For example, suppose our researchers were concerned with the spread of ages among the subjects. They could restrict the subjects to those children who were between their fifth and sixth birthdays. Thus, age would be a control variable. And suppose the class decorum, noise level, were thought to be an important factor which could influence the study. The researchers could take steps to insure that each group had equivalent classroom decorum thus neutralizing the potentially influential effect of this variable. Classroom decorum then does not vary from class to class, thus becoming a control variable. Most well done experimental studies have several control variables. As more and more potentially influential variables are controlled, the effects of the independent variable may be viewed with more confidence in their veracity. Good experimental research is typified by the conversion of important extraneous variables to control variables.

Variables in Descriptive Research

In descriptive studies the variety of research methods is quite wide. In some methods such as the causal-comparative (to be presented in a subsequent chapter) many of the same types of variables discussed above may be identified for the purpose of understanding what the researchers have done. In one type of descriptive study though there is a somewhat different terminology for variables of which we should be cognizant. Suppose, for example, researchers seek to identify and measure a relationship between school attendance and school achievement in junior high school students. They select a group of students and take measurements of the two variables, school attendance and school achievement. They analyze the measurements on these two variables and say, use their analysis to allow them to predict one variable from another—for instance, if they know how often a student comes to school, they can predict (within limits) his or her school achievement.

If after analyzing the relationship between the two variables the researchers seek to use this information to predict achievement from attendance, then attendance is labelled the *predictor* variable since it is used to predict the other variable. Achievement is the variable to be predicted and is labelled the *criterion* variable. If the direction of the prediction were to be reversed, that is, attendance predicted from achievement, then the labels would be reversed too: achievement would be the *predictor* variable and attendance would be the *criterion* variable. Thus, two variables are measured and their relationship analyzed. Either one can be a predictor variable and either one can be a criterion variable; it depends upon which way the prediction is made.

In some studies, the relationships among several variables are analyzed. Again the assignment of labels, predictor or criterion, depends upon the purpose for which the researchers want to use the analysis. There is nothing inherently predictor-like or criterion-like about a variable. It depends on its use. Typically in studies of this sort, one variable is designated as a criterion variable and the others act as predictor variables, each predictor variable adding to the others to increase the accuracy of the prediction. For example, if our researchers wished to predict school achievement, they might not only analyze its relationship with school attendance, but also analyze its relationship with say, IQ, sex, age, aptitude, and education of parents. In this case school achievement is the criterion variable and all the others are predictor variables. The use of several of these predictor variables, rather than just one, will probably increase the accuracy of the prediction of school achievement.

In reading a research study, it is very important to know which variables are which so we can know what the researchers have done. In experimental studies, sometimes the independent and dependent variables are identified for us with those specific names: the other variables are rarely labelled at all. When they are not so identified, we need to infer the label from the text of the study itself: 1) locate the treatment and think of it as the independent variable, 2) locate the measurements which were analyzed and think of them as the dependent variable, 3) see if the independent variable was dichotomized in some way, those are moderator variables, 4) note what aspects of the research environment were controlled and not controlled; these are the control and extraneous variables respectively. In descriptive studies in which relationships are analyzed, the variables are usually identified for us as predictor or criterion, but again, if this is not the case, observe the use of the variables in the study and label them accordingly.

Sampling

A crucial element in any educational research endeavor concerns the nature of the sources of data. The data sources could be people, such as high school juniors; they could be objects, such as social studies books; they could be documents, such as census reports for a period of years; they could be buildings, artifacts—the educational enterprise is sufficiently broad to allow the inclusion of virtually anything as a potential data source. Any clearly defined collection of people or things is called a *population*. Examples of populations are all pupils currently enrolled in the 6th grade in the elementary schools of Hawaii, all mathematics textbooks selected for adoption in Indiana, all existing high school buildings (Grades 8–12 and 9–12) in the U.S.A. built before 1945, all pupils with multiple physical handicaps enrolled in the 1st grade in a certain five counties of Idaho.

Researchers must decide on how many of each population of data sources their study will use. Sometimes this is determined by the size of the population. For example, if a descriptive study were planned in which the attitudes of multiple physically handicapped pupils in the first grade in a certain five counties in Idaho were to be surveyed, there might not be more than a handful of such subjects who could be identified and otherwise found suitable for inclusion in the study. As another example, in a study which uses pre-1900 school buildings as data sources, a researcher needs to ask, "How many are there around?" When the population of data sources is small, often all cases in the population are used in the study. On the other hand, sometimes a decision as to how many data sources to use is based upon the nature of the research question posed. If the research question is involved with an in-depth description of a given phenomenon which is thought to be universal, then perhaps just a few sources are needed. For example, if researchers were investigating the problem solving ability of children, they might select just a few children from a given population and make in-depth observations or analyses of their behaviors.

Typically, when a large population is available and the research strategy to be utilized requires the use of a group of subjects or objects, researchers select a portion of the population to serve as data sources. This portion of the population which will serve as data sources is called a *sample*. Most research in education employs sample data drawn from a population rather than data from the population itself.

Researchers are primarily concerned with two characteristics of a sample: 1) how many are needed for an adequate explanation and 2) how representative is the sample of the population. Regarding the size of the sample researchers consider the extent to which adequate resources are available to them in order to gather data from the sample. The larger the sample, the more resources needed. For example, imagine the human and material resources needed to interview ten high school principals compared to what would be needed to interview three hundred. A second consideration regarding sample size is how many sources are needed to have confidence in any findings resulting from the study. Researchers select a sample which is large enough to satisfy the requirements of the analysis procedures they plan to use, yet not so large as to represent a waste of resources. For example, if a population of 500 high school principals was identified for a survey study, a sample of 5 or 10 would probably not be sufficiently large for a rigorous analysis to be conducted, but a sample of 150 or more would be unnecessary. A quality sample of 40 or 50 might do nicely for a particular analysis.

The second concern of researchers is the method by which a sample is selected. If the researchers seek to generalize from the sample that is used in a given study to the larger population from which it was drawn, then the sample should be representative of the population. That is, the characteristics of the sample should be similar to the characteristics of the population. This issue of the representativeness of a sample is usually dealt with by using an unbiased method of selecting a sample. The most common method is a procedure called *random selection* which when employed yields a group called a *random sample*. To engage in a random selection procedure each element of a population must be identified and then each element must have an equal opportunity to be selected for the sample. The word "random" in *random sample* refers specifically to a procedure which allows for equal probability of selection among the elements. The selection procedure itself rather than being random in the sense of haphazard is quite specific. In the example above for instance, the researchers wanted a random sample of fifty high school principals. They might assign a number to each principal of the population of 500 and perhaps select the sample by taking the first fifty numbers between 1 and 500 from a table of random numbers.

The random selection procedure is based upon the idea that the laws of chance will operate if allowed to, and a sample drawn randomly from a population will be unbiased, proportionate, and will be similar in characteristics to the population. The larger the random sample the more similar to the population it will be. But sometimes researchers need to be sure that even with a large sample certain characteristics of the population are truly representative. For example, suppose our researchers who plan to survey a group of principals want to insure the correct proportion of women principals to men principals in the sample because they believe that these two groups of principals may differ substantially in their responses. If one group or the other were overrepresented, the responses of that group would be overrepresented in the findings of the study. To insure the correct proportion of these two subgroups, researchers employ a technique called *stratified random selection*. In this technique, the subgroups identified are considered *strata* of the population. The proportion of each strata to the population is computed and a random selection within each strata is conducted. For example, if 150 of the 500 principals are women and a stratified random sample of 50 is desired, then 15 women will be randomly selected from the subpopulation of 150 women principals, and 35 men will be randomly selected from the subpopulation of 350 men principals. The resultant random sample of 50 principals will have the precise proportion of women to men ($15/35 = 3/7$) as the exists in the population ($150/350 = 3/7$).

Theoretically, researchers can stratify a sample on more than one variable. Stratification could be done for example on age of principals, (20–39 vs. 40–65) educational level (masters vs. specialist vs. doctoral degrees) and a host of other seemingly pertinent variables. This generally is not done because for technical reasons the total size of the sample becomes quite large. Some researchers believe that stratified random sampling is not needed—one should have confidence that the laws of chance will insure proportionality. Sometimes researchers, in lieu of a random selection procedure will employ a procedure in which the elements of a population are systematically selected by choosing every, say, 10th person from a list. This is called *a systematic selection* procedure. If the list from which the selection is made is ordered randomly, then there is probably no bias in this procedure. But if the list is not ordered randomly such as in an alphabetical listing, there may be a subtle but present bias of which the researchers may not be aware.

An unbiased, representative sample which results from a random selection procedure is necessary in order to use many of the best analytical techniques available to researchers. The importance of this to the entire research enterprise can not be overstated. The logic behind the techniques of design and analysis which will be discussed in subsequent chapters is based upon the idea of unbiased representative samples. The degree to which samples have these qualities is the degree to which researchers can use these research procedures with confidence. Unfortunately, in the real world of educational research where studies are frequently conducted in conditions which are less than ideal, a random selection procedure is impossible to use. This can be due to administrative, logistical and/or political considerations. In such situations, researchers sometimes use *available samples* which are derived from a sample of the population which was available at the time of the study. Or *grab samples* are sometimes used: these are already aggregated intact groups. When samples which were selected by procedures other than random selection are used, we need to attend to the possible biases which may be present in the sample and follow carefully the procedures the researchers used in accounting for or controlling these biases. There are statistical procedures as well as organizational procedures which have been developed in order to control for these biases. But ultimately we need to consider these biases when we observe the generalizations made by the researchers as they move from the data derived from the sample to a statement about the population.

Hypotheses

When researchers plan a research study, a good portion of their planning culminates in the development of one or more hypotheses, as was discussed in Chapter 3. The hypothesis is the heart of a research study; it is an operational statement of the purpose of a study. When we want to find out precisely what a study is examining, we locate the hypothesis and find the information there.

An hypothesis which guides a research study is an assertion of a tentative answer to a research question. The syntactic format in which an hypothesis is stated will vary according to the needs of the analysis and the style of the researcher. In whatever form, the specific hypothesis represents the end product of a narrowing process which starts with a general purpose and develops into a question. For example suppose researchers are interested in investigating the relationship of long distance running to task perseverence among high school boys. From this point, the narrowing process might proceed as follows:

Purpose: The purpose of the study is to determine the effect of a long distance running training program on the task perseverence abilities of high school boys.

Research question: Is there a difference between the task perseverence abilities of high school boys who have had a long distance running training program and those who have not?

Hypothesis:

Research hypothesis style: High school boys who have had a long distance running training program will have a higher task perseverence ability than will high school boys who have not had this training.

Null hypothesis style: There is no significant difference in the mean task perseverence ability scores of high school boys who have had a long distance running training program and high school boys who have not.

We see that the *purpose* of the study is phrased as a declarative sentence which indicates fairly directly why the study is being conducted, what it seeks to find out. The *research question*, takes the purpose and restates it as a question with a specific focus: "Is there a difference. . . ?" This question impels the researchers to conjure up a tentative answer so they can proceed with the study. This tentative answer to the research question is the *hypothesis*. It is a statement which purports to answer the research question. Whether it does or not will depend upon the evidence the researchers gather which may or may not support the assertion of the hypothesis. This evidence will then be used to test the hypothesis.

You will note the use of "support" and "not support" when referring to the effect evidence has on any hypothesis, and the specific avoidance of the terms "prove" and "disprove." This is not an exercise in humility nor a statement of conservatism necessarily. Rather it is a reflection of the fact that in a research endeavor, we never know all there is to know—all the facts are never in, and if all the facts were in, we may be dead wrong anyway. So, researchers state that their evidence supports or does not support an hypothesis knowing that other additional evidence may possibly yield a contrary conclusion.

Research vs. Null Hypotheses

The hypothesis for this study in our example above is stated in two different styles. (This is done for exemplary purposes. In an actual study either one or the other would be stated but probably not both). In the *research style* hypothesis an assertion is made in a positive phrasing, "High school boys . . . will. . . ." This seems to be a natural way of making an assertion: to state that something *is* the case. In contrast, the null style hypothesis is a negatively phrased assertion: "There is no significant difference. . . ." This seems highly unnatural—we generally do not make assertions that something *is not* the case; we are usually uninterested in what is *not* happening, but rather we are interested in what *is* happening. Why then are hypotheses sometimes stated in null form? What advantage is there in this form? Why do some researchers choose the null form rather than the research form or vice versa?

The decision as to whether researchers use the research or null form of hypothesis is based upon the nature of the evidence they secure and the type of analysis to which the evidence will be subjected. If quantitative data, scores for instance are used as evidence and these scores are subjected to a statistically based analysis then the null form is necessary in order to employ certain decision making procedures to be discussed later in this chapter. If other data or analyses are used, then the null form of hypothesis is unnecessary and the research hypothesis may be appropriately used.

For example, let us suppose that two researchers are interested in investigating this matter of the long distance running training program and task perseverence but decide on different strategies. One researcher, Gretchen Rooms, decides to do a descriptive study using interviews as her data base. She adopts the research style hypothesis as the focus of her efforts. She locates a group of high school boys who have completed the long distance running training program and a comparable group of boys who have not. She interviews each boy in both groups asking questions dealing directly and indirectly with task perseverence. By analyzing what each subject said and did not say and tempering all this information with her observation of body language and the situational context, she arrives at the judgment that there is no difference between these two groups of boys regarding task perseverence ability. She applies her judgment to the research hypothesis and states that her findings do not support the hypothesis.

The other researcher, Fred Overshoe, takes a difference route in answering the research question. He adopts the null style hypothesis as the focus of his efforts, after having devised an experimental study yielding data to test this hypotheses. He locates a school which has a training program of this sort and works with the coach to identify a sample of boys to participate in the study. The boys in the sample are assigned at random to a group which engages in the training program or to a group which does not. One month after the termination of the training program, he administers a task perseverence test to all the boys in both groups. In this study the training program is the independent variable, and the scores on the task perseverence test are the dependent variable. This dependent variable represents the evidence he will use to test the hypothesis.

Now, let us return for a moment to the beginning words of the null hypothesis, "There is no significant difference between the mean task perseverence ability scores of . . . (the two groups). This hypothesis tells the Fred specifically what to do. First, he needs to take the dependent variable scores for each group and compute a mean average for each. Then he needs to observe whether the mean averages for each group are different. Then he needs to employ a statistical test to determine whether the difference between the means which he observed is likely or unlikely to have occurred by chance.* If the difference between the means *is* likely to have occurred by chance, then he would judge that the null hypothesis should be left alone—not rejected: there *is no* significant difference between the mean averages of these two groups. But on the other hand if the difference between the means *is not* likely to have occurred by chance, that is, it is probably a genuine indication that there is a real, bona fide difference between these two groups, then he would judge that the null hypothesis should be rejected: there *is* a significant difference.

Now, this same decision making process could have been employed with a positive phrasing of the content of the null hypothesis: "There is a significant difference . . ." rather than the actual negative phrasing used: "There is no significant difference. . . ." The reason for using the negative phrasing is based upon the limitations of the statistical tests involved. Without getting too technical at this point we can summarize the test by saying 1) there is an observed difference between the means 2) but the means might really be the same 3) the test can not tell us if the means are the same 4) but *it can tell us the chances of the means being truly different*. So, the null hypothesis states there is no true difference, the statistical test tells us what the odds are that this is so, and on the basis of this we decide whether we should change our minds. The logic behind the statistical test simply can not handle the positive statement.

You may feel that the use of null hypotheses in some research studies needlessly confuses the reader with its seemingly convoluted syntax. There are some people inside and outside the research community who would agree with you. However, most researchers and statisticians feel obliged to stay with null statements of no difference because such statements will allow them to be faithful to the logic behind the statistical test to which the hypotheses will be subjected. They are mindful of the possibility of errors which can result from many sources. Strict adherence to the hypothesis testing procedure removes one additional source of error.

*This chance factor refers to the concept of significance which will be discussed later in this chapter.

Inferential Statistics and Decision Making

In many research studies after having gathered and analyzed the data generated by the procedures, researchers go an extra step. They seek to generalize from the particular research situation in which they have been involved to a larger context outside of the research situation. For example suppose in one experimental study researchers find out that a sample of fourth grade pupils learns mathematics better when it uses certain materials. This fact in itself has little utilitarian value although it may be of passing interest to the researchers. But if the researchers were able to conduct their study in such a way that the findings of their study could be generalizable to all fourth grade pupils, then the results of their study would be much more valuable. It is this type of generalization which is the focus of procedures called *inferential statistics*—researchers seek to infer that certain qualities exist in a population that were actually found in a sample. In order to make such an inference and be able to defend it logically, they rely on procedures which are based upon theories of probability. In this section we will present three concepts which are basic to understanding the logic of statistical inference and decision making: the normal curve, levels of significance, and errors in statistical inference.

The Normal Curve

The *normal curve* is a hypothetical model which serves as the basis for much decision making. It is bell shaped in appearance and represents a certain collection of events (be they scores, sequences, measurements or anything else) which is referred to as a *normal distribution* to be further discussed below. Figure 4.1 shows a normal curve. Since the comprehension of a normal distribution and the normal curve are fundamental to understanding decision making, let us build our understanding with an easily conceptualized example.

Let us assume we possess a coin, freshly minted, that is in absolute balance. It has a head on one side and a tail on the other, and if we were able to slice this coin down the middle to produce two coins each half as thick as the original, the two resultant coins would have identical weights. This coin is a technological marvel, a precision device: it is completely without bias. If we were to flip this coin, the chances of it coming up heads would be exactly equivalent to the chances of it coming up tails: The chances of a head are exactly 50–50 each time we flip it. Now suppose we flip this coin 100 times. Each time we flip it it has a 50–50 chance of being heads because it is

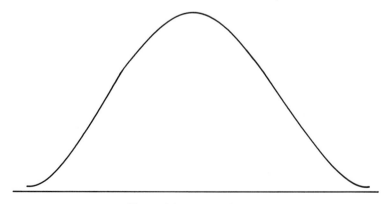

Figure 4.1. A normal curve.

unbiased, but when we consider all 100 flips taken together as a sequence it may or may not turn up heads 50 times. This is because there is an element of chance involved. Sometimes lady luck favors the head side of the coin and we get more than 50 heads in the sequence, and sometimes she favors the tail side of the coin and we get fewer than 50 heads in the sequence. When this happens, we know it is not the fault of the coin because the coin is in perfect balance, so it must be chance.

Now, suppose we wanted to know something about the effect of chance on coin flipping. We could engage in a series of coin flipping sequences, each sequence comprised of 100 flips, and keep track of how many times the coin turns up heads. In order to keep track of the results of each sequence, let us record each one on a graph as shown in figure 4.2. The horizontal axis is a continuum which can indicate the number of heads in a sequence from 0 to 100. The vertical axis helps us keep track of how many times a particular result of a sequence occurred. Each time a sequence has been conducted, we record the resultant number of heads on the graph by placing an "X" in the appropriate place. Already recorded on this graph are sequences with 43, 51, 55, 74 and two with 46 heads. When scores, measurements, events or in this case, sequences are spread out on a continuum we say that they are *distributed* on a continuum. Figure 4.2 shows a *distribution* of six scores.

If we were to continue flipping our coin until we had completed say 100 sequences, the distribution might look like figure 4.3. Notice how most of the sequences result in about 50 heads—they tend to gather around the mid-point of the continuum. Some of these sequences have exactly 50 heads but many more are *approximately* 50 heads. In general, the further you move from the 50 point on this continuum, the fewer sequences you find. Note that the sequence of 18 only occurred once in the 100 sequences.

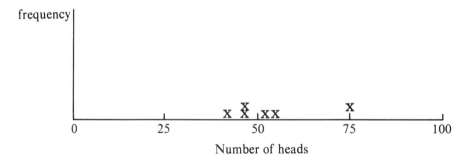

Figure 4.2. Recording of six coin-flipping sequences.

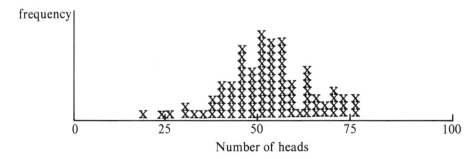

Figure 4.3. Recording of 100 coin-flipping sequences.

74

If we were to continue our flipping sequences until we had completed say 10,000 sequences, the distribution might look like figure 4.4. In graphing this distribution, all the "X"s we used to record each sequence by necessity become very small and appear as a solid mass of ink. But the height of the distribution still reflects the frequency of the sequences at that point on the continuum. You have probably noticed the resemblance of the distribution in figure 4.4 to the representation of the normal curve in figure 4.1. If we were to connect the top points of the distribution in figure 4.4 and leave out the black ink underneath, it would resemble the normal curve in figure 4.1 even more. These two curves are similar but not identical. This is because the normal curve is theoretical, therefore it is perfect; our coin-flipping sequence curve is taken from the real world of coinflipping so is tainted with imperfection. Also, the normal curve is based on an infinite number of events; our coin-flip sequence curve is based on a finite number of events, specifically 10,000. The more sequences included in our distribution the more closely its shape will approximate a normal curve.

So, we see that a normal curve is a graphic representation of a normal distribution. The normal distribution is characterized by having a clearly recognizable midpoint, a gathering of most cases near that midpoint and a gradual tapering towards the ends or *tails* of the distribution. You will note that the normal curve is symmetrical. If you were to fold it at the midpoint and lay the left half on the right half the two halves would be congruent. The slope of the curve from the midpoint to the tail is identical for both halves. In presenting this explanation of the normal curve, we showed how it could be developed from an experientially based procedure of sequences of coin flipping. In actuality, the normal curve in all its wondrous perfection is developed mathematically and need not rely on experiences. It is, however, somewhat reassuring to know that the theoretical model it represents can be demonstrated in real life experiences. With this basic understanding of the normal curve let us see how it can be used to make inferences.

From our discussion in a prior section of this chapter, you will recall that a sample is a portion of a population. A random sample is an unbiased portion of a population which if sufficiently large will be fairly representative of the population. In our coin flipping sequence distribution shown in figure 4.4, the entire distribution of 10,000 sequences is a population of sequences. Each sequence is one element of the population. As you observe the distribution, you will note that most

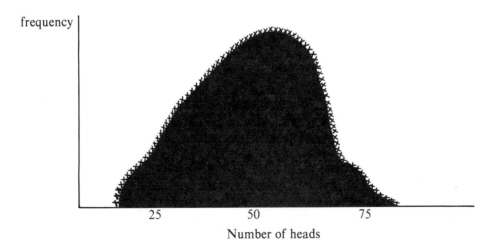

Figure 4.4. Recording of 10,000 coin-flipping sequences.

elements are near the middle of the distribution, but some are quite far away. Remember, that this distribution was composed of elements whose number of heads was derived from flipping an *unbiased* coin 100 times.

Now suppose someone comes to us with two coins and wants to determine whether these coins are biased, that is, whether they tend to favor the head side or the tail side. We could take each coin, flip it 100 times and repeat the sequence 10,000 times. This would mean one million flips per coin. Then we could compare resultant distributions from each coin to the more-or-less normal distribution derived from our perfect unbiased coin. The extent to which each of the two distributions differ from the normal distribution is the extent to which each coin is biased. This is an effective way of determining bias but unfortunately it is very time consuming. We can save time and trouble by using our knowledge of probability. While we will never *know* if the coins are unbiased or not unless we flip them indefinitely, probability theory will let us know how much confidence we can have if we decide that a coin is *probably* biased or unbiased.

Let us first consider Coin #1. We do not know whether this is a biased coin or not. If it were an unbiased coin and we flipped it 100 times, a sample sequence, how many heads would we expect to show? You say, fifty. Exactly fifty? Well, about fifty. Why do you say that? Because when you flip a coin 100 times if there were no chance factor and the coin were indeed unbiased you would get fifty heads. Since there is a chance factor you may come out with more or fewer heads. All right, we conduct a sequence of 100 flips. We get 53 heads. Is this a biased coin? You say, no. Why? Because 53 is pretty close to the theoretical 50 being only off by 3. Besides, lots of sequences with the unbiased coin had 53 heads, and a lot more were off by 4,5,6 or more from the theoretical 50. Noting where in the distribution this particular sequence falls, we ask *what is the probability* that the 53 head sequence which is three removed from the theoretical 50 heads *is the result of chance* rather than the result of bias in the coin? All things considered, you will probably judge that the probability is high that this deviation from 50 resulted from chance and conclude that this is an unbiased coin, relatively speaking. It is not necessarily a perfectly unbiased coin, but probably contains insignificant amounts of bias. After all, we flipped it 100 times—surely a bias would have shown up if it were present. Maybe, but maybe not. We will never know for sure; all we can do is state the probability.

What we have done in comparing the sequence of 53 to the entire distribution is try to determine how much chance was involved in the 53. Chance is really *error*. In theory, an unbiased coin turns up 50 heads every time because there is no chance, no error. But in practice, an unbiased coin usually turns up more or fewer heads because there is chance or error. The theory of probability seeks to specify chance or error. But let us return to our coins again.

We will consider Coin #2. We again conduct a sequence of 100 flips and the sequence yields 87 heads. You say, "Wow! Far out" (You think the "far out" expression is really a cute metaphor, but we shall see that it is an excellent description of the phenomenon from which it was elicited). We observe our distribution in figure 4.4 and compare the sequence of 87 to it. We note that 87 is indeed "far out"—it is quite some distance from the midpoint of the distribution. We would have expected the sequence to have been approximately 50, give or take a few heads. But this is off 37 from our expected 50. So again, we ask ourselves, *what is the probability* that the 87 heads sequence which is 37 removed from the theoretical 50 heads *is the result of chance* rather than the result of bias in the coin. You will probably judge that this occurrence would happen very infrequently with an unbiased coin, so infrequently that the probability is high that this did *not* result from chance, but rather is the result of a bias in the coin. So you conclude that the coin is *probably* biased. You can not be certain, after all, even the perfect unbiased coin yielded a sequence of 87. This *could be* one of the unusually high sequences from an unbiased coin. It could be but it is improbable. Suppose you want to check this out further. We might conduct a second sequence of 100 flips. This time we get 84. So we ask ourselves, what is the probability that two sequences of 87 *and* 84 are the result of chance. The probability is much higher than with one sequence that this did not happen by chance. We can be even more confident that this is a biased coin although we may never *know* for sure. After all, our original perfect unbiased coin yielded sequences of 87 and 84, too.

Confidence Limits

Let us move now from coins to research, reserving the right to return to coins for additional conceptual background. So far in our discussion, we have been stating our conclusions in broad general terms: we said that Coin #1 was *probably* unbiased and Coin #2 was *probably* biased. We can be more accurate in our statements of probability. Statisticians have through use of the theory of probability and the normal curve, developed procedures which enable us to state a level of probability in quantitative terms. These statements can be expressed in many verbal styles. We could say for example that the odds of Coin #2 being biased are 99 to 1, or the odds of Coin #2 being unbiased is 1 to 99; or there is a one in a hundred chance that Coin #2 is unbiased; or the chances are 1% that Coin #2 is unbiased. These expressions tell us in quantitative terms how confident we can be that Coin #2 is biased. We may interpret this the same way we do when the TV weather reporter tells us that there is a say, 20 per cent chance for rain tomorrow. This is a statement of a probability—it might rain or it might not but the chances are greater that it will not rain.

In educational research, confidence limits are often expressed in terms of the normal curve. Statisticians have divided the continuum on which the normal curve rests into units (called standard deviations, which will be discussed in a subsequent chapter.) This divided normal curve is shown in figure 4.5. Each unit may be described in terms of the percentage of events included in it. From the midpoint to one unit *above* the midpoint *or* one unit *below* the midpoint 34.13% of the events are included. Taken together from one unit below the midpoint to one unit above the midpoint are included approximately 68% of the events. Similarly from one unit *below* the mid-

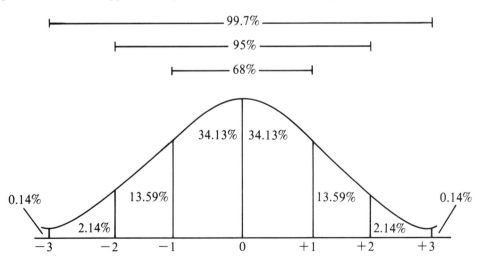

Figure 4.5. A normal curve subdivided into units.

point to two units *below* the midpoint *or* from one unit *above* the midpoint to two units above the midpoint 13.59% of the events are included. The remainder of the graph may be interpreted in like manner.

Now, when we conducted a sequence of 100 flips with Coin #2 and we compared the resultant yield of 87 heads to the distribution in figure 4.4, we noted it was indeed far out—it was at the extreme end of the continuum in the right hand tail. We judged that it was highly improbable that this was an unbiased coin. By using the normal curve in figure 4.5 we can quantify our judgement. We note the location of the sequence of 87 as being at the very end of the right hand tail, and observe that this is further than three units above the midpoint. By noting the percentage of sequences included from the midpoint to the three unit mark (49.86%) we can conclude that a sequence of 87 or more can be expected to occur fewer that 0.14% (.0014) of the time. This is less than 1%, so we can state that the chances of this coin being *biased* is over 99%. Stated otherwise, the chances of this coin being *unbiased* is less than 1%. Our confidence limits are 99%. Researchers do not need to actually make visual comparisons of a sample to a population. This information is available in statistician's tables which present the values needed by the researchers.

In educational research, we may administer a treatment to a sample of students. When we measure the effect of the treatment we then want to know whether the sample is now different from the population from which it was drawn regarding the attribute measured. The statistical procedures which are available to us to compare the sample to the population are based upon the procedures used to compare a given sequence of coin flips to the distribution of all possible coin flips. When the actual data based on a sample of students is compared to the hypothetical data from the population from which it was drawn, if it is different we can determine 1) the probability of the difference being solely due to chance and if so 2) what confidence limits there are on our judgment.

Levels of Significance

Confidence limits are usually expressed in terms of *levels of significance*. When researchers observe that two groups, a sample and a population, or perhaps two samples, are different they seek to determine the probabilities that the differences occurred by chance. They do this by testing the values associated with the two groups and noting if they exceed the confidence limits. If they do exceed the confidence limits, then the difference between the groups is said to be at or beyond a *level of significance,* and the observed difference is said to be a *significant difference.* By convention, most educational researchers adopt a level of significance at the .05 level or the .01 level. What this means is if for instance the level of significance is set at .05, when a difference between two groups is tested and found to occur by chance alone in five or fewer times out of one hundred, the difference is said to be *significant*.

For example, suppose researchers investigate the effects of two different methods of teaching spelling; one group is taught with method A, a second group is taught with method B. The average spelling achievement score for Group A was 7 points higher than the average spelling achievement score for Group B. The researchers note that this is not a large difference but it is not a small difference either. Could it have occurred by chance due perhaps to errors or bias in sampling? A test of the significance of the 7 point difference is made. The results show that this difference could not have happened by chance more than three times out of 100. The difference is significant at (or beyond) the .05 level. This is usually stated $p < .05$ and is read "the probability is less than .05"* that this finding would have happened by chance alone.

*The term *.05* may be read a "point-oh-five" or "five percent."

Errors in Statistical Inference

The purpose of much experimental research is to infer a characteristic of a population from data gathered from a sample of that population. This is the culminating point for most experimental studies: a statement that this is what the researchers found and this is what it means. Many of the ideas and concepts presented in this chapter will be drawn together in this section and then extended.

Suppose a group of researchers decide to study the effect of a speed reading program on college students. They are specifically interested in whether the program's techniques improve the students' comprehension of written material. The existence of funding and logistical problems precludes the random sampling they would like to do from a large population of college students. So instead, they select one Mid-western university which they believe is fairly typical of a certain class of universities. They obtain a computerized print-out of the junior level students and randomly select 150 students. They contact these students offering each one $25.00 if they will participate in the study. One hundred forty-three of them agree to participate and 140 actually show up when they are supposed to.

In planning the study, the researchers wrote the following hypothesis:

There is no significant difference in mean reading comprehension scores between junior level college students who complete the XYZ speed reading course and those who do not take the course. The .05 level of significance is adopted for the test of this hypothesis.

The researchers randomly assign the 140 students to the treatment group which gets the course or the non-treatment group which does not. The students assigned to the treatment group take the course. The students assigned to the non-treatment group bide their time. Of the 70 students in the treatment group, 65 complete the course. Four weeks after the termination of the course, the students in both groups take a test of reading comprehension. Of the treatment group, all 65 showed up for the test; of the non treatment group, 69 take the test.

The mean* score of the treatment group is 62.55; for the non-treatment group the mean score is 60.17. The difference between these two mean scores is 2.38. A statistical analysis is made of the difference between the two mean scores to test whether the difference is attributable to chance rather than reflecting a genuine difference in ability. Results of the analysis show that the size of the difference, 2.38, is too large to be attributed solely to chance. The difference is significant at the .05 level. The probability of a difference of this size occurring by chance alone is less than .05. On the basis of this finding the null hypothesis is rejected and its alternative is expressed: it appears that there is a significant difference in mean reading comprehension scores between junior level college students who complete the XYZ speed reading course and those who do not take the course. Note the expression "*it appears that there* is a difference. . . ." This indicates the researchers cognizance that this judgment is based on probability, and that what appears to be may not really be. This is comparable to the weather reporter who when interpreting the probability associated with his forecast for rain (5%) says, "*Looks like* it'll be a nice day tomorrow."

After presenting this finding, the researchers discuss the weaknesses in their study, the meaningfulness of the findings, the implications of the study, and various other matters. But let us return to their decision to reject the null hypotheses. The hypothesis stated "There is no significant difference. . . ." The analysis showed that the difference they found was indeed significant beyond the .05 level. On that basis they rejected the null hypothesis. Their rejection was based upon the

---

*A *mean* is an arithmetic average which will be discussed in a subsequent chapter.

idea that a difference of 2.38 points in that research setting could only happen by chance in fewer than 5 times out of 100. But suppose, this was one of those times. Suppose this was one of those five times in 100 when it did happen by chance. Remember the unbiased coin which once turned heads 87 times out of 100? It happens sometimes. So, too, does it happen that lady luck permits an observed difference of 2.38 in a research setting of that kind when in fact no real difference exists. If this was one of the chance occasions and the researchers, not knowing this of course, rejected the null hypothesis when they should not have rejected it, then an error has been committed. This is called a *Type I* or *alpha* error: a null hypothesis was rejected when in reality it should not have been rejected.

Now suppose the experiment ended a different way. Suppose the mean difference between the groups of 2.38 was found to be not significant at the .05 level. In other words, the difference could have happened by chance six or more times out of 100. In fact, a computation revealed that that finding could have occurred by chance 9 times out of 100. On the basis of this, the researchers do not reject their null hypothesis: yes, indeed, "there is no evidence to support rejection of the null hypothesis." They cannot conclude a significant difference does exist. But what really happened was that lady luck was not functioning this time and although the probability is high that the difference of 2.38 *was* attributable to chance, the fact is that it was *not* caused by chance. It is a genuine difference which reflects the differences in the training of these two groups. The researchers not knowing lady luck was out to lunch did not reject this null hypothesis, but in truth they should have rejected it. In this case they committed a *Type II* or *beta* error: a null hypothesis was retained when it should have been rejected.

These errors, Type I and Type II, reflect the dilemma researchers are in when they have to decide on rejecting a null hypothesis. Their decisions are based on probabilities and they can be wrong sometimes. The situation is quite analogous to the predicament you might find yourself in when confronted with true false examination questions. You are pretty sure you know the answers; let's say the probability of your answers being the correct answers is 95%. Now each time you answer a question, one of four possible situations can occur.

1. You answer *true* and the statement is *true*—no problem.
2. You answer false and the statement is false—no problem.
3. You answer true but the statement is false—this is a Type I error.
4. You answer false but the statement is true—this is a Type II error.

Thus a type I error is when you "true" when you should have "falsed." A type II error is when you "false" when you should have "trued."

Setting Significance Levels

The avoidance of Type I or Type II errors is a major concern to researchers as well as to students taking exams. An error free decision making process is impossible to achieve when the basis for making a decision is a probability. However, the significance levels can be set in such a way as to reflect the researchers' concern for error. For example, researchers can minimize the risk of a Type I error by setting the significance level needed for rejection at .01 or .001 or .0001. This reduces the probability of a Type I error to one in hundred, a thousand or ten thousand respectively—very slim chances. But this also increases the probability of a Type II error. There is an inverse relationship between Type I and Type II errors: as the probability of one decreases, the probability of the other increases, but not in exact proportion though. You can not minimize the probability of both types of errors at the same time—you can not have your cake and eat it too. So researchers have the problem of finding a happy medium—minimizing the likelihood of Type I error but not at the expense of overly maximizing the Type II error probability past the limits of good sense. This requires a judgment on the part of the researcher and in most cases .05 or .01 is considered an appropriate significance level at which to test a null hypothesis. You should note that the commonly encountered significance levels of .05 and .01 are arrived at really quite arbitrarily rather than being reflective of some great truth.

The basis for the selection of a significance level is determined in large part by the consequences of the decision to reject or retain the null hypotheses. If a study is exploratory in nature, such as studies found in basic research then a fairly low level of significance may be appropriate. For example, if researchers were to conduct a study concerned with developing a theory of language processing in children, they might adopt a significance level of .05, .10 or even .20 to test their hypotheses. This allows a lot of room for a Type I error but reduces the size of a Type II error. In setting the significance level at these figures the researchers are saying that they would rather risk being wrong in saying they found something important that really was not there, than risk being wrong in saying they did not find anything important when something important was there. The consequences of a Type I error in this study would be that if they or someone else were to continue the investigation their efforts might be fruitless, but this would be found out in the course of time. On the other hand, the consequences of a Type II error would be that further investigation of the problem might cease, when there was really something there to follow up on. Since the study was exploratory in nature, an unnecessary cessation of the exploration should be avoided. Thus the probability of a Type II error should be reduced.

Now if a study were confirmatory (rather than exploratory) in nature as would be the case in most applied research, then a higher level of significance would be appropriate. For example, if researchers conducted an experimental study to determine if a new language arts program were more effective than the existing program used in a school corporation, they might want to adopt a significance level of .01 or .001. In setting these significance levels they are saying that they would rather risk being wrong in saying that the program is not effective when it really is, than risk being wrong saying the program is effective when it really is not. The consequences of a Type I error are great. If the new program were said to be more effective than the old program then the school corporation might spend hundreds of thousands of dollars on new textbooks, materials, consultants, in-service education for teachers, and other things as well. If the program really was not effective, then all these resources, material and human, would be wasted. The consequences of a Type II error are in many respects not as great. If the new program were said to be no better than the old program the school corporation would keep the old program until such time as another new program were found to be better. The students in the school corporation would still be receiving an education, and the money that would have been spent on the new program would be spent on something else instead. In this example the consequences of the Type I error, an expenditure of money are irreversible; the consequences of the Type II error keeping the old language arts program are reversible.

We may look to our system of jurisprudence for a good analogy to the statistical decision making process and errors. Suppose a man is accused of a crime and is brought to trial. He is considered *not guilty* until proven guilty—this is in essence a null hypothesis. Evidence is presented by both a prosecutor and a defense attorney, and the jury is left to decide his fate: guilty or not guilty. The prosecutor works to induce the jury to reject the null hypothesis of not guilty: the defense attorney works to induce the jury to retain the null hypothesis of not guilty. The burden of proof is on the prosecutor, and the judge will instruct the jury that the prosecutor must prove guilt *beyond a reasonable doubt.* This is analogous to a statement of a significance level. Now, the jury has to interpret the phrase "beyond a reasonable doubt" in making their decision. The nature of the crime and the anticipated consequences of their decision may influence them. If the crime was embezzlement a Type I error might send the defendant to jail inequitably because he is really not guilty. A Type II error might free him when he really should have gone to jail. The consequences of their decision are serious but not grave. Probably a .05 level of significance would be the appropriate doubt level. But suppose the crime were first degree murder and a conviction would mean the defendant's death. A Type I error would result in the killing of an innocent man. A Type II error would result in a murderer being sent back out on the streets. The phrase "beyond a reasonable doubt" might be interpreted more stringently in this case since the consequences of a Type I error are irreversible. Perhaps a .01 or .001 level of significance would be more appropriate here.

There is always a trade off involved when setting significance levels which effect Type I and II errors. How we view the consequences determines the levels, and our view of the consequences is itself influenced by our values. In our society, we are more willing to risk freeing a guilty man than to risk convicting an innocent man. Thus the burden of evidence is upon the prosecutor, and the jury which judges the evidence has a fairly high level of significance used in making a decision. In other societies in which individual rights are less important and are subordinate to collective rights there is more of a willingness to risk conviction of an innocent person. Their levels of significance might well be lower.

The Meaning of Significance

It should be noted that the term *significance* has a very special meaning in a research context. It refers to *statistical significance* and is based upon the probability of something happening by chance. When researchers want to present statistical significance in terms of a verbal category rather than a quantitative expression such as $< .05$ or $< .01$, they sometimes use the word "significant." If the chance probability is between .05 and .01 then the finding is referred to as "significant." If the chance probability is at .01 or beyond, then the finding is referred to as being "highly significant."

Now, whether a finding is *practically significant,* that is, meaningful outside the research situation itself, is another matter entirely. For example, a large scale study may find that the mean average achievement score for Method A is 63.4 and for Method B is 63.6. And let's say this difference is significant at the .01 level. What does this mean? It means that the odds of this happening by chance are 1 in 100. That is statistical significance. When large samples are used, even very small absolute differences between means will often be statistically significant. This is because the larger the sample the more representative it is of the population from which it was drawn, hence the less sampling error involved. And so with less sampling error, the probability is less that the observed difference between means is attributable solely to chance. In our example, although the difference of 2/10 of a point between the means is significant at the .01 level, the difference is so small that it has no *practical significance.* For all practical purposes, the two means are the same. To a practitioner, this finding of statistical significance would have little if any value: one method is the same as the other.

Summary

The specialized techniques used in educational research are based upon several key concepts which when understood allow readers of research to understand better the research they encounter.

Researchers identify *variables* when engaged in a research study. A variable is a property or attribute of a subject, object or event which may vary from case to case. The *independent variable* is the variable upon which researchers focus their efforts: they seek to determine the effect of this variable. The *dependent variable* is the variable which consists of measurements taken on the subjects, objects or events. *Extraneous variables* are variables which are uncontrolled and which may have an effect upon the dependent variable. *Moderator variables* are independent variables of secondary importance. *Control variables* are extraneous variables which have been neutralized, or controlled. In correlational studies, variables are sometimes labelled *predictor* and *criterion* depending upon their use in an analysis. A *predictor variable* is used to predict a *criterion variable*; conversely, a *criterion variable* is predicted by a *predictor variable*.

The subjects, objects or events from which data are taken usually represent a portion of all the possible sources of data. The entire collection of potential data sources is called a *population*. A portion of a population from which data is taken is called a sample. If a sample was selected by means of a procedure called random selection, then the sample is called a *random sample*. If the population was divided into subpopulations and the random selection was done so as to insure the proportionality of each subpopulation, then the sample is called a *stratified random sample*. The sample selection procedure is of extreme importance in a research study.

Researchers develop *hypotheses* to test: their efforts focus on this testing. A *research hypothesis* states the research question in a positive wording. A *null hypothesis* is a negatively worded statement of the research question and is often used when researchers plan to use a statistical analysis of their data.

Inferential statistics are procedures which allow researchers to generalize from the data collected on a sample to the population from which the sample was obtained. Much of inferential statistics is based upon the *normal curve*—a symmetrical, bell-shaped curve which represents a *normal distribution* of measurements. This hypothetical model is very useful in allowing researchers to quantify their statements of probability. Statements of probability are usually expressed in terms of a *level of significance* such as the .01 or .05 level. Statements of probability are used to retain or reject null hypotheses. If a null hypothesis is rejected when it is true, a Type I error has been made. If a null hypothesis is retained when it is false, a Type II error has been made. Researchers set limits on the chances of a Type I or II error based on the type of study in which they are engaged and the consequences of each type of error.

Further Readings for Chapter 4

Huff, Darrell and Geis, Irving. *How to Take a Chance.* New York: Norton, 1959.
> This is a highly readable and entertaining exposition of probability theory. It is highly recommended to those who want a good understanding of probability.

Kerlinger, Fred N. *Foundations of Behavioral Research.* New York: Holt, Rinehart and Winston, 1973.
> Parts I and III of this excellent text present detailed explanations of the considerations presented in this chapter.

Willemsen, Eleanor W. *Understanding Statistical Reasoning:* San Francisco; Freeman, 1974.

Part Three
The Design of Research

Author's comment:

At this point in the text we begin considering the specific techniques used by researchers. The three chapters in this part deal with the overall approach researchers use to gather data. Chapter 5 is concerned with experimental methods. Rather than listing the various designs and pointing out strengths and weaknesses of each, I have presented a discussion of the most frequently encountered designs in a setting of the potentially confounding variables they seek to control. In this way, you will be able to appreciate more fully the rationale underlying the use of each design. This chapter is not meant to be a compendium of all designs ever used in educational research— just most of them. The readings at the end of the chapter may be consulted for a more extensive exposition.

Chapters 6 and 7 deal with the methods used in descriptive research. I think they are the most interesting chapters in the text: the range of possible approaches in descriptive research is quite large. In order to give you a handle on this whole area of descriptive methods I have organized them into four general categories. But be aware that these categories are not mutually exclusive, that is, a given descriptive study may be categorized in more than one way.

The section on evaluation was particularly enjoyable for me to write because the field of evaluation has recently come to be considered an independent field in its own right: much of what has been happening in this field has happened fairly recently. Another reason explaining my personal interest in evaluation is that it touches all our lives (and our pocketbooks, too). And a third reason is that the scope of evaluation includes all of the research techniques discussed in this text but in addition gets into politics, economics and related fields. The context of evaluation is richer and infinitely more complex than research *per se*. The portion of this section dealing with so-called outside evaluation represents a genuine concern of mine in the field of education as well as in other fields. I have tried to develop the idea of the mythology of outside evaluators to heighten your awareness of this problem without creating an aura of despondency.

Chapter 5
Experimental Design

Researchers start with an idea for research, a question perhaps. They develop background on it, meditate, review prior research, explore possibilities and ultimately refine their idea into an *hypothesis,* which is an operational and testable statement of their question. If the hypothesis requires an experiment in order to provide data which can test it, then the researchers will need to set up a controlled research situation so they can collect data appropriate for testing the hypothesis. The conditions under which the data are collected, that is the conceptual framework in which the experiment is conducted, is called *experimental design.*

The development of a suitable experimental design is a major step in the planning of a research study. If a given design is weak, loose, carelessly determined or otherwise faulty, one cannot have much confidence in the findings of the study regardless of what the findings are. And if this is so, what was gained by doing the study? Therefore, the researchers take great pains to set up their experiments in such a way that their designs are strong, tight and will provide them with data which can be relied on, and which will survive the onslaught of their critics.

You may feel that the phrase "the onslaught of their critics" is an overstatement of sorts. Well, actually, it is a pretty serious situation. When researchers complete a study, no matter what the findings someone somewhere is not going to like it. Perhaps the findings are contrary to "conventional wisdom" or current thinking; they can expect criticisms from persons supporting those opposing positions. "If you don't like the findings, attack the method," is a popular strategy among closed-minded people. On the other hand, if their findings support present thinking then those associated with a counter movement will be carping on the sidelines. Unanimity of esteem is virtually impossible to achieve—all researchers can really hope for is to proceed in the most scientific, unbiased manner, report their findings with due regard to the limitations and weaknesses of their study, and let the chips fall where they may.

You will recall that in Chapter 4 we discussed several key concepts which are related to research matters—hypotheses, variables, sampling and others. In our present discussion of experimental designs, these concepts assume great importance as researchers seek to conduct their studies in a scientific manner. In order to design an effective study, researchers must think defensively. They start by designing their study and projecting its anticipated findings, positive or negative. They usually want to demonstrate causality through their research. They hope to be able to say, "If we do *this,* then *that* will happen." So they arrange for the manipulation of the independent variable and measure the effect of that on the dependent variable. For example, they may design an experiment in which two methods of teaching spelling are used with two groups of students, and the spelling achievement of these students is measured. When the study is complete, they would like to say that either one method is better than the other or that they are both the same. In other words, they would reject or not reject the null hypothesis which was posed based upon the data gathered.

Suppose, for instance, they found that one method was indeed better than the other. Now, someone with another view of reality might say, for example, "It wasn't the spelling method that made the difference in achievement. It was the time of day. You taught the experimental group in the morning and the control group in the afternoon. Everybody knows that kids learn better in the morning." Whether the last statement is true or not is debatable. But the time of day *could* have made a difference. The time of day in which the teaching took place is a variable which never should have varied. You will recall that this type of uncontrolled but should-have-been-controlled variable is referred to as an *extraneous variable*. The statement above, made by a critic of the study offers an alternate explanation of the findings: the time of day of the teaching made the difference, or at least contributed heavily to it. This weakness in design has the effect of *confounding,* or confusing the findings. Its presence allows for an alternate explanation, called a *rival hypothesis.*

Other rival hypotheses might also become apparent due to design defects. Each legitimate rival hypothesis has the effect of attenuating the findings of the study to the point where there is virtually no confidence in the study at all. This is a situation which the researchers seek to avoid, and this can be done through carefully thought out design decisions.

There are two major benefits which accrue to a research study which has a good, tight, solid, well thought out design. The first benefit is *accuracy*. If a design controls extraneous variables to the point where they are effectively neutralized, the accuracy of the findings of a study are greatly enhanced. This is because for each controlled extraneous variable there will be one less plausible rival hypothesis to explain the findings of a study. If the independent variable is the only important variable which is left to vary, then its effect alone will influence the dependent variable. This is a highly desirable situation, and is one which researchers seek to promote. When a design so controls extraneous variables as to allow researchers to study the unambiguous effect of one or more independent variables, the design is said to have *internal validity*. In the example presented above dealing with spelling methods an important extraneous variable, the time of day, was not controlled. Accordingly this design is said to have poor internal validity. You may feel that it is unduly harsh to condemn a design (and concomitantly the findings of the study itself) because of one single extraneous variable. But all it takes is one extraneous variable to invalidate a study as we shall soon see in a following section of this chapter.

The second benefit of a good design concerns the usefulness of a study. Research studies are typically conducted in order to understand a particular phenomenon. The idea is to set up a research situation, study the given phenomenon in the particular research setting and then generalize the findings of the study to other situations *outside* of the particular research situation. If the findings of a study can logically be generalized to other situations outside the research situation, then this study can be quite useful. A design so constructed to promote this usefulness by allowing logical generalizations to other non-research environments is said to have *external validity*. For example, suppose a new program in elementary school science was being compared to an existing science program. The new program in its shiny red boxes was taught by enthusiastic teachers backed by a cadre of company paid consultants, and was initiated with a great deal of hoopla. If this program were found to be more effective than the existing program we are left with a nagging question: if the program were to be initiated when 1) the red boxes have lost their shine and/or 2) the teachers were not so enthusiastic and/or 3) the company paid consultants were no longer in attendance and/or 4) the hoopla were gone, would the program be as successful? The question is somewhat analogous to the old lover's dilemma, "Will you love me tomorrow the way you love me tonight?" This issue is external validity: would the same findings have occurred in a nonexperimental setting?

The relationship between internal and external validity is a dependent one but not as simple as it would seem. Internal validity is a necessary but not sufficient condition for external validity; that is, if a study has poor internal validity it cannot have external validity, but if it does have internal validity that does not necessarily mean that it has external validity too. This is because if the findings of a study are not accurate within the given research situation (lack of internal validity) in which the study took place, we can not assume that they would be any more accurate outside of the research situation (lack of external validity). But if a study does have internal validity, there are still other matters which may jeopardize its external validity.

The complexity of the relationship between internal and external validity can be appreciated by the plight of researchers as they design their studies. Sometimes these two types of validity work against each other. In an effort to enhance internal validity, researchers seek to control as many extraneous variables as they can. However by so doing they may create a research environment which is so artificial that it could not exist except as part of a contrived research situation. How then can they generalize from it? Research conducted in a laboratory is typified by tight control of extraneous variables, but the outside world is quite different from a laboratory. The other approach is to conduct research in the real world so the results of a study can be generalized to other portions of the real world. But by so doing, the researchers may lose control over a multitude of extraneous variables; they may have a finding but they might not know what it really is.

In situations in which internal and external validity are in opposition to one another, researchers often have to decide on where they want to take their chances: bolster external validity and take a chance on internal validity or bolster internal validity and take a chance on external validity. A decision of this sort will depend upon the nature of the research problem as well as the training and temperament of the researchers themselves. Typically, in the real world of educational research the designs actually used are compromises of one sort or another. Researchers select for control the extraneous variables which have the greatest potential for causing mayhem (or perhaps those which are most controllable) while attempting to retain most of the real world characteristics of the research situation. The determination of an experimental design is the culmination of a balancing act—internal vs. external validity. As consumers of research we need to note carefully whether the design is in balance considering the research problem and the anticipated use of the findings.

This chapter will focus on three major types of designs. First, the *classic experimental designs* will be presented in a setting of extraneous variables they seek to control. Then the *factorial designs* which emerge from the classic designs will be presented. And finally, *behavioral designs,* which represent a distinct contrast to the previously described experimental designs, will be discussed.

The Nature of Judgments

Before considering the specific designs used in experimental research, we should consider the issue of the quality of our judgments. Now, we make many judgments everyday, in our personal lives as well as in our professional lives. We are constantly confronted with choices from which we need to select specific options: which brand gasoline to buy, which teaching method to use, which candidate to vote for.

A fundamental maxim of decision making is that *all judgments are relative.* That is, when judging the value or worth of something, it must be compared to something else in order for its value to be meaningful. However, what "something else" to which the "something" is actually compared is crucial in the judgment process. For example, a research study could demonstrate that ABC Brand gasoline will power your car effectively, and you are advised accordingly to use this brand. The choices implicit in this statement are 1) use ABC Brand or 2) do not use ABC Brand. Obviously, there are other options available, such as using other available brands. The point is that the study was limited to the one brand of gasoline, and the implicit choice was between using that brand of gasoline or not using that brand. This is not a realistic choice. The value of ABC Brand is not in its comparison to no gasoline at all, but rather its comparison to other available brands of gasoline. The issue involved here is the problem of the *critical comparison:* what is this brand of gasoline being compared to?

Another example of this problem is a research study which finds that DEF gasoline with its exclusive XYZ additive performs better than DEF gasoline without that additive. However it happens that DEF gasoline is only marketed *with* the XYZ additive. So, the comparison is between a real gasoline and a fictitious gasoline, but this does not present a realistic choice selection for us. The consumer has no really useful information because the critical comparison is absurd.

In experimental research, the issue of the critical comparison is of paramount importance. Our judgments as to the effect of an experiment are, as is the case with all other judgments, relative. But relative to what? That is the question which focuses on the issue of the critical comparison.

Most judgments of the effects of treatments used in traditional experimental research are made by using as a critical comparison the measurements obtained from an *experimental group* which received a treatment compared to the measurements obtained from another similar group which did not receive a treatment. This other group used for comparison purposes is referred to as a *control group*. A control group, in order to fulfill its purpose should be as close to identical as possible to the corresponding experimental group. This attribute is usually achieved through the processes of *random selection*. It is the use of a randomly selected, unbiased control group in an experiment that typifies true classic experimental design; the existence of this group allows the most meaningful critical comparisons to be made.

Typical behavioral designs involve comparisons within a person, such as his or her behavior prior to, during, and after a treatment. In essence, the subject serves as his or her own control, and the critical comparison is between various stages of the experiment.

The next section of this chapter will deal with specific factors which threaten the validity of experimental research and will show how classic experimental designs are developed to neutralize their potentially detrimental effects. In order to assist in the presentation of this discussion, a uniform notation system will be used. These particular symbols and their spatial arrangements are the conventional symbols used in most discussions of research design.

O Symbolizes an observation or measurement. This is often the dependent variable. It could be a test score, a rating, an observation or any other expression of the magnitude of a given attribute.

X Symbolizes a treatment or experimental condition. This is usually the independent variable which a given group of subjects may or may not receive.

R Symbolizes a random assignment of subjects to a group.

The Os and Xs in a given *row* refer to a specific group of subjects. The temporal order is shown by the left to right directionality. For example: O X indicates an observation was made and then a treatment was administered. When two groups are notated the verticle dimension shows whether the Xs and Os were simultaneous. For example:

$$X \quad O$$
$$O$$

shows that one group received a treatment before an observation while the other did not receive a treatment, but both groups received their observations at the same time.

An R placed to the left of an X or O shows that the subjects were randomly assigned to the groups. Subscripts applied to Os are used to differentiate between the Os in a discussion external to the symbolic notation. For example:

$$R \; O_1 \; X \; O_2$$
$$R \; O_3 \quad O_4$$

shows two groups whose subjects were randomly assigned. Each group received two observations (O_1—O_2 and O_3—O_4) but one group received a treatment between its two observations.

Classic Experimental Designs

There are many situations which can threaten the internal and external validity of a study. If any of these situations is present, it could produce an effect that could be confused with the effect of the independent variable. Accordingly, procedures have been developed in recent decades which control these potentially dangerous factors. These procedures have resulted in designs which are referred to as *classic experimental designs*. To show the rationale for the development of these classic designs, each threatening factor is presented and explained separately. The particular features of each design will be seen as emerging from the need to control the potentially damaging effects of one or more threatening factors.*

IN AN EXPERIMENTAL STUDY, HOW WELL DID THE DESIGN
CONTROL THREATS TO INTERNAL AND EXTERNAL VALIDITY?

1. *History*. Sometimes specific events occur during the span of a study which influence the dependent variable. For example, suppose a researcher hypothesizes that if teachers change their behavior from cool and aloof to warm and sympathetic, the achievement of their students will improve. So the researchers design the study so as to measure achievement while the teachers are cool and aloof, have the teachers change to warm and sympathetic, and then measure achievement again. The design would be symbolized $O_1 \; X \; O_2$. The critical comparison would be the gain or loss between O_1 and O_2. But suppose during the span of the study the school's principal, a respected and popular person, dies prematurely. Was the difference, if any, between O_1 and O_2 caused by the teacher's change in behavior or the principal's death? A design to control for this factor would use an equivalent control group and be symbolized:

$$R \; O_1 \; X \; O_2 \text{ (experimental)}$$
$$R \; O_3 \quad O_4 \text{ (control)}$$

---

*Many of the ideas and much of the terminology used in this discussion of experimental designs are adapted from the seminal work of Donald T. Campbell and Julian C. Stanley, *Experimental and Quasi-Experimental Designs for Research*. The present author as well as virtually all other writers in this area are greatly in their debt.

The first group which received the treatment is called the experimental (E) group. The second group which did not receive the treatment is called the control (C) group. The critical comparison would be the difference between E group's O_1 and O_2 compared to the difference between C group's O_3 and O_4. The rationale for this comparison is that if the principal's death had an effect on the difference between E groups O_1 and O_2, then it would have had a similar effect on the difference between C groups O_3 and O_4. Thus, any difference between their respective Os would logically be attributed to the independent variable, the teacher's changed behavior.

This design and its corresponding critical comparison will control for many of the extraneous variables presented in this section. It is referred to as a *two group, pretest-posttest* design. If the composition of the groups was determined by random selection procedures, then this design is considered a true experimental design.

Sometimes it is not possible to have a control group, and accordingly, this history variable is uncontrolled. There is not much a researcher can do about this except to 1) shorten the time span between O_1 and O_2, thus limiting the absolute time in which confounding historical events could take place; and/or 2) describe in detail those events which transpired between O_1 and O_2 which conceivably could have effected O_2, and let the research consumers judge for themselves.

2. *Maturation.* The passage of time can produce changes in people by itself without the aid of a treatment in an experimental study. People grow, get tired, lose motivation, get hungry or change in many ways merely as a result of the normal passage of time. This variable, maturation, is similar to history and is controlled in a similar manner. For example, a researcher wants to investigate the effect of manipulative materials on the development of basic mathematical concepts in young children. An experiment is set up where mathematics concepts are measured, the manipulative materials used, and measurements taken again. The design is symbolized O_1 X O_2, and the critical comparison is the difference between the pretest and posttest. But between these two measurements a period of six months elapses—sufficient time for these children to mature in their understanding of mathematics through the natural development of their abilities. Was the change from O_1 to O_2 the result of the treatment or maturation independent of the treatment? The two group pretest-posttest design as indicated above under History would control for this variable in some way. If no appropriate control group is available, a shortening of the duration of the treatment would offset partially this variable.

3. *Pretesting.* If a pretest is given a posttest, the pretest can have the effect of influencing the posttest in several possible ways. It could provide practice in test taking, in which case a gain from pretest to posttest could be the result of the advantage of doing something better the second time than the first time it was done. Or the pretest could be a tip-off to the subjects that those test items included in the pretest are important in some way. This could result in the test taker being extra sensitive to content in some way related to those pretest items.

For example, some researchers might want to measure the effect of a social studies curriculum on the ability of students to predict economic conditions from a region's geographical features. A pretest and posttest are developed to measure this. The experimental treatment, the social studies curriculum, is presented to the students between these two measurements. Now, in order for the posttest to reflect any real cognitive gain, the pretest will have to measure essentially the same thing. In fact, the two tests should really be alternate forms of the same test. The problem is that after having taken the pretest, the students may have been sensitized to its content; if there were questions which they were unable to answer, they might very well attend more carefully to information presented subsequently which did answer those questions. Indeed, many teachers use some kind of prequestioning technique, pretest or otherwise, as a useful *teaching* technique for the very purpose of focusing students' attention on what they want them to learn. This interactive effect of pretesting and treatment is fine for teaching, but for testing in an experimental setting should be controlled. If a two group pretest-posttest design were used as follows

$$R \ O_1 \ X \ O_2 \ (E)$$
$$R \ O_3 \quad O_4 \ (C)$$

history and maturation would be controlled, but would the gain from E group's O_1 to O_2 be the main effect of the treatment or rather the interaction of the pretest and treatment, O_1 and X? You may question the need for this precision. "After all," you say, "if the E group's O_1-O_2 gain is significantly larger than the C group's O_3-O_4 gain, what difference does it make?" Well, actually, as far as this experiment goes, the issue is not crucial. But if the researchers' concern is also with *external validity,* they can only generalize the findings to similarly pretested groups. In other words, if the treatment were found to be effective, then would it also be effective with another similar group which had *not* been pretested? The two group design indicated above would not demonstrate this. However, a three group design is helpful. Note the following *Solomon Three-Group Design:*

$$R \ O_1 \ X \ O_2 \ (E)$$
$$R \ O_3 \quad O_4 \ (C_1)$$
$$R \quad \ X \ O_5 \ (C_2)$$

This is the two group design used previously to which has been added another control group (C_2) which has not been pretested. There are two possible critical comparisons to be made. The first is E group vs. C_1 group. If the E group's pre-post gain is significantly higher than C_1 group's pre-post gain, it could be the result of a treatment main effect or the interactive effect of the pretest and treatment. So the second critical comparison is between E group and C_2 group. We have a problem though: The C_2 group was not pretested so we cannot compute a "gain" from pretest to posttest. However, since the groups were composed by the process of random assignment we may assume that if C_2 had been pretested it would have scored the same as E group did. So, we can assign a hypothetical pretest score to the C_2 group which is equivalent to the actual pretest score of E group. If the pre-post gain of the E group is the *same* as the pre-post "gain" of the C_2 group, then the treatment effect is probably responsible for E group's gain being larger than C_1 group's gain. This is shown in Case 1 below. If, on the other hand, E group's pre-post gain is *larger* than C_2 group's, then the pretest-treatment interaction is probably responsible. This is shown in Case 2 below.

Case 1:	Pretest		Posttest	(difference)
E group	23	X	37	14
C_1 group	23		25	2
C_2 group	(23)	X	37	(14)

Case 2:				
E group	23	X	37	14
C_1 group	23		25	2
C_2 group	(23)	X	25	(2)

You can see how the additional control group directly addresses the issue of pretest bias by allowing a second critical comparison. It might be mentioned in passing that even more rigorous control of the pretesting variable can be had by adding another control group which receives neither pretest nor treatment. This is called the *Solomon Four Group Design* and it is an extremely tight design, but it is seldom used because of the additional resources needed to carry it out and other problems related to analysis.

4. *Instrumentation.* The instruments used in measuring the effects of a treatment must be reliable. That is, they must provide consistent measurements during a given administration, and between different administrations. This will be discussed in detail in a subsequent chapter. No matter what design is used, unreliable instrumentation will yield unreliable data and cause any findings to be suspect.

Sometimes, even when fairly reliable instruments are employed, a single pretest or posttest may not be appropriate. This is especially true when measuring an attribute which is subject to change over a short period of time, such as pupil behavior or attitude. In such cases repeated measurements help develop a more stable measurement of the attribute. A design which employs multiple measurements is referred to as a *one group time-series* design and is symbolized as follows:

$$O_1 \; O_2 \; O_3 \; X \; O_4 \; O_5 \; O_6$$

As indicated by the notation, only one group is present in this design. Three observations are taken before a treatment is administered, and three observations are taken after the treatment.

Not only is this design helpful in developing stable pre and post measures, but in addition it provides a check on maturation already discussed and statistical regression which will be discussed below.

Usually when well developed standardized tests or other good measuring procedures are employed, the issue of instrumentation is not a problem. But when measurement devices are used which are essentially judgmental in nature, the researcher needs to be very careful to develop judging procedures from which most bias or error has been systematically eliminated.

Intentional bias refers to bias or error which occurs as the result of a false judgment made by someone who bases his judgment on what he *wants* his judgment to be rather than being based on what he actually observes. Human beings have human failings: often they cannot be objective (or choose not to be) when rating something in which they have a subjective bias. Teachers have favorite students, raters have favorite subjects. This type of measurement bias which takes place can be controlled by having several raters agree unanimously on what the rating is. This is, in essence, how the jury system in Anglo-American jurisprudence operates. Another way of attenuating bias with fewer raters is to have each of several raters judge a subject on some attribute and average their ratings after omitting the highest and lowest ratings made. This was the technique used in the judging of the diving competition in the 1976 Olympics. Predispositions toward divers from countries with certain political leanings were toned down quite effectively. In fact, the variation in ratings among the judges was really quite small.

Non-intentional bias refers to bias or error which also results from human nature, but which is less under the control of the judges than is intentional bias. This type of bias can be *random,* that is, it can happen any time, any place, perhaps without warning and is usually distributed equally over all subjects. Or non-intentional bias can be *systematic,* occurring only under certain conditions and effecting certain subjects. If the bias is indeed random, effecting all subjects equally, we can control it by having more than one rater and averaging the ratings. Let us look at a situation in which non-intentional bias presents itself.

Suppose researchers want to find out if children will write better compositions when they are free to select their own topic than when a topic is assigned. They set up the experiment and gather compositions from the subjects under both experimental conditions. The compositions are scored in several ways: total length, T-unit length and a variety of judgmental variables such as clarity of expression, sophistication of style and overall pazaaz. There are two major problems with the ratings of those last three variables.

(1) The first problem with ratings is that they can vary widely among the judges, because the judges may define the variable differently. This can be controlled by specifying the usage of, say, a 5 point scale and *anchoring* points 1, 3, and 5 with descriptions and/or examples of what that variable should be to be rated at that point. For example, in the variable "clarity":

Ratings: 1. Very unclear and ambiguous. Almost impossible to understand what the writer is expressing.
3. Moderately clear. Mostly understandable but with a few ambiguities.
5. Perfectly clear. Everything understandable and nothing ambiguous.

These anchoring descriptions allow a rater to judge the clarity of each composition by comparing it to the description offered. Ratings at points 2 and 4 can be interpolated from the descriptions given. In addition to providing an anchored rating scale, the judges should be trained so that they generally agree with one another.

(2) The second problem with ratings is that even with trained judges using specified scales the problem of rating deterioration over time exists. That is, as judges rate the compositions over a period of time, they tend to get fatigued by the task. This has the effect of introducing systematic error to the compositions rated in the later stages of the time period; the compositions rated last may be rated higher (or lower) than they would have been if they had been rated first. If the compositions from the first experimental treatment are rated in toto before the compositions from the second experimental treatment, then the second experimental treatment papers might be judged quite differently from the others. This can be controlled presumably by having short rating sessions which terminate before judge-fatigue sets in. Another way to control this is to wait until all compositions from both experimental conditions are completed. Then assign a random number to each composition to keep track of which numbers went to which experimental condition, thoroughly randomize the order of the compositions, and give them to the judges to rate. In this way, as judge-fatigue sets in, the compositions of both experimental conditions will be equally effected by it. In essence then, this procedure has the effect of substituting random error for systematic error.

No arrangements or measurements, treatments and control groups can really control for unreliable measures. Rather, the development of the measuring instruments themselves and the procedures with which they are used are the determining factors. Multiple measurements and counterbalanced designs afford some assistance, but do not make up for any inherent unreliability of the measuring instrument.

5. *Statistical regression.* This factor is similar to number 2, Testing discussed above in that the relationship between the pretest and the posttest alters the actual value of the difference between them. What happens in statistical regression is that a population is tested and a sample is selected from that population on the basis of how far it is (up or down) from the mean average of the population. If that sample is tested again at a later date it will be closer to the mean average of the population than it was before. At least some of this movement toward the mean average of the population (and perhaps all of it) is attributable to the *regression phenomenon.*

To understand this phenomenon, we need to delve briefly into measurement theory. The actual raw score we obtain from a test or rating is called an *Observed Score*. As fallible human beings using fallible measuring instruments, our observed score probably has some error in it; that is, the observed score is not an absolutely precise measurement. The absolutely precise measurement exists only in theory and is known only to God or Nature; it is called the *True Score*. The difference between the observed score and the true score is called the *Error Score*. The relationship can be expressed mathematically by the following:

Observed score = True score + Error score.

Now, in any distribution of scores the extreme observed scores, high or low, are presumed to have more measurement error than those scores close to mean average. At least some of this error is random error, and the further away from the mean the observed score is, the more error it is presumed to contain. If the subject who received the extreme observed score is tested again, the chances are good that the second observed score will have less error than the first observed score. The less error it has, the closer to the mean it will be. The movement toward the mean on the part of the second observed score is called *statistical regression*. It is a result of the error in observed scores and the effect of retesting.

To observe this phenomenon in action, let us look at the following example. Suppose a researcher wants to measure the effect of smaller class size on the achievement of students in a remedial reading class. He measures their reading achievement, reduces class size by half, and four weeks later measures their reading achievement again. The design is symbolized:

$$O_1 \ X \ O_2$$

and the gain from O_1 to O_2 is used as evidence of the effectiveness of the treatment.

The problem with this design is that because the subjects were remedial readers who were specifically selected for this class on the basis of their low reading achievement scores, one would expect a gain from O_1 to O_2 as a result of statistical regression. This can be controlled easily by the familiar two group pretest-posttest design:

$$R \ O_1 \ X \ O_2 \quad (E)$$
$$R \ O_3 \qquad O_4 \quad (C)$$

if and only if the C group is composed of comparable remedial readers. The critical comparison would be the gain of the E group and the gain of the C group.

6. *Selection.* This is a very obvious source of bias. If a critical comparison is to be made between an experimental and control group, as in the two group pretest-posttest design

$$O_1 \ X \ O_2 \quad (E)$$
$$O_3 \qquad O_4 \quad (C)$$

each group must be truly equivalent at the start or be made equivalent in order to have confidence in the results. For example, suppose a researcher wants to investigate the effect of extensive use of media on fifth grade children's social studies achievement. He randomly selects Mr. Bradley's class as the E group and Mr. Tallow's class for the C group, and proceeds with the experiment. There are several possible biases in this selection procedure. For one thing, although the selection of which class is the E group and which is the C group may have been random, the original assignment of pupils to the classes might not have been. In this case, the groups might not have been equal at the beginning of the school year much less at the beginning of the experiment. Secondly, even in the unlikely case that the pupils had been randomly assigned to Bradley's and Tallow's classes at the beginning of the school year, we may presume that the two teachers have different teaching abilities and that after a few months with each teacher, one class might be better educated than the other. This is a *selection bias*—the two classes may not be equivalent at the outset of the experiment and it threatens internal validity.

A similar problem is encountered when a study is set up in which volunteers are used for the experimental group and non-volunteers for the control group. Now, volunteers are different from non-volunteers in one very obvious way: they volunteered. Perhaps not so obvious are the attributes associated with volunteerism. We may expect volunteers to be more confident, more eager and excited, and more willing to take a chance than non-volunteers. When volunteers are pitted against non-volunteers, the odds are in favor of the volunteers no matter what the treatment effect. This type of selection bias threatens external validity.

The probability of a selection bias is so prevalent and its effect so devastating that the exclusion of it requires eternal vigilance on the part of the researcher. Its nature is insidious because a study could be beautifully designed and executed, with suitable numbers of subjects, control groups, sophisticated analyses and its findings reported cogently and coherently, yet the study could be virtually worthless because of the group selection procedures.

This bias can be controlled by using a rigorous random selection procedure. In the example above dealing with Mr. Bradley's and Mr. Tallow's classes, if all pupils in both classes could be conceived of as one group, and pupils from this one group were randomly assigned to either the E group or the C group, then the selection bias would be eliminated. (There may be other problems with generalization however; these will be discussed later.) In a like manner, if all volunteers were pooled and group assignments were made randomly so both E and C groups had volunteers, the selection bias would also be eliminated.

This procedure will control for the selection bias by insuring that the subjects in each group are similar and thus comparable. The critical comparison between the two groups will not be invalid due to a selection bias. However, a larger problem may still remain—the question of external validity. Suppose, for example, a study was conducted in which the cognitive gains of an experimental group of volunteers was compared to the gains of a control group of comparable volunteers, and the experimental group did significantly better. As far as the particular study is concerned, the treatment was effective. Now the question is, would the treatment have been effective with non-volunteers? The results of the study cannot necessarily be generalized to another different population such as non-volunteers. Thus, it is seen that selection procedures can influence both the internal and external validity of a study, and the matter should be treated with great care.

Unfortunately, in the real world researchers often are not free to select their groups as they would like, They have to take what they can get, and they may be lucky to get anyone considering the typical procedural restrictions placed upon them. There is another way to deal with the selection bias, and although it is not as effective as randomization, it is nonetheless an appropriate procedure. Rather than controlling selection bias through randomized design features, the control is achieved through statistical analysis. The specific procedure is referred to as Analysis of Covariance (ANACOVA), and it will be discussed in a subsequent chapter.

7. *Experimental mortality.* In the course of an experiment, often some subjects drop out. This is referred to as *experimental mortality* and it is a strong, but subtle, bias which can influence the results of an experiment. "Mortality" is perhaps too strong a word since few subjects actually

die in a typical study; more often they drop out due to disinterest, poor health, lack of motivation and similar reasons. However, as concerns the experiment they might as well be dead since they are no longer part of it.

An example of experimental mortality would be an experiment to determine the effectiveness of a speed reading machine. Seventy-two volunteers are recruited into the study and are randomly assigned to E and C groups. The design is familiar:

$$R \; O_1 \; X \; O_2 \quad (E)$$
$$R \; O_3 \quad\;\; O_4 \quad (C)$$

The critical comparison will be between the O_1-O_2 gain of E group, and the O_3-O_4 gain of C group. During the treatment phase, ten of the E group's subjects drop out. Interviews revealed that three of them just became bored, three others were not doing well and were frustrated by the treatment and the remaining four had varied reasons. So when posttest time, O_2, arrives, only twenty-six of the original thirty-six in the E group are tested.

Now, we started with a mixed group of thirty-six volunteers in E group, but we have ended with only those twenty-six who stuck it out—apparently these twenty-six subjects do not tire as easily and were not as frustrated by the treatment as were some of the drop-outs. The posttest, O_2, obtained from the E group is from these twenty-six subjects. But the posttest, O_4, from the C group is from all thirty-six of its subjects, presumably some subjects who would have tired easily or been frustrated by the treatment if they had received it. Thus, the comparison is invalid. One would expect the E group's posttest to be higher regardless of treatment.

8. *Experimental Participation (Hawthorne Effect).* Sometimes an experimental group changes substantially during a study merely because it is an experimental group. Although the group may be composed of subjects randomly assigned to it, and is quite comparable to its corresponding control group, when it finds that it is the focus of attention it changes. Perhaps its self-concept improves, or perhaps it tries harder or longer. Whatever the specific change, it seems that the group's knowledge of its participation tends to have a beneficial effect on its achievement.

The medical profession knows this from its drug research. When some patients are given new drugs, they may claim that they feel better when there has been no actual change in their physical condition. Suppose, for example, a new pain killer is developed and is put into a white aspirin-type tablet in order to administer it to a group of subjects. If a one group design is used:

$$O_1 \; X \; O_2$$

in which pain measurements are taken for O_1 and O_2, and X represents the administration of the tablet, a critical comparison between O_1 and O_2 could be made but any improvement may be the result of the attention given to the group. If a control group were added to yield a design such as:

$$R \; O_1 \; X \; O_2 \quad (E)$$
$$R \; O_3 \quad\;\; O_4 \quad (C)$$

and a critical comparison made between E group's O_1 and O_2 and C group's O_3 and O_4, we have still not controlled the participation factor. So we can give the C group a tablet similar in taste and appearance to E group's tablet, but the ingredients are inert. This tablet is called a *placebo* and it has the effect of controlling the participation variable because now both groups think they are the experimental group, since they are both getting a treatment of sorts. The best procedure for using a placebo is a *blind,* in which case no one in either group knows which group he or she is in and whether he or she is getting the experimental medication or the placebo. If, in addition, the person administering the tablets does not know which is being given to whom, this is called a *double blind*. In such a case, any subtle but possibly important investigator bias is removed and as such, the double blind procedure is a highly desirable research procedure.

In social science research, it is not quite as easy to disguise a placebo so it appears to have no difference between it and the real treatment. However, the design can include multiple control groups so several comparisons could be made. For example, suppose researchers want to measure the effects of new materials on science achievement—let's call these materials X_1. They can set up a typical two group pretest-posttest design but add a third group, which also gets other new science materials—we'll call these X_2. The design looks like this:

$$O_1 \; X_1 \; O_2 \quad (E_1)$$
$$O_3 \quad\;\; O_4 \quad (C)$$
$$O_5 \; X_2 \; O_6 \quad (E_2)$$

Two critical comparisons can be made, E_1 group's O_1-O_2 compared to E_2 group's O_5-O_6. This will tell them the effect of the treatment, X_1 with the participation variable controlled. Then E_1 group can be compared to C group for further analysis; E_2 group can also be compared to C group. Several possible cases are apparent as we observe the mean pretest-posttest gains.

Mean Gain		**Cases**				
		1	*2*	*3*	*4*	*5*
E_1 group	+5	5	5	2	2	
C group	+2	2	5	2	5	
E_2 group	+2	5	5	5	5	

In case #1, E_1 group gained more than both C group which had no treatment, and E_2 group which had the other treatment. E group's treatment is probably effective. In case #2, E_1 group did better than C group, but E_2 group did, too. Probably it was the participation in the experiment which made E_1 group do so well or perhaps E_2 group's materials were equally effective. In case #3, all groups did as well as one another, so no treatment effect was observed. In case #4, E_2's treatment was more effective than E_1—in this case, E_1 serves as "other" treatment for E_2. This is also true in case #5.

In a study of this sort, a double blind procedure is highly desirable. The participants and the data gatherers should merely know that a treatment is being administered and not know which is experimental and which is the "other" treatment. Then when the data are analyzed, the chips can fall where they may.

9. *Multiple treatment interference/interaction.* In some experimental studies, a prior treatment received by an experimental group can have an effect on the experimental treatment itself. For example, suppose a researcher seeks to determine the effectiveness of a new mathematics curriculum in teaching computational skills. A two group design is set up.

$$R \; O_1 \; X \; O_2 \quad (E)$$
$$R \; O_3 \quad\;\; O_4 \quad (C)$$

The results of the study show that E group made significantly larger gains than C group. Hence, the treatment is judged to be effective; the new mathematics curriculum does its job.

There may be a problem with external validity though. The subjects in the study have had some training in mathematics prior to the beginning of the study. Suppose the training had been concerned with the development of background for computation. Then would the results of the study be caused by the experimental treatment exclusively, or rather caused by the combination and interaction of the prior mathematics curriculum with the experimental mathematics curriculum? If the results of the experiment were due to the combination of the two curricula, then how would the experimental curriculum work when combined with still a different mathematics curriculum?

Now, it could have gone the other way, too. That is, the prior mathematics curriculum might have, in some way, *interfered* with the potential beneficial effect of the experimental curriculum. In this case, the study might have shown negative gain from pretest to posttest in the experimental group.

This is a particularly vexing problem for researchers because they have to know much about the subjects prior to training. Often this information is not accessible. The best way to control for this is to identify a population which is large enough to include many different possible prior treatments and to select an experimental sample randomly to minimize the effect of any one prior treatment.

A similar problem occurs when several experimental treatments are administered to the same group. In a one group design, as shown below, the group acts as its own control. This is called a *repeated measures* design.

$$O_1 \ X_1 O_2 \ X_2 \ O_3 \ X_3 \ O_4 \qquad (E)$$

A pre-measurement is taken (O_1), and then each of three treatments is administered and followed by a post measurement. O_1 is the pre-measurement, O_2, O_3, and O_4 are all post measures. The problem with this design is that the effect of X_2 may really be an accumulated effect of X_1 and X_2; or possibly the effect of X_3 may be an accumulated effect of X_1, X_2, and X_3.

Let us see how this might work in reality. Suppose some researchers want to study the effect of three methods of teaching sight words to first grade children. They devise three methods:

X_1—a "phonics" method. The child is directed to attend to the sounds of the letters in each word.

X_2—a "visual" method. The child is directed to attend to the shape of each word.

X_3—a "kinesthetic" method. The child is directed to trace each word with his finger.

O_1 is a pretest to insure that the words given to a child are unknown.

O_2, O_3 and O_4 are posttests which measure how many words the child learns after each of the methods, X_1, X_2, and X_3, respectively. The design is as follows:

$$O_1 \ X_1 \ O_2 \ X_2 \ O_3 \ X_3 \ O_4 \qquad (E)$$

The problem is that X_2 and X_3 may represent a cumulative effect. In X_1 the child was directed to attend to the sounds of the letters. But when the child came to X_2 and was directed to attend to the shape of the words, does this mean that he or she no longer attended to the sounds of the letters? Do children *do* what we tell them to do and *only* what we tell them to do? There is probably no sure way of knowing what a child is actually thinking when instructed to do something. The effect of this design is to complicate the interpretation of any findings other than how well the children did on X_1, which had no prior treatment with which it might have interacted.

This problem can be relieved by randomly dividing the experimental group into six subgroups, each having a different order of presentation.

Subgroup	Order of Methods		
(R) A	1	2	3
(R) B	1	3	2
(R) C	2	1	3
(R) D	2	3	1
(R) E	3	1	2
(R) F	3	2	1

This looks very complicated, but in actuality it really requires careful record keeping as to which child was in which group. The process of changing the order is known as *counterbalancing* and is fundamental in reducing multiple treatment bias.

In this section we have seen the development of several classic experimental designs: two group pretest-posttest, Solomon three group, Solomon four group, one group time series, repeated measures, and counterbalanced. Each of these designs, in its own way, seeks to control factors which threaten internal and/or external validity.

These designs have been aptly labeled "classic," for they are classic in several meanings of the word. For one thing, they are traditional and enduring designs characterized by simple, straightforward lines; they serve as a standard by which other designs may be judged. But of equal importance is that like classical architecture and music, they represent a point of departure for the development of still more designs to be used in other circumstances and for other purposes. The remainder of this chapter is devoted to a description of other, non-classic experimental designs.

Factorial Designs

In the previous section, we have discussed the classic experimental designs which are characterized by the manipulation of one independent variable. Factorial designs are an extension of the classic designs, and allow two, three, or more independent variables to be manipulated simultaneously within one experimental setting. For example, suppose researchers want to find out the effect of programmed instruction in history on achievement compared to traditional textbook usage. They could set up the design as a classic two group posttest-only design, and randomly assign students to either condition as shown below:

$$R \ X_1 \ O$$
$$R \ X_2 \ O$$

where X_1 is the programmed method and X_2 is the text method. However, they have reason to believe that a student's reading ability might have an effect on his or her success with either method since the programmed instruction consists of shorter passages which would ostensibly be easier to read. A simple factorial design will allow them to consider this additional independent variable, reading ability. They could divide their sample of, say, 80 kids into good and poor readers and then assign them to one or the other treatment groups. The format for this design is shown in table 5.1.

Table 5.1.

	Instructional Method	
Reading Ability	*Programmed*	*Text*
Good	N = 20	N = 20
Poor	N = 20	N = 20

This is a 2 x 2 (read "two by two") factorial design. There are two independent variables: 1) Instructional method, referred to as the *experimental variable* and 2) Reading Ability, referred to as the *control* or *moderator variable*. This design yields four distinct groups of subjects; the spatial location of each group on the table above is referred to as a *cell*. In this example, each cell has twenty subjects. Various analyses can be made when each cell is viewed separately or when different combinations of cells are synthesized. This arrangement enables the researchers to answer more questions than merely, "Which method results in higher achievement?" They can also ask, "Which method works better with good readers or poor readers?"

When researchers ask, "Which method results in higher achievement for all subjects?", they are investigating a *main effect*. They do this by lumping together all forty subjects, both good and poor readers, in the Programmed Instructional Method and comparing them with all forty of the Text Instructional Method subjects, both good and poor readers. In essence, this analysis reduces the design to a classic two group posttest only design.

However, when they ask, "Which method works better with good readers and which method works better with poor readers?", they are investigating an *interaction* between instructional method and reading ability. Now, they could have done this by conducting two, two-group posttest only studies. One would use only good readers; the other experiment could have used poor readers only. And then they could have compared each group's achievement. But they would be comparing results from two different experimental settings, which makes interpretation of findings somewhat difficult. Fortunately, the factorial design allows them to investigate this question simultaneously with the investigation of the main effect of the instructional method. This is one main advantage of a factorial design.

The researchers might also be interested in investigating the differential effects of the instructional method on boys and girls. Do boys learn better from one method than from another? Do girls? This can be done by extending the 2 x 2 (method x reading ability) design to a 2 x 2 x 2 (method x reading ability x sex) design. In tabular form this design would look like table 5.2.

Table 5.2.

		Instructional Method	
Reading Ability	**Sex**	*Programmed*	*Text*
Good	Boys	N = 10	N = 10
	Girls	N = 10	N = 10
Poor	Boys	N = 10	N = 10
	Girls	N = 10	N = 10

We still have our experimental variable, Instructional Method, but now have *two* control variables, Reading Ability and Sex. Rather than four cells, we now have eight cells. And rather than one possible interaction, Method x Reading Ability, we have two additional possible interactions, Method x Sex, and Reading Ability x Sex (although the latter interaction is somewhat removed from the focus of the study, namely, Instructional Method) plus a triple interaction, Method x Reading Ability x Sex.

If desired, the researchers could add still more control variables such as socioeconomic class (high, medium, low), race (white, non-white), and birth order (first/only, middle, last). This would yield a 2 x 2 x 2 x 3 x 2 x 3 factorial design consisting of 144 cells, a mass of possible interactions and utter confusion for all.

There are practical limits to how complex a factorial design can get. Take the above example. In order to use powerful tools of analysis you cannot have one or two subjects in a cell. For some stability of the mean score in each cell, ten subjects would be all right. For 144 cells at ten subjects per cell, the total number of subjects needed at the end of that study is at least 1,440. And due to attrition problems, you need many more than that at the outset of the study. This presents major problems which would preclude the use of such a design for most researchers.

The interactions become fascinating, however. Would it not be interesting to know that programmed history instruction works better than texts for middle socioeconomic white first born girls of low reading ability? But, then, what does one do with such enlightening information? The practical value is nil.

Returning, however, to our simpler 2 x 2 factorial design measuring the effect of two instructional methods (independent/experimental variable) on a sample of good and poor readers (independent/control variable) on achievement in history (dependent variable), let us look at two possible outcomes. The mean average achievement score appears in each cell of table 5.3.

In table 5.3 we see that for both good and poor readers in total, the programmed approach appears to have resulted in higher achievement than the text approach, 78.5 and 68.0, respectively. Good readers did better than poor readers in both approaches, 82 to 75 in the programmed approach and 71 to 65 in the text approach. This is reflected in the total means over both approaches, 76.5 to 70.0. These findings show a main effect, but no interaction between experimental and control variables. If the means of the four cells were to be plotted as in figure 5.1 where the cell values for each approach are connected, the lines would not intersect. Indeed they are almost parallel.

Table 5.3.

	Instructional Method		
Reading Ability	*Programmed*	*Text*	*Total*
Good	82	71	76.5
Poor	75	65	70.0
Total Group	78.5	68.0	

Table 5.4.

	Instructional Method		
Reading Ability	*Programmed*	*Text*	*Total*
Good	74	83	78.5
Poor	80	70	75.0
Total Group	77.0	76.5	

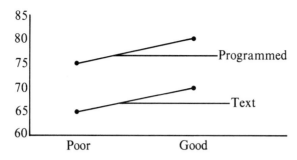

Figure 5.1. A representation of no interaction.

Now let us consider another possible situation.

In table 5.4, we see that for both good and poor readers considered together, there is no substantial difference between the programmed and text approaches, 77.0 and 76.5, respectively. And for both approaches collectively, good readers did better than poor readers, 78.5 and 75.0. But poor readers do much better on programmed than on text, 80 to 70, and good readers do much better on text than programmed, 83 and 74. These findings show an absence of main effect (77.0 and 76.5—the difference appears negligible) but a substantial interaction of method and reading ability. The charting of the means of each cell appears in figure 5.2. The lack of parallelism shows the interactive effect of the two variables. Indeed the lines which represent them intersect.

The two examples charted in figures 5.1 and 5.2 are obvious examples of no interaction and interaction, respectively: almost parallel lines with intersecting lines. One might ask, "What about the cases in between these extreme examples? How lacking in parallelism do two lines have to be before you can say that there is an interaction?" These questions cannot be answered by eyeballing the data. Rather, a statistical analysis of the variables which takes into consideration 1) the distance between the means; 2) the overlap of the scores in both groups; and 3) the number of subjects involved will indicate the chances of a possible interaction being a real or spurious finding. This will be considered more fully in Chapter 11 when statistical significance is discussed.

The possible investigation of the interactive effects of variables is a very important feature of factorial designs. It is especially important in the social sciences where the variation between subjects and complexity within subjects necessitates a closer look at research findings than a main effect analysis can give. Accordingly, these designs are frequently found in the literature.

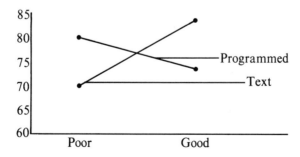

Figure 5.2. A representation of an interaction.

Behavior Analysis Designs

Behavior analysts have developed a unique set of designs for use in their own and related disciplines. These designs* reflect their own particular view of learning, causality and what is an appropriate research format. In contrast to the classic experimental designs described above, these designs typically are characterized by: a) small numbers of subjects (often only one at a time); b) continuous measurement of the dependent variable(s); c) presentation of data in graph form to obviate the use of statistical analyses. Behavior analysis designs permit the determination of functional relationships between environmental events of the behavior of *individuals*. Classic experimental designs can not do this—their focus is on variation in *group* behavior rather than individual (intra-subject) behavior variation.

The demonstration of changed behavior caused by the intervention of a treatment is of major concern to behaviorists. In essence, the research procedures begin with the selection of a target behavior in a specific subject (or subjects). The target behavior is to be changed through the application of some treatment. Then the frequency of the existence of that behavior in that subject is determined. This is done through systematic observation and recording. This phase of the design is known as the *baseline* phase. It is analogous to a pretest or preassessment.

Following the baseline phase, a treatment is administered and the frequency of the behavior is again systematically observed and recorded. This phase is called the *treatment* or *experimental condition* phase. Then, depending upon the particular design, there can be a return to baseline conditions or introduction of slightly different experimental conditions. Let's look at three basic behavior analysis designs and see how they operate.

The Reversal Design

In this design, a target behavior is measured (Baseline$_1$) and then an experimental condition is administered (Treatment$_1$). Following this is a return to baseline condition (Baseline$_2$) and then a return to experimental condition (Treatment$_2$). The "reversal" procedure or reverting to a baseline condition from treatment may be repeated several times depending upon the nature of the particular study. At all times and through all conditions, the target behavior is being measured continuously.

For example, suppose Peter, a fourth grade boy, is constantly engaging in disruptive behavior in his classroom, and his teacher, Susan, wants to try a positive reinforcement type technique to change his behavior. The procedures might develop like this:

Baseline$_1$ For five days, Susan observes and records Peter's disruptive behavior. His disruptive acts numbered 7, 4, 5, 7, 6 on each of these days. Following each disruptive act, she yells at Peter as she always has done.

Treatment$_1$ For the next five days, every time Peter engages in a disruptive act she ignores it, but later gives verbal praise to him when she sees him engaged in non-disruptive behavior. She continues to observe and record the number of disruptive acts which do take place. For these five days these acts number 3, 2, 3, 1, 2.

Baseline$_2$ For the next five days she reverts to yelling at Peter when he commits a disruptive act and she continues to observe and record. The acts number 5, 6, 7, 8, 5.

---

* There are several names for these designs: single case, intra-subject replication, operant, time series, and behavior analysis. For the purpose of consistency, the latter term will be used in this discussion.

Treatment$_2$ For these next five days, she reverts to the treatment condition of ignoring and praising. She observes and records the following number of acts: 4, 1, 0, 3, 1.

These four phases are represented graphically in figure 5.3. It is readily apparent why the design is called a "reversal" design: after having effectively reduced a given behavior by initiating a treatment condition, the experimenter seeks to reverse its effect by reverting to a prior condition. Causality is inferred by a critical comparison of the frequency of occurrences of the target behavior in baseline conditions and treatment conditions. The initiation and cessation of the treatment is considered analogous to a light switch. When the switch is turned on, the target behavior decreased; when the switch is turned off, the target behavior increased. The inference of causality is determined by the relationship of the timing of the decreased frequency of the behavior with the timing of the initiation and cessation of the treatment condition.

Multiple Baseline Design (MBD)

This design, too, uses baseline and treatment conditions but several subjects, behaviors or situations are monitored simultaneously. Three examples are shown below:

1. *MBD across behaviors*: Several behaviors on one subject. For example, a student, Barbara, has three problems in her English class: a) getting her assignments completed b) engaging in study behavior c) bringing her books back from home to school. Her teacher, Jay, seeks to change her behavior by applying token reinforcement (poker chips to be cashed in for a prize later on). Previously, he had given her long lectures about her deficiencies.

He observes and records the frequency of each of these behaviors from day 1 to day 10. On day 11, he applies the token reinforcement to behavior (a) and records the frequencies while continuing to record the frequencies of behaviors (b) and (c). On day 15 he applies token reinforcement to behavior (b) and on day 20 he applies it to behavior (c). Figure 5.4 shows how these data might appear in graph form.

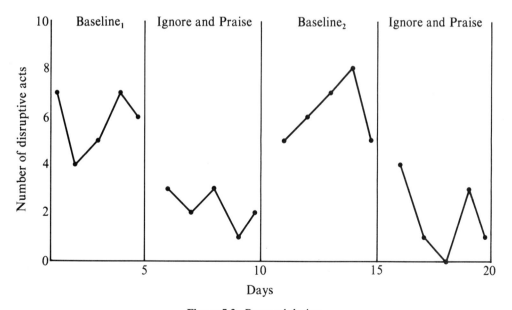

Figure 5.3. Reversal design.

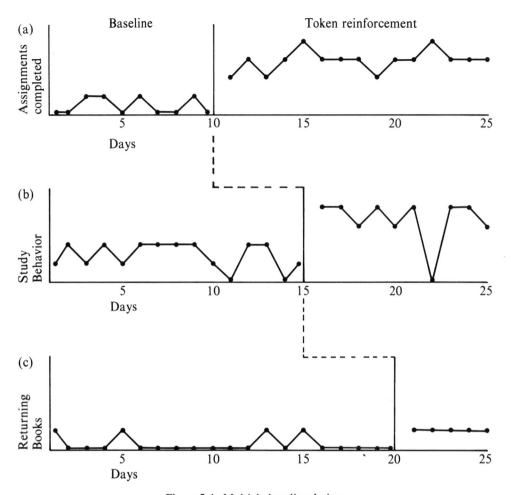

Figure 5.4. Multiple baseline design.

This design gets its name from the fact that more than one baseline is established. Because of the staggered entrances of the treatment condition, the baselines vary in length, making them readily distinguishable.

2. *MBD across situations:* The same behavior on one subject across situations. For example, a fourth grade boy, Jerry, has the habit of yelling out during instructional time in Social Studies, Mathematics and reading. His teacher, Conrad, develops a treatment: a response cost which consists of the loss of one minute of recess per yell. Conrad records the frequency of yells during the three instructional times and initiates the response cost treatment on a staggered basis, one subject area at a time. The charting of this endeavor would resemble the chart in figure 5.4.

3. *MBD across individuals:* The same behavior on several subjects. For example, four boys on the football team are always late for practice. The coach develops a treatment, time in the whirlpool bath contingent upon their punctuality. In this example, each boy would have his punctuality charted on a separate baseline and as in the example above, the coach would stagger the initiation of the treatment.

Changing Criterion Design

This design is an extension of the multiple baseline design. In essence, a baseline is followed by a treatment which is contingent upon a subject achieving a certain criterion level. When the subject achieves the criterion level, that level becomes a baseline for a treatment at a higher criterion level and so on until the ultimate criterion level is reached. For example, Darryl, a sixth grade boy, does poorly on his weekly spelling tests. His teacher, Penny, seeks to increase his achievement by allowing him extra time at recess for improved achievement. She records his spelling scores for six weeks during baseline. Then she informs him that he can have increased time at recess if he gets four out of ten words correct. After he achieves this criterion for a few weeks, she changes the criterion, making additional recess contingent upon his getting five words right. After this criterion is reached, she changes the criterion to six, then seven, and so on. Figure 5.5 shows how these data might appear in graph form. The distinct phases, baseline and different criterion treatment levels are referred to as panels. The solid horizontal lines represent the criterion level.

Comments on Behavioral Designs

A discussion of the efficacy of behavioral designs must begin with a determination of whether these designs fulfill their intent: the demonstration of causality. Can experiments using behavioral designs show that a treatment causes a change in behavior? Indeed, can any experimental design—behavioral, classic, or factorial—show this? The answer to these quasi-rhetorical questions is not straightforward, but this apparent ambiguity is somewhat resolved when we view experimental designs as having various degrees of quality depending upon their ability to control extraneous variables. In conservative operational terms we are better off viewing causality as being *inferred* rather than *demonstrated*. Our question now becomes, "How strongly can causality be inferred from experimental designs?"

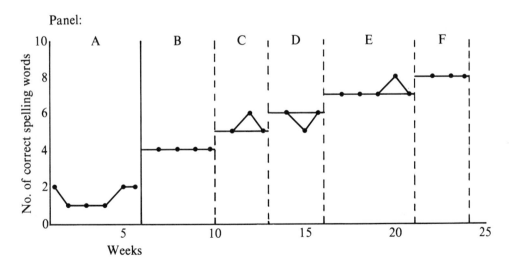

Figure 5.5. Changing criterion design.

Several of the classic group experimental designs which use randomized subjects—two group pretest-posttest, two group posttest only, Solomon three and four group, and factorial—are sometimes referred to as *true experimental designs* (other designs are often called *pre-experimental* or *quasi-experimental*). These true experimental designs probably allow the highest inference of causality because they control more effectively those factors which can threaten internal validity. Behavior analysis designs also allow high inference of causality, but only to the extent that they also control these threatening factors. It would be instructive here to consider how behavior analysis designs control each factor.

History is not really controlled. But it is assumed that the daily monitoring and measurement of the subject would reveal the effect of a given historical event. The reversal design seems to handle this best since it is highly unlikely that a given historical event would occur in both baseline phases or both treatment phases. A multiple baseline design also handles history well since it is highly unlikely that a historical event would occur at two points in time coincident with the introduction of the treatment. *Maturation* in most cases would not be a problem since the duration of most behavioral studies is quite short. *Pre-testing* (pre-assessment) in the baseline phase may or may not be a problem depending upon whether the subject knows he is being observed, and if so, whether he changes his behavior because of it. *Instrumentation* is fairly well controlled by 1) the simplicity of the measurements involved (typically frequencies of occurrences of a specific behavior) and 2) the high accuracy of the measurement typically caused by the corroboration of a second and third observer with the primary observer—inter-observer reliability.

Regression may not apply since there is no observed group mean to which a subject could regress. Yet, one might ask that if a subject were selected because of his abnormal or undesirable behavior, what are the chances that a treatment might make his behavior *more* abnormal or *more* undesirable. *Mortality* does not apply since the loss of the subject terminates the experiment. The interaction or interference of a prior treatment which would cause a *multiple treatment* effect may or may not be in existence. Sometimes the sequence of the phases can induce an effect; sometimes there is a carryover effect resulting from alternating treatments.

Experimental participation (Hawthorne effect) may be a problem in the external validity and long range effect of the treatment. Typically, the subject in a behavior analysis design knows that he or she is the object of experimentation. If repeated measures are taken over a long period of time, then this problem is lessened. Very problematic is the *selection* factor and its effect on external validity. Suppose the treatment did work on a given subject, as was the case with Peter in our example, Would it necessarily work on other subjects? Was Peter randomly selected from a population of disruptive students? Or was he selected because he was the most disruptive? Would it make a difference? This question may be investigated through extensive and systematic replication of the experiment. If it were found, for instance, that the treatment which worked on Peter also worked on virtually all other subjects on whom it was tried, then the selection factor would be dealt with satisfactorily. External validity is enhanced by systematically repeating the study with other subjects outside the original study.

In addition to these threats to the validity of a behavioral study, there are other concerns to be considered when evaluating these designs. Two concerns are with the baseline data to which the treatment data will be compared in the critical comparison. First, how long is the baseline? Is it long enough and stable enough to serve as a true index of a subject's pre-treatment behavior? Secondly, what was the slope of the baseline? Was a trend already in effect, and did the treatment happen to coincide with the trend? How long is long and how sloped is sloped—these are questions of judgments to be made.

Another matter to consider is whether the treatment effect, if any, lasted. What was its permanence? The duration of behavioral studies is typically quite brief: a question of days or weeks. Was some kind of follow-up made? A post check of treatment effects? Also, what was the role of the researchers in the analysis of the data in the study. What biases did they bring to the task? This is especially important when the effects are not strong since in most behavioral studies the data are charted and the determination of the efficacy of treatment is made by "eyeballing" the graph. Might not researchers bring predispositions to the data which would influence their judgment in drawing conclusions from ambiguous data? We consumers are obliged to do our own "eyeballing" too.

And finally, could a treatment effect, if any, be an interactive effect of the treatment with the person who administers the treatment. For example, when Jay gives the token reinforcer, a poker chip, to Barbara is his routine to smile and speak to her in addition to giving the reinforcer? And if so, what is the treatment—the reinforcer or Jay or both? This problem exists in all designs but is exacerbated in behavioral designs because of their limited numbers of participants, both experimenters and subjects.

Despite these problems, behavior analysis designs provide a valuable means of investigating causal relations with individuals. We consumers must be careful, however, to read studies using behavior analysis designs quite thoroughly, especially with regard to matters of external validity. The directness of the behavior analysis designs and the simplicity of the approach may lull us into a sense of false security. All designs have potential trouble spots—behavior analysis designs are no exception.

Summary

Experimental designs are conceptual and procedural frameworks in which experimental research is conducted. The purpose of an experimental design is to control the extraneous variables which might influence the results of the study. Researchers are concerned with the internal validity of a study: whether the procedures in a study allow the researchers to have confidence in their findings and conclusions. Also of importance is the external validity of a study: whether the results of a study can be generalized to other nonresearch environments. In experimental research, judgements of the effectiveness of the treatment are made on the basis of a *critical comparison*—thus a judgement is a relative matter.

Classic experimental designs are used to assess the effect of an independent variable by controlling extraneous variables; history, maturation, pretesting, instrumentation, regression, selection, mortality, experimental participation, and multiple treatment effect. *Factorial designs* achieve the same purpose but allow for the study of more than one independent variable and for the study of the interaction of two or more of these variables.

Behavioral designs are used typically by behavioral psychologists when they study the behavior of a small number of subjects. The behavior in a pre-treatment condition which occurs in the *baseline* phase is compared to the behavior in the *treatment* condition to determine if a change has occurred.

The following question needs to be asked by consumers when they encounter experimental designs:

IN AN EXPERIMENTAL STUDY, HOW WELL DID THE DESIGN CONTROL THREATS TO INTERNAL AND EXTERNAL VALIDITY?

Further Readings for Chapter 5

Campbell, Donald T. and Stanley, Julian C. *Experimental and Quasi-Experimental Designs for Research.* Chicago: Rand McNally, 1966.
> This is a classic in the field of experimental design. Virtually all discussions of the topic make reference to this monograph. Highly recommended.

Collies, Raymond O. Jr., and Elam, Stanley M. *Research Design and Analysis.* Bloomington, Indiana: Phi Delta Kappa, 1961.
> This book from a Phi Delta Kappa symposium is worthwhile reading. Two papers in particular are of interest: one by Cornell on sampling and another by Stanley on measurement and manipulation.

Denenberg, Victor H. *Statistics and Experimental Design for Behavioral and Biological Researchers, An Introduction,* Washington, D.C.: Hemisphere, 1976.
> A nice presentation of some experimental designs is found in this text. Chapter nine in particular deals with nested, randomized block and factorial designs.

Kerlinger, Fred N. *Foundations of Behavioral Research.* New York: Holt, Rinehart and Winston, 1973.
> A thorough treatment of experimental designs is found in Part 6 of this text.

Kirk, Roger E. *Experimental Design: Procedures for the Behavioral Sciences*, Belmont, California: Brooks/ Cole, 1968.
> A very thorough treatment of complex experimental designs is found in this widely used text.

Lindquist, E. F. *Design and Analysis of Experiments in Psychology and Education.* Boston: Houghton Mifflin, 1953.
> The text by Lindquist is a classic in the field of experimental design.

Winer, B. T. *Statistical Principles in Experimental Design.* New York: McGraw-Hill, 1962.
> An excellent advanced treatment of factorial designs will be found in this book.

Improving Experimental Design and Statistical Analysis. Chicago: Rand McNally, 1967.
> This book contains papers from a Phi Delta Kappa symposium on educational research. One paper by McLean and one by Baker especially will extend your knowledge of designs and in addition develop a perspective on the field.

Chapter 6
Descriptive Methods

Much of the research in education is descriptive research. Descriptive research seeks to answer questions which require a description of the present status of one or more phenomena. Researchers, rather than manipulating variables as in experimental research, arrive upon a scene and take measurements of the subjects or objects in which they are interested. The type of measurements employed vary with the nature of the research question: sometimes the measures are first hand observations made on site; in some studies interviews and questionnaires are used; but in most research in education test scores and ratings prevail although other types are used as needed. Some of the measurements already exist at the outset of a study such as IQ scores on school records; other measurements may need to be derived specifically for the purpose of a given research study, such as a measure of attitudes toward school gained from a researcher-developed questionnaire. In any case the researcher collects data to describe a phenomenon but does not intervene in such a way as to influence the phenomenon being investigated.

Descriptive studies in educational research abound because they serve several useful functions as discussed in Chapter One. The nomenclature for different types of studies varies widely and includes the following terms: prediction, growth, causal-comparative, survey, document analysis, case study, trend, correlational, census, ex post facto, longitudinal, cross-cultural, job analysis, cross sectional and other terms as well. Some of these terms are synonymous, few are mutually exclusive of others. There is little agreement in the field of research as to how these studies should be classified. In order to assist the reader in understanding the nature of descriptive research the following mini-taxonomy has been developed.

Descriptive research may be classified according to four characteristics.

1. *Depth vs. Breadth*: How many data sources were used? Some studies take a few sources of data, for example mentally retarded 12 year olds, and probe them deeply to describe many phenomena. This is referred to as a *case study* approach. On the other hand a study might use large numbers of subjects and make fewer observations on each one. This is called a *survey* research.

2. *Unicultural vs. Cross Cultural*: From how many environments were data collected? Most studies take place within a given culture. Some however, especially those seeking to investigate universality and causality collect data from several cultures or sub-cultures. These studies are called *cross cultural*.

3. *One shot vs. More than once*: How many times were data collected? Some studies collect data at one and only one point in time. Other studies collect data continuously for a period of time. These are called *longitudinal* studies.

4. *Simple description vs. Analysis of relationships*: What research purposes were served by the analysis of the data? Some studies present a simple description of the data, perhaps in tabular form. Other studies provide this description and in addition do sophisticated correlation or variance analysis on the data.

This taxonomic scheme will be used to provide a framework for a discussion of the major types of descriptive methods used in educational research. The remainder of this chapter and a portion of the next will present the various methods and discuss the strong and weak points associated with each.

Depth vs. Breadth
How many data sources were used?

When planning a study, researchers need to make a fundamental decision as to whether the purposes of their study would be served better by an in-depth analysis of a few subjects or a surface analysis of a large group of subjects. Each approach has its pros and cons. Two types of studies, *case studies* and *surveys* exemplify the differences between the two approaches.

Case Studies

The case study method involves researchers making an intensive study of one situation. The situation may be an individual, a social unit, a school, or element of a subculture or other small units. Through intensive in-depth probing, the researchers hope to uncover not merely the apparent, surface-type phenomena characteristic of the subject, but also the deeper knowledge, skills, values, and beliefs and the interrelationships among these factors within the subject. The researchers are seeking answers to *how* and *why* questions in addition to determining *what* and *when* information.

When a person is the object of a case study, researchers typically spend hours and hours with the person, interviewing and interacting with him or her or observing the responses to many stimuli. For example, the work of Sigmund Freud is case study research; his findings resulted from his many sessions with relatively few subjects. The work of the Swiss psychologist Jean Piaget is essentially case study research, too. The research of both these men has provided great insights in understanding personality and cognition respectively. Research in language development accomplished by linguists is typically case study research. Sociologists and anthropologists often use a case study approach in researching a community. They will spend days, months, even years getting data as they probe to uncover facts. Sometimes the researchers will become members of the group they are studying; this technique is referred to as *participant observation*. Information theretofore only available to members of that group would then become available to them.

Case studies are usually presented as narratives with little if any statistical analysis. They are generally easy and interesting to read. Considered as a research method, a case study approach has some important merits. The depth of the research uncovers information which may never have presented itself in other methods. Furthermore, the interrelationships of more easily accessible information may only be visible in the understructure of the person or object being studied. Hence, a case study approach is a useful tool in the development of a model or paradigm as well as in the subsequent development of testable hypotheses.

IF GENERALIZATIONS ARE MADE FROM A CASE STUDY, IS THE ATTRIBUTE CONSIDERED SUFFICIENTLY UNIVERSAL TO ALLOW A GENERALIZATION TO A LARGER GROUP?

There are problems in the use of the case study method. The main problem is that of external validity: how generalizable are the findings to other, different situations. Was the particular situation studied typical or atypical of the broad class to which generalizations might be made. There is an implicit assumption of universality when generalizations are made from a very few subjects. Were Freud's subjects, middle class Viennese women, typical of all women? Were Piaget's children like all others? There were so few subjects relatively speaking that the chances of confounding the findings due to the inclusion of an atypical subject are noteworthy. A favorite joke among linguists is about the researcher who studied the phonology of an esoteric language by listening to one native speaker for five years, only to find out that the subject had a lisp.

IN A CASE STUDY, WAS THE SELECTION OF THE SUBJECT/OBJECT APPROPRIATE TO THE PURPOSE OF THE STUDY?

Since a case study uses very few subjects or objects for analysis, it is important for those few to be selected very carefully. The purpose of the study should dictate the procedure involved in the selection. For example, if a study seeks to generalize its findings, then the subjects/objects should be fairly representative of the broad class to which generalizations are to be made. On the other hand, if the purpose of a study is to do some basic exploration of a certain type of subject/ object such as a schizophrenic, then the researcher should select a really good example, such as a person who is an extreme case. Such a person would afford the researcher a greater potential for analysis than a milder case.

Another problem with case studies is their inherent subjectivity. The researchers determine 1) the object of their research, 2) the questions to be asked, 3) the depth of their probing and other important factors as well. Their observations are subject to the effect of their predispositions toward their observations—they may observe only what their perceptual field and prejudices allow them to see. As a result, their research may lack objectivity and unfortunately the finding of a case study due to its technique does not lend itself to verification through exact replication.

Surveys

A survey is a method aimed at collecting surface-type data from a large number of subjects. In this method the individual respondents are considered as anonymous members of a group and the data from the group are collected at one point in time. The purpose of a typical survey is to find out *what* a certain group of subjects knows, or feels, or believes. The questions of *why* and *how* a group knows, feels, or believes are usually not posed, however inferences of why and how can sometimes be drawn from analyzing the responses of separate but related questions. Surveys are characterized by an apparent directness and simplicity of approach to gathering data and an uncomplicated method of reporting the findings, usually simple descriptive statistics in tabular form. Yet this seemingly straightforward approach to gathering and reporting data may obscure some possible methodological weaknesses whose effect on the findings could be profound. Two methodological features of a survey method on which our attention should focus are *sampling* and *instrumentation*.

Some surveys include as subjects an entire population, that is, all possible respondents in a group. This type of survey is called a *census*. For example, in its census every ten years, the U.S. government tries to get information from every citizen in the country. A PTA chairperson who asks each of the 250 members of the organization if they will be participating in a bake sale is conducting a census. More typically, however, a survey collects information from a sample of a population, and how that sample was determined is crucial. As we have seen in earlier discussions, the potential for bias, indeed perhaps out-and-out fraud in sample selection is enormous. Good research should report in very specific terms exactly how the sampling was achieved.

IN A SURVEY, WAS THE SAMPLE SUFFICIENTLY LARGE AND REPRESENTATIVE?

Samples should be as large as feasible: The larger the sample, the more representative of the population it will be, hence the less sampling error involved in the study. The tough question for which there is no definitive answer is, "How large is large enough?" The sample must be large enough to be representative of the population, and in addition, be large enough to utilize the analytical procedures employed in the study. Some generally accepted guidelines are available for different kinds of studies. For most survey-type research, 15–20% of the population yielding at least 30 subjects/objects is usually considered acceptable.

A sample should be drawn from a well defined population. If generalizations from the sample to the population are to be made, then procedures specifically designed to insure the representativeness of the sample should be revealed. For most studies, a random sample should be employed. In cases where this is not possible, then the procedures in selecting a sample should demonstrate a conscious effort to avoid bias.

IN A SURVEY, WAS THE RESPONSE RATE SUFFICIENTLY LARGE TO RETAIN THE QUALITIES OF THE ORIGINAL SAMPLE?

A population may be defined and a good sized representative sample drawn from it. But in survey research, typically not all subjects in the sample respond to the survey. Telephone interviewers may find that 40% of the sample choose not to speak to them. A mailed questionnaire may yield only 25% returns. The two general issues discussed above—representativeness and size—need to be reexamined. In reality, the sample in survey research is not the subjects from whom the researchers *plan* to obtain data, but rather those from whom they actually *do* obtain data. Our question again is how much is enough, and again there is no definitive answer. Assuming the final number of actual respondents is sufficient to use the necessary analytical procedures, we may say that if 75–100% of the sample respond, that's fine; if 50–74% respond, that's acceptable; if 25–49% respond, it is weak but acceptable if all conclusions from the findings are tempered accordingly. Any response rate of less than 25% should probably not be taken as an accurate reading of the original sample.

IN A SURVEY, HOW UNBIASED WAS THE MEASUREMENT INSTRUMENT?

The measuring instrument used in a survey, be it an interview, questionnaire, or opinionnaire needs to be scrutinized for bias. How a question is phrased can have an important effect upon the response elicited from a subject. As we shall see in a later discussion of instrumentation, the nature of the conclusions of a survey can hinge upon the phrasing of a few items. Since uninformed consumers of research tend to look at the findings and not the items themselves they may be easily misled. Good research reporting should include in its presentation the specific content of the measurement instrument.

Most surveys seek information about people by using people as subjects. However, descriptive information which is useful in education can be derived from an analysis of documents, books, records, and other printed materials. Studies using printed materials as sources of data are often referred to as *document analysis* or *content analysis studies*. These studies may be viewed as special cases of survey research, and thus they share the same problems as other surveys. For example, suppose researchers want to investigate the degree of anti-feminine bias in children's textbooks. They select the books, proceed with the analysis and draw conclusions from the data. In evaluating the study, the consumer needs to evaluate the procedure used to determine the sources of the data, that is, how many (census or sample) of which books from what population of books were used in the study. Also, the criteria for judging the existence of the bias in question should be evaluated: What was examined? Pictures? Narrative content? Pronoun usage? And if the task was judgmental in nature, what procedures were employed to insure that unbiased and reliable judgments were made? Good documentary analysis research reporting should be quite explicit about the specific procedures employed.

Unicultural vs. Cross-Cultural
From how many environments were data collected?

The typical descriptive study takes place in one well defined environment: a school, a factory, a community, etc. The population from that environment shares its definition and is a source of data on which the findings of a study are based. Sometimes, researchers may want to extend the conclusions derived from a study by determining how universal the findings are, that is, would the same type of data derived from other research environments yield similar conclusions. This is a quest to determine *universality* and is one major purpose of a *crosscultural study.* For example, researchers may make observations over a period of time dealing with the needs of people. They may find that in a given society people strive to fulfill certain needs among which are food/clothing/shelter, to belong to a group, to love, and to self-actualize. With this information they now want to know if the particular society in which these people live induces these needs or would the needs exist in other, different societies, too. Stated otherwise, are these needs society-bound or universal? To answer this question, they extend the data base to include other societies and make observations which serve to substantiate or refute the possibility of universality. Thus their study becomes crosscultural and the variables being investigated may be analyzed not merely within one culture but in addition, among many cultures. The extent to which the data collected from the various cultures are similar is the degree to which the claim of universality can be made.

On some occasions, a researcher may want to extend his conclusions to investigate possible *causality* among the variables in his study. The investigation of causality is a second major purpose of crosscultural studies. For example, suppose researchers conduct a study of remedial reading programs in a given society. They examine many variables and among their findings is the fact that the overwhelming number of clients in remedial reading programs are boys. They now want to know why this should be. Is there something in the inherent genetic makeup of boys which causes them to read poorly as compared to girls, or is it an environmental societal influence which causes it? To find an answer to this question, they search for societies where girls predominate in remedial reading clinics and if and when such societies are identified they extend the data base to include them. Although they can never demonstrate causality directly, a potential causality can be inferred from a comparison of each society's set of data.

It should be noted that the terms *society* and *culture* which have been used interchangeably in this discussion are not necessarily restricted to usage reflecting geographical differences. There is an American society (or culture) and a French society, but there are also many American subcultures based upon race, country of national origin, religion and a host of other variables which may exist within a given geographical location. For example, within New York City can be identified such prominent subcultures as white middle class, black middle class/Puerto Rican/

Spanish surnamed. Research studies which include as subjects members of subcultures, and which identify the subcultures as elements for analysis may be considered crosscultural if universality and/or causality are investigated by comparing the subcultures.

Problems in the availability, comparability, and quality of data in *cross-subcultural* studies are fewer than in cross-cultural studies and can usually be dealt with satisfactorily. But when two or more entirely separate cultures are included in a cross-cultural study the problems can be formidable.

IN A CROSSCULTURAL STUDY, ARE THE NECESSARY DATA AVAILABLE AND COMPARABLE?

One prominent problem is the availability of data. Some cultures keep records, some do not. Some cultures exhibit behaviors which appear to reflect certain feelings, while other cultures consider the behaviors to be taboo. Comparability of data, too, presents problems. Words and gestures may mean different things in different cultures, even in closely related ones. An American *public school* is not the same as an English one. A gymnasium in Munich, Germany is not comparable to one in Muncie, Indiana. An unwillingness to look a person straight in the eye means different things when done by a white middle class child or a Navajo child.

IN A CROSSCULTURAL STUDY, DID THE RESEARCHERS POSSESS THE SPECIAL COMPETENCIES TO OPERATE EFFECTIVELY IN AN UNFAMILIAR CULTURE?

An evaluation of crosscultural research must include a special assessment of the background and competency of the researchers: do they know a language and culture sufficiently to interpret meaning? And this goes the other way too: do the researchers know their own culture sufficiently to enable themselves to make observations and provide stimuli that are not culturecentric and biased with culture-laden values.

Furthermore, we should question if the researchers are sufficiently familiar with the foreign culture to engage in research procedures independent of external assistance? Or did they need to be "guided" to data sources by a potentially biased member of that culture, perhaps a government official. This is a key question, especially when dealing with crosscultural studies which include data from relatively closed societies.

One Shot vs. More Than One Shot
How many times were data collected?

Often researchers conduct studies to determine if change has taken place over a period of time. The changes to be studied may be changes in people such as students or parolees, or changes in events such as birth rates or word usage. Such studies of change are sometimes referred to as *developmental studies*. Within each type of change studied—people or events—two approaches may be employed as research methodologies: collecting data at one point in time or collecting it more than once, perhaps continuously, over a period of time. Let us examine both approaches within each type of change.

Changes in People

One method of observing changes in people is to select some people and keep on observing them for months, years or even decades. Studies using this methodology are called *longitudinal*. Changes among subjects on the specific target variables being studied are observed along with other changes in the environment. Because of the intensive nature of the procedure itself direct conclusions regarding growth and change may be made. A contrasting method of observing change is the *cross-sectional* approach in which at one point in time data are collected on a group of subjects of different ages or at different points of development. Conclusions regarding growth and change are much more inferential and less direct than can be made from longitudinal studies. As we shall see both methods have their pros and cons.

Longitudinal Studies

Researchers interested in growth and change who have sufficient time, money, patience and anticipated longevity may choose a longitudinal approach to investigating a research question. For example, suppose researchers are interested in describing cognitive and affective growth, and determining the child rearing practices associated with different growth patterns. First, they might identify contrasting practices in certain aspects of child rearing such as feeding, toilet training, discipline, mother/father roles, etc. Then families with infants might be identified and data on these variables might be collected through observation or interviews. The researchers would stay in contact with families as the infants matured into toddlers, pre-schoolers, school age, adolescents and perhaps further. They would be collecting data continuously on the subjects' social, emotional, and intellectual growth by means of tests and/or observations. At the termination of the study, the researchers could present their findings in many different ways: for instance, the subjects could be grouped according to a given child rearing practice and then traced to see how they turned out; or the subjects could be grouped according to how they turned out and then traced backwards to see how they were reared; or individual cases could be traced separately, or a combination of these reporting formats could be used.

A longitudinal study is considered a highly satisfactory method for investigating change over a period of time. Since the same subjects are used in all phases of the study the inherent abilities of the subjects remains constant. In essence, each subject serves as his own control. Another advantage is that the variation in growth between individual subjects may be readily ascertained. However, this methodology creates a host of other problems which must be considered in evaluating its appropriateness.

IN A LONGITUDINAL STUDY, WAS THE INITIAL SAMPLE SUFFICIENTLY LARGE AND REPRESENTATIVE?

The main problems in this method concern sampling. Because of the intensity of the data collection and the concomitant resources needed to actualize the study, a small sample of subjects is typical. This has the effect of reducing the potential variability in the group of subjects, as was seen in our earlier discussion of sampling. Now the problem is one of external validity—can findings on this small group of subjects with restricted variation be generalized to a larger population?

117

IN A LONGITUDINAL STUDY, WAS THERE AN IMPLICIT OR AN EXPLICIT SELECTION BIAS?

There are other problems, too. You will recall from the previous chapter on experimental design the insidious effect of a selection bias on external validity. This problem exists in longitudinal studies as well. In order to conduct a study such as that described above, the cooperation of the subjects' parents must be enlisted. Did all parents contacted for inclusion in this study agree to participate? What was the proportion of those who agreed to participate to those who did not? Could this be a biased sample? In order for a study like this to be conducted, families need to be relatively stable in the location of their residence so the researchers may stay in contact with them for the duration of the study. If the families in the study are stable, but the larger population is mobile then the subjects of the study may be atypical. On the other hand, if the families in the study are as mobile as the larger population, thus allowing themselves to be considered typical, many of them may lose contact with the researcher during the course of the study. This natural attrition of subjects may result in a situation in which the subjects still in the study at its termination are atypical, although at the outset of the study the non-attrited larger group of subjects was typical. It is a no-win situation for the researchers.

The researchers have other problems as well. If decisions about sampling, instrumentation or other procedural considerations turn out to be wrong, the researchers are stuck with them. Sometimes, during the course of a study new measuring devices are developed which are far superior to those used in the study. Or new measuring devices may permit the measurement of variables of interest not theretofore possible to measure, but the point in time of the study for their use may be past. And finally, longitudinal studies are expensive in terms of time and money. Ongoing support from a governmental, private foundation, or other organization is usually needed to complete this type of study. One must ask what effect if any this financial support has on the researchers, their methods and findings.

Cross-sectional studies

Some of the problems of longitudinal research may be overcome by using a *cross-sectional* methodology. Suppose, for example, researchers seek to investigate the same issue as the previous example: a description of cognitive and affective growth patterns and the child rearing practices which are related to them. They may select a sample of subjects at ages 4, 6, 8, 10, 12, 14, 16 and 18 and take measurements on them through tests and observations. Then, in order to collect data relative to their early childhood, interviews with their parents may be conducted. This approach would *seem* to yield the same type of data as the corresponding longitudinal study, the data having been collected in the space of a few weeks rather than over eighteen years.

For the purpose of description, the cross-sectional data may be superior because typically it is gathered from larger numbers of subjects than longitudinal studies. This reduces the chance effect of sampling bias, and includes more variability among the subjects than a smaller sample would. However, the full description of this variability may be masked by incomplete data description. For instance, growth patterns—physiological and intellectual—vary widely among adolescents: there are early maturers and late bloomers. When lumped together and considered as a group, the average growth of the group may predominate the analysis. Even the statistical measures of the variability discussed later would probably not do justice to this phenomenon. However, a case study type approach characteristic of a longitudinal study would make this information more or readily apparent.

IN A CROSS-SECTIONAL STUDY, HOW ACCURATE ARE DATA BASED ON RECOLLECTIONS?

It is in the inference of causality that this cross-sectional method suffers most. The first problem is with the data on child rearing practices. Data collected after the fact are inherently weak; the longer the duration of elapsed time between the event reported on and the recollection of that event the weaker the data. How accurate is the best recollection of a parent? How much has it been tempered by time, experiences, new knowledge? Is the information recalled a true account of what happened, or is it rather what would have happened if the parent knew then what he or she knows now? And is the recollection the best recollection or rather the most acceptable recollection in present circumstances?

IN A CROSS-SECTIONAL STUDY, HOW WELL WERE THE VARIABLES OF HISTORY AND SELECTION CONSIDERED?

Problems in inferring causality and in the accurate description of growth are caused by the existence of extraneous, uncontrolled variables. History could have a confounding effect. If the study in our example were conducted in 1962 then most of the subjects of 14–18 years of age would not have experienced television in their early years whereas most subjects aged 4–10 would have. One might suspect that television has had a profound effect on the variables being studied. Other historical events (e.g. war, recession) or social trends (e.g. single parent families, geographical mobility) may exert a similar influence on the findings. A selection bias may also be present. As children mature some may become less accessible to the researcher (dropouts or runaways) or totally inaccessible (premature deaths: natural, accidental or suicidal). This is completely out of the control of the researcher and may represent a real selection bias: the 14–18 year old group may not contain all the types of kids the 8 year old group contained. Thus the sample at the different age levels may not be comparable.

The choice of which method to use, cross-sectional or longitudinal, should depend upon the major purpose of the study. If researchers are interested in describing the *status* of typical subjects at various age levels at one point in time, then a cross-sectional method is appropriate. If, however, researchers are interested in describing *change* in subjects and perhaps inferring causality, then a longitudinal approach is more appropriate.

Changes in Events

The effective administration of social institutions requires extensive planning in order that social services be available when needed. Research methods which can collect data allowing for an analysis of trends which may help to predict the future are extremely valuable. As was the case in methods for examining changes in *people*, changes in events can be examined at one time or over a period of time.

Trend Studies

Typically, trend studies are a combination of historical research, document analysis, and longitudinal research techniques. Existing social, economic, demographic or other data are observed and based on their analysis a trend may be noted. This trend may be used to predict the future, and that information may be used to plan needed services. For example, suppose a growing community, Middle City, is concerned that sufficient school space be available to its residents.

The school board needs to plan its construction program so the right size schools are located in the right places. A *trend study* examining certain variables would yield this information. For instance, the question of school location requires information concerning housing patterns: Where is the greatest population growth? The question of school size requires information as to the anticipated birth rate. But in order to project enrollments, more than just birth rate information is needed. One needs to know how expensive the housing is in the growth areas. If it is too expensive, then perhaps young parents with small children may be excluded. If the housing is comprised of one bedroom apartments, this too would exclude most family units with children. The point is that the two variables—location of housing, and birth rate—must be not only considered individually but also as they interact with one another. A trend study including these and other relevant variables can be extremely helpful to the school board in helping make wise decisions.

Trend studies may also be conducted by making repeated surveys at given fixed intervals rather than relying on existing historical data. For example, suppose a school district wants to assess the adequacy of its vocational curriculum for the vocational needs of its community. Each year it might survey the local business and industrial community in order to determine trends in employment opportunities. Based on such data its curriculum may be revised to prepare its students for anticipated jobs. This type of trend analysis is concerned with immediate short term needs and data collection is focused on the present and near future rather than the past.

Among trend studies there is a wide variation in scope. Some are restricted to one or two obvious variables, others deal with a multitude of interdependent and interactive variables, but the problems inherent in this type of research are present in most studies. The problems are focused upon the *description* of the presumed trend and the inferred *prediction* from it.

IN A TREND STUDY, ARE THE SETS OF DATA USED TRULY COMPARABLE?

A major problem when analyzing data from over a period of time is its *comparability*. For example, suppose researchers are analyzing trends in kindergarten age children. Are current figures comparable to figures from 50 years ago when there were many fewer kindergartens into which children could be enrolled? Another example concerns any research over time involving money. Suppose a researcher is analyzing trends in teacher salaries. All data are reported in dollars but 1980 dollars are not comparable to 1970 dollars or 1960 dollars. Good reporting would adjust the figures in terms of some constant (e.g. 1960 dollars or how long a teacher needs to work to earn enough to pay for a car) in order to make the data more meaningful.

Data of this type often need to be presented in several ways in order that their significance not be twisted. For example, in a trend analysis of the number of high school graduates over time, the raw figures which show increasing numbers may be misleading since the population has been increasing too. Good reporting should also include the *proportion* of the 17–20 year old population that is represented by the actual number of high school graduates.

Predicting the future of complex social or economic phenomena from past events is always a risky business. In evaluating a prediction of this sort, two questions should be asked in order to test the plausibility of the prediction.

IN A TREND STUDY, IS AN OBSERVED TREND TEMPORARY OR PERMANENT?

We need to ask ourselves if a trend has been observed long enough to determine whether it is cyclical (temporary) or long range (permanent). For example, an analysis of stock prices in the 1960s would reveal a trend toward higher and higher prices. However, if the analysis went back to the 1920s a rather different picture would emerge.

IN A TREND STUDY, IS THE TREND OF THE VARIABLE BEING STUDIED INDEPENDENT OF OTHER SIGNIFICANT VARIABLES?

Some variables whose trend is being studied are interactive with other variables rather than being independent. For example, birth rates seem to vary with economic conditions (more births in good times), social lifestyles (fewer births with delayed or fewer marriages), minicatastrophes (more births following power blackouts and sustained blizzards), and prior birthrates (more births due to the existence of more women of child bearing ages), as well as with other relevant factors. Reasonable prediction of one variable needs to be based in part on the prediction of other covarying and possibly causal variables.

Long range planning is the riskiest business of all. Unforeseen and unimaginable events can completely undermine the apparent logic of a prediction. Historical and timely examples abound. In the 1940s magazine ads for insurance companies pictured for instance a man in his 60s fishing from a rowboat—a picture of contentment—with a caption, "How I retired at 65 with $400 per month income." No one foresaw the rampant inflation subsequent decades would witness, thus rendering absurd the idea of a comfortable retirement on that amount of money. Mass starvation was predicted for the population of Asia. No one predicted the Green Revolution whose use of high yield hybrid grains boosted food supplies enormously. Lenin predicted the demise of capitalism based upon his analysis of events, but did not predict the rise of labor unions. The problems of accurate short term prediction are formidable; the problems of accurate long range prediction are staggering.

Summary

There is a wide variety of methods used in descriptive research. Each method is appropriate for a given research question, although sometimes any of several methods may be effectively utilized. Often the specific techniques used in a given study are a combination of the techniques associated with several methods.

A *case study* involves the intensive study of one or just a few cases. The researchers are interested in the depth and interaction of the variables being studied. On the other hand, *surveys* collect data of lesser depth but from more cases. Each of these methods has its strengths and weaknesses. *Cross-cultural* studies collect data from two or more separate cultures. These studies are useful to determine causality and universality. *Developmental studies* observe changes in subjects. In *longitudinal studies*, a group of subjects is followed over a period of months, years or decades with observations or measurements being taken periodically. However, *cross sectional studies* observe characteristics of subjects of many ages but at one point in time. *Trend studies* observe changes in events and often seek to predict the future on the basis of the observed trend.

The following questions need to be asked by consumers when they encounter these methods.

IF GENERALIZATIONS ARE MADE FROM A CASE STUDY IS THE ATTRIBUTE CONSIDERED SUFFICIENTLY UNIVERSAL TO ALLOW A GENERALIZATION TO A LARGER GROUP?

IN A CASE STUDY, WAS THE SELECTION OF THE SUBJECT OR OBJECT APPROPRIATE TO THE PURPOSE OF THE STUDY?

IN A SURVEY, WAS THE SAMPLE SUFFICIENTLY LARGE AND REPRESENTATIVE?

IN A SURVEY, WAS THE RESPONSE RATE SUFFICIENTLY LARGE TO RETAIN THE QUALITIES OF THE ORIGINAL SAMPLE?

IN A SURVEY, HOW UNBIASED WAS THE MEASUREMENT INSTRUMENT?

IN A CROSS CULTURAL STUDY, ARE THE NECESSARY DATA AVAILABLE AND COMPARABLE?

IN A CROSS CULTURAL STUDY, DID THE RESEARCHERS POSSESS THE SPECIAL COMPETENCIES TO OPERATE EFFECTIVELY IN AN UNFAMILIAR CULTURE?

IN A LONGITUDINAL STUDY, WAS THE INITIAL SAMPLE SUFFICIENTLY LARGE AND REPRESENTATIVE?

IN A LONGITUDINAL STUDY, WAS THERE AN IMPLICIT OR AN EXPLICIT SELECTION BIAS?

IN A CROSS SECTIONAL STUDY, HOW ACCURATE ARE THE DATA BASED ON RECOLLECTIONS?

IN A CROSS SECTIONAL STUDY, HOW WELL WERE THE VARIABLES OF HISTORY AND SELECTION CONSIDERED?

IN A TREND STUDY, ARE THE SETS OF DATA USED TRULY COMPARABLE?

IN A TREND STUDY, IS AN OBSERVED TREND TEMPORARY OR PERMANENT?

IN A TREND STUDY, IS THE TREND OF THE VARIABLE BEING STUDIED INDEPENDENT OF OTHER SIGNIFICANT VARIABLES?

Chapter 7
Descriptive Methods II

In the previous chapter, we discussed several descriptive methods used in educational research. These methods were classified according to the number of data sources used (depth vs. breadth), the number of environments from which data were collected (uni-cultural vs. cross cultural), and how many times data were collected (one-shot vs. more than once). In this chapter we shall complete the fourth classification of descriptive methods which deals with the research purposes served by the analysis of the data—simple description vs. analysis of relationships. Following this, a special case of descriptive research, evaluation, will be discussed.

Simple description vs. Analysis of relationships
What research purposes were served
by the analysis of the data?

Data collected in descriptive research may be treated by a variety of descriptive and analytical treatments. At one extreme is the reporting of data in tabular form, perhaps with a smattering of common descriptive statistics. For example, a trend study might show an incremental change over a period of years by reporting the mean average salary of teachers and the range of salaries. At the other extreme, some studies use the most sophisticated multivariate correlational analyses available in seeking to predict accurately one variable from a slew of others. The particular analysis used in a given study is determined by the purpose of the study. In this section is a discussion of two descriptive methods which are frequently encountered in the literature and which use relatively complex analytical procedures. Both methods, the *causal-comparative* and the *correlational* seek to describe a phenomenon and its relationship to other phenomena.

Causal-comparative studies

Researchers live in a world which places certain reasonable restrictions on their activities. Often they cannot manipulate variables as they please due to logistical or ethical considerations, yet they may still be interested in investigating causal relationships. For example, if researchers were interested in investigating the effect on human beings of nutritional deprivation in early years on health in later years, they might randomly assign children to differing nutritional conditions, follow them longitudinally and measure their health at maturity. This experimental design would allow for high inferences of causality. Fortunately, civilized societies do not permit such experimentation on their members. Causality must be investigated by other, ethically acceptable methods. The *causal-comparative method*, also called the *ex post facto method* is often substituted for an experimental design in cases like this. This method is a descriptive method: the researchers do not *manipulate* the independent variable as they would in an experimental design. Rather, the researchers *identify* the independent variable—nutritional conditions—and select subjects for study based upon the prior existence of that variable in the subjects. Because the method is descriptive the inferences of causality are somewhat lower than those possible in experimental designs. Yet the method is still valuable in the investigation of causality, subject of course to its methodological limitations.

A causal comparative method might be employed effectively to investigate the effect of poor nutrition in early years on health at maturity in the following way. Researchers might 1) locate a community in which a natural or man-made catastrophe (e.g. Germany in 1943–45) caused a food scarcity 2) identify subjects who would have been, say, 3 or 4 years old at the time of the shortage 3) determine which subjects had had good and poor nutrition at that time and 4) assign the subjects to two groups on the basis of this information. Then various measurements of health could be taken and an analysis of the differences of the health of the two groups could be made. If a difference between the groups were found, an inference of causality could be made.

Note the fundamental difference between an experimental design and a causal comparative method in this example. In the former, researchers assigned subjects to receive the nutritional condition—they directly manipulated this variable. In the latter, the subjects had already been subjected to the nutritional condition—the researchers merely determined who had been in which condition. They made the determination *ex post facto*, after the fact.

Causal comparative methods are often confused with some experimental and factorial designs because superficially they resemble each other. Note how the following tabular arrangement of variables appears like the two group posttest-only experimental design.

$$X_1 \quad O$$
$$X_2 \quad O$$

The Xs are the nutritional conditions, the independent variable: X_1 could be good nutrition, X_2 could be poor nutrition. The Os are the measurements of health at maturity, the "dependent variable." Indeed, some causal comparative studies will label the groups experimental and control. The analysis of the dependent variable may use the same technique as would be used in an experimental study. When we as consumers seek to determine whether a given study is experimental or causal-comparative, we need to inspect the development of the independent variable. If it was developed by manipulation on the part of the researchers, then it is an experimental design. If the variable existed before the researchers came on to the scene, then it is descriptive: specifically, causal comparative.

When reading causal-comparative studies, the consumer must focus on several of the same questions which are typically focussed on when reading an experimental study. First, what exactly are the variables? How is, for example, poor nutrition defined? How poorly fed did a person have to be in order to be assigned to the "poor nutrition" group? In other words, what were the criteria for assignment to this level of the independent variable? Similarly with regard to the dependent variable what specifically constitutes "good health?" What indices were used to judge this attribute? In research of this type, often decisions as to criteria for classification are made arbitrarily. Sometimes, however, generally acceptable criteria do exist. Did the researchers seek to determine the existence of acceptable criteria? And if so did they use them? And if not, was there any *rational* basis for a seemingly arbitrary decision concerning criteria? The decisions made in regard to operational definitions of the independent and dependent variable can have a profound effect on the conclusions derived from a study. Good research reporting demands not only information concerning the operational definitions of the variable but also a rationale for the decisions which were made.

IN A CAUSAL COMPARATIVE STUDY, HOW REASONABLE IS THE INFERENCE OF CAUSALITY?

The major factor to consider concerns the interpretation of the findings. Suppose a study does find a relationship between the independent and dependent variables which allows for an inference of causality. There are three possible explanations if a causal relationship exists: 1) the independent variable caused the dependent variable 2) the dependent variable caused the independent variable and 3) a third variable—an unstudied independent variable which subsumes the studied independent variable—caused the dependent variable. The determination of which of these three possibilities is indeed the case relies on the plausibility of the possibilities as they apply in a particular research study. Common sense and intuition play an important role in a decision of this sort.

For example, suppose in the study described above it turns out that adults who had poor nutrition in early years have poor health at maturity and those with good nutrition had good health. It would be reasonable to conclude that the independent variable caused the dependent variable, that is, the nutritional condition caused the health condition and not vice-versa because it is consonant with our knowledge of human physiology and also because of the time relationship involved: the nutrition in question came many years before the measurement of health. It is absurd to posit that the dependent variable caused the independent variable, that is, that good health at age 21 caused good nutrition at age 4. In another example, a study might show that in 1973 when speed limits were 65 or 70 mph there were more accidents than in 1975 when speed limits were 55 mph. A reasonable inference could be made that lowered speed limits caused fewer accidents and not vice-versa. This is in keeping with our knowledge of the effect of speed on driving and similar information. Also, the reduction of accidents came after the decreased speed limit; the temporal arrangement of these variables preclude a conclusion that fewer accidents caused lower speed limits. Besides, we know that the reduction in speed limits was a result of legislation aimed at saving gasoline, and this entire situation was caused by a Mid-East oil embargo.

Other situations are not quite as obvious though. Suppose a study investigated self concept and achievement in Junior High School students. Either one of these variables, self concept or achievement, could be designated as the independent or dependent variable. The study found that students with high achievement had high self concepts and students with low achievement had low self concepts. Our knowledge of human functioning allow us to infer a causal relationship between self concept and achievement. But which way? It can be argued that when Carolyn Gale, a 7th grade student, demonstrates high academic achievement she feels good about herself so achievement causes self concept. On the other hand, it could be argued that when she feels good about herself she achieves highly, so self concept causes achievement. Maybe it goes both ways: she feels good about herself so she does well, which makes her feel good about herself so she continues to do well, which in turn makes her feel good about herself etc. *ad infinitum*. Which came first: achievement or self-concept? That information would help us determine the cause from the effect. But therein lies a major weakness of a causal comparative study: data are collected at one point in time, and if both variables are present we simply cannot *know* which came first. In a case of this sort, an experimental design can address the issue of causality more fruitfully.

Sometimes a cause and effect relationship of an independent and dependent variable is inferred but the cause may be only a symptom of a larger, broader, superordinate cause reflected by the presence of larger, broader, superordinate independent variables. For example, suppose a study showed that drivers who used seat belts have fewer accidents than drivers who do not use seat belts. Is it plausible that wearing a seat belt would lower the risk of having an accident? Hmm.

125

We can rule out the possibility that having an accident causes a person not to have worn a seat belt, but can merely buckling up prevent accidents? We need to delve further into this phenomenon. What kind of person uses a seat belt? A prudent person would. If a person is prudent in this regard, might not he or she also be prudent in other driving habits such as speed, changing lanes, car maintenance, drinking habits, etc.? In other words, might not the use of seat belts merely be one observable manifestation of a prudent person, and the real cause of fewer accidents be a result of a general prudency? This explanation is more intuitively appealing. In another example, a study might show that school children who have high achievement in reading also have high achievement in mathematics. Does one cause the other or are both caused by high intelligence? The superordinate attributes of prudency and intelligence in our two examples provide more plausible explanations of the findings than the initially utilized independent variables alone.

At the root of the problem of interpreting the findings of a causal comparative study is the fact that our subjects, human beings, are unbelievably complex. Researchers may select subjects on the basis of a particular independent variable, but there are always other variables associated with the independent variable which may need to be considered too. Some of these variables may be known to the researchers, others may not be. Good research recognizes this fact and accordingly presents rival hypotheses honestly and openly or shows how the variables upon which they were based were controlled procedurally.

Correlational Studies

The complexity of human beings and the interrelationship of the variables associated with them invites researchers to engage in exploration. The analytical procedures used in most such explorations are classified under the generic name of *correlation**, and studies using any of these procedures are often called *correlational studies*. Correlational studies are frequently encountered in the educational and psychological literature. They are relatively easy to conduct, and sophisticated and powerful techniques are readily available for purposes of data analysis.

The purpose of a correlational study is to examine two or more variables in order to see if a relationship between them exists. If such a relationship does exist, then the researchers note first the magnitude of the relationship, that is, is the relationship strong or weak and the nature of the relationship, that is, is it a positive relationship such as when one variable goes up so does the other, or is it a negative relationship such as when one goes up the other goes down or vice-versa, or is it a non linear relationship, sometimes positive and sometimes negative.

Correlational studies are conducted for two distinct purposes. One is to *generate hypotheses*. For example, suppose researchers are interested in examining the relationship between self concept and achievement among Junior High School students. (You will recall that this same research question was used earlier in a discussion of the causal-comparative method.) They identify a sample of students, take measurements on self concept (variable 1) and achievement (variable 2), and submit these data to a correlational analysis. Let's say the analysis shows a high positive correlation between them—the higher a student's self concept the higher his achievement tends to be and vice versa. The researchers are now in a position to use this finding to generate hypotheses. Now, the findings of this correlational study can *not* be interpreted as meaning that self concept causes achievement or vice versa. This was also true when the question was investigated with a causal comparative method. But of equal importance is the fact that *it can not be interpreted as meaning that it doesn't. Causality is neither demonstrated nor precluded by a high correlation.*

---

*The elements of the statistical procedure used to develop a correlation index will be discussed in a subsequent chapter.

But the existence of a strong, positive relationship can allow the researchers to hypothesize a causal relationship and conduct an experimental study to confirm or reject this hypothesis. For instance, they could use a two group post test only design as shown below.

R   X   O   (E)
R   O   (C)

in which a sample of low self concept students are randomly assigned to an experimental or control group. The experimental group is given a program, X, designed to boost their morale and make them feel good about themselves. The program is judged to be successful. The control group receives no treatment. Then an achievement test is administered and the E group and C group achievement is compared. The results of this comparison will confirm or reject the hypothesis that self concept causes achievement. The point is that the hypothesis which guided this experiment might not have been generated if a correlational study had not shown the existence of any relationship between the two variables.

A second purpose of correlational studies is to provide information which would allow someone to *make predictions* from one variable to another. Note the very specific use of the word prediction in this context. It does *not* mean if you do one thing that something else will happen, e.g., if you are holding a pen above a table and you let it go, you predict it will fall to the table. This type of "prediction" is a cause and effect statement. In the research context, the term *prediction* refers specifically to the prediction of one variable from knowledge of another; for example, predicting grades in college from knowledge of grades in high school—these two variables have a high positive correlation. If as in a prior example, a strong positive correlation were found to exist between self concept and achievement then you could predict one from the other; that is, if you know how a person feels about himself you can predict what his school achievement will be, subject to a certain amount of error. You will recall that the same example of self concept and achievement was used earlier to illustrate a causal-comparative design. Both causal-comparative and correlational designs serve to analyze relationships. But if prediction is desired the coefficient of correlation derived from a correlational study will be a more valuable statistic than a summary statistic derived from an analysis of difference between groups as would be found in a causal-comparative study.

IN A CORRELATIONAL STUDY, WAS A CAUSAL RELATIONSHIP BETWEEN THE VARIABLES STATED?

The major problem in correlational studies as is the case with causal comparative studies is in interpretation of findings. There is an urge—irresistable in some folks—to leap from relationship to causality. As mentioned earlier, the existence of a high positive correlation neither affirms or precludes a causal relationship: the logic behind the analytical process itself just does not allow for a causal inference. But it does allow for prediction of one variable from another. The distinction we consumers must make is between causality which is not allowed and prediction which is. For example, a recent UPI news article reported several folklorists who predict weather in upcoming winters by examining certain phenomena appearing in nature. A woman in Missouri notes that in some years the wolly worm caterpillars who reside near her home have the appearance of being "thin, light brown with black tips," and this tells her that the impending winter will be mild. In the past three winters which had been quite severe, the caterpillars had been fat and black. If it were to turn out that mild winters are indeed usually or perhaps always preceded by the presence of caterpillars with light coats, and severe winters preceded by caterpillars with heavy coats, then one could predict the weather from the appearance of the caterpillars in the preceding months. However, one is hard put to explain this phenomenon in causal terms—can one state that a bunch of caterpillars can cause the vast and profound vagaries of Nature? Prediction, if the facts bear it out?—yes. Causality? Probably not. Then we are left with the question of why do caterpillars dress more warmly for an impending severe winter? Perhaps they know something we don't.

As another example, a sportswriter in Palo Alto, California has noted a relationship between the Super Bowl and the stock market. Since 1967 when the Green Bay Packers, a National Football League Team, won the first Super Bowl competition the following has occurred in almost every year: If a National Football League (NFL) team wins the Super Bowl, the stock market in December of that year will be *higher* than it was in the previous December. And if an American Football League (AFL) team wins the Super Bowl the stock market will be *lower* in December of that year than it was the previous December. This pattern has held true almost every year even after the two leagues merged: an old NFL team win precedes a higher stock market, an old AFL team win precedes a lower stock market. Prediction? Maybe—it seems to work. Causality? Highly unlikely.

Evaluation

In the field of education, evaluation studies have become increasingly important in recent years. Virtually every piece of social legislation emanating from Federal sources has mandated the inclusion of an evaluation component in the program it funds. In addition, local and state projects have found it wise to engage in systematic evaluation partly in recognition of its usefulness as a management tool and partly in a defensive posture as a reaction to calls for accountability. The result of such interest is the development of the field of evaluation from the status of sleepy-weak-sister-of-experimental-research/ho-hum-after-thought of a project to a vibrant, exciting, and stimulating independent field in its own right. Evaluation has attracted talented people and has stimulated much creative thinking. We need to examine the field of evaluation in order to understand its dimensions and interpret the studies it produces.

We might begin by focusing on the word *evaluation* itself. This will alert us to the existence of several major problems to be discussed below. The denotation of the word *evaluation* is straight-forward: to evaluate is to determine the value of something, to examine, to judge. The connotation of the word is something else. When a person is told, "By the way, you're going to be evaluated this month," that person usually does not view this as a desirable event. Indeed, the word evaluation tends to strike terror into the hearts of those whose programs or who personally are the objects of this activity. Such a reaction can militate against the cooperation of those associated with the object of the evaluation. Thus, the word evaluation itself can be an impediment to the conducting of an evaluation study.

Evaluation may be best viewed as a special case of descriptive research. It is similar to other research activities in that it is a method of inquiry which seeks to find answers to questions and it often uses the same tools of measurement and analysis as other research. But evaluation is different from other research in three very important ways.

1. Evaluations tend to focus on a specific situation. They are not necessarily designed to generalize to other situations; the intended scope and usefulness of their findings are often quite limited. This is in contrast to most educational research which seeks to extend its findings to other situations external to the research environment in which the study was conducted.

2. An evaluation is typically mandated by statute or policy and the evaluator is commissioned to perform it. This is in contrast to most research in which the researcher himself or herself initiates the research activity. The evaluator is working for someone—a decision-maker who may be a project director, an agency representative or the like. The findings must be presented in such a format as to be useful to the decision-maker. Thus the information resulting from an evaluation is *action oriented* enabling the decision-maker to indeed make a decision—expand this, eliminate this, check into that, fish, cut bait, whatever.
3. Evaluations are not restricted to using the conventional tools of measurement and analysis which are used in most experimental and descriptive research. Rather, the options are wide open and the procedures and methods currently in use include those usually associated with anthropology, journalism, and criminal/legal investigation, as well as those used in other educational research efforts.

There is an important formal distinction between evaluation studies that needs to be made. This distinction deals with the purpose of the evaluation, and it is important because the intent of the evaluation, as is the case in the intent of any research study, has a profound influence on the decisions made concerning procedural matters. And the decisions concerning procedural matters of course will have a similarly profound influence on the findings of the evaluation. As consumers of research findings, we need to understand clearly what the intent of an evaluation was in order to judge the appropriateness of its methodology and concomitantly, the credibility of its findings.

Formative vs. Summative Evaluations

It was discussed above that a unique feature of evaluation studies as compared to other types of educational research is that the impetus for conducting an evaluation comes from a decision-maker rather than from researchers or evaluators themselves. The question to be asked is, "What is the purpose of the evaluation?" That is, "Why did the decision-maker commission the evaluation?" Now, some decision-makers will respond to such a query by saying, "We are required to evaluate our program so we're doing it." Others have no response, and one wonders if the purpose for the evaluation is to punish or harass those persons upon whom the responsibility for an uncomplimentary evaluation would fall. Such, sometimes, is life in the field!

However, most qualified decision-makers commission evaluations to answer one of two possible questions.

1. "What's going on? What's right and what's wrong?" Information which provides answers to these questions can be used to improve a situation.* It can point the way to better procedures, changes in methods, or different personnel. An evaluation yielding such information is called a *formative evaluation*, so called because the situation being evaluated is still being formed, that is, it is capable of being changed. The findings of a formative evaluation will allow a decision-maker to make the necessary changes to improve a situation.

Examples of formative evaluations abound. When a manufacturing company introduces a new product to a small group of people and measures their response to it, the company seeks

*In the ensuing discussion of evaluations, the term *situation* will be used in a generic sense to represent the object of an evaluation. The specific situation could be a program, a person, a book, a set of materials, a course of study, a product or anything else which could be subjected to an evaluation.

information about what are the desirable and undesirable features of the product. Based on that information the company would develop the product further to eliminate the undesirable features. The product may be an underarm deodorant or a social studies curriculum: good product development requires formative evaluation. Most field testing of products is formative.

2. A second question to which an evaluation could be addressed is: "Is this any good?" Information of this sort enables a decision-maker to make a judgment as to the worth of a situation; he or she can then decide whether to continue a situation. Or a decision can be made as to whether the quality of the situation is high enough to be considered successful. An evaluation yielding information of this type is called a *summative evaluation*, so called because it yields a summary of the quality of a situation. Summative evaluations are conducted on situations which have been already developed. In continuing with the example above, after a manufacturer has developed a product, it is test-marketed. Depending upon its acceptance by its potential customers management will make a decision as to whether or not the product should be continued to be marketed. Again the product may be a deodorant, a textbook or anything else.

It is very important to distinguish between these two purposes of evaluations. A confusion between them can make the assessment of the evaluation techniques involved difficult to determine and the interpretation of any findings difficult to assess. For example, Linda Rivers comes to an auto mechanic and says, "Here, look this car over." Now, the mechanic might assume that Ms. Rivers wants to buy this car and that he is expected to render a judgment as to whether the car is sufficiently roadworthy to be purchased and used. Accordingly the mechanic might take it out on the road to drive it, then take it back to the shop, put it in the rack, look under the hood, etc. After making these observations, the mechanic says to Ms. Rivers "It doesn't run well! You shouldn't buy it." In this instance the mechanic performed a summative evaluation. He made observations which enabled him to render a judgment concerning the value of the car; he made a summary judgment about the car which was expressed as a recommendation not to buy it. But suppose Ms. Rivers then says, "I didn't buy it. My ex-husband gave it to me. I want you to fix it up." The mechanic responds, "Oh, that's a different story!" Now he changes his mind set to observe specifically what is wrong with the automobile, how bad it is, and how much it will cost to repair. He will probably spend more time with the car on the rack, more time under the hood using diagnostic equipment, and less time driving the car. The whole focus of his evaluation will have changed because his concept of the type of information needed by Ms. Rivers has changed. Accordingly the tests to which the automobile will have been subjected are changed and when the evaluation is completed the format of the report will have changed too. The mechanic might say, "You've got some problems with the ignition system, but a tune up will take care of it. The chassis is good, the body is good, but the carburetor will need to be replaced, and the battery and voltage regulator ought to be replaced soon. All in all, it will cost about $175 to put it into good shape." The mechanic has performed a formative evaluation and has provided information to Ms. Rivers which informs her of the changes necessary to improve the automobile.

Another example illustrating the difference between these two purposes are medical examinations given by physicians so they can prescribe medication (formative purpose) contrasted with medical examinations given so they can report to an insurance company whether a person is a suitable risk (summative purpose). An educational program such as a secondary school mathematics program can be evaluated to determine how it could be made more effective in accomplishing its goals (formative) or whether it is sufficiently effective to be continued rather than be replaced by another program (summative).

In some evaluation studies, both purposes are served. In some studies the purposes are not stated explicitly but rather have to be inferred by the methods used, the data gathered, and a piercing analysis of the surrounding verbiage. In some studies, an evaluation may be labeled (explicitly or implicitly) for one purpose but its findings used for another; this is a very unethical state of affairs. Decision-makers need to be open and honest about the use to which the evaluation results will be put. It is highly unethical, for example, to evaluate teachers ostensibly to improve their effectiveness in the classroom (formative) but then use the results of the evaluation to adjust their salaries because of good teaching or poor teaching, (summative). In addition to being unethical, it is probable that the observations made were inappropriate for the purpose.

Judging Evaluations

The methods used in evaluation studies vary widely with the needs and desires of the decision-makers. Formative evaluation methods show the most variety because they take their cue from the specific situation being evaluated. We need not overly concern ourselves with judging formative evaluations because typically these evaluations are not performed for nor reported to those outside the situation being evaluated: a formative evaluation is usually an "in-house" project the results of which are shared among the in-house staff. Traditional summative evaluations often resemble quite closely the experimental research discussed in an earlier chapter. As such they may be evaluated by the same criteria as experimental research studies are. However, an additional element to be considered in judging either a formative or summative evaluation study is the person performing the evaluation: What is his or her relationship to the situation being evaluated?

The Evaluator

Evaluators who are a part of a situation being evaluated are called *inside evaluators*. These persons have been associated with the situation for a long time, perhaps since its inception. They are acquainted with the day to day operation of the situation and know it well, probably better than anyone not associated with the situation could. Inside evaluators often function as "trouble shooters." locating problems and doing what is necessary to solve them. On the other hand, evaluators who are not associated with the program are called *outside evaluators*. These are persons brought in to a situation specifically for the purpose of performing an evaluation. Now, which ones, the inside or the outside evaluators, are the better ones to perform an evaluation? Let us consider formative and summative evaluations separately.

IN A FORMATIVE EVALUATION, HOW KNOWLEDGEABLE AND UNBIASED IS THE EVALUATOR?

With regard to formative evaluations, a good case can be made for using inside evaluators. After all, these persons are intimately acquainted with the operation having been participants in its functioning. These persons would have firsthand knowledge of processes and personnel and would know about problems—indeed, they may have contributed to them. On the other hand, this very intimate relationship with the situation may militate against a useful formative evaluation. The inside evaluators may be so close to the situation that they cannot see larger problems which may exist; they cannot see the forest for the trees. Moreover, they may have formed friendships among the personnel in the situation, thus rendering themselves unable or unwilling to perceive and report negative aspects of the situation. The degree of autonomy and independence possessed by the inside evaluators is a crucial feature of their effectiveness. If this autonomy and/or independence is compromised, then the possibility of an effective formative evaluation is reduced. Probably, a more effective evaluation format would include both inside and outside evaluators.

IN A SUMMATIVE EVALUATION, HOW INDEPENDENT AND UNBIASED IS THE EVALUATOR?

Summative evaluations are focused on output or product; they yield information regarding the worth or effect of a situation. Thus the strengths of inside evaluators are wasted for the most part; an intimate knowledge of the day to day operations of a situation just is not necessary to judge the ultimate value of a situation. Indeed it may interfere: inside evaluators may be absolutely certain that the product of a situation is good because it has worked so well everyday its effect *has to be good*, whether in reality it is or not. Thus outside evaluators are typically the better persons to perform a summative evaluation: they may not be subjected to the pressures to which inside evaluators would be subjected. The perceptions of outside evaluators have not been restricted by the daily operations; they do not have to remain working with the personnel in the situation. It would seem that outside evaluators have the autonomy and independence necessary to render a fair and unbiased opinion as to the worth of a situation. But, is this in reality the case? Perhaps, but perhaps not.

The Myth of the Outside Evaluator

The mere fact that evaluators come to a situation from the outside does not guarantee their independence. The major question we must ask is, "Who hired the evaluator and to whom will the evaluator report?" For example, suppose an evaluator, Janice Swan, is hired to perform a summative evaluation on a funded project. The purpose of the evaluation is to determine whether or not the project is sufficiently worthwhile to justify its continued funding. The project director hires the evaluator. Figure 7.1 shows the relationship of the elements in the administrative structure. The relationship of the evaluator and the project director is displayed by the dotted line labeled "Case #1". Note that the evaluator reports to the project *director* who hired her and the project director reports to the *funding agency*, which could be a governmental agency or private foundation. Now we must ask ourselves how much autonomy and independence does Janice, our evaluator, really have. The project director's job may depend upon the continuation of the project, which in turn may depend heavily upon a favorable evaluation. If Janice ever expects to do another evaluation of this project, she will need to develop a favorable evaluation otherwise the project may go out of existence. Indeed, if the word were to get around the funded project community that she actually turns in unfavorable evaluations, she might find her services no longer solicited by project directors. Therefore, Janice being under pressure (implicit or explicit) from the project director and looking out for her own self interest might very well be predisposed to submit a positive evaluation whether or not the facts call for one.

Now suppose instead of a project director hiring an evaluator, the funding agency does the hiring and is the party to whom the evaluator reports. This is shown in figure 7.1, Case #2. In this situation, the evaluator is independent of the direct influence of the project director. But the project director's influence on the funding agency may have a substantial although indirect effect on the evaluator. We must ask ourselves to what extent is it in the best interests of the funding agency for the project to be successful. If the project represents a major portion of the activities of the funding agency the evaluator might be pressured by the funding agency to submit a favorable evaluation. After all, the funding agency would look bad if it were found to be funding ineffective or unworthy projects.

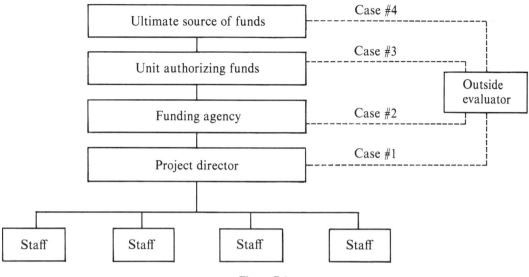

Figure 7.1.

This can be carried one step further. The evaluator could be hired by the unit which authorized the funds initially, for example, a congressional committee or a foundation's board of directors. This is shown in figure 7.1, Case #3. Here the external influence on the evaluator is less than in either Case #1 or Case #2. Ultimately, the very least degree of influence would occur in a situation whereby the evaluator was hired by and reports to those persons supplying the money originally: the taxpayers or the foundation's sponsor. This is shown in figure 7.1, Case #4. Such evaluators are sometimes referred to as "self-styled" or "self-appointed" with a distinct pejorative connotation. This is unfortunate. The mere fact that they appoint themselves (who is there to do the appointing?) is not necessarily a negative feature. They are called "whistle blowers" or "muckrakers" and their efforts are often belittled by those in funding agencies. Yet, these people—evaluators in the larger sense of the word—serve a unique and important role in our society. They are influenced little by those they are evaluating and they can report directly to the ultimate source of funds. These outside evaluators are sometimes journalists, sometimes attorneys, sometimes an organized group such as Common Cause. Their power and effect are increasingly felt in our society. They are valuable, but they are not necessarily incorruptible.

It is of interest to note, but saddening too, that evaluation in educational research is not alone in its problems of objectivity, influence, compromise, and full disclosure. Other fields of endeavor suffer equally, perhaps even more than education. For example, financial evaluation—accounting and auditing—has been a party to so many large scale financial debacles as to make the efforts of educational evaluators appear puerile in comparison. The questions which investors need to pose are similar to those which need to be posed by consumers of research: Who hired the auditors and to whom do the auditors report. In an example from the corporate world, the auditor is analogous to the evaluator, management analogous to the project director, the SEC (Securities and Exchange Commission) roughly analogous to the funding agency (in that it requires audits of publicly owned corporations) and the investors in the company analogous to the taxpayers.

Theoretically the stockholders of a given corporation are responsible for the selection of the accounting firm which will conduct an audit of the corporation's finances. In reality however, management selects these auditors and the stockholders ratify their choice at the corporation's annual meeting. The purpose of the audit is ostensibly to describe fully the financial status of the corporation giving a statement of its worth and of its earnings. Its earnings in particular will be compared to its earnings in comparable periods of time and also to the earnings of other similar corporations. These are the critical comparisons. Usually management is considered to be effective if the corporation's earnings increase year by year and if the earnings represent a good return on the capital invested. Management would look favorably upon auditors who could show such happenings. Now, accountants have what they call Generally Accepted Accounting Procedures (GAAP) which they use as standards to regulate their methods of description and analysis. However, there is much leeway within these standards—so much that the same financial information can be treated one way to show a healthy, prosperous company or it can be treated to show a company on the verge of bankruptcy. Obviously it is in the best interests of management to have their company shown to be in the former situation. In this way they can keep their high paying jobs longer and sell their stock while there is still someone willing to buy it. Many of the greatest financial busts of recent decades were given clean bills of health, financially speaking, only months before their stocks crashed which preceded their ultimate demise. It seems hardly plausible that they turned around financially in such a short span of time.

The issue is, can an auditor who is selected by and beholden to management be considered a true *outside* auditor, when its own well being can be influenced by the result of its audit? Perhaps a securities analyst independent of management but beholden to the stockholders could render a more honest, impartial and complete judgment as to the worth and earnings of a corporation.

One might surmise from having read the above paragraphs that the author is somewhat pessimistic and perhaps paranoid as well. Are outside evaluators—educational or financial—crooked, self-serving, and not to be trusted? Are those who evaluate trying to pull the wool over the eyes of the public before they are fleeced? Of course not—necessarily. Evaluators, as a subspecies of mankind, share mankind's strengths and weaknesses. It is not possible to determine the proportions, but probably most outside evaluators are honest while some are not. The point of this somewhat lengthy discourse on the role of the outside evaluator in a summative evaluation is that the *mere fact that an evaluation was performed by an outside evaluator is no guarantee of its accuracy, honesty, and completeness*. To merely state that an evaluation is credible because it was performed by an outside evaluator is absurd: this is the *myth* of the outside evaluator. When the stakes are high, one's values are more easily compromised; and when such a compromise does occur credibility is attenuated. The integrity of the evaluators is the *sine qua non* of an honest evaluation.

Perhaps the entire concept of an outside evaluation needs to be reexamined. It has been said that war is too important to be left to the generals; health is too important to be left to the doctors; education is too important to be left to the educators. Perhaps educational evaluation is too important to be left to the educational evaluators. Perhaps summative educational evaluation should be conducted by outside evaluators who are outside the area of education entirely and beholden to no party with a vested interest in the outcome. Until such a time comes, if ever, we consumers of educational evaluations need to scrutinize well those who conduct them.

Naturalistic Inquiry

Traditional evaluation methods rely heavily upon the techniques associated with experimental research: control groups, random selection, quantitative measures, and the like. These techniques assume a conception of the setting in which the evaluation takes place as being a laboratory in which the researchers are in full control of the research environment. Variables are identified, then they are controlled or manipulated as needed and the results are presented in precise mathematical terms perhaps with some verbal commentary. These techniques of experimental research are an important means of uncovering truth. They have served us well, although better in some situations than in others.

The application of experimental methodology to evaluation studies is somewhat problematical, though. You will recall that in a previous discussion of evaluation studies, it was mentioned that one way in which they are different from other research efforts is that they tend to focus on specific situations. The specific situations exist in the real world—this is a world in which variables are confounded, subjects do not always show up, test scores get fudged, etc. This is a world in which if anything can go wrong it will: Murphy's Law Lives! It is often extremely difficult for researchers who are conducting evaluations in the real world, as opposed to a laboratory situation, to control extraneous variables sufficiently in order that an experimental methodology be reasonably applied. Yet, often we see exactly this being done. We see from time to time utter mayhem in data gathering procedures followed by classy, ultra-sophisticated analyses of data. This is, in effect, a subversion of the experimental methodology. Unfortunately, some researchers persist in using an experimental paradigm even when it is clearly inappropriate for a given evaluation situation. They frequently claim an inability to accept an inference of causality from any other research paradigm. Earlier in this book, such thinking was characterized as being associated with researchers who are prisoners of their training.

But the use of an experimental paradigm is not the only way to uncover truth. Other approaches also exist and have been used successfully in situations in which laboratory type conditions are impossible or impractical to achieve. These approaches and techniques and their underlying rationales and philosophies are labeled *naturalistic inquiry*. The term is apt in that the naturalistic paradigm operates in a *natural* rather than a laboratory or contrived situation. Moreover, it tends to use methods of observation and analysis which are more natural, that is, more spontaneous and unobtrusive, than the quantitative techniques used in conventional experimental paradigms.

The techniques of naturalistic inquiry (which incidentally include experimental techniques when appropriate) borrow heavily from techniques used in other fields. Three fields in particular—anthropology, criminal investigation, and investigative reporting—utilize techniques which are naturalistic in character. And what they all have in common is their lack of obtrusiveness. Let us develop this concept a bit.

When experimental researchers conduct a study they identify the research variables (dependent/independent), design the study to exclude the effect of potentially confounding variables, and proceed with the collection of data. Usually these research procedures obtrude on the natural setting in which the experiment is taking place. For example, the subjects may take tests which they would not have taken if an experiment were not taking place. As another example, a new element like the experimenter's presence may obtrude in the setting. If the experiment had not been taking place 1) the test would not have been taken and 2) the experimenter would not be present. These two occurrences detract from the naturalness of the setting in that they react with the setting to form a new different setting. In other words, the setting from which the experimenter gathers data, subjects taking tests and the experimenter being present, is different from the setting in its original condition in which the subjects were not taking tests and the experimenter was not present. This is because the experimenter by performing the experiment has changed it. Thus, the experimental paradigm is *obtrusive* in that it obtrudes on the setting before and during the time at which data are gathered. This results in data being gathered in an artificial, unnatural setting from which it may be difficult to generalize. You will recall the problems in external validity discussed in an earlier chapter.

In contrast, naturalistic methods tend to be applied after the fact. They tend to be descriptive rather than experimental, they sometimes *emerge* from the particular situation rather than *contribute* to the formation of the situation. In short, they tend to be nonobtrusive; they tend to react *to* the situation, not cause a reaction *in* the situation.

Many people find a naturalistic mode of inquiry very appealing because of its variety of acceptable methods and its openness to new ideas and paradigms. Because the types of data utilized differ so greatly from that of most of the research in education it would be instructive to examine the techniques of three fields of inquiry from which naturalistic methodology borrows freely.

Anthropological field methods, often utilize methods low in obtrusiveness. In *participant observation*, observers live among those people they are studying. They eat with them, sleep with them, talk with them, join in their customs and rituals; in effect they almost become one of them. They do not use measurement instruments—tests, scales, devices. Rather observers use their keen powers of observation. They do not use measurement instruments—they *are* measurement instruments. As such, observers often try to keep a low profile and do not intrude upon that which they are observing.

The methods of criminal investigation are quite naturalistic in character. Detectives come on to the scene of an alleged crime after the deed has been done. Their first task is to determine if a crime has been committed. Following this they determine the identity of the victim, the location of the offense, the means by which the crime was committed, the time, motive, object and intent of the crime and finally the identification of the criminal. Now, the methods employed by detectives have to be nonobtrusive because the actual offense being investigated is past history. The television series, *Columbo*, illustrates this methodology well. In essence, Columbo has two types of evidence available to him: physical evidence from the scene of the crime and testimony from those connected in some way with the crime. Using the physical evidence available and the testimony he elicits from various people, he applies his background knowledge of crime and criminals, e.g., *modus operandi*, and a good deal of deductive logic to piece together the event which transpired. He constantly verifies the accuracy of the testimony he receives by comparing it to other verifiable sources. For example, when a suspect states that he arrived at the scene just ten minutes before, the detective finds the suspect's car and feels the engine block to determine if it is still warm. If such physical evidence for corroboration is lacking, he will perhaps seek other testimony, perhaps from a witness who would have seen him arrive. Such cross-checking is called *triangulation*. In effect, the process of triangulation uses two or more sources to establish a fact. With these means— physical evidence, testimony, and logic he is able to reconstruct the crime.

When the crime is reconstructed and the suspect is brought to trial, the defense attorney will try to discredit the evidence by presenting other evidence which does not agree with the original evidence offered, or by stating other explanations or other deductions which conflict with the explanation and deductions already presented. In such a rivalry, evidence is constantly challenged and evaluated.

Investigative journalism uses many techniques similar to criminal investigation. Leads for stories often come from tips from informers, examination of public records, or systematic observation of everyday phenomena. Reporters often verify their information by triangulation. When this is impossible, they can sometimes force documentation from a source by demanding repeated retellings which they examine for consistency. Or they check with other reporters. Investigative reporters use records, interviews, their own observations and use a good deal of logic to piece all the information together. Sometimes they use a variation of the participant observation method by going undercover and passing themselves off as someone they are not. Laura Hobson's book *Gentleman's Agreement* tells of a reporter who passed himself off as Jewish in order to write about anti-Semitism. A book from the early 1960s, *Black Like Me*, by John H. Griffin is an actual account of a person who passed himself off as a black American. Such methods of inquiry are based on the observation that you don't know what it's like to be a certain person until you've walked a mile in his shoes.

The point is that naturalistic inquiry borrows its techniques freely from other fields as is appropriate for particular situations. For the most part, it uses multiple sources of data in natural settings and is not restricted to any one type of description or analysis. Its style of reporting tends to be non-technical and informal, stressing the qualitative rather than the quantitative aspects of the data. Frequently, it bears strong resemblence to journalistic style. Because its outlook and stance are so wide open it is no surprise that naturalistic inquiry and its proponents have spawned a multitude of specific evaluation designs. The degree to which each design is naturalistic varies considerably, but they all represent divergencies from traditional methods toward naturalistic ones.

Earlier in this section, we discussed two major questions which need to be considered when judging an evaluation. Both of these questions dealt with characteristics of the evaluators: their knowledge, independence, and lack of bias. Considering our discussion of naturalistic modes of inquiry we need to pose one additional question:

IN ANY EVALUATION, HOW APPROPRIATE, MEANINGFUL AND VARIED ARE THE TYPES OF DATA?

Because they take place in the real world, evaluations need not and probably should not rely exclusively on methods used in traditional experimental and descriptive paradigms. Furthermore, a multiplicity of sources each of which affirms the others (triangulation) is a better basis for a decision than merely one source of information, and evaluations, you will recall are aimed at the needs of a decision-maker. However, there are some members of the scientific community who are loathe to deviate from the traditional, generally accepted data sources and research paradigms. Indeed, some may cast aspersions on any efforts typified by non-traditional methods—these efforts have been labeled "unscientific" in an attempt to discredit them. This is an unfortunate use of the term *unscientific*. Perhaps a better way to describe these methods is to refer to them as being *different* from the methods associated with most educational research endeavors but not necessarily inferior. It is hardly appropriate to call them "unscientific" as if to denote a careless or haphazard approach to inquiry. This is usually not at all the case.

The attitudes toward evidence held by us as research consumers will have a significant effect upon how believable we judge research studies to be. It seems most appropriate for the acceptance of many different types evidence which are scientifically gathered and evaluated. We might take our cue from our system of jurisprudence. Our legal system is firmly rooted in the concept of evidence which is gathered, presented, and critically evaluated. Those who have studied comparative judicial systems rate our stystem as among the very best, and one would suspect that the chief reason for this opinion is the rules on evidence which have been developed over many decades of English and American judicial experience. These rules permit a wide variety of evidence to be utilized as long as an opportunity is given to critically evaluate each piece of evidence.

The attitudes of some consumers of research toward the admissibility of *testimony* as evidence in educational research shows an unfortunate incongruity. In a courtroom, testimony from a witness is a key type of evidence presented and evaluated, and in some instances it is the only evidence. It is indeed strange that some thoughtful research consumers can accept the fact that a person can be sent to prison or even to death based upon the testimony of witnesses to a crime, yet these same consumers will not consider to be admissible scientifically elicited testimony in an educational research effort, the effects of which may be much less devastating than those of a legal trial.

We must remember that in the real world with all its complexity and resultant confounding variables we must find truth as best we can in each unique situation. The judgments that are made in the real world are only sometimes based on quantified data and rarely are those data collected in a controlled research environment. The *appropriateness* and veracity of the evidence presented are the issue, not its type and style.

Summary

Causal comparative studies are used by researchers to investigate causal relationships when experimental methods are unsuitable. Inferences of casuality must be based on a good deal of common sense and intuition. *Correlational studies* seek to determine the existence of a relationship between two or more variables. This is done for the purpose of generating hypotheses or allowing predictions of one variable from one or more other variables. An important distinction needs to be made between correctly using a high correlation for prediction purposes and incorrectly using a similarly high correlation to infer causality.

Evaluation is a special case of descriptive research which differs from it in that it is situation-specific, initiated by someone other than the evaluator, and uses many techniques in its methodology. *Formative* evaluations are aimed at improving a situation. *Summative* evaluations make a summary judgment as to the worth of a situation. The crucial issue which determines the credibility of an evaluation is the characteristics of the evaluators themselves. The mere presence of an outside evaluator is no guarantee of the objectivity of the evaluation.

Naturalistic inquiry in evaluations is a reaction to traditional evaluations which were often based upon experimental paradigms. The techniques of naturalistic inquiry tend to occur in natural settings and do not obtrude on these settings.

The following questions need to be asked by consumers of research when they encounter causal-comparative, correlational or evaluation studies.

IN A CASUAL COMPARATIVE STUDY, HOW REASONABLE IS THE INFERENCE OF CAUSALITY?

IN A CORRELATIONAL STUDY, WAS A STATEMENT OF A CAUSAL RELATIONSHIP BETWEEN THE VARIABLES AVOIDED?

IN A FORMATIVE EVALUATION, HOW KNOWLEDGABLE AND UNBIASED IS THE EVALUATOR?

IN A SUMMATIVE EVALUATION, HOW INDEPENDENT AND
UNBIASED IS THE EVALUATOR?

IN ANY EVALUATION, HOW APPROPRIATE, MEANINGFUL AND
VARIED ARE THE TYPES OF DATA?

Further Readings for Chapters 6 and 7

Anderson, David and Benjaminson, Peter. *Investigative Reporting.* Bloomington, Indiana: Indiana University Press, 1976.

    The techniques of investigative reporting are discussed in some detail in this volume. The case studies included (such as the Boys Town story) are fascinating reading and demonstrate the results of good investigation.

Anderson, Scarvia and Ball, Samuel. *The Profession and Practice of Program Evaluation.* San Francisco: Jossey-Bass, 1978.

    This is an excellent book to provide an overall view of program evaluation. Part one deals with evaluation practices including methods and evidence. Part two explores the ethics and values in evaluation, and deals with matters such as an evaluator predisposition toward methodology and corruptibility. Excellent reading.

Armer, Michael and Grimshaw Allen (eds.). *Comparative Social Research: Methodological Problems and Strategies.* New York: John Wiley, 1973.

    The problems involved in cross cultural studies are discussed extensively in this collection of papers. Chapters one and two deal with the general problems especially the concepts of appropriateness and equivalence. Chapters three and four are first person accounts of problems which occurred in specific studies. Chapter eleven deals with the assessment of children's language and is of particular interest.

Backstrom, Charles and Hirsch, Gerald. *Survey Research*, Evanston, Illinois: Northwestern University Press, 1963.

    If you want to delve into the specific techniques used in surveys this book will be helpful. It is written as a manual and includes very specific information on the details of the survey technique from planning, data generation, and data processing stages.

Blalock, Hubert M. Jr. *Causal Inferences in Non-Experimental Research.* Chapel Hill, North Carolina: University of North Carolina Press, 1964.

    The issue of causality in descriptive research is discussed effectively in this text. It is written in a reasonably nontechnical style and explores the issue globally. Chapters one and three will be of particular interest.

Blalock, Hubert M. Jr. (ed). *Causal Models in the Social Sciences.* Chicago: Aldine-Atherton, 1971.

    And if you are truly excited about the idea of causality in descriptive research, you might try some of the papers in this text. They are not for the faint hearted though.

Briloff, Abraham J. *More Debits than Credits, The Burnt Investor's Guide to Financial Statements.* New York: Harper and Row, 1976.

    For an exciting analysis of the world of financial evaluation—accounting—this volume is highly recommended. An accountant himself, Briloff reveals the scope of creativity which exists within GAAP.

Doby, John T. *An Introduction to Social Research.* Harrisburg, Pennsylvania: Stockpole, 1954.

    Two chapters, eight and nine, in this book will extend your knowledge about cross-sectional research and the participant observation technique.

Guba, Egon, G. *Toward a Methodology of Naturalistic Inquiry in Educational Evaluation.* Los Angeles, California: Center for the Study of Evaluation, 1978.

    The most definitive statement concerning naturalistic inquiry (as of this writing) is presented in this monograph. Scholarly and erudite in tone, this source shows very effectively the characteristics of naturalistic inquiry especially its contrast to traditional evaluation. Highly recommended.

Idstein, Peter. "The Great Train Robbery," *Phi Delta* Kappan, Vol. 53 No. 2 (October, 1971).

    A humorous narrative showing how decisions concerning a design of an evaluation can be used to guarantee a result is presented in Idstein's article. It shows how the possibilities for fraud in "scientific" experimental type research are limited only by the creativity of the experimenters and the gullibility of the readers. *Highly recommended.*

Krenkle, Noele and Saretski, Gary. "Evaluation a la Machiavelli," *Phi Delta Kappan*, Vol. 55, No. 4, (December 1973).

    This is a tongue-in-cheek flow chart showing how evaluations work from beginning to end. Most people who have done evaluations find this to be hilariously funny, probably because there is a good deal of truth to it.

Pelto, Pertti, J. *Anthropological Research, The Structure of Inquiry*. New York: Harper and Row, 1970.

    This book is a classic in its field, and will give you an excellent idea of the framework in which research in anthropology is conducted. Chapters 1 and 5 in particular will be helpful.

Webb, Eugene J. and others. *Unobtrusive Measures: Non-reactive Research in the Social Sciences*. Chicago: Rand McNally, 1966.

    An interesting and very useful presentation of ideas concerning non-quantitative data is found in this text. Your perspective on the nature of data will be extended by this book.

Part Four
The Development of Data

Author's comment:

A scientific method of inquiry relies on the use of evidence to answer the questions it poses; the evidence used by educational researchers is usually in the form of data of some sort. Thus the focal point of an entire research study is its gathering of high quality data. In this section I present information about the types of data consumers encounter in the literature.

In Chapter 8 I present some theoretical aspects of psychological measurement which underlie the development and understanding of the specific techniques used by researchers. I have tried to present these simply and directly but with intellectual integrity. Understanding these theoretical aspects of measurement is crucial to your understanding of data gathering techniques. And since the raw data are the basis for all subsequent analyses and decisions it will be worth your while to try to comprehend this information as fully as you can.

The actual generation of data is treated in Chapter 9. I have tried to present to you the scope of the measurement scene—the techniques are varied and numerous but all of the measurement devices can be classified as being a certain type. However, the heart of this chapter is the section dealing with the assessment of measuring instruments. Most lay people and indeed many professionals have what might be best described as a blind faith in psychological measurements. Yet upon examination many instruments seem to be based on assumptions which may or may not be reasonable. A key issue I have tried to develop is the situational appropriateness of tests: there is no such thing as a good test any more than there is a good way of behaving—it is the specific situation which dictates the appropriate test or behavior. I have tried to point out to you some of the considerations involved in evaluating the use of a specific test.

There is a lot of frank discussion here about issues some people would rather not think or talk about. This discussion is included because without it I believe that consumers will not be in any position to evaluate research critically.

Chapter 8
Basic Concepts of Measurement

The most important characteristic of scientific inquiry is its reliance on evidence usually found in the form of carefully gathered data. We have seen in previous chapters how procedures and paradigms have been developed in order to collect data; experimental designs and descriptive methods are frameworks in which data are generated. And these frameworks allow us to use data as a component in the process of scientific inquiry. But the actual generation of these data, the development of these facts directly from the data sources (persons or objects) is of crucial importance to our understanding of the research process because of the strong effect they can have on the entire research enterprise. No matter how tight the design, how appropriate the method, how unbiased the researcher, how sophisticated and accurate the analysis, if the raw data used in a study are inaccurate, invalid or inappropriate the study will suffer.

No chain is stronger than its weakest link. The collection of data is the first link in a chain of procedures which culminates in a decision about an hypothesis. The degree to which the raw data are of poor quality is an indication of the weakness of this link which will reflect itself in a lack of credibility in the completed study. Computer people have a saying: "GIGO: Garbage in, garbage out." If you use poor data as input into a computer analysis the computer cannot improve it and the result is an analysis devoid of usefulness. For this reason, our attention as consumers of research must focus upon the issue of the credibility of the raw data used in a research study. In this chapter we will discuss some background information needed to make a judgment about measurements used in educational research. First we will consider the types of data yielded by measurement procedures, then we will consider the necessary qualities of good measuring instruments.

Types of Data

Much of the data used in educational research are measurements of one kind or another. *Measurement* is the process of assigning numerals to measured properties of subjects, objects, and/or events. The type of measurement that is made characterizes the type of data available for analysis. Let us examine the various types of data.

Enumeration data, as implied by the name, are data derived from counting. They answer the question, "What is the frequency in this classification." An example of enumeration data is classroom enrollments, or the number of children qualifying for free lunches. These are not really measurement data—actually nothing is being measured. Researchers can do little with such data except to report them and compare them perhaps with other enumerations in the same classification, e.g., compare one class enrollment with another. In contrast, *measurement data* are data derived from measuring attributes of people or things; they represent differences in the magnitude of an attribute. Most data used educational research, scores for instance, are measurement data.

There are four levels of measurement which will determine the type of data we have. It is important to make a distinction between these levels because the assignment of these measurement levels will influence in large part the statistical technique which can be appropriately employed in the analysis of the data.

Nominal Data

The lowest level of measurement yields *nominal data,* also referred to as *categorical* data or *discrete* data. As implied by these three terms these are data which are fit into separate categories each with its own name. The categories are quite separate, that is if represented graphically they would appear to have empty space between them as shown in figure 8.1. Often the categories are polar opposites. For example if a questionnaire yields data which are comprised solely of *yes* or *no* responses, these data are nominal; a response is either yes or no, there is no middle ground. Similarly the sex of subjects, male or female, represent separate categories: a person is either male or female, although perhaps a special category could be formed for people who have a sex change through surgery. Other examples of nominal data are types of illnesses (such as measles, mumps, etc.), color eyes (brown, blue, grey) etc.

In educational research these data have their chief value in allowing researchers to describe subjects or simplify more complex data. There is not much that researchers can do with these data except count them and report them. The data are similar to enumeration data in their inherent characteristics and the simplicity of possible treatment.

Ordinal Data

Nominal data show how things differ qualitatively. If in addition to this, data can be shown to differ in level or size, then they are referred to as *ordinal data.* Ordinal data are data that can be ordered or ranked, that is, it can be said that one thing is "greater" than or "less" than another. One can express differences among data and reveal their relative position to one another by using ordinal numbers: 1st, 2nd, 3rd, 4th, etc., or verbally stated wordings: largest, next largest, large, medium, small, etc.

Now, this can not be done with nominal data. One can not say that a yes response is "greater" than a no response or that *brown* eyes are ranked "higher" than *blue* eyes. One can say, of course, that there were more brown eyed subjects than blue eyed subjects, but one can not state that the category of brown eyes is ranked "higher" than the category of blue eyes. One *can* say this about shirt sizes though. *Large* is larger than *medium, medium* is larger than *small,* etc. Shirt sizes like this are ordinal measurements.

A representation of ordinal data appears in figure 8.2. You will note that there are three categories on the variable socio-economic status—low, middle and high—and these categories are ordered. Also note that the space between them which separates them into categories is uneven:

Variable: Response to question

Figure 8.1. Representation of nominal (categorical) data.

Variable: Socio-economic status

Figure 8.2. Representation of ordinal data.

the space between the low and middle positions is less than the space between the middle and high positions. This reflects the fact that high socio-economic status is generally considered to be well above low or middle status.

Examples of ordinal data found in educational research are grade-equivalent scores, socio-economic status, academic ranks, and most attitude scales. These data can be counted *and* ranked and as such, are often more useful to researchers than nominal data.

Interval Data

Also referred to as *continuous data, interval data* are measurements of an attribute which can be represented by a continuum on which the scale units are of equal size. A good example of this is the face of a clock. It can be easily noted how the distances between the numbers are the same. Inches on a ruler or points on a thermometer show the same continuity of equal intervals. The particular points on a continuous scale are for reference—the attribute is thought to flow unimpeded on the continuum. Thus, on a ruler with only whole inches marked off, the area of the continuum represented by the marks at, say, 5 inches, is from 4.5 inches to 5.499 . . . inches. The 5 inch mark is considered the center of the area on the continuum it represents.

A representation of interval data is shown in figure 8.3. The variable *mathematics ability* is represented on a continuum which ranges from low to high. On the continuum are many points equidistant from one another. This is in contrast to the two categories of nominal data shown in figure 8.1, or the three ordered levels which have different distances between them shown in figure 8.2. Most data used in educational research are presumed (sometimes mistakenly) to be interval data and are treated accordingly. These data may be counted as with nominal data, ranked as with ordinal data, and furthermore may be subjected to almost every other analysis available to researchers.

Ratio Data

Ratio data are derived from a scale which has a *true* zero point. The existence of this true zero point allows one to state differences among data in the form of ratios. For example, height and weight are ratio scales. One can say that Frank is twice (2/1) as tall as his son, Morgan, but only three quarters (3/4) the height of his brother Bill. These statements are possible because there is a true zero point (theoretically) on the continuum of the attribute length.

Note the use of the word "true" in referring to the zero point on a ratio scale. Not all zero points are true zeros. For example, zero degrees Farenheit (or Celcius) is not a true zero point, since temperatures below it exist. This zero point was assigned arbitrarily and although it serves as a useful reference point it does not represent the absence of the attribute of temperature. Accordingly, one *can not* say 60°F. is twice as cold as 30°F. On the other hand, the attribute of weight has a true zero point. Thus one *can* say that 60 lbs. is twice as heavy as 30 lbs.

Low   High

Variable: Mathematics ability

Figure 8.3. Representation of interval data.

Interestingly, temperature does have a true zero point, $-459.70°$F. at which point all molecular motion stops, resulting in a complete absence of heat. Physicists refer to this temperature as "absolute zero." When measured on this scale, expressions of ratios of temperature are meaningful.

In educational research, few measurements are made on ratio scales, which somewhat limits the statements one can make about some faimilar concepts. Take intelligence as measured by an IQ test for example. The IQ scale has a reference point of 100 and all points are spread out on a continuum of presumably equal intervals on both sides of the 100 point. There is no zero point: no one can have zero intelligence. An IQ score is interpreted by noting how far it is from the reference point of 100, not by how far it is from zero. Therefore, one cannot say that a person with an IQ of 150 is twice as smart as a person with an IQ of 75.

Ratio data can be subjected to all the analytical treatments that interval data can and in addition the expression of ratios is admissible. Little educational data are ratio data: the chief importance in understanding ratio data is in recognizing the limitations of interval data.

Limitations of Data Types

It has been noted that researchers attempt to secure data at the highest level of measurement possible. This enables them to use the most powerful and sophisticated analyses with which to treat the data. In so doing, however, the limitations of the data type should not be violated. Unfortunately, violations of this sort abound in many areas of educational research.

One problem occurs when a statistical treatment appropriate for a given level of measurement is assigned to data derived at a lower level of measurement. For example, one reads that the average American family has 2.3 children. This figure was probably produced by counting the number of children in all families and dividing that figure by the number of families. This computation of a mean average assumes that the number of children possible in a family exists on an interval scale and that the 3rd child for example represents a child who exists between 2.5 and 3.499 on the child continuum. This, of course, is an absurd assumption. Children can not be represented on a continuum—they are discrete entities. There is such a thing as one child, two children, three children, and there is such a thing as a first child, a second child and a third child, but there is no such thing as .3 of a child (unless, with a stretch of the imagination perhaps one is referring to a fetus in its first trimester). The violation inherent in the notion of "2.3 children" is that a mean average was computed on nominal or ordinal data when this statistical procedure is only suitable and appropriate for interval or ratio data. The more appropriate treatment of these data would have been the assignment of frequencies in categories (one child, two children, etc.) and the computation of the modal average.* This would allow for a more reasonable statement to the effect that the average American family has two or three children.

---

*The mean and modal averages will be discussed thoroughly in Chapter 10.

IF THE DATA WERE TRANSFORMED FROM NOMINAL OR ORDINAL TO INTERVAL, WAS THE TRANSFORMATION AND SUBSEQUENT ANALYSIS REASONABLE AND APPROPRIATE?

Of course, we all know that *2.3 children* is purely a "statistical" description; we know that what the statement refers to is 2 or 3 children. Not so obvious though is the computation of a mean average from transformed data. For example, sometimes, in order to use a statistical treatment reserved for interval or ratio data, data which are nominal are transformed in appearance to an interval scale. We say "in appearance" because the transformation may assume equal intervals when indeed equal intervals do not exist. As an instance, in many schools and colleges letter grades are awarded to students based upon their achievement: A, B, C, D, F. To summarize many of these grades a Grade Point Average (GPA) is computed by transforming the letters into numbers according to the following schedule: A=4, B=3, C=2, D=1, and F=0, and computing a mean average of the grades over the number of courses. This transformation gives the impression of an equal interval scale. But one must ask if the difference between an A and a B is the same as the difference between a B and a C. And are any of the differences between adjacent grades as large as the difference between a D and an F? If visualized spatially would the grades look like this?

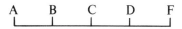

or would they look like this?

```
A        B   C      D                    F
|____|____|____|____|____|____|____|
```

The first case assumes equal intervals and if this assumption is justified then a mean average computation is appropriate. Many persons would say however that the second spatial arrangement is probably more accurate in its reflection of the perceived weights of the grades. If this is the case, then it is hardly interval data. Rather it is ordinal data and should be treated accordingly. But on the other hand if grades are judged to be on a continuum but not at equally distant points, then perhaps the 4, 3, 2, 1, 0 scale points should be reallocated such as 4, 2.3, 2.1, 0.8, 0.0. In this case the computation of a mean average would be appropriate.

Another example of problems with transformed data can be seen when rating scales with verbal descriptions are transformed into numerical scales. For instance, a self report rating instrument might ask, "How often do you do these activities? Lie, Cheat, Steal." The response format might be: Never, Seldom, Sometimes, Often, Always. Numerals are often assigned to each response, 1, 2, 3, 4, 5 respectively, indicating a presumed interval scale. This is shown graphically in figure 8.5, Scale A. Again, one wonders whether the distance between "Never" and "Seldom" is the same as the distance between "Seldom" and "Sometimes". Are not "Never" and "Always" absolutes which are rarely achieved and are not "Seldom" and "Often" relatively minor deviations from "Sometimes?" Might not a more realistic spacing of these points be represented by Scale B in figure 8.4?

The essence of this problem is the difference between a number and a numeral. A number is a mathematical expression of a quantity existing on an interval scale—it represents a concept. A numeral, however, is the symbol used to represent the concept. The problem in transforming data

How often do you lie, cheat, and steal?

	Never	Seldom	Sometimes	Often	Always
Scale A	1	2	3	4	5
Scale B	1		2	3	4	5

Figure 8.4. Example of transformed data.

from nominal or ordinal to interval is that one may assign numerals to categories but then mistakenly treat the numerals as if they were numbers when they might not necessarily be so. Perhaps Roman numerals should be used for categories—they are much more difficult to manipulate than Arabic!

Importance of Data Types

One may wonder, why in a consumer oriented book about research is so much space devoted to a seemingly abstract and theoretical issue such as types of data. The reason for this inclusion is that the determination of the type of data researchers have to analyze comes fairly early in the sequence of data collection and analysis, and any error involved in the determination will be compounded several times. The problems begin when a researcher selects an instrument with which to obtain measurements. The instrument to be utilized has had its accuracy judged, and even in the case of the very best instruments available the accuracy is never absolute: The instrument is probably *fairly* accurate. The inaccuracy of the instrument is error. Because of this the measurements obtained with the instrument have error too.

Then the instrument is used and the data are obtained. The measurements may or may not be true interval data but usually they are treated as if they were. The degree to which they are not constitute more error. Additional error is found in the sampling error that exists when less than an entire population is measured. Hence, error is piled upon error.

This picture is gloomy enough but to make matters worse the data may then be subjected to highly sophisticated statistical procedures. These procedures are easily managed using programs run on high speed computers which are capable of making the most precise, accurate computations frequently expressed with decimals of more than 6 places. Then, based on these computations, researchers reject or do not reject hypotheses at various levels of confidence (another potential source of error), and decisions are made on the basis of the hypothesis testing. Thus, errors are compounded as additional procedures are employed. The earlier an error occurs in the procedural sequence, the larger is its potentially deleterious effect at the end. A similar snowballing effect can be seen with compound interest; the earlier in a chronology in which interest is calculated and added to the principal, the greater magnitude its contribution to the final balance. The "data-type" error comes near the beginning of a research sequence, hence its potential for compounding is formidable. It is for this reason that a decision to view data conservatively by not assuming they are at a higher level than justifiable is considered a wise choice. The alternative is to risk unnecessary compounding of errors which ultimately weakens one's confidence in the test of the hypothesis.

The Quality of Measuring Instruments

In most educational research, the data collected usually represent measurements taken on subjects or objects. These measurements are derived from the application of a *measuring instrument* to the subjects or objects. The total range of possible instruments is quite broad and will be discussed in the next chapter. Whatever the instrument used in a study, it must have two characteristics to be useful in a research enterprise: it must be *valid* and it must be *reliable*. As consumers of research we must make a judgment about the measurement instruments used in a study. This is true whether the instrument is a published test used in prior research efforts or an *ad hoc* questionnaire thrown together for a specific occasion. Especially in the latter instance researchers often present information about the development of the measuring instruments used. In order for us to understand such a presentation and in order to judge instruments we need to have a basic understanding of the concepts of validity and reliability.

Validity

An instrument ought to measure what it purports to measure. This is a definition of validity. A ruler purports to measure the attribute length. Most people would agree that it does. An IQ test purports to measure intelligence, but this issue is debatable. The validity of an instrument is not a yes/no question. It is a matter of degree and a matter of judgment, depending upon the accuracy of the measurement, the nature of attribute measured, and the intended use of the measurement.

At this point we should be aware that an instrument itself cannot be said to be valid or invalid. Rather the *use* of the instrument in a specific situation may be *judged to be valid or invalid*. For example, a standardized reading test may be a valid test to describe certain reading behaviors of a given group of students compared to a larger norming group. But the very same test used on the very same students may be invalid when used to divide the students into groups for instructional purposes. This is because the reading behaviors sampled probably do not represent the specific reading behaviors occurring in an instructional setting.

If an instrument is accurate and furthermore is used in a situation appropriate to its intent, then we may judge it to be valid. (Accuracy, called *reliability,* will be discussed in the next section.) Let us concern ourselves now with the use to which a measurement may be put; this use indicates the most appropriate assessment of validity. The three major uses of a measurement instrument are: 1) to establish a relationship between two variables; this is called *predictive validity* (and also *empirical* or *statistical validity*); 2) to represent a specific universe of content; this is called *content validity* (and also *face, intrinsic* or *circular validity*); and 3) to measure a psychological trait: this is called *construct validity* (and also *factorial validity*).

1. *Predictive Validity.* Sometimes a measurement of an attribute is made in order to predict another attribute. The Scholastic Aptitude Test (SAT) for example is used to predict success in college level academic work. A reading readiness test is used to predict success in first grade reading achievement. In constructing a test for this purpose, a *criterion variable* to which the test will be related is determined: in the above examples the criterion for each would be college GPA and reading achievement test scores. Then a test is constructed which would appear to have a content which is prerequisite for the criterion: reading and writing ability for the SAT, and say, letter recognition and spatial orientation for the readiness test. This test is called the *predictor variable*. The validity of this test (let's use the readiness test as the example) is determined by administering the test to a group of kindergarten or early first grade pupils and then administering to the same pupils a reading achievement test at the end of first grade. A correlation analysis (see

Chapter 10) is performed and the degree which the two tests are related becomes the index of predictive validity. So we see that the determination of predictive validity is made upon an analysis of the relationship between the predictor test (the test being validated) and a criterion test (the test of the target attribute). This validation procedure is entirely statistical; for this reason, predictive validity is sometimes referred to as "empirical" or "statistical" validity. Tests which seek to predict, such as aptitude or readiness tests, should have a high degree of predictive validity.

2. *Content validity.* A test is sometimes devised to measure the extent of a person's knowledge about something. Final examinations and achievement tests are examples. For tests of this sort, the assessment of a test's content is used as an index of its validity. This assessment can be made at two stages in the development of a test.

Stage 1: The validity of a test can be built into the test by using appropriate plans and procedures during its construction. The test items should be truly representative of the domain being tested. For example, in the development of a mathematics test, a decision needs to be made concerning the scope of the test. Will it measure computation, understanding, memory, application or other aspects of mathematics? Following that decision, a suitable number and type of items dealing with each component should be included. Mathematics computation, for example, should probably include several items each in columnar addition, subtraction without exchanging, subtraction with exchanging, etc.

Stage 2: After the test is constructed its content could be validated by administering the test before and after a training routine which was previously judged to have been effective. If the scores of the second administration were higher than those on the first administration, this might be an index of the test's content validity. However, it also could be the result of a practice effect from pretest to posttest (see Chapter 5). Another validation method is to correlate the test being validated with another older/and established test. However, this is no guarantee of the test's content validity since both tests may be measuring the same wrong things. This particular validity assessment which correlates a new test with an already established test is called *concurrent validity.*

The assessment of a test's content validity can be done without statistical analysis. It can be handled very well by the judgment of experts in the field which is being measured. The problem is that experts in any given field may differ substantially as to what the field comprises. For example, one math expert might expect a math test to determine whether a pupil has memorized certain formulae; another expert might expect a pupil to use the formulae effectively in a problem solving situation without necessarily having memorized it. As another example, there is great divergence of thinking in the field of reading education. Some experts believe a pupil should be able to pronounce words out of context; others insist that reading is a process in which words are encountered in context so an out-of-context subtest is inappropriate. The point is that experts differ, and in the assessment of a test's content the most important determiners may be who the experts are, what are their biases, and where are they coming from.

3. *Construct validity.* Some tests are designed to measure a construct*. Such a test should possess construct validity. The steps in determining the construct validity of a test are as follows:

Step 1: Domain specification. You recall that a construct is composed of several observable variables, and the existence of a construct is inferred from measurements taken of those variables. Which variables are included in a construct depends upon the theory behind

---

*A *construct* is a complex attribute made up of several simpler observable attributes. Examples are intelligence, anxiety, and self-concept.

the construct. For example, one might theorize that intelligence is comprised of vocabulary, listening ability, and awareness of spatial and numerical concepts whereas someone else might theorize intelligence to be verbal reasoning, aesthetic judgment, and moral judgment. Each set of variables represents an operational definition of the construct intelligence.

Step 2: Relationship analysis. Following the specification of the variables which comprise the construct, tests of each variable are administered to a group of subjects and the interrelatedness of the variables is analyzed through correlational procedures (see Appendix C). The degree to which the variables are related is an indication of the construct validity of the group of tests. The tests which do relate highly to one another are said to be measuring a similar thing; that similar thing is the construct. For example, if a theorist states that intelligence is comprised of vocabulary, listening ability, awareness of spatial and numerical concepts, and if furthermore, correlation analysis shows these variables to have a high relationship with one another, then one can say that the test has construct validity. On the other hand, if a second theorist states that intelligence is comprised of verbal reasoning, aesthetic judgment, and moral judgment, and correlational analysis shows that this set of variables has a high relationship, then this test, too, has construct validity. Thus construct validity is determined by the relationships among the set of variables. In one sense it resembles content validity in that the specification of content is crucial. In another sense it resembles predictive validity in that it requires correlational analysis in its procedure.

You may be asking yourself, how can two tests which purport to measure the same construct—intelligence—be comprised of such different content, yet both have construct validity. Simple. This is because the tests were developed on the drawing boards and have not yet been tested against reality. This leads to the third step.

Step 3: Theory validation. If a test with construct validity is to be useful, then it should discriminate between people who are thought to possess the construct and those thought not to. An intelligence test, for example, should discriminate between people who have "a lot" of intelligence and those who have "little" intelligence. A good way to validate a test is by the "known group" method. An administration of the test to, say, bright capable independent people and to slow, incapable, dependent people should show the former scoring higher than the latter. Similarly, one would expect to find high anxiety scores in neurotic people and low anxiety scores in non-neurotic people—high self-concept scores in happy people, low self-concept scores in unhappy people.

A problem occurs when two tests with dissimilar content purport to measure the same thing, as is the case with intelligence tests. The content of each test may have high interrelationships thus high construct validity. And the theory behind each test may be validated using known groups, although the groups may be different (Test A might use "bright, capable, independent" people as a criterion group while Test B uses honor students at a suburban high school as its criterion group). Which test is measuring intelligence? As evidence that the test is measuring the "real" construct, the test developers may point to the theory and show how the test fits the theory. Such reasoning, however, is fallacious. It is begging the question to state that a theory is valid because a test has been devised to measure the theory. This assumes that the theory was valid to begin with.

150

Which of the two tests is measuring the "real" construct? Perhaps both are, perhaps neither is or perhaps there is no "real" construct. There are different kinds of "intelligence". There is intelligence as measured by the Otis-Lennon Test. There is intelligence as measured by the Peabody Picture Vocabulary Test. And there is "street-smart" intelligence as measured by survival in a hostile environment. The test *is* the construct, operationally defined. This accounts for the fact that a person can take several different intelligence tests and come out with several different scores, some of which may vary widely. In summary then, construct validity is determined by specifying the constituent variables of a theory of a construct, analyzing their inter-relationships and checking out the test with reality.

It should be mentioned that the key concepts included in the discussion of validity of tests applies in general to all types of measurements in research and evaluation procedures. Judgments as to value, appropriateness, validity and the like are highly relative. The questions are seldom either/or or yes/no. More likely the questions are How much? To what extent? Under what conditions? Situational appropriateness is the key to judging quality.

Reliability

The reliability of an instrument is a more simple, straight-forward concept than validity. It deals with the accuracy of the measurement rather than its appropriateness and can be determined by computation rather than judgment.

A reliable automobile is one that starts up easily and takes you where you need to go day after day. A reliable worker is one who gets to work on time and does his or her work properly day after day. A reliable rifle sends bullets to the same place when aimed at the same place time after time. Reliable things or people are dependable, consistent and predictable. Measuring instruments are also said to be reliable when they exhibit these traits. A reliable air pressure guage should yield almost identical readings when applied to the same tire twice consecutively. A reliable ruler should have inches of the same length, none shorter or longer than the others. A reliable psychological test, too, should demonstrate consistency upon repeated application.

To understand the concept of reliability of psychological measurements we need to make a brief excursion into measurement theory. Now, the individual scores in a set of scores may be seen to differ from one another; this difference is referred to as *total variance*. These are the differences we observe in a distribution of scores. This total variance is presumed to be comprised of two elements: *true variance* and *error variance*. True variance reflects the real differences in the attribute being measured. This is the variance among scores which would occur with a perfect measuring instrument administered under perfect conditions. True variance reflects those sources which contribute to the accurate measurement of an attribute; such sources are the skill or ability being measured and test-taking skills. Error variance on the other hand reflects random and independent error in the measurement process. Error variance may be composed of *ad hoc* problems the subject had on the day of the test such as fatigue or illness, clerical errors such as mismarking an answer sheet, or may be due also to an inadequate number of items which sought to measure the attribute. There may be great truth to the response of a 5th grade pupil who when confronted with the fact that she got only 3 items correct on a 15 item social studies test replied, "I know more than that. The teacher asked me the wrong questions!"

Total variance is composed of true variance plus error variance. Stated symbolically

$$\text{Variance}_{total} = \text{Variance}_{true} + \text{Variance}_{Error}$$

Using a simplified illustration we may say that 10 units of total variance are comprised of 8 units of true variance and 2 units of error variance

$$10 = 8 + 2$$

As can be seen by this relationship, when error variance goes up, true variance goes down.

total = true + error
$$10 = 6 + 4$$

Conversely, when error variance goes down, true variance goes up

total = true + error
$$10 = 9 + 1$$

The less error variance present, the more true variance possible, and the closer the true variance approximates the total variance. *The proportion of total variance that is true variance is the reliability of the measurements.* Stated symbolically:

$$\text{Reliability} = \frac{\text{Variance}_{true}}{\text{Variance}_{total}}$$

A perfectly reliable set of measurements would have no error variance, in which case total variance and true variance would be identical.

total = true + error
$$10 = 10 + 0$$

As error variance increases true variance and thus reliability decrease.

total	= true + error	reliability =	$\dfrac{\text{true}}{\text{total}}$
10 =	10 + 0	$\dfrac{10}{10}$ or	1.00
10 =	9 + 1	$\dfrac{9}{10}$ or	.90
10 =	8 + 2	$\dfrac{8}{10}$ or	.80
10 =	7 + 3	$\dfrac{7}{10}$ or	.70
10 =	6 + 4	$\dfrac{6}{10}$ or	.60

When it gets to the point that there is so much error variance that the true variance is obscured we cannot have much confidence in the accuracy of our measurements. Exactly where this point is will be explained later in this section.

Types of Reliability

A measuring instrument should have the quality of *stability* over a period of time. A scale would not be very helpful to you if you step on it, note your weight at 145 lbs, step off and then step on again and note your weight at 147. Similarly an aptitude test, for example, would have little value if it showed that you have an aptitude for, say, engineering on Monday, but did not have the aptitude on the following Wednesday. There are two ways in which the stability of a test may be estimated*. In one way, the *test-retest* method, a test is administered to a group on two occasions and a correlation of the test scores is computed. In the second way, the *equivalent forms* method, two equivalent or near-equivalent forms of the test are administered to a group on two occasions. In this method, too, a correlation of the two tests is computed. In both methods, the resulting correlation coefficient is an index of the test's stability.

A measuring instrument ought to be consistent within itself. If a yardstick has some inch marks off by a quarter inch or so and a measurement of, say, 15 inches is taken it should not make any difference whether you measure the 15 inches from the left or the right side of the yardstick. Similarly the pounds at the top of a scale should represent the same units of weight as the pounds at the bottom or middle of the scale. The items on a psychological test should all contribute equally to the total score. There are two ways of estimating the *internal consistency* of a test. In one method, the *split half* technique, the test is administered to a group on one occasion and the test is divided into two halves, usually odd items and even items. Then a correlation between the two halves is computed. Other methods developed by Kuder and Richardson correlate each test item with each other test item and the test as a whole.

Which type of reliability—stability or internal consistency—is better depends in large part upon the type of measurement instrument involved. If an instrument is measuring an attribute with different kinds of items then the test-retest method would be appropriate. For example, a questionnaire with items dealing with educational level, residence, place of birth, attitude toward government, and television viewing habits would use the test-retest method to estimate its reliability. The items are so heterogeneous that to measure the internal consistency is absurd—there is no internal consistency.

Stability is an important aspect of reliability, but in some cases it is difficult to estimate, and internal consistency is estimated instead. For example, if an attribute like paragraph comprehension is being measured, if the duration between the test and the retest is brief then the subjects taking the retest may remember their responses from the first test. This would make the correlation spuriously high. On the other hand if the duration between the test and retest were too long, then differential growth rates among the subjects might make the correlation spuriously low. In such cases, a consistency reliability estimate may be a better choice.

If the test were a speed test in which not all items were completed or attempted by all the subjects then still other problems may arise. For example, say a timed test of mathematical computation was administered and there was virtually no expectation that the subjects would get to every item. Because there were omitted items and secondly because the tendency for most subjects is to score correctly on virtually all items attempted on this type of test, any internal consistency method would give poor estimates of reliability—too high or too low depending upon the nature of the score distribution. A test-retest method might be good, but there might well be

---

*The use of the term "estimated" is deliberate. There are many factors other than the quality of the test that effect reliability. Thus reliability can not be determined but merely estimated.

a practice effect causing the retest scores to be higher for those subjects who benefitted from the practice. This would lower the reliability estimate. A better way might be to develop two alternate forms and have them administered one after the other.

In research that involves qualitative judgments or ratings by someone other than the subject, a special problem exists. The instrument itself may be a check list or a taxonomy—a sterile form though perhaps laden with validity. A person, the examiner perhaps, observes a subject's behavior and notes its occurrence directly on the instrument. The question is whether other examiners would have rated the behavior the same way. For example, in behavioral research an examiner may be tallying the frequency of non-study behaviors. In a given five minute period of time he noted 12 such occurrences. Would another examiner have also noted 12 occurrences? As another example, a rater might judge the creativity of a written composition as being "fair". How would other raters have judged it? In both examples, if others would have rated or judged differently can we say that the rating was accurate? The issue in these cases is one of *inter-rater reliability* and is endemic to all such judgmental type measures. It is handled in two ways. First, the operational definition of the behavior being observed may be specified more precisely including perhaps examples and non examples. Second, the raters or judges should be given training to establish some uniformity in their perceptions and their operational definitions of what they are judging. In either case an index of reliability should be computed based on a sample of many ratings. This index is usually the percentage of agreement among the raters and serves to indicate the consistency of the ratings in the study. Ratings or judgments presented without some indication of their reliability should be viewed with suspicion.

Relationship of Reliability and Validity

A test can be reliable and not valid but not vice versa. For example, we can use a very precise and reliable micrometer to measure a man's bicep in order to determine his strength. However, strength is determined by more than just the size of the bicep. This is a case of a reliable instrument used for an invalid measurement of strength. Instead we could use a thin rubber tape measure for this purpose, but then we have an unreliable instrument used for an invalid measurement. The presence of reliability does not guarantee validity; a micrometer though reliable does not render its measurement of a bicep a valid index of strength. A low level of reliability however, virtually precludes a high level of validity; even if a man's strength could be determined by the size of his bicep, a thin rubber tape measure is so unreliable a measuring instrument that the bicep measurement could not be judged valid. Figure 8.5 shows the relationship of reliability to validity by using a target analogy. The bull's eye is the attribute being measured, the bullet holes represent the test. Note that the mere presence of close shot groupings does not mean we hit the bull's eye; the accuracy of our marksmanship must be directed to the right place on the target in order to score points.

The relationship between reliability and validity is a dependent one: there must be a certain amount of reliability in order for a measurement to be considered valid. How much, though, is a matter of judgment. This relationship is somewhat analogous to the relationship between the internal and external validity of experimental designs. You will recall from Chapter 5 that internal validity is concerned with the mechanics of an experimental design, whereas external validity deals with the usefulness or generalizability of the findings from a study using a given design. If a design does have internal validity then it may have external validity as well. But if it does not have internal validity it can not really have external validity. In designing an experiment sometimes researchers have to trade off one kind of validity for another: they might sacrifice some internal

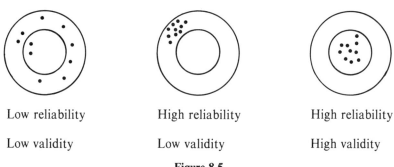

| Low reliability | High reliability | High reliability |
| Low validity | Low validity | High validity |

Figure 8.5.

validity in order to increase external validity. In measurement, the same type of trade-off occurs sometimes. For example, a teacher's judgment of a child's achievement may lack the precision and objectivity of a standardized test, yet may be based on a much larger sample of a child's behavior. This could be described as moderate reliability but high content validity. As another example, the ratings of gasoline consumption of automobiles made by Consumers Union (CU) are based on highly valid tests done in the real world with real drivers on real roads. The Environmental Protection Agency (EPA) tests cars for the same information but does its testing in a highly controlled laboratory situation which is somewhat less valid. EPA's measures are very precise; CU's are reasonably precise. Which information is more useful in predicting the gasoline mileage the car will get when you are driving it on the road? CU's has been judged to be more valid for this purpose. Trade-offs of this sort are common in measurement. When evaluating the quality of a measure one must consider whether the concept of the measurement is valid and if so, question whether or not there is sufficient precision to have confidence in it. Validity must be considered first.

Summary

Much of the data used in educational research are comprised of measurements of attributes of persons, things, or events. There are four levels of measurement which characterize the data obtained. Nominal data which are derived from the lowest level of measurement are data which fit into separate categories. Ordinal data are data which can be ordered or ranked. Interval data are derived from a scale with equal intervals. The highest level of measurement yields ratio data, which is similar to interval data but is derived from a scale which possesses a true zero point. The type of data is a major determinant as to the specific analytical techniques which may be appropriately applied. The higher the level of measurement, the more sophisticated the admissible analyses.

Data are sometimes transformed by researchers from one type to another. There is often a loss of accuracy which results when this takes place. Researchers seek to avoid losses in accuracy which are possible at this stage of a research endeavor because the inaccuracies may become compounded and result in a distortion of the findings of a study.

The two major qualities which measuring instruments should possess are validity and reliability. An instrument is considered valid if it measures accurately what it purports to measure. There are three basic indices of an instrument's validity—predictive, content, and construct validities. The appropriateness of these three indices to a given measurement is determined by the use to which that measurement will be put. Tests which seek to predict, such as aptitude tests, should possess predictive validity. Tests which seek to describe an attribute, such as survey tests, should have content validity. And tests which seek to describe a construct, such as intelligence tests, should have construct validity.

Reliability refers to a test's accuracy as reflected by its stability and consistency. A test's stability is measured by its ability to yield similar measurements of the same phenomenon at different times—this is called test-retest reliability. A test's consistency is measured by the degree to which its items all contribute to the total test score—this is called its internal consistency. Tests need to be reliable in order to be considered valid, but the mere fact that they are reliable is no guaranty that they are valid.

The following question needs to be asked by consumers when they encounter psychological measurements in research:

IF THE DATA WERE TRANSFORMED FROM NOMINAL TO ORDINAL OR INTERVAL, WAS THE TRANSFORMATION AND SUBSEQUENT ANALYSIS REASONABLE AND APPROPRIATE?

Chapter 9
The Generation of Data

In the previous chapter we discussed the various types of data which can be obtained through measurement procedures, and examined the characteristics of measuring instruments—validity and reliability—by which their quality can be assessed. Using this information as background we will now consider the various types of measurement instruments often used in educational research and how to evaluate their use in a given research endeavor.

Types of Measurement Instruments

Educational research uses a variety of measurement instruments to generate data. *Psychological tests* pose questions or provide tasks to a subject, whose responses are scored. *Attitude scales* require a subject to react to a question or statement; an attitude is inferred from the reaction to that stimulus. *Questionnaires* and *interviews* seek opinions from subjects in a pencil and paper format or face-to-face respectively. Finally, *direct observation* may be used to gain information about a subject's knowledge, attitudes, opinions, or behavior. All these methods find their way into the research literature. Let us consider each of these several devices.

Psychological Tests

By far the most prominent source of data in educational research is the psychological test. These tests are typically pencil and paper affairs and are given for a variety of purposes. Some tests are called *speed tests* and have a definite time limit for completion but most tests are *power tests* and have no such stringent time limit. Other tests combine these formats.

Achievement tests seek to measure what a person knows or has achieved following a learning experience. These tests may be classified according to three qualities:

1. Content. A *survey test* seeks to measure a person's general knowledge of a subject by sampling the different kinds of knowledge in a given area. For example, a mathematics survey test would have items which were representative of the level of mathematics being tested. A specification of the content of the level needs to be made quite clear. The resulting score from a survey test would indicate in general a subject's achievement in that area. A *diagnostic test,* however, seeks to determine precisely what a subject does and does not know. Accordingly it has to include not merely a sample of possible items but specifically several items on each possible task. Because of this requirement, the scope of a diagnostic test is usually quite limited. Otherwise the test would be too long to administer. For example, if one were *surveying* mathematics ability a few items on subtraction would suffice. But for *diagnostic* purposes we would need to have several items for each possible skill: a) one digit from two digits without exchanging; b) one digit from two digits with exchanging; c) two digits from two digits without exchanging; d) number facts; etc.

2. Administration. *Standardized tests* are quite formal in their administration. Instructions are explicit and should not vary from one administration to the next. These tests are usually published and come with norms for interpretation. They are used to describe the achievement of a group of students: a class, a school, a district. *Informal tests* are often teacher made and administered individually to students. Their purpose is to assist in instruction. Procedures for administering them are less rigid and meaningful norms are infrequent.

3. Reference. In interpreting a test score, the score needs to be compared to some other score in order to be meaningful. A *norm referenced test* is developed in such a way that a given score may be compared to the scores of comparable subjects. For example, if a fifth grade pupil takes a norm referenced test and achieves a raw score of, say, 38, this score may be compared to the average score of a large group of other fifth graders (referred to as the *norming group)*. Then it can be determined whether this pupil scored higher than, lower than, or the same as the average of pupils in the norming group. The average raw score for the norming group is often referred to as *grade level,* so that when one speaks about a pupil reading below grade level this refers to the average achievement of his grade level peers. It should be noted that the determination of the point at which a certain grade has its average achievement is done empirically—grade level is the point at which most kids in the norming group score. There is no *a priori* determination of grade level. It is a relative concept based on average achievement rather than an absolute point at which mythical fifth graders *should* be reading.

In a *criterion-referenced test,* a subject's score is compared to a criterion score to determine whether or not his or her performance is satisfactory. For example, in a test of addition facts which includes 15 items, a pupil's score of, say, 14 correct would be compared to a criterion of, say, 13. In this case, his achievement would be judged to be satisfactory which would allow him to proceed in the program and take more tests. Mastery tests used in diagnostic-prescriptive programs are criterion referenced. It should be noted here that the determination of the criterion score, that is, the cutoff point above which signifies success and below which signifies failure, is usually made quite arbitrarily. One would assume that the proportion of items necessary to enable a pupil to advance to another task with a good chance of success would be carefully researched; such is rarely, if ever, the case. Typically the test developers pick a number representing 80–90 percent. This shows that the pupil can do it very well yet there is room for an occasional careless error.

Intelligence tests are instruments which purport to assess a general ability rather than a specific knowledge. This ability may be assumed to be inborn, learned or a combination of both, depending upon your point of view. As discussed in the previous chapter, intelligence is a construct and the content of a particular intelligence test will depend heavily upon the theory from which the construct was derived. The grand-daddy of all intelligence tests is the Stanford-Binet which was originally developed in the early 1900's and which underwent several revisions to arrive at its present state. This test measures a variety of abilities such as vocabulary, logic, and common information and is highly verbal in format. Originally a subject's score was transformed into a mental age (MA) which was divided by his chronological age (CA) and multiplied by 100, which yielded an intelligence quotient (IQ). In its present form, however, the IQ score is a standard score based upon a distribution of an age group's scores with a mean of 100 and a standard deviation of 15.* Because of the wide acceptance and historical significance of the Stanford-Binet many intelligence tests base their validity upon their correlation with it.

*These terms will be discussed in detail in Chapter 10.

Intelligence tests vary considerably from one another. They may be classified according to two qualities:

1. Content. Most intelligence tests are highly *verbal* in nature, requiring the examinee to understand language and to respond in language. However, *non-verbal* tests exist which minimize language skills. For example, the Ravens Progressive Matrices test has the examinee match a pattern with other patterns. The performance portion of the Wechsler Intelligence Scale for Children has the examinee duplicate a color design by manipulating colored wooden blocks. One verbal test, the Peabody Picture Vocabulary Test (PPVT) uses a non-verbal response mode: a page with four pictures on it is presented to the examinee as the examiner says a word. The examinee points to the corresponding picture.

2. Administration. Some intelligence tests need to be administered individually by trained personnel; such tests include the Stanford-Binet, Wechsler, and the PPVT. This is an expensive and time-consuming procedure. Accordingly, group administered pencil-and-paper tests have been developed, such as the Otis Lennon.

Aptitude tests are instruments which purport to indicate if a subject has the prerequisite skills and/or abilities for success in a given endeavor. Some intelligence tests, especially those which are highly verbal, are considered to be indicative of an academic aptitude since much academic work is verbal in nature. Aptitude tests are sometimes administered in batteries. For example, a battery might include subtests of verbal intelligence, clerical speed, spelling, and mechanical ability. These tests are often used for guidance purposes as counselors seek to channel students into courses or vocations in which they will be successful. The composition of an aptitude test will reflect the test developer's beliefs as to what skills are needed for success. For example, a music aptitude test might measure a subject's ability to distinguish pitch, rhythm, loudness. A clerical aptitude test might measure a subject's simple arithmetic ability, speed and accuracy with routine chores, alphabetizing, and eye-hand coordination. *Readiness tests* are a special type of aptitude test. They seek to determine whether a pupil has the requisite skills to experience success in learning a more advanced or sophisticated skill. Readiness tests are often given to young children to predict success in learning to read and do mathematics. Here, too, the content of the test is heavily dependent upon the views of the test developer. As a result, the content of readiness tests, especially in reading, varies considerably from test to test.

Personality tests purport to describe subjects' personalities by analyzing the responses to test stimuli. As a field of endeavor personality testing is fraught with numerous problems of reliability and validity. Yet these tests are used in educational research although their usefulness is suspect. Personality tests fall into two categories. *Self-report inventories* are instruments which present subjects with a series of statements. The subjects then indicate whether they agree or disagree with the statement, or whether the condition in the statement is characteristic of them. For example, in a test of introversion a subject might be presented with these statements: "I often prefer to be alone." "Groups of people make me uncomfortable." "I like team sports." If a subject agreed with the first two statements and disagreed with the third, this might be interpreted as an indication of an introverted personality. Some inventories measure only one personality trait, while others measure several at one time.

Projective tests present subjects with ambiguous stimuli to which they can respond as they choose. The type of response elicited from the stimulus is thought to reveal a type of personality; the subjects "project" their personality through the responses. One type of popular projective stimulus is an ink blot which the subject is asked to tell about. Another type is a picture about which a subject is asked to tell a story. Trained clinical psychologists interpret the responses to

159

the stimuli and infer a type of personality from them. Other projective techniques include: a) *sentence completion tasks,* for example "I enjoy . . . " or "I am most afraid of . . . "; b) *constructive tasks,* for example a subject is asked to draw a picture or play with toys; c) *role-playing tasks,* for example a subject is asked to act out a role as a teacher or a parent. In each of these methods the range of possible responses is virtually unlimited and an examiner must infer a personality type from the interpretation of the responses.

Attitude Scales

The measurement of attitudes is often accomplished through the use of scaling techniques. Unlike most psychological tests which present *questions* to a subject and elicit answers which are scored right or wrong or otherwise interpreted, *attitude scales* present stimulus *statements* to which a subject responds. This response may be in one of several possible forms, and is used as the basis for inferring an underlying attitude.

Likert-type scales (summated rating scales) present subjects with a number of positive and negative statements about a subject or object. Subjects responding to the scale indicate the degree to which they agree or disagree with the statement. For example, in order to find out the attitude of a woman toward running as exercise we might present her with the statements in figure 9.1. Then she is asked to indicate her agreement with each statement by placing a check mark under one of the categories: strongly agree, agree, uncertain, disagree, strongly disagree. Each category is later assigned a number 5 through 1, respectively; negative statements such as item 3 are coded 1 through 5. The numerical values for each statement are summed and divided by the number of items to which the subject responded. This mean value is compared to the mean of 3.0 which represents a neutral point. If a person's mean value is above 3 this indicates a positive attitude toward a subject; a mean value below 3 indicates a negative attitude.

Place a check mark to indicate how you feel about each statement.

	Strongly Agree	Agree	Uncertain	Disagree	Strongly Disagree
1. Running is good exercise	_____	_____	_____	_____	_____
2. Running improves the mind as well as the body	_____	_____	_____	_____	_____
3. Too much running can lead to dizzy spells	_____	_____	_____	_____	_____

Figure 9.1. Example of a Likert Scale.

Some researchers use values of 2, 1, 0, −1, 2 for the five categories. Sometimes the middle category, "uncertain" is left out. These are stylistic variations of the Likert technique and typically have no effect on the findings.

Thurstone type scales present subjects with a large number of statements, 30–50 usually, from which they select those statements which reflect their attitude. Prior to the administration of the scale, each statement was judged as to how favorable or unfavorable an attitude it expresses, and a numerical value from 1 to 11 was assigned to it. Figure 9.2 shows an example of some

Check each statement that expresses your opinion about running.

_____ I believe running makes people happy. (7.1)

_____ I think runners are people who enjoy pain. (4)

_____ I believe that runners are crowding cars off the street. (2.5)

_____ I think that people who attend road races are bored. (4.8)

_____ I believe that running is a truly fantastic experience. (10.7)

Figure 9.2. Example of a Thurstone-type scale.

items from a Thurstone-type scale. The numbers in parentheses are the assigned values. A subject's score which reflects an attitude toward running is the mean average of the items selected.

Guttman type scales are similar to the Thurstone scales in that they also present subjects with a series of statements from which they select those with which they agree. But the Guttman scale items differ in that they are cumulatively inclusive. Figure 9.3 shows four items which exemplify a Guttman scale. Return to figure 9.2 for a moment. Note that the five items all deal with running but with different dimensions. The first item deals with the effect running has on happiness, the second item deals with the personality of runners, the third with traffic conditions, and so on. The Guttman scale items in figure 9.3 are *unidimensional;* the items deal only with the effect of running on health. Because the item content is unidimensional the items may be viewed cumulatively. That is if a subject agrees with item 2 he also would have to agree with item 1, but not necessarily with items 3 or 4. If he agrees with item 4, then he would have to also agree with items 1, 2, and 3. A subject's score on a Guttman-type scale is the highest item number he or she agrees with.

Place a check mark on the one item which best represents your belief.

_____ 1. I believe running is somewhat beneficial to the body and could be tried if medication is ineffective.

_____ 2. I believe running is helpful in maintaining a healthy body and should be done by anyone who is inclined to do so.

_____ 3. I believe that running is a very good thing for body and mind and it should be done to some extent by everyone.

_____ 4. I believe that running is the best thing a person can do for body and mind and it should be done every day by everyone.

Figure 9.3. Fxample of a Guttman-type scale.

The *Semantic-Differential Scale* is a unique approach to measuring attitudes. Subjects are presented with the name of a subject or object and respond to it on several seven point scales. Each scale is anchored at the ends with bipolar adjectives. Figure 9.4 shows several semantic differential scales for the subject running. The points on the seven point continuum range from $+3$ to -3, with the positive adjective assigned the $+3$ rating. The degree to which a person's attitude toward something is positive or negative is indicated by which side of the zero or neutral point most of the ratings fall. A mean rating may be computed, and can be compared to a group mean to determine if an individual's attitude is different from that of a comparison group.

A *Q Methodology* is somewhat similar to a semantic differential scale. Subjects are presented with a number of stimulus cards on which appear statements, objectives, or names of objects. Then, they have to sort them on a bipolar scale which is shaped in a symmetrical distribution.

Place a check mark on each line where it best shows your feeling.

RUNNING

1. good	____	____	____	____	____	____	____	bad
2. clean	____	____	____	____	____	____	____	dirty
3. healthy	____	____	____	____	____	____	____	weak
4. constructive	____	____	____	____	____	____	____	destructive

Figure 9.4. Example of a semantic differential scale.

Figure 9.5 shows an example of a seven point continuum onto which the statements about running can be sorted and shows three such statements. Note how the continuum specifies how many stimuli go at each point. These numbers 2, 5, 8, 10, 8, 5, 2, will yield a symmetrical normal-type distribution. The respondent sorts the cards into piles corresponding to the specifications of the continuum. For this example, 50 cards would be used.

Q sorts are sometimes used as a means of pre-assessing and post-assessing a variable. A correlation can be computed to determine the extent to which the positions of the stimuli changed. A high positive correlation would show little change. A high negative correlation would show substantial change. Another type of analysis could examine the mean value of a given group of items in a pretest and posttest by utilizing a *t* test or Analysis of Variance technique.*Another application of the Q sort is in determining the relative importance of each stimulus by having several people do the Q sort and compute the mean value for each stimulus.

Questionnaires and Interviews

A variety of useful information can be gained through the use of *questionnaires* and *interviews*. Both techniques are used extensively in the research literature and both techniques appear simple to an observer. But examination of a questionnaire developed by an amateur, or observation of an interview conducted by a neophyte will show that there is more to these techniques than meets the eye.

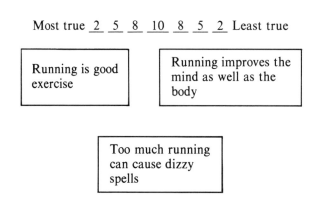

Figure 9.5. Example of a Q-Sort continuum.

*These techniques will be discussed in Chapter 11.

162

Questionnaires are information gathering devices in which a respondent answers specific questions. Sometimes a researcher will distribute questionnaires personally to the respondents, but more typically they are mailed. There are two major formats for questionnaires.

1. *Closed form.* In this format, questions are presented and a choice of possible answers is provided. For example, to determine a person's educational level, the item might read

How many years of schooling have you had? Circle one.

8, 9, 10, 11, 12, 13, 14, 15, 16, more than 16.

2. *Open form.* In this format, questions are presented and a space is provided for a written response. The same question as above might be used, for example

How many years of schooling have you had?

_____
_____

A closed form makes the tabulation of the responses much easier; the researcher merely tallies how many respondents gave which responses. However, the open form can reveal information not tapped by the closed form. For example, a respondent to the open form might have written, "Graduated from high school but learned radar in the Army," or "I dropped out of college in my 3rd year, and returned later. But I had to redo some courses at the sophomore level." Respondents with tales like this would have to circle a response if that is all that was presented, and valuable information would never surface. Some researchers prefer a combination of open and closed forms. For example

How many years of schooling have you had? Circle one.

8, 9, 10, 11, 12, 13, 14, 15, 16, more than 16

Comments _____

Closed form responses are tabulated from the responses circled. Open form responses are analyzed, categorized, and then tallied within the categories.

Interviews resemble questionnaires in their intent but can allow for a greater depth of response. Some interviews are highly *structured;* interviewers can follow a schedule, asking prepared, specific questions of a respondent. There is such uniformity in each interview that the technique might be best described as an oral questionnaire. On the other hand, *unstructured* interviews are much more flexible in their approach. After initial responses to interviewers' questions, interviewers can ask for clarification, follow-up, probe—they can shift gears as needed by the situation. Unstructured interviews closely resemble the techniques used by mental therapists in getting to understand their clients. Interview data on a number of respondents are often presented as tabulations in categories with sample comments to add clarity and flavor.

Direct Observation

Thus far in this section we have discussed tests, scales, questionnaires and interviews. All these instruments have one thing in common: they are applied directly to a subject who interacts with them. The last measurement type we shall consider, observation, does not usually interact with the subjects. Rather another person, a rater or observer, provides the data based on direct observation.

Checklists are sometimes used to facilitate the recording of observations. A checklist is a simple listing of possible observations. A check mark or tally can be made when a listed behavior is observed. For example, the following checklist could be used in observing the classroom behavior of a junior high student:

1. In seat: study behavior   _____

2. In seat: non-study behavior   _____

3. Out of seat: in motion   _____

4. Out of seat: talking to teacher _____

5. Out of seat: talking to classmate _____

6. Out of seat: other   _____

Since the behaviors observed are quite specific, there is little interpretation needed by the observers unless they seek to generalize from these data.

Rating scales are sometimes used to record a more general impression than a checklist offers. For example, an observer might note the behaviors described in the checklist above and record them like this:

How often does the student engage in study behavior?

Always   Usually   Occasionally   Seldom   Never

Behavioral diaries are narrative accounts of a subject's behavior. When several narratives have been recorded the researcher can compare them and note trends and tendencies which become the data for analysis.

Evaluating Measurements

In the previous section we described a variety of measurement instruments used in educational research. The scope of the research literature is sufficiently broad to allow for the use of each type at one time or another. The measurements derived from the application of these instruments form the data base from which all subsequent analyses, interpretations, and conclusions are made. It follows that the findings of a given research study can not be any better than its data base.

Producers of research sometimes appear to have a blind faith in the quality of their data— a faith which may or may not be justified when the measurement techniques and procedures are examined carefully. In this section, we shall take a careful look at the qualities of measurement instruments in general and the problems associated with their specific use.

The Qualities of Good Measurement Instruments

We have observed a great variety in the number and types of measuring instruments encountered in educational research. There is also a great range in the characteristics among instruments which purport to measure the same attributes. The better instruments possess certain qualities which are frequently absent from those instruments of lesser value. These qualities refer to the inference level needed for interpretation and the test's inherent assumptions.

Inference Level

A test yields data about an attribute; the data are gathered in a testing situation. In order to be useful, the test data must be interpreted in such a way as to provide meaningful information about the attribute as it exists outside of and independent of the testing situation. This requires an inference to be made—the researcher must infer a true description of the attribute from its measurement. Inference is not an either/or type of decision; rather it is a question of degree. Generally, the lower the level of inference needed to interpret the test data the better the test.

> IS THE LEVEL OF INFERENCE REQUIRED IN ORDER TO PROCEED FROM THE TEST DATA TO THE ATTRIBUTE SUFFICIENTLY LOW TO JUSTIFY A DESCRIPTION OF THE ATTRIBUTE?

We are constantly called upon to judge levels of inferences in our daily lives as we interpret information. For example, a consumer organization recently tested a small car and found it to be unacceptable because they found it to be inherently unstable. The procedure used in this test was to drive the car at a given speed, turn the wheel sharply, let go, and observe the car's response. Most other cars straighten themselves out shortly after the wheel is let go, but this model car gyrated back and forth several times. From this fact, the examiners concluded that the car was inherently unstable, hence dangerous, hence unacceptable, hence not recommended for purchase. The inference was that the measured behavior, gyration, demonstrates instability. However, the manufacturers of the car performed the same test with the same results but stated that the test was not a valid one because drivers do not act that way—turning the wheel sharply and letting go. Then later some owners of the car responded to the publicity by relating episodes in which precisely these events involved in the testing procedure happened to them in a real driving situation. The question is whether the test involved is sufficiently low in inference to warrant the conclusions made from the results. If the test had resulted in the car's overturning rather than merely gyrating, the inference of instability would be far less. The question is an old one: how much is enough? The potential consumer must consider it carefully.

In psychological measurement, potential mis-inferences abound, especially when dealing with pencil and paper attitude or personality measures. The reason why these measures often lack demonstrated validity is that they require high levels of inference. Items may or may not reflect what they are thought to. In order to deal with this problem, often direct observation of behavior is substituted for direct questioning, but this too can be highly inferential. For example, a pupil's self concept can be inferred from the number of times he looks at himself in the mirror; pupils with high self concepts look at themselves more often than pupils with low self concepts, it may be thought. But this interpretation assumes that a pupil looks in a mirror because he is proud of himself or of his appearance. He might be looking to see if a rash is clearing up or he might be looking out of idle curiosity or because he is bored. Thus, the number of times a person looks in a mirror could just as easily be interpreted as an index of self concern, insecurity or boredom as it could high self concept. To measure self concept by counting the number of times a pupil looks in the mirror assumes that looking in the mirror reveals a high self concept. The entire procedure begs the question. This type of observation for the purpose of determining self concept is highly inferential. Similarly, the observation of a man going to a baseball game with his son may indicate a love of baseball, a love of his son, a boredom with staying at home, all of these, none of these, or other motives.

Assumptions

Psychological measurements are based on implicit or explicit assumptions of which we should be aware.

ARE THE ASSUMPTIONS UPON WHICH A MEASUREMENT INSTRUMENT IS BASED REASONABLE?

A basic assumption in most standardized tests is that the attribute being measured is normally distributed, that is, the attribute in a population exists in the shape of a normal, bell shaped curve with most people in the middle and fewer and fewer at the ends of the distribution. The rationale for this assumption is that most readily observable attributes of people such as height or weight *are* distributed more or less normally. For example, the average height of the American adult male is 5′10″ and the further one gets from this height the fewer people there are at a given height. This can be demonstrated empirically by measuring the population with a commonly accepted valid device such as a ruler. The issue is whether psychological traits, especially those which reflect training such as school subject achievement, are also distributed normally. This may or may not be the case and the issue has at its foundation some basic ideas concerning human nature and its responsiveness to the environment. Whatever the case, the fact remains that the developers of many standardized tests *assume* that the attribute is normally distributed (whether it is or not) and accordingly construct the tests in such a way as to show this normal distribution. The degree to which this assumption is indeed a reality is one indication of the validity of the test.

This issue of the reasonableness of a test's assumptions is one which is philosophical in nature and may never be resolved. An even more fundamental problem is whether a given attribute or construct even exists. Is there such a thing as a "rigid" personality? A test of rigidity would assume so but is there other evidence of the existence of this attribute, or does it merely exist in the minds of those interested in describing personality? Questions of this sort are judgmental in nature and their answers effect the very essence of research studies in a given area.

In order to assess adequately the merit of a measuring instrument, one needs to have extensive knowledge about the attribute being measured and also the techniques of test construction. This information is beyond the ken of most research consumers but fortunately there is some help available. *The Mental Measurements Yearbooks* edited by the late Oscar Buros is a consumer reference source for virtually all published tests. The entries for each test are comprised mainly of reviews which include a description of the test and an assessment of its quality. The reviewers themselves are often well known authorities in their respective fields and in test development and their thoughts are very helpful to our deliberations. It should be noted though that the reviewers are not without biases. As individual human beings as well as scholars they bring their particular views to the test. When the test involves a construct such as intelligence, reading, self concept, or personality traits, we can expect the assessment of a test's validity to reflect the reviewer's biases.

If a test is not published then we need to examine the details of its construction as best we can. The developer of the test should provide information concerning theoretical background, item generation, item selection, field testing, and indices of validity and reliability. We may scrutinize this information with all we know about tests plus a good deal of common sense. If this information is not presented to us, then it is debatable whether the entire study should be taken seriously.

Assessing the Specific Use of a Test

A test may possess the qualities of low inference and reasonable assumptions mentioned in the previous section, but the mere presence of these qualities in a test do not necessarily mean that it will yield high quality data in a specific research situation. There are questions which are occasion-specific to which our attention should be drawn.

The Test and the Research Question

When researchers identify a research question, one of their major strategic decisions concerns the type of measurement they will utilize in their efforts to answer their research question. As we discussed earlier in Chapter Three there is often some room for a variety of divergent but acceptable procedures.

WAS THE MEASURING INSTRUMENT USED THE BEST WAY TO OBTAIN DATA RELEVANT TO THE PURPOSES OF THE STUDY?

Ultimately a decision is made to utilize one measurement procedure rather than others. As consumers of research we need to ask ourselves whether the use of the particular measurement procedure actually employed in the study was the *best* way of getting relevant data rather than the most convenient way. For example, a questionnaire may ask a person how he feels toward educational opportunity for minority children. A respondent may indicate one sentiment on the questionnaire, but his actions in a real situation may reveal something else. A questionnaire respondent may state that she does not drink, yet testimony from the liquor store clerk and examination of the garbage generated from her household may reveal another story. The major assumption involved in the use of questionnaires and other self-report instruments is that people tell the truth when they respond to them. The experience of this author is that some people do indeed tell the truth, some people do not consciously, some people do not unconsciously, while others have no idea what the truth is. Is the data generated by a self-report device valid? Without some corroborating evidence such as that gained through a validation study, the question is open. A sub-problem in this issue is whether the respondent to a self-report device takes the matter seriously. Some people consider such matters a waste of time and fill in anything in order to be done with the task. Others may be deluged with such devices and knock them off without even a modicum of thought.

Convenience of the researchers is but one reason for the specific use of a given measurement. Other factors discussed in Chapter Three such as the training and preexistent biases of the researchers may also influence their decisions on this issue.

Situational Validity

The key attribute of any measuring instrument is its validity. It must have a reasonable usefulness in describing the phenomenon to which it is applied. The type of validity—content, construct, or predictive—will depend upon the particular type of measure and its stated purpose. For example, achievement tests should have content validity; so should questionnaires and interviews. Aptitude tests, too, should have content validity but more importantly should have predictive validity since their purpose is to predict success on another task. Projective personality tests do not show content validity but should have construct validity since they seek to describe a construct, and they should have concurrent validity, that is, a high relationship with another source of measurement; unfortunately projective tests rarely show such validity.

IF A MEASUREMENT INSTRUMENT IS GENERALLY CONSIDERED VALID, WAS ITS USE IN THE SPECIFIC RESEARCH STUDY VALID?

The issue of the type of validity a test possesses is an important one for consumers of research to consider. As was discussed in the last chapter, it is the use of a test which is valid, strictly speaking, not merely the test itself. And the specific type of validity assessed by the validation procedure is determined by the anticipated use of the test. Occasionally we encounter misinterpretations of test results because the interpreters of the test results are seemingly not aware of the differences in the intended and appropriate use of the tests involved. For example, the recent decline in *Scholastic Aptitude Test* (SAT) scores has been interpreted by some as revealing a decline in the general level of achievement in high school students. This interpretation has set the stage for a critical attack on the entire American educational system, and a call for "Back to Basics." Perhaps our educational system deserves to be attacked— perhaps we should go "back to basics." But the SAT score decline is hardly a valid justification for this.

The SAT is an excellent instrument for predicting academic success in college. It has a high degree of predictive validity: it was validated specifically for use as a predictor of academic success. But to judge a level of curriculum achievement by observing the SAT scores is to ask the test to do something for which it was not intended. The SAT does not have sufficient content validity for the task. It was not constructed to reflect the overall curriculum which exists in our schools. Examination of its items will reveal this readily. Thus, to use the SAT for purposes of curriculum evaluation rather than its intended use as a predictor of collegiate success is inappropriate. The developers of the SAT know this and have stated it but the mininterpreters of social phenomena seem to conveniently ignore the issue.

Sensitivity Sufficiency

Measurement instruments vary in their ability to register change in a given attribute on their scales: they differ in their sensitivity. For instance, when measuring weight change in a 5 lb. baby, a typical household bathroom scale is not refined nor sensitive enough to show the changes of an ounce or two at a time. When small changes in measured psychological attributes are thought to have occurred, the instrument utilized ought to be sufficiently sensitive to show the change.

IS THE MEASUREMENT INSTRUMENT SUFFICIENTLY SENSITIVE TO MEASURE THE ATTRIBUTE OR A CHANGE IN THE ATTRIBUTE IF SUCH A CHANGE INDEED OCCURRED?

The exact nature of the specific attribute being measured needs to be considered carefully. For example, a skills oriented mathematics program might actually be effective, but its effectiveness might not register on a survey achievement test, whereas a diagnostic criterion referenced test might show a gain the survey test missed.

As another example in mathematics, an experimental study might seek to compare the effects of two types of mathematics instruction, one stressing conceptual understanding and computation, the other stressing just computation. A standardized, norm-referenced, mathematics survey test could be used as the dependent variable index. But if this test were to measure only computation and not conceptual understanding (as most such tests do), then its use in this study might be invalid, since it is not sensitive to changes in conceptual understanding. On the other hand, if a test *only* measured conceptual understanding it too might be invalid because it did not register changes in computation. The goals of instruction would need to dictate the type of test used in the study.

Another aspect of sensitivity concerns a procedure's ability to deal with the honesty or acceptability of a subject's responses, especially in attitude or personality measurement. For example, in a study of attitudes in a delicate area such as religion, a good interviewer can pose questions, probe when needed, and evaluate responses on the basis of what the subject said, how it was said, what he didn't say, and his body language during the interview. If a questionnaire was used, only the original questions would be answered. Even with attitude scales not all the beliefs of the subject are tapped as fully as might be by a good interviewer.

Appropriateness for Subjects

A given measurement instrument might work out fine when applied to one type of subject, but be completely inappropriate for other subjects.

IS THE MEASUREMENT INSTRUMENT APPROPRIATE FOR THE SPECIFIC SUBJECTS TO WHOM IT WAS APPLIED?

The issue of the appropriateness of an instrument breaks down into four related questions. 1) Could the subjects handle the test format; for example, if the test required subjects to read questions, did they have enough reading ability to accomplish the task? 2) Could the subjects handle the response mode; for example, if the test required them to write out answers, did they have the ability to do this? If a test required reading and the subjects could not read well, or if a test required writing and the subjects could not write well, then regardless of the ostensible content of the tests they were measuring reading and writing ability respectively. 3) Was the content fair for use with these particular subjects; for example, if a particular test measuring intelligence is comprised of information-type items which are typical of information encountered in a middle class WASP culture—then its content might not be suitable for subjects in minority groups who would not have had an opportunity to encounter such information. Such a test might show one result while the application of a culture fair test might show something else. And related to content-fairness is: 4) Are the norms (if any) reflective of the cultural and economic diversity of potential subjects? Were the type of subjects (for example, poor and rural or Spanish speaking-etc.) to which the instrument was applied included in the norming of the instrument?

Another issue in subject appropriateness concerns the problem of motivation. The validity of the score of a test is in part based upon the assumption that the subject taking the test is trying to do well. Observation of testing situations, particularly with school age children, shows a variety of degrees of motivation present. Some students approach the task diligently considering each item carefully. Others put down the first thing that comes into their heads. Still others delight in making clever patterns of pencil marks on the answer sheets, completely disregarding the test questions. Interestingly, some informal research on this matter has shown that a given group of pupils, when provided powerful extrinsic motivation, can score many, many months higher on a standardized test than they did a few weeks before when they took an alternate form without motivation. Another issue to consider is that for some subjects the consequences of a good performance on a test may not be desirable. Consider the child who does poorly on a reading test so he can stay in the same reading group with his friends. Witness the young man who does everything he can to flunk his physical in order to avoid being drafted for military service.

Special problems often develop when young children are used as subjects. For example, in a study in which a sociogram technique was used with elementary age children, the children were asked to write the names of the three classmates they would most like to have at a party they were giving. The teacher, who was administering the sociogram, noted that one girl had not invited her best friend. When the teacher asked the girl why, she responded embarrassingly, "I don't know how to spell her name." When a class roster was provided to all pupils this problem was solved. It is interesting to speculate what kinds of profound and momentous decisions have been made about children based on immense measurement error which could have been corrected by a careful monitoring of an instrument's administration.

Administration of Instrument

Even if all prior questions dealing with the occasion-specificity of the use of an instrument were answered favorably, there is still one more issue we need to consider: the person who administered the instrument.

WAS THE MEASUREMENT INSTRUMENT ADMINISTERED PROPERLY?

Administering a test is a seemingly easy task to accomplish, but there are many pitfalls that lie awaiting the naive and uninitiated. One question to be asked is whether the person administering the instrument was qualified. Had he done this before? Was he trained? Was he certified? In the administration of a standardized group test this point is not absolutely crucial, but in the case of an interview or an individual intelligence or personality test it is of the utmost importance. Another question concerns the events just prior to the application of the instrument. Was the subject's interest aroused? Did the examiner motivate the subjects? Did she establish rapport? And a third question relates to the test-taking abilities of the subject. Was the test format—stimulus presentation and response mode—new to the subject? If so, was sufficient practice given to make the subject comfortable with the test format? *Was the subject doing it right?* For example, in a cloze test a subject is asked to fill in deleted words in a text. The purpose of the test is to measure a subject's ability to predict words from context. The scoring procedures of most cloze tests require that only the exact word which appeared in the original text before deletion be scored as correct. Frequently, some subjects of elementary school age misunderstand the nature of the task and rather than predict the original word as instructed, write in the most imaginative word that could fit in that context. If an examiner had provided some practice and had checked to see that the subjects were indeed accomplishing their assigned task, then a gross error of this sort could be avoided and the measurements made more valid.

Reliability

All measurement instruments should have a demonstrated reliability. Without this quality we may never know how accurately we are measuring something. A consequence of inaccuracy is a lessening of validity which may lead to an increase in the tentativeness of any research findings. The determination of standards of reliability is somewhat easier than the assessment of validity because with reliability we have quantified indices—coefficients of correlation—to deal with rather than logical/philosophical issues. Yet there are elements of judgment involved. One needs first to determine the purpose for which a test is administered. If a test is used in basic research then reliability indices (expressed as correlation coefficients) of .50 to .70 would probably be sufficient, assuming that they are significantly different from zero correlation. To insist on higher correlations may be a waste of resources. On the other hand, in applied research situations correlations of .70 to .90 are usually necessary. This is especially true when important judgments are to be made on the basis of a cutoff point in a distribution of scores. For example, if a decision concerning admission into a training program depends upon a person having a score of 60 on an examination, then we ought to be sure that a score of 59 is not really a score of 60 in disguise, that is, there should be very little measurement error. If an IQ score of 75 is the borderline between assignment to a regular class and a class for the mentally retarded then very little measurement error can be tolerated; a reliability index of over .90 would be necessary.

A matter related to reliability concerns the time sampling of a test when the test is applied to one person rather than to a group. Is one administration of a test sufficient to form a judgment about one person? A number of years ago, William F. Buckley ran for mayor of New York City. When asked what he would do if elected, he replied, "Demand a recount." A few years ago, the present author had a blood chemistry test performed which revealed a high level of uric acid. When he asked his doctor what to do about it, the doctor suggested that before medication could be prescribed the test should be repeated in a few weeks. It turned out that Buckley was not elected and the author's high uric acid count showed the same level when the blood was tested again. The point is that some occasions can trigger physical, emotional and/or intellectual responses which can make test scores spuriously high or low. One administration of a test may not be enough to make an accurate assessment.

Special Problems of Questionnaires

The assessment of questionnaires requires our special consideration. They differ from most other instruments in two special ways: 1) They are usually occasion-specific, that is, a questionnaire is typically developed for a specific research study and is used only in that study. Consequently, there are few rigorously developed, standardized questionnaires in existence. 2) The respondents are usually well out of range of the questionnaire developer; typically the questionnaires are distributed by mail. As a result, there is no one to answer any of the respondent's questions about the instrument.

The development of a questionnaire appears to be a childishly simple chore: you ask a question and you get an answer. Simple. If you know the intent of a questionnaire item you know what the answer should be—a developer knows both. But the respondent to the item knows only the item, and if the item is *ambiguous* his response may not be accurate. For example, an open form item could read "Where do you live?" This could be answered in many ways by the same person: in a house, in New York on a quiet street, in a nice neighborhood, in a disco joint on Saturday night. This item may not seem ambiguous to the developer because he knows the intent of the item: to determine the city of residence. The item might read "In what city do you live?" and the response would be "in New York." But how about the person who is living temporarily in another location? A better item would read, "In what city are you now living?" Still other changes may need to be made to account for people who do not live in cities.

Even the matter of determining a person's age is laden with potential problems. An item might read "Age _____." A nine year old might give you his "going on" age: ten. A forty year old might give you an age of thirty-nine. Some people will only respond to this query if given an age range to choose from: 20–29, 30–39, 40 or over.

Sometimes closed forms do not allow enough choices for all people. For example, consider the following item:

Religious preference:

_____ Catholic

_____ Jewish

_____ Protestant

Where does a Buddhist respond? Or an atheist? This item needs two more choices: 1) _____ Other: _____ where a subject can indicate another and 2) _____ None.

Sometimes terms do not mean the same things to different people or sometimes people use different terms for the same thing. This author once assisted some researchers who had developed and administered a questionnaire surveying kindergarten facilities, philosophies and programs. One item asked, "Does your school have a step up room?" The responses to this item were quite removed from reality—indeed half the respondents left it blank. It turned out that in many sections of the geographical area surveyed this room (which incidentally is used for pupils who need another year of pre-first grade experience) is called a transition room. In all probability, many respondents did not know what the item was referring to.

The ambiguity of questionnaire items is a very serious matter because usually there is no one to answer a respondent's questions in cases of ambiguities. For this reason, a questionnaire should be field tested in order that the ambiguities be identified and omitted. Moreover the field testing should be done with a sample of the respondent population. The author had occasion to witness a "field testing" of a questionnaire which was developed by a professor done by other professors. There were no real problems in ambiguity because the developer and those who participated in the field testing spoke the same language, shared the same beliefs, and had had similar background experiences. But when the questionnaire was mailed to a teacher population, it was a disaster. Subsequent investigation revealed that the teachers applied substantially different meanings to words in some items.

The validity of questionnaires is often *assumed* rather than verified because its content is obvious; but content validity alone is not sufficient. There should be an external criterion used to establish concurrent validity. For example, in the development phase a questionnaire could be sent to a sample of respondents who would be interviewed somewhat later using the same items as the questionnaire. A correlation between the responses of the questionnaire and the interviews would be an index of concurrent validity. If a questionnaire seeks to elicit observable data, then a high correlation between the questionnaire responses and an actual on-site observation would indicate concurrent validity. Reliability, too, needs assessment but is often ignored. A test-retest procedure is easy enough to accomplish and would give a good indication of the stability of the instrument.

A major problem concerning the use of mailed questionnaires is the rate of return. Many people receive questionnaires in the mail and throw them away summarily, others procrastinate and never get around to mailing them back. Researchers often make valiant follow-up efforts to increase the return rate, but often the efforts have negligible effects. As a result, return rates of 20–30% are not uncommon in research utilizing questionnaires. The problem is ultimately one of external validity: how does one interpret the findings? For example, a population of 1,000 junior high school language arts teachers could be identified and a random sample of 150 selected from it. A mailed questionnaire to the 150 teachers yielded a return of 40 questionnaires, 27%. After tabulating the responses, the researchers can not say that the responses reflect the opinions of the original population of 1,000. If all 150 of the sample had responded, then they could. But those who actually did respond are merely a sample of the 150, and *not* a random sample. They can not logically generalize to the larger population. All that can be reported is, "Of those responding to the questionnaire, n or % stated. . . ." Or as they now say on television commercials, "Nine out of ten doctors *who participated in our survey* chose Brand X. . . ." Return rates on questionnaire mailings should be noted carefully. There are no standards to guide us but in general the lower the return rate the less confidence we can have that the returned questionnaires represent adequate data.

Summary

The range of measuring instruments used in educational research is quite large. *Psychological tests* are frequently encountered. These tests pose questions or provide tasks to a subject whose responses are scored. The tests include survey and diagnostic tests which may be standardized or informal, and which may be interpreted by reference to a norming group or to another external criterion. Psychological tests includes tests of achievement, intelligence, aptitude and personality.

Attitude scales provide a stimulus question or statement to a subject whose response reveals an attitude about something. Methods of attitude scaling include Likert, Thurston, Guttman and Semantic Differential scales and the Q Methodology. *Questionnaires, interviews* and *direct observation* are other methods of obtaining data from a subject.

Consumers of research need to evaluate carefully the measurement instruments used in the research they encounter. The instruments should have a low level of inference needed to proceed from the data obtained to the actual accurate description of the attribute being measured. In addition, the assumptions upon which a given instrument is based should be reasonable. These issues should be considered in relation to any given instrument regardless of its use.

The validity of a given test, however, needs also to be considered with regard to its use in a specific research situation. The use of the instrument should be shown to be the best way to generate the data needed to answer the research question. The determination of its validity when developed should coincide with its use as applied to the specific research occasion. It should be sensitive enough to register a measurement or change of measurement of the attribute; it should be appropriate for the subjects, and it should be administered correctly and carefully. Finally, it should have sufficient reliability for its purpose.

Questionnaires have special problems caused by item ambiguity and inappropriate format. Low response rates cause further problems in interpretation.

The following questions need to be asked by consumers of research when they encounter measuring instruments.

IS THE LEVEL OF INFERENCE REQUIRED IN ORDER TO PROCEED FROM THE DATA TO THE ATTRIBUTE SUFFICIENTLY LOW TO JUSTIFY A DESCRIPTION OF THE ATTRIBUTE?

ARE THE ASSUMPTIONS UPON WHICH A MEASUREMENT INSTRUMENT IS BASED REASONABLE?

WAS THE MEASUREMENT INSTRUMENT USED THE BEST WAY TO OBTAIN DATA RELEVANT TO THE PURPOSES OF THE STUDY?

IF A MEASUREMENT INSTRUMENT IS GENERALLY CONSIDERED VALID, IS ITS USE IN THE SPECIFIC RESEARCH STUDY VALID?

IS THE MEASUREMENT INSTRUMENT SUFFICIENTLY SENSITIVE TO MEASURE THE ATTRIBUTE OR A CHANGE IN THE ATTRIBUTE IF A CHANGE INDEED OCCURRED?

IS THE MEASUREMENT INSTRUMENT APPROPRIATE FOR THE SPECIFIC SUBJECTS TO WHOM IT WAS APPLIED?

WAS THE MEASUREMENT INSTRUMENT ADMINISTERED PROPERLY?

Further Readings for Chapters 8 and 9

Cronbach, Lee J. *Essentials of Psychological Testing*. New York: Harper and Row, 1969.
> This is a complete and excellent survey of the entire field of psychological testing. Many widely used tests are presented and discussed in great detail.

Edward, Allen I. *Techniques of Attitude Scale Construction*. New York: Appleton-Century-Croft, 1957.
> This is a classic text in attitude scale measurement. Chapters 4, 6, and 7 deal with the Thurstone, Guttman and Likert procedures in some detail.

Hopkins, Charles and Antes, Richard. *Classroom Measurement and Evaluation*. Itasca, Illinois: Peacock, 1978.
> This is an excellent overall text on applied measurement. It is highly readable and very inclusive.

Murstein, Bernard I. (ed.) *Handbook of Projective Techniques*. New York: Basic Books, 1965.
> This is a comprehensive collection of articles on projective techniques. Following a section on theory and general matters are sections containing numerous articles on Rorschach, Thematic, Draw-a-Person, Bender-Gestalt, and Sentence Completion Test.

Nunnally, Jum. *Psychometric Theory*. New York: McGraw-Hill, 1967.
> The chapters on reliability and validity will extend the concepts presented in this chapter. Part Four deals with the theoretical aspects of most of the measuring devices discussed.

Osgood, C. E., Suci, G. J., and Tannenbaum, P. N. *The Measurement of Meaning*. Urbana Illinois: University of Illinois Press, 1957.
> This is the basic source for extending knowledge about the semantic differential technique.

Stephenson, William. *The Study of Behavior: A Technique and its Methodology*. Chicago: University of Chicago Press, 1953.
> This is the basic source for information about the Q technique.

Tyler, Leona E. *Tests and Measurements* (2nd ed.). Englewood Cliffs: Prentice Hall, 1971.
> This is a short, highly readable, and concise treatment of the topic.

Part Five
The Analysis of Data

Author's comment:

Arnold Palmer has called the golf shot taken in a sand trap "the easiest shot in golf." For some reason, though, I have trouble with it—I do much better with short irons as I approach the green. Perhaps this is an idiosyncracy of mine. Or perhaps Palmer is just trying to bolster my confidence. Similarly, researchers and statisticians often comment that data analysis is not difficult. They too may be trying to bolster the confidence of neophytes in research. An alternate explanation is that Palmer and the statisticians are telling it the way that they see it, and that they are right. In any case, the fact remains that most readers of this book will be uncomfortable with the thought of learning about how data are analyzed—indeed some will be terrified. I am here to tell you not to worry. If you have understood the contents of this book so far, you should have no problem with this section. I have tried to present data analysis in these two chapters in a manner which I believe is consistent with the intent of this book: a focus on the understanding of the results of data analyzed by others. There is no computation involved, and there are no formulae presented except when needed to help explain a concept.

Chapter 10 presents statistical techniques used to describe data. I have organized these techniques according to what questions about the data they answer. Chapter 11 presents inferential statistical techniques, introduces non-parametric procedures, and contains a special section dealing with techniques used in summarizing research. The content of these chapters represents the mainstream thinking of researchers and statisticians in education. You should be aware however, that there are other points of view regarding the content of these chapters. I have chosen not to include a full treatment of these matters in order to keep the presentation brief. I have tried to keep the narrative moving along by being direct and to the point while still providing sufficient background and numerous examples to clarify things. Three appendices to this text contain further information which may be of help to you. One appendix, a glossary of symbols, should prove valuable to you as a quick reference and review; another deals with some infrequently encountered non-parametric procedures. A third appendix presents a discussion of multivariate statistical procedures—factor analysis and the like. You may run into a study using these techniques from time to time.

Chapter 10

The Analysis and Interpretation of Data: I

Researchers conduct studies in order to find answers to questions they pose. They set up procedures for the collection of information which is relevant to their research questions; these procedures are called the *designs* of their study. The information they collect is referred to as *data*. Data come in many forms: test scores, opinions, ratings, frequencies and the like. But in whatever form the data are originally generated, typically they have little value to the researchers until they have been organized, summarized, and analyzed so as to yield information in a form appropriate to the specific research problem being dealt with. The techniques involved in the analysis of data range from very simple to very complex. Researchers try to select the most powerful techniques suited to the type of data they have obtained and which will provide them with the information they need to answer the research questions.

Data come in two basic forms: *qualitative* and *quantitative*. Qualitative data, sometimes referred to as *soft data,* are usually verbal; they may be expressions of opinions, beliefs, or feelings. Quantitative data, sometimes referred to as *hard data* are usually in numerical form such as test scores, frequency counts, ratings, etc. The terms "hard" and "soft" used to describe quantitative and qualitative data respectively may be somewhat misleading. Many people have a tendency to attach a pejorative connotation to the term "soft" data. This is unfortunate because increasingly nowadays the value of qualitive data is being recognized as being more appropriate than quantitative data for some research questions. This is especially true in evaluation research.

The analysis of small amounts of qualitative data is straightforward and requires little in the way of sophisticated techniques. Usually, these data are presented in their original form perhaps with comment by the researchers. However, when the amount of these data becomes quite large then the data need to be grouped somehow in order to be presented effectively to the reader. When this happens the techniques associated with quantitative analysis are used. The grouping has in effect transformed the data from qualitative to quantitative. This transformation caused the data to lose some of its flavor but a simplicity of presentation is gained.

When qualitative data are left in their orginal form when presented and analyzed in a research study, readers of research will find few if any, new or unusual techniques which might interfere with their comprehension. But when they are quantified, or when quantitative data are presented with or without analysis, the methods of description and analysis actually utilized can be quite technical in nature. The remainder of this chapter and the next one present these techniques so readers of research will understand and appreciate most of the frequently used methods employed by researchers.

Statistics

Quantitative data is analyzed through use of a body of procedures called *statistics*. The term, statistics, is also used in its singular form to indicate the result of a particular procedure: for example, we refer to a correlation coefficient of .78 as a *statistic*. Statistics provides a way for researchers to treat data in a systematic way. It helps them answer questions about data in a concise manner. Specifically, statistics helps them *describe* and *infer* and these two activities lend their names to the two major kinds of statistics: *descriptive* and *inferential*.

There are five attributes of data which are typically described by statistics:

I. *Distribution:* How are the data distributed over the data source? How many got what scores?

II. *Central tendency:* Where do the data tend to gather? What is a typical score?

III. *Dispersion:* To what extent are the data spread out? How far from average are all the scores?

IV. *Relative position:* How do the data compare to one another? Who got the higher or lower scores?

V. *Relationships:* How do these data compare with other data on the same data sources. What relationship do these scores have with the group's other scores?

The procedures used to describe these attributes of data will be presented in this chapter. The techniques of *inferential statistics* allow researchers to infer characteristics of a large unexamined group of subjects from a small examined group. These procedures allow for generalizations to be made. A portion of the next chapter is devoted to an explanation of these procedures.

A word about statistics and mathematics: they are not the same but they are related. Statistics is an applied branch of mathematics. It represents one application of mathematics to the needs of the real world. From the viewpoint of the consumer of research however, statistics and mathematics are related only in that they both use numbers to express properties. The same could be said for accounting and mathematics. This chapter will not be concerned with the mathematical derivation of statistical procedures. Nor will it deal with matters of computation. Rather it will seek to develop a knowledge and background in the readers which will enable them to read research and understand its message.

Descriptive Statistics

Descriptive statistics are used to describe large bodies of data in summary form with regard to their inherent characteristics. A knowledge of descriptive statistics enables us to read a few symbols and understand what a body of data would look like in its original form. In presenting this section dealing with descriptive statistics we shall treat each type of description from the point of view of what attribute of the data it describes.

HOW COMPLETE AND APPROPRIATE IS THE DESCRIPTION OF THE DATA?

Data can come from a variety of sources which were subjected to a measurement process. The measurements obtained may be ratings, frequencies, scores or any other measurements. Most measurements may be subsumed under the term *scores* and accordingly for purposes of examples used in this discussion the term *scores* will be used to indicate the data being described. Also, data sources could be people or objects; for simplicity and uniformity all data sources will be referred to as subjects.

Attribute I: Distribution
How are the data distributed over the data source?

When measurements are taken on subjects, the researchers' first task is to arrange them in some orderly fashion so they may easily make some observations and summary statements about them. Usually they receive the data in the form presented in table 10.1. This is an unorganized listing of subjects and raw scores on three variables: X, Y, and Z. For the moment let us observe the first column which contains the names of the subjects, and the second column which contains the raw scores for variable X.

There are several ways of organizing these data. If researchers are going to derive summary statistics from the data, a *frequency distribution* will serve them well. A frequency distribution of some of the data in table 10.1 is presented in table 10.2. All possible scores on the X variable in table 10.1 from highest to lowest are shown in the left hand column in table 10.2. The middle column is used to tally the scores as they are taken from the unorganized listing in table 10.1; the frequency count in the right column is derived directly from the tallies in the center column. This organization scheme shows quickly the *frequency* with which all scores are *distributed* on the

Table 10.1. Raw Scores of 25 Subjects

Subjects	Variables		
	X	Y	Z
Tom	34	42	47
Dorothy	29	31	57
Ed	35	41	42
Ken	26	33	65
Linda	35	43	48
Don	28	28	58
Yetta	25	32	65
Fred	31	35	49
Inta	29	37	63
Mildred	23	20	59
Ted	26	32	58
Sandy	21	28	63
Bernie	30	38	45
Van	29	36	60
Mary	26	29	43
Nita	29	27	45
Judy	20	28	68
Vivian	27	26	62
Dave	33	39	42
Susan	21	28	53
Lelon	31	32	44
Larry	24	23	45
Conrad	31	36	44
Cathy	29	30	59
Karen	27	27	50

Table 10.2. Frequency Distribution of Variable X

Scores	Tally	Frequency
35	//	2
34	/	1
33	/	1
32	/	1
31	///	3
30	/	1
29	ʬ	5
28	/	1
27	//	2
26	///	3
25	/	1
24	/	1
23	/	1
22		0
21	/	1
20	/	1
		N = 25

continuum of possible scores from 35 to 20: hence, its name: a *frequency distribtuion*. The researchers may now proceed to develop other analyses of these data using the frequency distribution as a working source.

Sometimes it is convenient to transform a frequency distribtion into a graphic representation of the data. Two such common forms are a *histogram* (bar graph) and a *polygon* (line graph). Samples of these two graphs based on the data from table 10.2 are presented in figure 10.1 and 10.2. In both graphs, the score points are laid out on the horizontal axis (abscissa) and the frequencies are indicated on the vertical axis (ordinate). This type of presentation of data is often used by researchers when presenting data to lay audiences and/or when a brief, general view of the distribution is needed. Readers of research should be aware however that the transference of

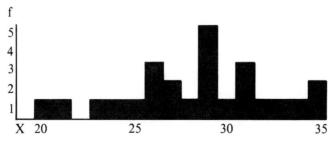

Figure 10.1. A histogram.

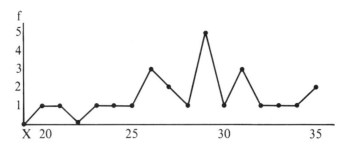

Figure 10.2. A frequency polygon.

data from a frequency distribution to a graphic representation can, and sometimes is done in such a way as to distort the data and leave an erroneous impression with the reader. The specific technique of graphic misrepresentation will be discussed in some detail in a subsequent chapter.

Attribute II: Central Tendency
Where do the data tend to gather?

An important question about a set of data concerns its central tendency. What is the average score, or what is a typical score, or what score did most people get? Each of these questions addresses the issue of central tendency.

Researchers may inspect the frequency distribution, histogram or polygon to determine which score most people got. Figure 10.1 shows that the score of 29 is found to be the most frequent score. This is called the *mode* of the distribution and is the simplest measure of central tendency to derive. When used in a research report the term mode may be spelled out or abbreviated *Md*.

Another useful measure of central tendency is the *median* (sometimes abbreviated *Mdn*). This is derived by finding the midpoint in the number of people represented in a distribution and noting the score that that person had. In the distribution in table 10.2, the scores of twenty-five subjects are listed. The median is the score associated with the thirteenth person. In this case that score is 29.*

The most useful and most used statistic to describe central tendency is the *mean* (usually abbreviated M or $\bar{X}$). This is the arithmetic average determined by adding up all scores and dividing by the number of subjects in the distribution. In the case of the data in table 10.2, the mean is 27.96.

You will note that the three indices of central tendency derived from the distribution in table 10.2—mode, median, and mean, 29, 29 (or 28.3), and 27.96 respectively—are quite close together. Indeed one could be substituted for the others with little loss of accuracy. This phenomenon occurs when the statistics are derived from a fairly symmetrical distribution. Observation of figures 10.1 or 10.2 show the highest point at score 29 is near the center, and then to the right and left of this point the configurations seem fairly similar: high points at 26 and 31 and fairly smooth otherwise. This distribution approaches the shape of the *normal curve* discussed extensively in Chapter 4. The more a distribution approaches the shape of the theoretical normal curve, the closer the mode, median and mean become. Indeed, in a perfect normal curve these three indices are identical.

---

*Actually the median is 28.3. This is because in the actual computation of the median, significance is given to the fact that one person below the thirteenth and three people above the thirteenth got the same score of 29.

The shape of a distribution will determine the relationship between these indices. Figure 10.3 shows a *normal curve* with a mode, median and mean at the same point. Figures 10.4 and 10.5 are *skewed*. Skewed means stretched. A distribution is said to be *negatively skewed* if it is stretched towards the negative end of the abscissa. This would be caused by the existence of a few very low scores in a distribution. Figure 10.4 shows a *negatively skewed distribution*. In this distribution the mean is lowered because of these low scores at the negative end of the abscissa. If five low scores (say 7, 8, 8, 12, 13) were added to the distribution shown in table 10.2 it would be negatively skewed.

In a similar manner, a distribution is said to be *positively skewed* if it is stretched toward the high or positive side of a distribution. This would be caused by the existence of a few very high scores. Figure 10.5 shows a positively skewed distribution. Here, the mean is raised as these high scores affect its computation. If five high scores (say 43, 44, 49, 52, 57) were added to the distribution in table 10.2 it too would be positively skewed.

With this information about the causes of skewedness and the effect of these causes on the central tendency indices, and with additional information about the dispersion of the scores to be

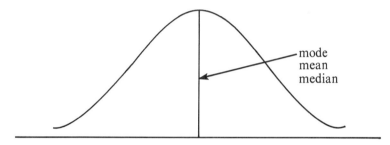

Figure 10.3. A normal distribution.

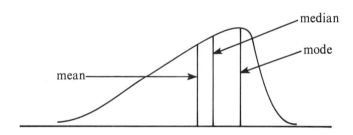

Figure 10.4. A negatively skewed distribution.

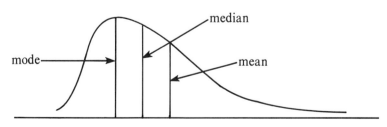

Figure 10.5. A positively skewed distribution.

discussed next, one can visualize the skewedness of a distribution from examination of the differences between the measures of central tendency.

Which of these indices is the most appropriate to use? That depends on two factors: the number of scores involved and the characteristics of the data.

If there are few scores involved, the median will probably describe the central tendency best. Note this distribution

2, 3, 5, 7, 8, 10, 12

The median is 7. The mean is 6.7. There is no mode. Either statistic is acceptable; each shows the middle of the distribution. But suppose a score of 48 is added to the distribution. The median would become 7.5 but the mean would leap to 11.8. This mean is higher than all but two scores; its tendency is not central. The addition of that one high score to only seven other scores has a negligible effect on the median but a strong effect on the mean. Hence, the median is a better statistic to use in a small distribution: it is more stable.

However, if researchers are working with a large distribution, examination of the characteristics of the data will help their decision as to which statistic should be used. You will recall our previous discussion of types of quantitative data—nominal, ordinal, interval (continuous) and ratio. The type of data being described can determine the best descriptive technique. For example, let us take three attributes of men aged 21–49 in Fort Wayne, Indiana: their height, monetary income, and hat sizes. Height is a continuous variable and probably is normally distributed over the population. For height the mean would be the most appropriate index. Monetary income, too, is continuous but probably not normally distributed. For one thing, there is a zero point on the income continuum—it is possible to earn nothing. Then there are some people who have a subsistence level income of less than $5,000. Then there are most people who work and earn $7,000–30,000 per year. But there are lots of people who through high paying positions, investments or inheritances earn from $50,000 to several hundred thousand or more per year. Their income might be distributed as shown in figure 10.6. You will note that the distribution is very positively skewed. Those subjects represented on the far right side of this distribution are responsible for this skewedness. Now, a *mean* income would *not* accurately reflect the midpoint of this distribution. A median however would be much less influenced by the high income group and accordingly is the better choice. Also, the fact that some people in the distribution have zero income causes some additional computational problems when the mean is used.

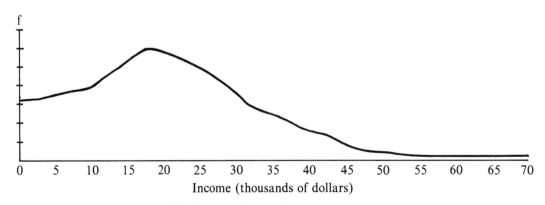

Figure 10.6. Example of a distribution of monetary income.

The hat sizes of our population are probably equally distributed but they are not continuous data—rather they are discrete. A mean hat size might be computed to be 7.43. Unfortunately, hats do not come in that size, you have your choice of 7⅜ or 7½, but not 7.43, so a mean hat size is not helpful. The mode would be a better index of central tendency than the mean in this case. There is a tendency for data to be subjected to the mean, arithmetic averaging, process whether it is appropriate or not. This is something for which research consumers must be on guard. The point is nicely illustrated by the story about the fellow who had one foot immersed in boiling water and the other in ice water. When asked if he was comfortable he replied, "I feel fine on the average."

Sometimes a mode needs to be considered along with a mean in order for an accurate representation of data to be rendered. For example, suppose data were to be gathered on how late a sample of thirty clients show up for their counseling sessions. The data are summarized in table 10.3 below.

Now, there are several ways in which these data may be summarized and reported:

a. One might say that "the average client was late five minutes"; (150 client-minutes divided by 30 clients).

b. One might say that "of the clients who come late, the average lateness is ten minutes" (150 client-minutes divided by the 15 clients who come late.

Neither of these statements tells the whole story. A better description of the data would indicate the mode as well as the mean: "Half the clients did not come late; of the remaining half the average lateness was ten minutes." Reporting of the modal data is easily overlooked in descriptive statistics, and if the mode is zero the mere reporting of the mean is misleading.

Thus, we see that although there are three indices of central tendency, researchers must take care to choose the one or ones which most accurately reflect the nature of the data. The choice of statistic used should depend upon the type of data, the amount of data, and the shape of the distribution. The consumer of research needs to evaluate the statistic used in terms of its appropriateness in a given situation and must judge this appropriateness by looking for gross violations rather than fine differences.

Table 10.3. Lateness of Clients for Counseling Sessions

Number of Clients	Lateness (minutes)	Lateness in client-minutes
15	0	0
7	5	35
3	10	30
3	15	45
2	20	40
N = 30		150

Attribute III: Dispersion
To what extent are the data spread out?

In the previous section, we saw how researchers would describe a distribution in terms of its central tendency. They would present the information to us with a mean, median, or mode depending on the type of data and type of distribution. This is helpful in informing us of the nature of the distribution but it alone is not enough; central tendency is but one dimension—we need to know more; we need a fuller description than just where scores gather.

Suppose a friend wanted to describe to you the shape of a person. He told you that this person, a man, was 6 feet tall. How well could you visualize the man to whom he was referring? You know but one dimension: his height. In order to visualize him you will need to know his weight, too. This might be anywhere from, say 125 lbs. to 350 lbs. With this additional information you would know another dimension of his size and could visualize him better.

In describing a distribution of scores, we are faced with the same problem. Suppose a distribution of scores was described to you as having a mean of 10. This is not enough information. Observe the following four distributions, f_1, f_2, f_3 and f_4 in table 10.4.

Table 10.4. Four frequency distributions

X	f_1	f_2	f_3	f_4
14	1	10		1
13	1			
12	2			
11	3		5	5
10	6		10	8
9	3		5	5
8	2			
7	1			
6	1	10		1
N	20	20	20	20
Mean	10	10	10	10
SD	1.89	4	.7	1.44
Range	9	9	3	9

Each distribution has a mean of 10 and an N of 20 yet they are hardly alike, any more than a 6 foot, 125 lb. man is like a 6 foot, 350 lb. man. The description must tell you more than the central tendency of the distribution; it must also tell you how the scores differ from one another. This information is referred to as the *dispersion* of the scores. The scores of f_1 are widely dispersed, they range from 6 to 14. The scores in f_2 are also widely dispersed; they range from 6 to 14 but in a different way; f_1 is a fairly normal distribution, and f_2 is *bimodal* (it has two modes; 14 and 6). The scorees in f_3 are not dispersed very much; they all collect near the center of the distribution. And the scores in f_4 are different yet; they resemble aspects of both f_1 and f_3.

Well, how can the dispersion of the scores in these distributions be described. There are several ways, each way with its own special characteristics.

1. *Range.* The dispersion of the scores can be described in terms of the outer limits of the distribution, that is, the highest and lowest scores. The f_1 distribution has a range of 6 to 14. Note that the range of the scores from 6 to 14 is not 8 but 9. This is because the scores are counted inclusively rather than by subtracting the smaller from the larger. That helps the description.

Unfortunately, f_2 and f_4 have the same range, 6 to 14. The range of f_3 however is quite different from either of these; its range is 3—from 9 to 11.

The range is a useful statistic but its main shortcoming is that one unusual score can distort it very greatly. Imagine, if one subject in f_3 got a score of 6. The range of f_3 would then change from 9 to 11, to 6 to 11, just as a result of that one subject's score. One method researchers use to avoid the effect of a few widely disparate scores is to divide the distribution up into quarters based on frequencies and then report the range of the inner two quarters (the middle half). This is referred to as the *interquartile range*. In the f_1 distribution the interquartile range is 9–11. Another still more restricted range is had by dividing the interquartile range in half so it represents the range of the middle quarter (the middle half of the middle half) of the distribution. This is known as the *semi-interquartile range*.

The problem with these refinements of the range statistic is that although they do not let extreme scores distort them, they do so at the cost of ignoring them completely. Fortunately there is a statistic which can be used to indicate how dispersed the scores are in general when considering the entire distribution, and also allow us to estimate the range by some calculations. This statistic is called the *standard deviation* (abbreviated SD, S, or σ) and it is the most useful of all measures of dispersion. It allows us entry into understanding sampling theory, standard scores, use of the normal curve, measurement error, and inferential statistics. In short, it is the basis for much of what statistics is all about. So, lets try to develop some understanding of this standard deviation.

2. *The standard deviation.* The dispersion of scores in a distribution can be described by the *standard deviation* (SD). This statistic is a improvement over the *range* because in its computation it considers every score in the distribution. In essence, each score is considered in relation to how far it deviates from the mean of the distribution. Then through a mathematical process of squaring and averaging the SD is computed. The most significant aspect of the computation of the SD is that it is done by considering each score in relation to the mean. And when presented along with the mean, the SD can give an excellent description of a distribution.

Now, let's take another look at the three distributions in table 10.4. You will recall that each of these distributions had a mean of 10 and an N of 20. Distribution f_1 has an SD of 1.89 and distribution f_3 has a SD of .7. According to our definition, the SD is based on each score's deviation from the mean and since f_1 has more scores further away from the mean than f_3 does, we can expect the SD of f_1 to be larger. And that is exactly the case. The SD will in most cases vary with the range: the larger the range the larger the SD. In fact the SD may be *estimated* from the range and vice versa using these simple formulas. This is valuable to know in case we are presented with an incomplete description of a distribution.

    a. For symmetrical distribution with large Ns (over 100)
        SD = 1/5 to 1/6 of the range.
    b. For symmetrical distributions with small Ns (15–20)
        SD = 1/4 to 1/5 of the range.

Thus, in our examples an *estimate* of the SD in f_1 might be 1/5 of the range (which is 9). That works out to be 1.80. The actual computed SD was 1.89. Not bad! For f_3 the estimate of the SD might be 1/5 of 3, which works out to be .6. Again, not bad as compared to the computed SD of .7.

One can estimate the range from the SD by reversing the formulas.

    c. For symmetrical distributions with large Ns (over 100)
        Range = 5–6 SD

d. For symmetrical distributions with small Ns (15–20)
   Range = 4–5 SD

Using this formula, based on an SD of 1.89 the estimated range for f_1 is 9.45, the actual range is 9. The estimated range for f_3, based on an SD of .7 is 3.5, the actual range is 3. (The rationale for these handy formulas may be noted by reviewing our discussion of the normal curve presented in chapter 4. You will recall that a normal curve may be divided into approximately six SDs).

So far, we have seen how the SD describes the dispersion of scores on both f_1 and f_3. But how about f_2 and f_4? When computed, the SD for f_2 works out to 4. This would seem to indicate that the scores in f_2 are much more widely dispersed than the scores in f_1 whose SD is 1.89. Is this the case however? Inspection of table 10.4 shows the range of f_2 to be the same as that of f_1, yet the SD is more than twice that of f_1, 4 vs. 1.89. How can this be explained?

The problem is that the SD is an inappropriate statistic for f_2. You recall that the SD is computed by comparing scores to the mean of a distribution. What is the mean of f_2? Theoretically it is 10 but actually, the mean never should have been calculated because this is not interval data—it is nominal data. The distribution is bimodal—only two scores occur: 14 and 6. There is no central tendency and so an index of dispersion based on central tendency (as is the SD) is inappropriate. Really, when you think about it, f_2 can be described very easily without any statistical terms: There were twenty subjects involved, ten got 14 and ten got 6. The other distributions are more complex and probably would require statistics to summarize them. The point of this discussion is that the SD like its companion, the mean, is only useful with interval or ratio data and when applied to nominal or ordinal data, it has little or no value: indeed it can be misleading.

It is of interest to note the effect of a few widely differing scores on the SD. Distribution f_4 is similar to f_3 except that two scores of 10 have been changed to 14 and 6. Recall that there were twenty scores in all, but the changing of only two scores has a formidable effect of the SD. The SD of f_3 is .7, but the SD of f_4 is 1.44, *more than double*. Like the mean, the SD is highly influenced by a few extreme scores.

Let's go back to the data in table 10.1. The following statistics have been computed.

	Mean	Mdn	Mode	Range	SD
X variable	27.96	29	29	16	4.11
Y variable	32.04	32	28	24	5.80
Z variable	53.36	53	45	27	8.38

Each variable has an N of 25. Examination of these statistics can reveal information about the distributions they represent.

a. Variable X: The closeness of the mean, median, and mode suggest a fairly normal distribution. But the size of the SD which is about ¼ of the range suggest a distribution whose peak is somewhat low. (Remember in a small distribution the SD may be expected to 1/5 of the range).

b. Variable Y: The closeness of the mean and median again suggests a fairly normal distribution but the mode which is 4 points lower suggest a flat distribution with a mode that barely is a mode. If the modal scores were more numerous, they probably would have had the effect of influencing the mean to be closer. The SD is about ¼ of the range which also shows a flat distribution.

c. Variable Z: This distribution probably approximates that of variable Y but is even flatter. The SD is about ⅓ of the range which indicates that the scores are quite spread out and without a strong central tendency.

3. *Variance*. A third measure of the dispersion in a distribution of scores is the *variance* (abbreviated σ^2 or s^2). As indicated by its abbreviated forms, the variance may be defined as the square of the standard deviation (indeed, it may be considered as another expression of the SD). Thus if the SD of a distribution were 2 its variance would be 4; SD = 2.8 : Variance = 7.84, etc. The variance of a distribution, like the SD, is computed by considering each score in relation to the mean. Some researchers prefer to report the dispersion of a distribution in terms of its variance, although the SD is more typically used for this purpose.

So, through our understanding of the statistics used by researchers in describing central tendency and dispersion we are able to visualize the shape of a distribution. Both dimensions are needed for a full description and both should be reported. You may have heard the story of the naive statistician who drowned while crossing a river with an average depth of two feet.

Attribute IV: Relative Position
How do the data compare to one another?

Researchers often need to make comparisons between elements in a given set of data and between elements in different sets of data. There are some special techniques they use in order to accomplish these tasks. Let's look at the data in table 10.1. If they wanted to know who had a higher score on variable X, Bernie or Dave, they could merely examine the raw data. They would find that Bernie's score was 30 and Dave's score was 33 and a simple comparison would tell them that Dave's score is three points higher. This presents no problem.

But instead suppose they want to know how Bernie did on variable X compared to how he did on variable Y. Inspection of the data shows that on variable X his raw score was 30 and on variable Y his raw score was 38. Did he do better on variable Y than X? His raw score of 38 on variable Y is 8 points higher than his score on variable X but does this mean he did better on Y than on X? Maybe variable Y is a much easier test, and although he scored higher he really did not perform as well as he did on variable X.

Or suppose they want to examine Don's scores on variables X and Y. Inspection of the data shows that he got a score of 28 on both variables. Does this mean he did equally well on both variables? These questions cannot be answered using these data in their present form of raw scores because the distributions in which the scores are found are different. They are not comparable—they have different means and different standard deviations. And until they can be made comparable it will be speculative to determine which scores are really higher than the others.

The context in which a number is located gives significance to that number. Suppose Bernie weights 82 kilograms and Dave weighs 15 stone. Who weighs more? Obviously 82 is more than 15 but the measurement units are not comparable. If we convert both to a common standard unit such as pounds, then the comparison becomes simple. Bernie's 82 kilograms equals 180 lbs. and Dave's 15 stone equals 210 lbs. Now the task of comparison is simple. Similarly, researchers use a procedure to make raw scores from different distributions comparable.

Standard Scores

A *standard score* is a derived score which researchers use in order to compare a score in one distribution with a score in another distribution, or to compare two scores in the same distribution. It is called standard because it is derived from a fixed, standard distribution with a mean of 0 and a standard deviation of 1. A standard score is defined as a score representing the distance of a given raw score from the mean of a given distribution. Figure 10.7 shows a continuum on which a distribution of scores could appear; the distribution is divided into 6 units, each representing one standard deviation. On this continuum, a distribution of raw scores with a mean of 35 and an SD of 5 has been placed. Inspection of this figure shows that a raw score of 40 is equivalent to a standard score of 1 (the raw score of 40 is 5 points or 1 SD above the mean of 35). A raw score of 37 is equivalent to a standard score of .4 (37 is 2 points above the mean of 35. The 2 points is .4 of the SD). A raw score of 28 is equivalent to a standard score of -1.4 (28 is 7 points below the mean of 35. 7 points is equal to 1.4 of a SD). When the mean and SD of a distribution is known, the standard score corresponding to any raw score can be easily calculated by applying the following formula: $\text{Standard Score} = \dfrac{\text{Raw Score} - \text{Mean}}{\text{SD}}$.

When raw scores on different distributions are converted to standard scores they then become comparable. Let's return to an earlier example. Bernie's raw score on variable X is 30, on variable Y is 38. On which variable did he do better? The presentation in table 10.5 shows a summary of the comparison. On variable X his raw score of 30 is ½ a SD above the mean resulting in a standard score of 0.5. On variable Y his raw score of 38 is 1 SD above the mean resulting in a standard score of 1.0. Bernie's score on variable Y is higher not only in raw score points (38 vs. 30) but also in relative standing in the distribution as shown by the standard scores (1.0 vs. 0.5).

Table 10.5

	Variables	
	X	Y
Mean	28	32
SD	4	6
Raw Score	30	38
Standard Score	0.5	1.0

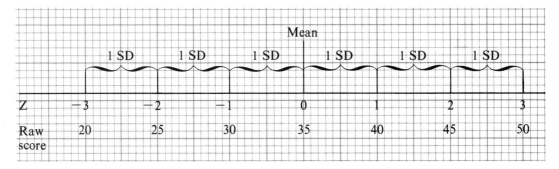

Figure 10.7.

188

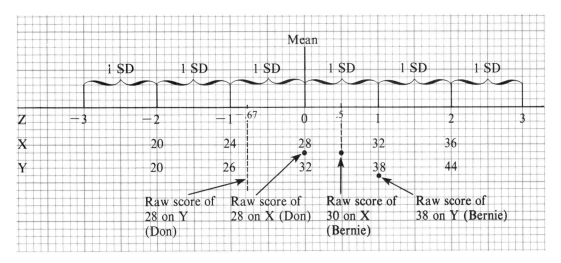

Figure 10.8.

This is also shown graphically in figure 10.8. The continuum shows a mean in the center and three SDs on each side of the mean marked off. The standard scores associated with each of these points are indicated below the continuum. Beneath those scores the X or Y variables have been adapted to the scales and now easy comparisons can be made.

Now let's look at our other example. Don has raw scores of 28 on both variables X and Y. Did he do equally well on both variables? Table 10.6 summarizes the relevant information.

Don's raw score of 28 on variable X was exactly at the mean of the distribution so his standard score is 0.0. However, his raw score of 28 on variable Y was 4 points (⅔ of an SD) below the mean of that distribution, so his standard score is −0.67. His relative performance on variable X is better than his relative performance on variable Y although the raw scores on each variable are exactly the same.

As you can see, the conversion of raw scores to standard scores is a relatively easy method of making comparable scores from different distributions. It is also useful if scores are to be combined in some way.

A word about terminology: When one speaks about "standard scores" and no further description is offered, it is assumed that a distribution with a mean of 0 and a SD of 1 is the reference. A standard score from such a distribution is called a z score. However, the term "standard scores" is also used in a generic sense indicating any derived score based upon its distance from the mean in units of the SD of its distribution. There are two other types of standard scores frequently encountered in the educational research literature. Their relationship is shown in figure 10.9.

Table 10.6

	Variables	
	X	Y
Mean	28	32
SD	4	6
Raw Score	28	28
Standard Score	0.0	−0.67

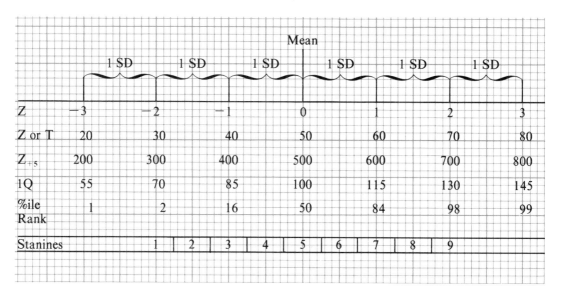

Figure 10.9.

    a. *T scores* or *Z scores* are derived from a distribution with a mean of 50 and a SD of 10, with a usual range from 20 to 80. This improves upon the z scores by avoiding negative numbers. For example, a z of -1.5 equals a T or Z of 35.

    b. *Z scores* typically used by testing services (noted here as Z_{ts} to distinguish them from the Z scores mentioned above) are another transformation of z scores. The Z_{ts} distribution has a mean of 500 and a SD of 100 (which is exactly 10 times the value of the Z or T distribution). Not only are negative numbers avoided by using Z_{ts} scores but decimal places as well. For example a z of $-.67$ is equivalent to a Z or T of 43.3 and a Z_{ts} of 433.

Stanines and Percentile Ranks

Two other methods of making scores comparable which are used by researchers are the use of *stanines* and *percentile ranks*. A *stanine* is a band of scores included in ½ or 1 SD depending upon the particular stanine. Figure 10.9 shows how a distribution is broken into stanines. The distribution is broken down into 7 stanines (2–8) each of which includes ½ of a SD. The two stanines at the extreme ends of the distribution each include one plus standard deviations. Thus the distribution is broken into stanines (the term stanine is derived from *standard nine*). Note that the mean of the distribution is in the middle of the 5th stanine which comprises ½ a SD. Thus the 5th stanine represents ¼ of a SD above and below the mean. Other stanines 6–8 and 4–2 are marked at ½ SD points but originate from the boundaries of the 5th stanine. This explains why the stanine points seem staggered in relation to the SD points on the continuum. The 1st and 9th stanines are open ended to reflect the fact that theoretically any distribtuion has no outer limits—you could always score lower or higher if the construction of the test allowed it.

Since stanines are bands of scores, researchers speak of a person scoring *in* the 6th stanine, rather than saying his score *was* the 6th stanine. Stanines are useful in conveying information to lay people because the stanines lend themselves to categorical labels. For example the nine stanines could be labeled: lowest, lower, low, low average, average, high average, high, higher, highest.

Another advantage is that referring to a score as being in a stanine recognizes the existence of measurement error which often makes small differences in raw scores meaningless. But this comes at a price: a person whose score is at the borderline of two stanines might really belong in one and not the other if there were no measurement error. After all, the division of the distribution into 9 units was arbitrary; it could have been divided into 7 units just as well and we would instead be talking about *stavens*.

A *percentile rank* indicates a person's relative standing on a continuum of 1–99. It answers the question, "What percentage of scores were exceeded by a particular score?" This can be readily understood by visualizing ninety nine women arranged in ascending order of height from left to right. We want to describe the height of the 12th person from the right relative to the rest of the group. We can say that she is at the 87th percentile. This means that her height exceeded the height of 87 women in the group of 99. This description is particularly useful with ordinal data since a large number of uneven spaces between scores might make standard scores inappropriate.

Attribute V: Relationships
How do these data compare with other data
from the same data sources?

So far in our discussion of descriptive statistics we have considered various ways researchers describe the scores obtained by a group of subjects on one variable (distribution, central tendency, dispersion) and the scores obtained by one subject on two or more variables (relative position). This exposition has indirectly revealed the great differences to be expected among subjects on one variable, and within a subject on several variables. But when researchers consider several subjects and several variables they are attending to the commonalities which also exist among subjects. Sometimes the variables associated with a group of subjects seem to go together as for instance intelligence and school achievement: for a group of students those with higher intelligence tend to have good grades in school. Sometimes variables associated with a group of subjects seem to have nothing to do with one another as for instance is the case with glove size and annual income: adults with small hands do not seem to be any richer or poorer than those with large hands.

Correlation

The technique researchers use for describing in quantitative terms the relationship of two or more variables associated with a group of subjects is called *correlation*. The term correlation is really a generic term for a group of statistical procedures which yield an index of a computed relationship. The index itself is called a *correlation coefficient* (abbreviated r) and is usually expressed as a two place decimal number ranging from 0 to $\pm$ 1.00. Thus the range of possible correlation coefficients is from -1.00 to $+1.00$. Examples of correlation coefficients are $+.72$, $-.34$, $+.11$, $.85$ (the absence of a plus or minus sign indicates an assumed plus sign).

A relationship can be graphed by plotting the scores on two variables for each person. Figure 10.10 shows such a graph. The absissa (horizontal axis) represents one variable and the ordinate (vertical axis) represents the other. A subject's score on the absissa variable is plotted from left to right and the score on the ordinate variable is plotted from bottom to top. Where these two scores meet is called a moment and a dot is placed there to represent that person's scores on the two variables. For example, Bob scored 75 on variable X and 24 on variable Y; Phil scored 78 on variable X and 29 on variable Y. The two scores for each of them are represented by two dots, moments,—one for Bob and one for Phil.

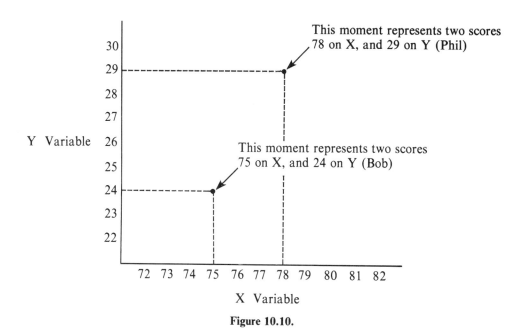

Figure 10.10.

The term *moment* is of passing interest to us. The most prominent procedure for the computation of a correlation coefficient is the product-moment correlation developed by Karl Pearson. An integral part of the computation is the multiplication of the two scores at each moment which yields the *product* of each moment. Hence the name *product moment*.

A graph in which such moments are plotted is called a *scattergram*. Four scattergrams showing four different types of relationships are shown in figure 10.11.

A relationship between two variables, if it exists, can be direct or invese or both. For example, knowledge of letter names and reading ability among first grade children have a direct relationship: kids who know letter names tend to read better than kids who do not. As one goes up or down so does the other go up or down. This is a *direct* relationship which would yield a position correlation and would be represented by a correlation coefficient in the neighborhood of, say .82. A scattergram showing this appears in figure 10.11a. On the other hand, weight and running speed among 6th grade kids has an inverse relationship: kids who weigh more tend to run slower than kids who weigh less. As weight goes up, speed goes down and vice versa. This is an inverse relationship which would yield a negative correlation and would be represented by a correlation coefficient of say, −.63. A scattergram showing this relationship appears in figure 10.11b.

Sometimes the relationship between two variables is both direct and inverse at different points in time. This type of relationship is called *non-linear* or, more specifically *curvilinear* and uses special computational procedures which yield a statistic called *eta*. For example, the relationship between anxiety and test performance among high school students is curvilinear. Subjects with absolutely no anxiety, that is, utter lethargy tend not to do well on tests. As they develop a little anxiety they try harder and do better. This peaks when they are so anxious that they prepare diligently for the test and "get up for it" at the actual test time. However some subjects get *so* anxious that their anxiety interferes with their test performance and they do less well than subjects

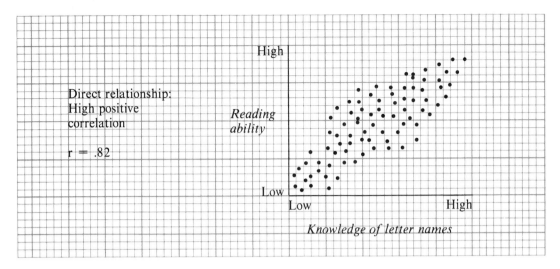

Figure 10.11a.

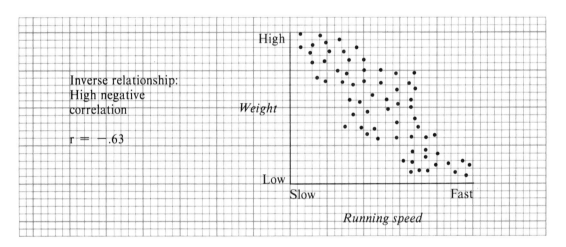

Figure 10.11b.

who have somewhat less anxiety. In fact so much anxiety can build that a subject can be in a state of shock and not be able to perform at all well on the test. That subject's performance might resemble that of the lethargic person who is completely devoid of any anxiety at all. This then is the curvilinear relationship between the variables anxiety and achievement. A scattergram showing this appears in figure 10.11c.

Two variables may have no relationship at all, as in our prior example of glove size and annual income. But note that the *absence* of any relationship is different from the presence of a negative relationship. A scattergram of these two unrelated variables which appears in figure 10.11d, shows a seemingly random distribution of moments over the graph. No pattern, positive or negative, linear or curvilinear, to these moments is apparent. Yet, if a correlation coefficient

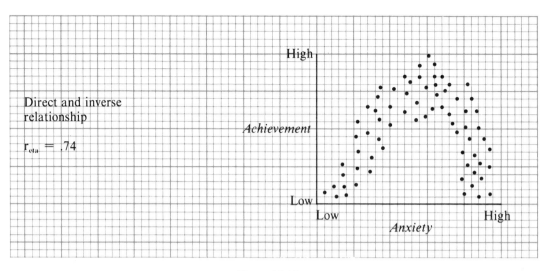

Figure 10.11c.

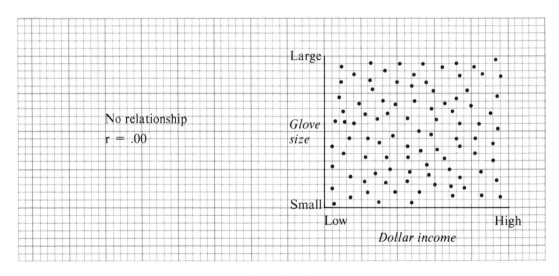

Figure 10.11d.

were computed it might be, say, .04 or − .07. These very low correlations are probably the result of chance and should not be taken as true indices of a relationship. Further discussion of this matter will appear latter under tests of significance.

Interpreting Correlation Coefficients

When confronted with a correlation coefficient presented in a research study we are faced with an index of a relationship between two variables. The sign of the coefficient—plus or minus— tells us the nature of the relationship. The difference between the coefficient and zero tells us the magnitude of the relationship. There are still several questions which need to be answered before we can convert this coefficient into meaningful and useful information.

First, how high does the coefficient need to be to be called "high" and conversely, how low need a coefficient be to be called "low?" This question is analogous to the question, "How tall does a person need to be to be called "tall"?" or "How high is up?" Obviously, there is no exact point at which categories of high and low may be distinguished. The real answer to this question must depend upon the use to which the coefficient is put. If the purpose of the correlation is to merely describe the extent of a relationship, then there are generally accepted characterizations which are useful to us. These characterizations assume the sample size from which the coefficients were derived was sufficiently large to represent a bona fide correlation, significantly different from a zero correlation. These characterizations apply whether the coefficient is positive or negative:

$r = .00–.20$	none, or negligible relationship
$r = .20–.40$	low relationship
$r = .40–.70$	moderate relationship
$r = .70–1.00$	high relationship

If however the purpose of the coefficient is to indicate the reliability of a test, anything less than .85 is generally considered too low; one needs coefficients in the 90's to be really valuable. On the other hand, if the purpose is to explore a purely theoretical problem then a coefficient of any magnitude as long as it is significantly different from zero (to be explained later) is important. Thus we see it is not just the size of the coefficient which determines its usefulness, but also the situation for which it was obtained.

It should be noted that a perfect correlation, one which yields a coefficient of ± 1.00 is virtually unheard of in the social sciences. Even in the physical sciences in which there is less variation, nature provides on occasion abberation to preclude the possibility of a perfect correlation.

Secondly, what does the numerical value of the coefficient mean? Let us examine first what it does *not* mean. A coefficient of say .60 derived from two variables does *not* mean that there is a .60 or 60% agreement between the two variables, it does *not* mean that the variables are related 60% of the time, nor that the variables are related in 60% of the subjects. The numerical value *cannot* be equated with a percentage. Nor does a coefficient of .60 mean a relationship twice as strong as that represented by a coefficient of .30. The scale in which the correlation coefficients exist is an ordinal sclae; there are uneven spaces between seemingly even intervals. For example, the difference between the coefficients .80 and .90 is far greater than the difference between .10 and .20. You will recall from our discussion of measurement scales that the forming of a ratio between points of a scale is only admissible on a ratio scale (whose properties include the existence of a real zero point). So to say that one correlation is twice as strong as another is inappropriate. Indeed, the computation of a mean average of several coefficients is suspect because such a computation requires an interval scale. So the numerical value of the coefficient is neither a percentage nor a number on an interval or ratio scale. Rather, *it is an index of a relationship.*

Why should this be? The underlying cause is in the computation of the coefficient which involves squared values rather than original values. This has the effect of reducing to almost .00 the existence of small degrees of relationship. Then when some relationship is indicated in a coefficient, the increases in relationship proceed geometrically rather than arithmetically, that is, the increases proceed in ever increasingly larger increments. This is shown graphically in figure 10.12 which shows the relationship of the percent of agreement between two variables and the coefficient expressing that agreement. You will note that even if a coefficient is about .00 there

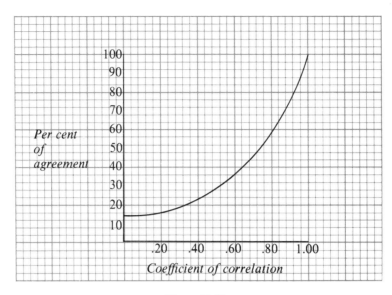

Figure 10.12.

will be some agreement between the variables, that is, in about 15% of the subjects a relationship between the variables will indeed exist. As the percentage of agreement goes up a little the correlation goes up faster and gains momentum until the agreement is 100% and the coefficient is 1.00. The percentage of agreement and the correlation coefficient are analogous to two trains starting at different distances and going at different speeds at various points on the journey, but ending up at the same place at the same time.

Thirdly, what conclusions may be drawn from an obtained correlation coefficient? Does it imply causality? No, but it does not preclude it either. Does it allow prediction from one variable to the other? Yes, within the limitations imposed by the coefficient itself. You will recall that the issue of causality was discussed fully in a previous chapter which described correlational studies.

Types of Correlation Methods

The most frequently encountered method of computing a correlation coefficient is the Pearson product-moment method. The use of this method assumes that the data involved in the computation meet certain assumptions: 1) the variables are linearly related, 2) the distributions of the two variables are fairly normal and have similar shapes, 3) the variables exist on a continuous (interval) scale and 4) there are 30 or more subjects in the sample. When any or all of these assumptions are not met, researchers may employ a variety of other computation procedures depending on the type of data available.

The most significant feature in determining which method of correlation researchers use with a given set of data is the *scale* from which the data were derived: categorical, ordinal, continuous (interval) or ratio. The distinctions between these data types were discussed at length earlier. When both variables are not continuous researchers choose from one of the alternate coefficients available to them: *phi, tetrachoric, point-biserial, biserial, rho,* and *tau.* Of these six correlation coefficients three of them—phi, point-biserial, and rho—may be considered to be equivalent to the product-moment correlation; they are merely different computations due to the differing nature of the variables. The biserial and tetrachoric coefficients are estimates of what the product-moment correlation would be if the variables were in a continuous form. One last correlation coefficient to be discussed is *eta*. Eta is often referred to as a universal measure of relationships because it can be applied to curvilinear as well as linear relationships and to categorical as well as continuous variables.

By far, the most prominent correlation coefficient in the existing research literature is the product-moment coefficient. This is probably because, with all its needed assumptions not-with-standing, it is the most widely understood by readers and most useful to researchers in extending their understanding of the relationship of two variables to more than two variables. The product-moment correlation procedure allows extension of bi-variable analyses to multiple-variable analyses.

Extensions of Simple Correlations

The product-moment correlation technique can be extended to deal with more than two variables at a time. These techniques are useful to researchers in analyzing a variety of problems and appear frequently in the research literature but tend to be quite complex. It is beyond the scope of this book to present a full development of the rationale for each of these procedures. Rather, the two most frequently encountered procedures will be discussed briefly in order that readers become familiar with them so they can avoid too many surprises while reading research.

Two noteworthy procedures, *partial correlation* and *multiple correlation* are used to explore the effect of other variables on a simple two variable correlational.

Partial Correlation

One of the goals researchers pursue is to understand the relationships among variables. Correlational analysis helps explain these relationships. Now, in terms of scientific theory the best explanations are the most direct, inclusive and simple; this is known as the law of parsimony. When a relationship between two variables is identified researchers are interested in knowing if the expression of that relationship in terms of a correlation coefficient is complete and simple? Or perhaps is there a better explanation of that relationship? This is a question which can be approached through the use of *partial correlation*.

Suppose for example a group of 50 subjects, aged 6–18, had two measurements taken on them: weight and arithmetic ability. To help understand the relationship between them a product-moment correlation coefficient was computed between these two variables: the result was a coefficient of say .83—fairly high. Researchers might ask, "Is there more to the relationship than this? Does the coefficient truly explain the relationship between these two variables? Is this the whole story?" They ask this because the two variables do not seem to have much to do with one another, yet they have a high correlation.

The unexpectedly high correlation might cause them to consider whether there might be another variable—perhaps a more inclusive, superordinate variable—which would explain this relationship better. The question now moves from, "Why are these two variables correlated?" to "Is there another variable which would explain this correlation?" So, what variable might researchers expect be related to both weight and arithmetic ability? A little speculation might suggest that *age* might be clearly related to both weight and arithmetic ability. The computation of correlation coefficients between weight and arithmetic ability, age and weight, and age and arithmetic ability might result in the following.

r — weight/arithmetic ability	= .83
r — age/weight	= .77
r — age/arithmetic ability	= .87

These coefficients show that age has a high correlation with weight (.77) and arithmetic ability (.87). Now, common sense indicates that as subjects, aged 6–18, get older they tend to weigh more *and* they tend to develop more arithmetic ability. This relationship is demonstrated by the obtained coefficient of .83. Researchers might want to know what the relationship of weight and arithmetic ability might be if we discounted the effect of age on this relationship. Their question is, does the high relationship between weight and arithmetic ability depend on age or is it independent of it? *Partial correlation* is the technique they would use to answer this question. The influence of age is "partialed" out of the relationship betweeen weight and arithmetic ability; that is, its influence is removed. What remains is a coefficient which indicates the relationship between weight and arithmetic ability excluding the effect of age. In this case such a coefficient might be .28—fairly low.

Thus, we see that a partial correlation is the net or residual correlation between two variables after the effects of a third variable are statistically removed. Partial correlation fulfills the researcher's need for parsimony in that it provides the best explanation and description of the relationship between the variables.

Multiple Correlation

You will recall from our previous discussion of correlational studies that in addition to describing relationships between variables, correlation analysis can be used by researchers to predict one variable from knowledge of another. For example, if leg muscle tone is highly correlated with running speed then researchers could predict how fast a person could run by determining his leg muscle tone. Conversely, they could predict his leg muscle tone by determining his running speed. The problem researchers encounter concerns the accuracy of their prediction. We know that the higher the correlation coefficient, the more accurate their prediction will be. Let us suppose that the correlation between leg muscle tone and running speed is .64, a moderately high relationship. How can researchers raise this coefficient to allow them to make even more accurate predictions?

First, they might decide that they want to predict running speed from leg muscle tone. Running speed will be called the *criterion* variable and leg muscle tone will be called the *predictor* variable. They will use the predictor variable to predict the criterion variable. Now, it is known that human beings are quite complex and that many variables, physical and psychological, can effect any other given variable. So the researchers might ask, in addition to leg muscle tone, what other variables might effect running speed? Common sense indicates that age, height, weight, stamina, perserverence, and competitiveness are probably related to running speed although it is not known to exactly what extent. What researchers try to do is to find additional predictor variables to improve the accuracy of their prediction. The *multiple correlation* technique (symbolized by R) is the basis for a regression analysis which enables researchers to make more accurate predictions.

In essence, the multiple correlation technique considers the correlations of each of the predictor variables with each other. What emerges from the analysis is a formula which weighs each of the predictor variables on the basis of how much it contributes to the best prediction of the criterion variable. For example, it might turn out that the simple product-moment correlation used to predict running speed from leg muscle tone is .64. When age is added as a second predictor variable the coefficient (now a multiple correlation coefficient) is .73. Adding weight and preserverence as further predictor variables might raise the coefficient to .77. Most analyses stop after three or four predictor variables are considered since little if any predictive ability is added beyond this point. The multiple correlation coefficient of .77 will allow researchers to make more accurate predictions than they could from a simple correlation of .64.

The logic of a multiple correlation is intuitively appealing: the more information you have the better prediction you can make. Tell me a man's wealth, I will take a guess as to what kind of car he drives. But give me more information about his age, residence, life-style, needs, dreams and my guesses will become increasingly better until they become genuine predictions with a reasonable degree of accuracy. Prediction from only one variable is much riskier than prediction from several.

Summary

Researchers collect data which is used as evidence to support or reject the hypotheses they pose. In their raw form, data are not generally useful for this purpose. *Statistics* are procedures which allow data to be reduced, described, and perhaps generalized in such a way as to allow application to the research question.

There are five attributes of a set of data which can be described by statistical procedures:

1. How are the data distributed over the data source? *Frequency distribution, histograms,* and *polygons* are used for this purpose.
2. Where do the data tend to gather? The *mean, median* and *mode* are indices of the central tendency of a set of data. The most appropriate use of each of these statistics depends upon the number of elements in a set of data and the characteristics of its distribution.
3. How are the data spread out? The *range* and *standard deviation* are the two most prominent indices of the dispersion of elements in a set of data. In order to describe more accurately a set of data an indication of its dispersion should accompany an indication of its central tendency.
4. How do the data compare to one another? Comparisons between the elements in a set of data often need to be made; the conversion of raw scores into *standard scores* facilitates such a comparison. Z and T scores, stanines and percentile ranks are some techniques used.
5. How do these data compare with other data from the same data sources. The *correlation* procedure enables researchers to express quantitatively relationships between two or more variables. The resultant correlation coefficient reveals the nature and the magnitude of the relationship. *Partial correlation* removes the effect of a third variable from the correlation of two other variables. *Multiple correlation* allows a criterion variable to be predicted by several predictor variables.

The following question needs to be asked by consumers when they encounter descriptive statistics.

HOW COMPLETE AND APPROPRIATE IS THE DESCRIPTION OF THE DATA?

199

Chapter 11

The Analysis and Interpretation of Data: II

In the previous chapter the procedures used in describing various attributes of data—descriptive statistics—were discussed. You will recall that a variety of procedures are used by researchers to describe the data generated by their efforts. In many research studies however, the research question being investigated requires the researchers to go beyond the particular data generated; they need to infer characteristics of a population from the data they collected which revealed characteristics of a sample. And they need to know how confident they can be in stating that the data from a sample is indeed a reflection of what the data from a population would look like if they had generated data from the population itself. The procedures used to make such inferences with certain levels of confidence are called *inferential statistics*. Data derived from a sample and summarized are called *statistics;* characteristics of a population are called *parameters*. Inferential statistics then, are procedures used to estimate parameters from statistics. Because the procedures are aimed at estimating parameters, these procedures are called *parametric statistics*.

Sometimes however researchers collect nominal or ordinal data to answer their research questions. These types of data can not be subjected to the same parametric statistical tests which can be appropriately applied to interval or ratio data. Instead, these data are treated with one or more *non-parametric* statistical tests. In this chapter we will discuss some of the more commonly used parametric and non-parametric procedures found in the educational research literature with a focus on how to understand and interpret what researchers present. Following this a brief discussion of presentations of research summaries will be presented. The logic behind many of the techniques presented in this chapter was presented in conceptual form in chapter 4. A brief review of that material would be beneficial to the reader at this point.

Differences Between Means

In some research studies, data are gathered from two or more groups of subjects and the mean average score for each group is computed. Typically there is a difference between the means of the groups: one group scored higher than the others. The researchers' problem is to determine if the difference between the means of the two or more groups was sufficiently large to be attributed to genuine differences between or among the groups, rather than being attributable to chance alone. Now, we know that chance is an important factor in determining any event; and you will recall that sampling alone, indeed merely considering the size of the sample involved in a study is a large determinant of credibility. So, chance will play its part in any event. The question is whether the difference between the means of the groups is so large that it probably could not have resulted from chance, or contrarily the difference between the means is not large enough to justify a belief that it probably could not have resulted by chance.

IF INFERENCES WERE MADE FROM A SAMPLE TO A POPULATION, WAS THE INFERENCE JUSTIFIED BY A TEST OF STATISTICAL SIGNIFICANCE?

In order to determine the probability of a difference between/among group means having occurred by chance, statisticians have developed two basic techniques to test the chance probability: the t test and the F test. Both techniques are based upon a ratio of information to error. The greater the proportion of information to error, the more probable the difference is genuine; the smaller the proportion of information to error, the less probable the difference is genuine. In our present research discussion, *information* is defined as the difference between/among means of groups. Error is defined as the chance factor which is comprised of the number of subjects in each group and the variance in each group.

The ratio between information and error may be best thought of as a fraction with information as the numerator and error as the denominator. This is shown below.

$$t \text{ or } F = \frac{\text{Information}}{\text{Error}}$$

Now, for exemplary purposes, let us assume the amount of information is 8 and the amount of error is 4 as shown below.

$$t \text{ or } F = \frac{\text{Information}}{\text{Error}} = \frac{8}{4} = 2$$

There is twice as much information as error and the t or F statistic is 2. Now, suppose the ratio of information to error is 8 to 6 as shown below.

$$t \text{ or } F = \frac{\text{Information}}{\text{Error}} = \frac{8}{6} = 1.33$$

Compared to the previous example, there is relatively more error in the ratio now: 6 as compared to 4. Accordingly the fraction reduces to 1.33 which is smaller than the 2 from the previous sample. Now, suppose the ratio of information to error is 8 to 10 as shown below.

$$t \text{ or } F = \frac{\text{Information}}{\text{Error}} = \frac{8}{10} = 0.8$$

In this case there is more error than information which results in the reduction of the fraction to less than one, specifically 0.8. The information was overwhelmed by the amount of error. Whenever a ratio of this sort reduces to one or less, there is just too much error present for a reasonable judgment to be made that the information is genuine.

The concept of an information to error ratio is crucial in understanding the t and F tests. As an aid in developing this concept, an analogy may be drawn between the ratios of informtion to error, and music to static. Suppose you are sitting in your car and turn the dial to a local radio station. You hear the music clearly and are aware of a little static which accompanies it but there is so little static that it does not interfere with your listening. Then you tune in to a radio station broadcasting from 30 miles away. There is lots more static but you can just make out the music. Then you tune in to a station broadcasting from 50 miles away and all you hear is static with the occasional note of music. The greater the proportion of music to static, the more you will hear the music. Information is the analog to music and error is the analog to static. The greater the proportion of information, (that is, difference between group means) to error, the more genuine the difference between means may be considered. The t statistic and the F statistic are each an index of the ratio of information to error. The larger the ratio the higher the t or F statistic will be. The higher the t or F statistic the more genuine the differences between/among the groups.

How high does a t or F statistic have to be in order for a researcher to have confidence that a difference between or among mean scores is genuine? That depends pretty much on how much confidence the researcher wants or needs. You will recall from our discussion in chapter 4 that levels of confidence are usually specified at one in twenty (.05) or one in a hundred (.01). The t or F statistic needed for confidence at the .01 level would have to be higher than the corresponding t or F statistic needed for the .05 level. In other words, the ratio of information to error needs to be greater in order to have the higher, more stringent level of confidence associated with the .01 level. Statisticians have prepared tables which show the t or F statistics needed for chance probability judgments at the .05 and .01 levels. The judgments of chance probability are referred to as *levels of significance* which you will recall from our discussion in chapter 4.

After completing an analysis which yields a t or F statistic, researchers consult the appropriate table to find out if the size of the obtained statistic exceeds the value needed for significance. In consulting these tables they must consider the size of the sample in the study; this sample size is expressed as *degrees of freedom* (abbreviated df). The concept of degrees of freedom is quite tricky and beyond the scope of this text. But suffice it to say that it is a function of the magnitude of the data: the number of subjects and the number of groups. A large sample will have many degrees of freedom; a small sample will have few degrees of freedom.

After comparing the obtained t or F statistics with those in the table, researchers judge whether the desired level of significance was reached and then this information is reported and interpreted. Let us now look at some examples of studies which present t or F statistics.

The t Test with Independent Groups

When researchers compare the means of two separate independent groups a *t test* is employed. Suppose, researchers seek to determine the difference in level of knowledge about chemistry between two groups of students at United college: last semester seniors who are 1) anticipated B.S. recipients majoring in chemistry and 2) anticipated B.S. in Education recipients majoring in education with a minor in chemistry. A random sample of 26 from each population is drawn and a test of knowledge in chemistry is administered. The raw data might look like the data in table 11.1.

The mean scores for each group were computed: 68.5 for Group 1, and 65.3 for Group 2. The information they have is that there is a difference of 3.2 points (68.5 minus 65.3) between the two groups. Now, the subjects in the groups are samples from their respective populations. The researchers want to infer characteristics of the populations from the data derived from the samples. The question is: is the difference of 3.2 points large enough relative to the error involved in the study to justify an inference from the samples to the populations? In other words, can they say with confidence that the chemistry majors—all of them: the entire population, not merely the sample—have a little more knowledge about chemistry than does the population of education majors? The t test will be useful in this endeavor.

The researchers will compute a t statistic by forming a ratio using the difference between the means of 3.2 as the numerator, and an error term which considers the variances of the two groups and their sample sizes as the denominator. This will be compared to the values of the t statistic

Table 11.1

Group 1 Chemistry Majors	Group 2 Education Majors
87	68
63	59
24	71
73	88
89	43
52	51
58	59
.	.
.	.
.	.
$\overline{X} = 68.5$	$\overline{X} = 65.3$

in the tables. Let us suppose that the obtained t statistic in this study was 1.850—apparently the error term was fairly large relative to the 3.2 difference between the means. The values from the table of t statistics shows that in order to be significant at the .01 level the obtained t statistic must exceed 2.678; for significance at the .05 level an obtained t statistic of 2.008 is needed. Both of these values from the table are based on a sample size which yields 50 degrees of freedom. As it turns out, the obtained t statistic did not exceed either of these tabled values and the researchers would need to state that the difference of 3.2 between the means of the two groups could be attributed to chance more than five times in one hundred. According, they could not infer a genuine difference between the populations based upon the data from the samples. This information might be expressed as follows:*

$$t \ (df \ 50) = 1.850 \ p > .05$$

We may read this as, "The obtained t statistic with 50 degrees of freedom is 1.850. The probability of the obtained difference between the groups being the result of chance is more than five in one hundred." The conclusion that researchers would be expected to make would be that there is no significant difference between the means of the two samples in the study. Thus, they could not then justify an inference from the samples to their respective populations. That pretty much ends the study, although the researchers might want to speculate as to why the study turned out the way it did, what it all means, and how other research studies might extend or improve their study.

The logic behind the decisions in using the other t statistic and the remaining F statistics is similar to that above. The remainder of this section will present examples of these other techniques with a discussion of how to read the presentation of results.

---

*There is no standardized method of presenting the results of statistical analyses. Sometimes the results are presented in the text narrative; sometimes they are presented in one of any of several tabular arrangements.

The t Test with Dependent (Correlated) Groups

Sometimes researchers utilize data from only one group of subjects. In such a case, a similar statistic called a *correlated* or *dependent t* is used in the analysis. Although its formula is slightly different it is interpreted similarly to the independent t. For example, suppose researchers are interested in determining if a group of reluctant readers would show a change in attitude toward reading as a result of a treatment stressing high motivational activities. Eight reluctant readers are randomly selected for the study and are given an attitude pretest before the treatment and a similar posttest afterward. The raw data might look like the data in table 11.2.

The mean difference between pretest and postest in these eight subjects is 1.88. This, of course, becomes the numerator in the ratio. The error term is calculated and a t statistic of 3.61 is figured. This value of 3.61 is compared to the values of the t tables of 2.365 for the .05 level and 3.449 for the .01 level. This information may be presented as follows:

$$t \text{ (df 7)} = 3.61 \text{ p} < .01$$

This may be read, "The obtained t statistic with 7 degrees of freedom is 3.61. The probability of the obtained mean difference having occurred by chance is less than one in one hundred." The researchers would be expected to conclude that there was a significant* positive change in attitude from the time of the pretest to the time of the posttest.

The F Test with Simple (One-way) Analysis of Variance

As we observed, the t statistic is derived from a ratio of information to error represented by the difference between means and an error term respectively. The F statistic is a ratio of two variances and is derived from a process called *analysis of variance* (abbreviated ANOVA). It is computed from a ratio of information to error which is based upon the variance *between* the groups *(information)* and the variance *within* the groups (error). You recall that a t statistic tests difference between two groups (or two sets of data from one group). The F statistic can be used to test differences between two or more groups.

In brief, the analytical procedure which produces an F statistic, ANOVA, analyzes the total variance which occurs among all the scores in all groups which are in a study. The analysis of the variance among scores is partitioned into two component parts: variance *between* the groups and variance *within* the groups. The relationship may be expressed as follows:

Total Variance = Between-group Variance and Within-Group Variance

Table 11.2

Subject	Pretest	Postest	Difference
1	4	5	1
2	6	8	2
3	5	4	−1
4	3	6	3
.	.	.	.
.	.	.	.
8	2	5	3

$$\overline{X} \text{ difference} = 1.88$$

*Some researchers use the term *significant* when chance probability is less than .05 but more than .01, and use *highly significant* when the chance probability is less than .01.

204

The *between* group variance is an indication of those differences between the groups in which the researchers are interested; this is the *information* or numerator part of the ratio. The within-group variation is the remainder of the variance which is unaccounted for: it is sometimes called residual variance. This variance is the *error* or denominator part of the ratio. The F statistic is the reduction of the ratio of between group variance and within group variance. This may be expressed as follows:

$$F = \frac{\text{Between-group variance}}{\text{Within-group variance}}$$

As was the case with the t statistic the higher the ratio of numerator to denominator, the higher the F statistic. The F statistic obtained from ANOVA will be compared to F statistics in statisticians tables. Then a judgment will be made as to whether or not the obtained F exceeds the tabled F values.

As an example, let us suppose a group of researchers are investigating the effect of three different junior high school science curricula. Upon entrance into the school, the students are placed into one of three groups, each representing a particular science curriculum. At the end of the first year, all students are administered an achievement test to measure knowledge of science. There was some attrition in the groups over the course of the year: originally there were thirty students in each group, now there are 21, 28, and 24. The mean achievement of each group was computed and is presented in table 11.3.

Table 11.3

Group	N	$\overline{X}$
1	21	40.9
2	28	38.2
3	24	45.0
Total	73	

* Researchers tend to use the term *between* rather than the more grammatically acceptable *among* when referring to three or more groups.

Inspection of these figures shows that there are indeed differences between* the means of the three groups. The question to be asked by the researchers is whether or not these differences are the result of chance or whether they represent genuine differences in achievement between the three groups. Since there are three group means involved the appropriate technique is ANOVA rather than a simple t test. The ANOVA is performed and the major elements of the computation and the resultant F statistic are presented in a format called a *source table*, so called because it shows the breakdown of the total variance into its component sources. The source table might look like table 11.4.

Although the item of interest to us as consumers of research is the F statistic located at the far right of the table, it would be instructive for us to understand some of the remaining elements. The first column at the left in table 11.4 shows the partitioning of the variance into between groups and within groups. The second column shows the degrees of freedom associated with each variance source. There were three groups studied: the degrees of freedom for these three groups is 2. There were 73 students in all the groups: the 70 degrees of freedom refer to this fact. The total number of degrees of freedom is a total of the between and within figures. The next column

Table 11.4. ANOVA Summary Table

Source of Variance	df	SS	MS	F
Between	2	604.00	302.00	1.73*
Within	70	12,239.92	174.86	
Total	72	12,843.92		

F .05 (df 2 + 70) = 3.13   * p > .05

headed SS refers to the *sums of squares*. This is the result of a computational procedure which reflects the variance between the groups and within the groups respectively. The next column headed MS refers to the *mean square*. The MS of 302 is the dividend of the SS, 604, divided by the df, 2, of the between variance. The identical relationship exists between the MS, SS and df of the within variance. The F statistic in the last column is computed by dividing the MS of the between variance by the MS of the within variance. Thus $F = \frac{302.00}{174.86} = 1.73$. This of course is appropriate because you recall that the between variance represents the information and the error variance represents the error. Thus information is divided by error. The asterisk after the computed F statistic draws our attention to the bottom right of the table where we are informed that this F statistic reveals that the differences between the group means could have occurred by chance more than five times in one hundred. The information at the bottom left of the table tells us that an F statistic of 3.13 is needed to be significant at the .05 level when 2 and 70 degrees of freedom are in existence.

The F Test with a Factorial Analysis of Variance

In the example above, the researchers were interested in determining the answer to one question: did one of the three methods result in significantly higher achievement than the others. Only one independent variable, the teaching methods involved, was the focus of the study, hence the name of the technique—one-way ANOVA. However, researchers are aware of the complexity of human beings and the environments in which they exist, and accordingly often seek to study two or more independent variables at the same time. Each independent variable so studied is referred to as a *factor,* and the ANOVA procedure used when more than one factor is being studied is called *factorial ANOVA.* If the factorial ANOVA is limited to two factors it is called two-way ANOVA; if there are three factors being studied it is called three-way ANOVA and so on. We will limit our exposition of this material to a two-way ANOVA, since the concepts may be developed sufficiently to our purpose.

Whereas a one-way ANOVA addresses one question dealing with the one factor being studied, and yields one F statistic, a two-way ANOVA addresses three questions: 1) The effect of Factor I, 2) The effect of Factor II and 3) The combined effect, or *interaction* of both Factor I and II. Accordingly, a two-way ANOVA will yield three F statistics. Let us consider an example to develop this idea.

.

Table 11.5.

Mathematics Aptitude

Level of Feedback	High	Low
Immediate		
Delayed		

Suppose researchers are interested in the differential effect of two levels of feedback on the achievement of tenth grade mathematics students. In addition, they want to know if the effect of levels of feedback would be different for students of differing mathematics aptitude. The design of this study might be visually portrayed as in table 11.5.

There are two independent variables—factors—in this study: level of feedback and mathematics aptitude. The feedback factor is divided into two levels and the mathematics aptitude is divided into two levels. The design is called a 2×2 (read "two by two") factorial ANOVA; this design yields four *cells* each representing a different combination of the two factors. The dependent variable will be the mathematics achievement test scores.

The researchers randomly select twelve low math aptitude students and arbitrarily assign six to each feedback condition; they perform a similar assignment with the high math aptitude students. Then they provide mathematics instruction under the two conditions of feedback and administer the achievement test. The results are shown in each cell in table 11.6.

Table 11.6.

Mathematics Aptitude

Level of Feedback	High	Low	Combined
Immediate	1 $N = 6$ $\overline{X} = 19.2$	2 $N = 6$ $\overline{X} = 20.9$	$\overline{X} = 20.1$
Delayed	3 $N = 6$ $\overline{X} = 20.2$	4 $N = 6$ $\overline{X} = 14.8$	$\overline{X} = 19.5$
Combined	$\overline{X} = 19.7$	$\overline{X} = 17.9$	

Table 11.7. Summary of Analysis of Variance

Source of Variance	SS	df	MS	F
Between columns (aptitude)	11.38	1	11.38	4.99*
Between rows (feedback)	32.21	1	32.21	14.13**
Columns X rows (interaction)	63.78	1	63.79	27.98**
Within groups (error)	45.50	20	2.28	
Total	152.87	23		

F .05 (1, 20) = 4.35	* p	.05
F .01 (1, 20) = 8.10	** p	.01

Each cell is seen to contain six students. Cell #1 contains high aptitude students who received immediate feedback. Cell #2 contains low aptitude students who received immediate feedback. The other cells may be read similarly.

An ANOVA is performed and the results are presented in the source table as shown in table 11.7.

Table 11.7 is read in much the same way as is the one-way ANOVA table in the previous example. There are a few differences though. Since there are two factors, they need to be identified separately. The aptitude factor is analyzed on the line labeled "Between columns". The "columns" refer to the spatial arrangement of the cells: you will note that the first column is high aptitude and the second column is low aptitude. The variance between the columns partitioned from the total variance is reflected in the F statistic of 4.99. Similarly, the feedback factor is analyzed on the line labeled "between rows". This variance is reflected in a F statistic of 14.13. The analyses of these factors are called a main effects; there are two factors so there are two main effects. The information at the bottom left of the table tells us that with 1 and 20 degrees of freedom an F statistic must exceed 4.35 to be significant at the .05 level, or must exceed 8.10 to be significant at the .01 level.

Inspection of the obtained F statistic of 4.99 shows that the main effect of aptitude was significant at the .05 level. Returning for a moment to the means of each cell we note that the means of the high aptitude students (cell #1: 19.2, and cell #3: 20.2) combined, exceed the means of the low aptitude students (cell #2: 20.9, and cell #4: 14.8) combined. Thus when not considering the level of feedback, high aptitude students as a group did better than low aptitude students as a group. The probability of this happening by chance is less than five in one hundred.

Inspection of the F statistic of 14.13 shows that the main effect of feedback was highly significant at the .01 level. Again returning to the means of each cell we note that the means of the immediate feedback students (cell #1: 19.2 and cell #2: 20.9) are higher in combination than the means of the delayed feedback students (cell #3: 20.2 and cell #4: 14.8) in combination. Thus when we do not consider aptitude, students who received immediate feedback did better as a group than did the students who received delayed feedback. The probability of this happening by chance is less than one in one hundred.

So far, we have noted the findings on the two main effects, aptitude and level of feedback, and we have considered them separately: high aptitude students did better than low aptitude students, and immediate feedback students did better than delayed feedback students. Our final F statistic of 27.98 appears on the line labeled "Column x rows", which is read "Columns by rows". This line deals with the interaction of the two factors previously analyzed; it shows the combined effect of the two factors on the students. For a third time, let us return to the means of each cell and make some observations. We need to examine each cell in relation to the other cells.

We note that in a previous analysis high aptitude students as a group ($\overline{X}$ = 19.7) did better than low aptitude students as a group ($\overline{X}$ = 17.9). But examination of cell #2 shows that the low aptitude students who received immediate feedback did very well, indeed their mean of 20.9 exceeds all other means in the analysis. Examination of cell #4 shows that the low aptitude students who received delayed feedback did quite poorly—their mean of 14.8 is substantially lower than the other means. This information is interpreted as an *interaction* between aptitude and level of feedback. It appears as if immediate feedback had a very beneficial effect on the low aptitude students. With regard to the high aptitude students, the level of feedback did not appear to have much of an effect: the means of cells #1 and #3, 19.2 and 20.2 respectively, seem quite close to one another. The observed interaction of these two factors is significant at the .01 level. The probability of this happening by chance is one in one hundred.

The F Statistic in Analysis of Covariance (ANACOVA)

When researchers conduct a study to determine differences between two or more groups, they tend to prefer a procedure which enables them to define a population, randomly select a sample, randomly assign the subjects in the sample to the different groups and proceed with the gathering of data. In the real world of educational research however, it is often not possible to engage in such a procedure. This is especially true in schools: principals and teachers are often uncomfortable with the idea of their students being assigned to special groups for research purposes because they believe, quite justifiably from their point of view, that the disruption in the students' routine will not necessarily be beneficial to them. As a result, researchers may find themselves in a position wherein the research question clearly calls for an experimental design, a crucial element of which is random selection, but they are unable to perform a random selection. If they are to use groups of students, they must use existing intact groups such as Ms. Gails fourth grade class or Mr. Vans second period tenth grade biology class.

You will recall from our discussion of experimental designs that the selection bias is an extremely important extraneous variable which must be controlled in order for a study to have internal and external validity. Random sampling and assignment to groups controls this bias and is the preferred method of control. But if random sampling is not possible, researchers may exercise control over the selection bias by utilizing a procedure known as *analysis of covariance* (ANACOVA). The details of computational procedures are well beyond the scope of this text, but we shall discuss the computational procedure in general terms. In essence, ANACOVA is a combination of its parent procedure, ANOVA, and correlation.

Suppose, researchers seek to investigate the differential effects of three methods of presentation on the learning of mathematics concepts by third grade pupils. Each method stresses a different presentation and reinforcement mode: Visual (V), Auditory (A) and Kinesthetic (K). Random selection and assignment is not possible, so three seemingly comparable third grade classes are identified and chosen to participate in the study. Each class receives instruction in one of the three

Table 11.8

Mean Scores

Group	Pretest	Posttest
V	23	28
A	19	26
K	20	25

presentation/reinforcement modes. A pretest on math concepts is given before the instruction begins. A posttest on math concepts is given after instruction ends, and represents the dependent variable in the study. Now, let us assume that the study yielded the results shown in table 11.8.

You will note that all three groups shown in table 11.8 scored better on the posttest than the pretest and that the posttest scores are different from one another. If the groups had been randomly selected, the researchers could perform an ANOVA to determine the significance of the difference between the posttest means. But this was not the case. If we examine the pretest means we note that there were differences between the groups regarding their knowledge of math concepts even before any instruction took place. The V group for example had the highest pretest mean of the three groups; it also had the highest posttest mean. Perhaps their high pretest score gave the group a head start which resulted in a high posttest. So, before an ANOVA can be performed on the posttest scores, the posttest scores have to be adjusted to reflect the preinstruction differences which existed between the groups. This adjustment is done on the basis of the correlation between the pretest and the posttest. You recall from our discussion of correlation that one of its uses is to predict one variable from another. If there is a high correlation between the pretest and posttest, that is, if one could predict the posttest from the pretest, then the V group did indeed have a head start on the other groups. The results of the correlation analysis between the pretest and posttest will be used to adjust the posttest means so as to reflect the preinstruction differences which existed. Following this, the adjusted posttest means will be subjected to ANOVA.

In this type of analysis, the pretest is referred to as the *covariate:* the extent to which it covaries with the posttest is considered in adjusting the posttest means. Often, studies will use more than one covariate in order to adjust the posttest means even more accurately. The results of ANACOVA are usually presented in a source table like that of ANOVA. Sometimes the unadjusted (original) means are presented along with the adjusted means. In any case, though, the F statistic is interpreted in exactly the same way as would be an F statistic from an ANOVA.

Multiple Comparisons

Before leaving the subject of F tests and ANOVA mention should be made of the tests of multiple comparisons which sometimes follow an ANOVA. You recall that if a t test shows a significant difference between two means, then one merely examines the two means to determine which is significantly higher. Similarly, with ANOVA of two groups, inspection of the two means shows which is significantly higher. But when ANOVA or ANACOVA is performed with three or more groups, and the resultant F statistic is significant, the researchers do not necessarily know where the significant difference is. Suppose, for example there were four means involved—18, 20, 21, and 27—and a significant F statistic was obtained. Is 27 significantly higher than 18? Is 27 significantly higher than 21? Is 21 significantly higher than 20? These and similar questions can not be answered by the F statistic alone. The F statistic tells the researchers that there is a significant difference, but it does not reveal between which pairs of means the difference lies. At this juncture, researchers employ one of several available *post hoc* analyses which make multiple comparisons of means. Such analyses will reveal specifically which means are significantly different. The various methods of multiple comparisons are referred to by the names of people who developed them. The most prominent methods found in the literature are those developed by Duncan, Newman-Keuls, Scheffe and Tukey. Researchers typically will report which of these methods (if any) was employed in their study.

Differences Between Frequencies

In the previous sections of this chapter we discussed statistical tests which analyzed the differences between means of groups. If the difference between the group means was large enough a statistically significant difference is said to exist. The fact that a *mean* was the object of the analysis tells us that the data in the studies to which these techniques are applied are interval or ratio data. You recall that interval or ratio data represent high levels of measurement. However, sometimes researchers gather nominal data in order to answer their research questions. This type of data is usually represented by frequencies of responses or observations which are categorical in nature, and as such can not be used in a computation of a mean average. In cases such as this a technique called *chi-square* (sometimes notated χ^2) is used to analyze the differences between sets of frequencies.

IF FREQUENCIES ARE PRESENTED, HAVE THE OBTAINED FREQUENCIES BEEN COMPARED TO THE EXPECTED FREQUENCIES BY A TEST OF STATISTICAL SIGNIFICANCE?

One instance of an appropriate use of *chi-square* is when researchers seek to determine whether the data from two *independent* groups are significantly different from one another. For example, they want to find out if there is a difference between boys and girls at Madison High School regarding how they feel about their school's athletic program. They identify the students who are associated with the athletic program; there are 100 of them—68 boys and 32 girls. They ask a variety of questions of these students and summarize each student's responses to indicate whether each student had a positive or a negative attitude. Then they tally the frequencies of students reflecting each attitude. The results of this tallying are called the *observed frequencies* and are shown in table 11.9 called a *contingency table*.

Table 11.9

Observed Frequencies

	Positive	Negative	Totals
Boys	29	39	68
Girls	22	10	32
Totals	51	49	100

Inspection of table 11.9 shows that the observed responses were about equal in the total group: 51 positive and 49 negative. But the research question is whether there is a significant difference between the responses of boys and girls. The researchers may observe that there are 68 boys and 32 girls in this group: the proportion of boys to girls is slightly more than 2 to 1. If there were no difference between the responses of the boys compared to the responses of the girls, they might expect a similar proportion of positive responses and a similar proportion of negative responses. In other words, they would expect about twice as many boys to have positive attitudes than girls because there are about twice as many boys in the study. Similarly, they would expect to have about twice as many boys to have negative attitudes than girls, again because there are about twice as many boys than girls in the study. These hypothetical expectations the researchers have are called *expected frequencies* and are shown in table 11.10 below.

Notice that the expected frequencies in positive responses—34.68 and 16.32—total 51, and are in exact proportion to the number of boys and girls in the study: 68 and 32. The same is true of the negative responses. Now the researchers need to know if the *observed frequencies* differ significantly from the *expected frequencies*. Or, in other words, are the differences between the observed and expected frequencies genuine differences, or could they be attributable to chance alone. The *chi-square* statistical procedure is applied to the data in both tables and the value obtained from this procedure is compared to previously calculated values in statistian's tables. As it turns out the *chi-square* statistic for this example is 5.94; this figure exceeds the tabled values at the .02 level of 5.41. So, the researchers would probably conclude that there *is* a significant difference in how boys and girls at Madison High School feel about their athletic program. Boys feel disproportionally more negative than girls do. The chances of this finding having happened by chance is two in one hundred.

Another instance of an appropriate use of the chi-square technique is when researchers seek to determine whether a set of data from *one* group of subjects is different from what might be expected. For example, suppose researchers want to know the preferences that special education-learning disability teachers have for three diagnostic procedures. There are 120 teachers whose preferences will be considered. In the absence of any information, the researchers might expect an equal number of teachers to select each method resulting in expectency frequencies shown in table 11.11.

When the teachers respond to the researchers' questions indicating their preferences the results are shown in table 11.12.

Table 11.10

Expected Frequencies

	Positive	Negative	Totals
Boys	34.68	33.32	68
Girls	16.32	15.68	32
Totals	51	49	100

Table 11.11

Methods	Expected Frequencies		
	A	B	C
Preference of Teachers	40	40	40

Table 11.12

Methods	Observed Frequencies		
	A	B	C
Preference of Teachers	42	48	30

As was the case in the last example, the chi-square procedure is used to determine if the differences between the expected and observed frequencies of preferences are genuine or rather are the result of chance. This use of chi-square in an analysis such as above is often called a *goodness-of-fit* analysis—how "good" do the observed frequencies "fit" the hypothetical expected frequencies. In this analysis a chi-square statistic of 4.2 was obtained.

The chi-square procedure is a very popular one because it is relatively simple to compute and interpret. It is frequently encountered in the educational research literature and it is the most used of the non-parametric statistical tests. In fact, it is a sub-procedure of several other non-parametric procedures.

Differences between Correlation Coefficients

When dealing with correlational data, researchers often need to consider the differences between the coefficients they obtain—are the differences genuine or are they the result of chance.

IF A CORRELATION COEFFICIENT(S) HAS BEEN PRESENTED, HAS IT BEEN TESTED FOR STATISTICAL SIGNIFICANCE?

There are two basic research situations which require a test of significance. In one situation, researchers obtain two (or more) correlation coefficients and need to determine if they are statistically different from one another. For example, suppose researchers seek to develop information regarding the relationship between scholastic aptitude and school achievement of two groups of high school students: dropouts and occasional truants. They identify a group of 39 dropouts and 72 occasional truants. They collect data on these two variables for each of the two groups of students and compute the correlation coefficients between them. The obtained correlation coefficients between scholastic aptitude and school achievement are: dropouts: .50, occasional truants: .55. A brief inspection of these coefficients reveals that they are different by .05. The researchers must ask whether this difference is attributable to chance. The procedure utilized to make this determination converts the coefficient and applies a technique called a *standard error*. The result of this analysis shows significance at approximately .74. In other words, the observed difference of .05 between these two coefficients derived from groups of 39 and 72 could have happened by chance 74 times in one hundred. Thus, the researchers could not have much confidence that these two coefficients are truly different.

A second situation in which researchers need to consider significance in relation to correlation is when they obtain *one* coefficient. For example, suppose researchers are investigating the relationship in multiply-handicapped middle grade pupils between the number of handicaps and school achievement. They identify 13 pupils so described, obtain measures on the two variables and compute a correlation coefficient which turns out to be .52. Their question now is, is there a real relationship between these two variables in these pupils or is the relationship really 0.00. Inspection of statisticians' tables shows that based upon the number of subjects in the study a coefficient of .58 or more is needed to be significant at the .05 level. The researchers would probably state that the relationship is questionable. It could have happened by chance more than five times in one hundred. The size of the correlation coefficient needed for significance drops as the number of subjects in the study increases. For instance, if a coefficient were derived from data from 100 subjects, a coefficient of only .19 would be significant at the .05 level. When the number of subjects in a study was low and/or the one obtained coefficient was low, researchers will state whether the obtained coefficient was significant. This refers to whether it was significantly different from zero.

Summaries of Research

All of the previous chapter and all of this chapter to this point have discussed the techniques used by researchers as they analyze and present data to consumers of their research efforts. The assumption has been that the consumers have the entire study to read and that they can apply their knowledge of procedures, logic and common sense to read critically what the researchers present. But the entire study done by researchers will not always be available to a consumer.

IF A SUMMARY OF RESEARCH IS PRESENTED, HAS THE ORIGINAL DATA BEEN DISTORTED BY EITHER OMISSION OR COMMISSION?

The consumer of research will, from time to time, come across summaries of research which will present data in a reduced form. The reduction of the data is usually done with the intent of retaining its primary characteristics. But just as easily, the data can be transformed in such a way as to highlight a certain point of view while playing down another. Through the use of a selective omission technique, writers without integrity can present data in such a way that their characteristics are distorted. Typically, this is done quite skillfully—writers do not change any of the data: rather they might report a portion of them conveniently neglecting other portions, or report them in a visual display which is misleading. Some writers believe it is not dishonest to engage in such devious activities. This text, however, takes the view that truth is the *whole* truth, as well as nothing but the truth, or, as the old Yiddish proverb states, "A half truth is a whole lie." The consumer of research should make every effort to obtain the original data for perusal. If this is impossible, then the consumer should be very wary of summaries of research.

There is little defense against a writer who is an out and out fraud save examination of the raw data or replication of the study. But for the devious presentations which do not exactly lie, but rather merely distort, we can be on guard to look for some common practices. In the readings at the end of this chapter will be found several excellent thorough treatments of this problem. In the short space provided here we will discuss a few frequently encountered distortions.

Graphics

In order to make a more effective presentation data are sometimes transformed from their raw state to tabular format and further to a graphic presentation. This is often done with the intent of presenting the data in a format in which comprehension is enhanced. Sometimes, however, a graphic display tends to distort the data. It is suggested that when data are presented graphically that the accompanying data in tabular form be scrutinized to determine if the graphic is a reasonable representation of the data. There are three popular methods of data distortion using graphics.

1. The floating zero

The meaning of data can be distorted by charting them on a graph without a zero point. For example, suppose researchers have data on the enrollment of students in the nursing program at XYZ college during the years 1970–1976. The data are presented in table 11.13.

Figures 11.1 and 11.2 are graphic presentations of these data. Figure 11.1 shows the enrollment figures on a vertical axis which ranges from 0–130. Figure 11.2 shows these same data, but the range of the axis is restricted from 70–100. Both graphs are accurate representations of the data, but figure 11.12 by focusing upon the restricted range shows the increase very dramatically. If one does not carefully note the calibration on the vertical axis, one might get the impression that during the years 1970–76 enrollment in this nursing program started from nothing and then skyrocketed.

2. The stretched axis

The distortion of the data as shown in figure 11.2 was accomplished not only by the restricted range of the vertical axis, but also by stretching out the calibration of the axis from ¼″ equals 10 units in figure 11.1 to ¼″ equals 2½ units in figure 11.2 The same restricted range might be utilized without stretching the axis as shown in figure 11.3, but the effect is not nearly as dramatic. Another effect can be had by stretching the horizontal axis instead, as shown in figure 11.4. This has the effect of showing slow but steady growth. Thus we see that the same data may be represented accurately on four different graph arrangements, each with its own special characteristics. Figures 11.2 and 11.4 show how the angles can imply great change or stability respectively.

The question now is which of these graphs presents the data most honestly. Probably figure 11.1 is the most conservative and from that point of view the least distorted, hence the most honest. But the others are just as accurate and the choice of which to use depends on the message the writer wants to get across. If a department chairman seeks more money for his program from a college president, then the chart in figure 11.2 would serve him well. But if a college president

Table 11.13

Year	Enrollment
1970	75
1971	80
1972	84
1973	80
1974	85
1975	89
1976	98

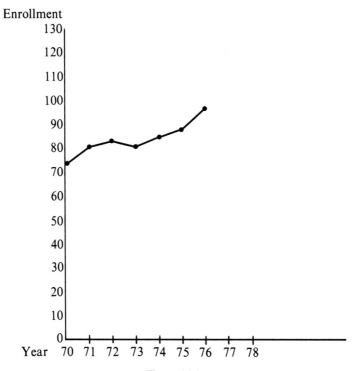

Figure 11.1.

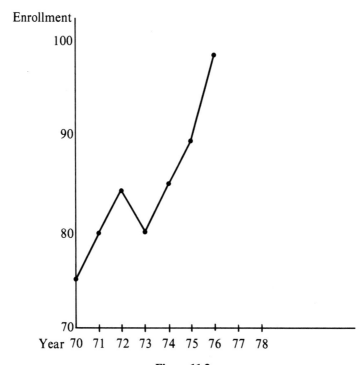

Figure 11.2.

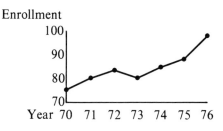

Figure 11.3.

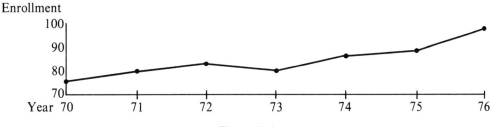

Figure 11.4.

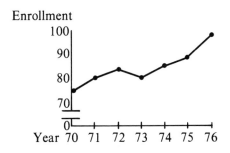

Figure 11.5.

wanted to show the department chairman why such funds were unnecessary, then she might use the chart in figure 11.4 effectively.

One way to get around the restricted range problem and still keep the graph small is to construct the graph with a *zero* break to show that the actual range of possible enrollment does go down to zero. This is shown in figure 11.5.

3. Deceptive scale comparisons

When two sets of data are to be considered together, they can be made to appear to be comparable by selective scaling. For example, suppose the teachers of Bottomville Heights are seeking a pay increase because their class size has increased substantially over the year while their salaries have not. The relevant data are presented in table 11.14.

Table 11.14

Year	Average Salary	Average Class Size
1977	$13,000	22
1978	$14,500	28

The board of education could respond with the charts shown in figures 11.6 and 11.7. To the naive observer, it appears that the salary increases have increased in exact proportion with the increase in class size: the identical 45° slope in both graphs gives this impression. But the more astute observer notes that the scaling of the vertical axes of these two graphs is not comparable. The change in the average teacher's salary in figure 11.6 is from $13,000 to $14,500—an increase of $1,500 or 11% of the lower figure. The change in the average class size for the same period as shown in figure 11.7 was from 22 to 28—an increase of 6 or 27% of the lower figure. The percent of increase in class size is more than double that of teachers' salaries. The same deception could be used if the class size had increased from, say, 22 to 34—an increase of 12 or 54%. Figure 11.8 shows this.

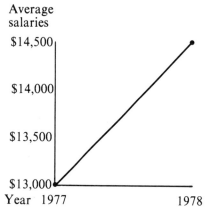

Figure 11.6.

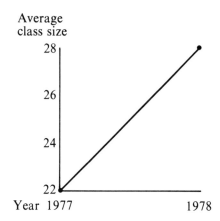

Figure 11.7.

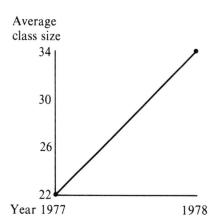

Figure 11.8.

218

Percentages

A useful way of making data easily understandable is to express them as a percentage. In essence, a percentage is a way of stating a quantity in terms of a proportion of a base of 100. Thus, 646 affirmative responses out of 1,219 can be stated as 53% which we recognize as a little more than half. But the use of percentages may obfuscate as well as elucidate as shown here.

1. Partial information

A mental health clinic proudly claims a success rate of 75% of its clients. They forgot to mention though that they only accept mild cases of depression; all the severe cases go down the block to the county clinic whose success rate, as might be expected, is much lower. A survey of 73 doctors reveals that 80% prescribe Brand A laxative. The researcher neglects to mention that this was the 26th survey they took; in all the rest of the surveys the figure was much lower.

2. Unknown sample size

A survey of new parents shows that 75% use disposable diapers on their infants. Does this 75% represent 3 out of 4, 30 out of 40, 1500 out of 2,000? Without this information we cannot judge whether the sample was adequate to insure representativeness.

3. Changing the base

This is a common deception which often goes unnoticed. Suppose in 1975 the daily occupancy at Central Hospital averaged 250 beds. In 1976, the occupancy rate fell 20%, but in 1977 it gained 20%, so now it is back to 250 beds. Or is it? Let's examine this in tabular form with the number of beds occupied indicated in actual numbers as well as percentages. This is shown in table 11.15. Examination of the actual numbers in table 11.15 shows that the increase of 20% did not cancel out the previous decrease of 20%. This is because the 20% increase was calculated on a base of 200, while the 20% decrease was calculated on a base of 250.

Manufacturers and retailers use this principle to minimize their profit margin when it is in their best interests to do so. For example, if an item costs $5.00 and is sold for $7.50, the $2.50 mark-up can be expressed as a) a percentage of cost in which case the mark-up is 50% ($2.50 mark-up divided by $5.00 cost) or b) a percentage of selling price in which case the mark-up is 33% (2.50 mark-up divided by $7.50 cost).

Two additional brief warnings: 1) Be wary of any data presented with excessive precision such as "82.87% of our sample said that. . ." Such precision is misleading: it purports great accuracy to a technique which is replete with large error possibilities. 2) Be very cautious in taking too seriously the accuracy of the results of public opinion polls conducted by nationally known pollsters. Their sampling techniques are generally very good, but they suffer from question bias, noncooperative respondents and insufficient reliability of those who do respond. Furthermore, the pollsters themselves should be examined for bias in the same manner in which evaluators are scrutinized.

Table 11.15

Year	Average Daily Occupancy	Percent Change
1975	250	——
1976	200	−20
1977	240	+20

Summary

Statistical procedures called *inferential statistics* enable researchers to infer characteristics of a population from data obtained from a sample. The basic approach is to compute the difference between the means of two or more groups and divide this by the error which is a part of the data. The *t* and *F* statistics result from such a procedure. The t test is employed when two sets of data are involved. The F test is used for two or more sets of data in a simple or factorial Analysis of Variance. An F test is also used in Analysis of Covariance which controls pre-existent differences in intact groups through statistical means.

An analysis of the differences between frequencies can be accomplished by means of the chi-square procedure. This is used to determine if two sets of frequencies are independent of one another, or if a set of frequencies fits well a hypothetical expected set of frequencies.

Two correlation coefficients can be tested to determine if they are significantly different from one another. A single correlation coefficient can be tested to determine if it is significantly different from zero.

When research is summarized it is sometimes presented in graphs which may distort the characteristics of the data. This can be easily accomplished by a floating zero, stretched axes, and deceptive scale comparisons. Percentages may be presented deceptively by providing partial information, or by changing the base from which the percentage was computed.

The following questions need to be asked by consumers when they encounter analyzed and interpreted data:

IF INFERENCES WERE MADE FROM A SAMPLE TO A POPULATION, WAS THE INFERENCE JUSTIFIED BY A TEST OF STATISTICAL SIGNIFICANCE?

IF FREQUENCIES ARE PRESENTED, HAVE THE OBTAINED FREQUENCIES BEEN COMPARED TO THE EXPECTED FREQUENCIES BY A TEST OF STATISTICAL SIGNIFICANCE?

IF A CORRELATION COEFFICIENT(S) HAS BEEN PRESENTED HAS IT BEEN TESTED FOR STATISTICAL SIGNIFICANCE?

IF A SUMMARY OF DATA WAS PRESENTED, WAS THE SUMMARY AN ACCURATE AND COMPLETE REPRESENTATION OF THE DATA?

Further Readings for Chapters 10 and 11

Campbell, Stephen K. *Flaws and Fallacies in Statistical Thinking.* Englewood Cliffs: Prentice-Hall, 1974.
This is a highly readable and entertaining explanation of how statistics are abused in research.

Guilford, J. P. *Fundamental Statistics in Psychology and Education.* New York: McGraw Hill, 1965.
This is a classic in the field written by one of the leading figures in psychology. It is computationally oriented and contains excellent explanatory material.

Huck, Schuyler W., Cormier, William H. and Bounds, William G. Jr. *Reading Statistics and Research.* New York: Harper and Row, 1974.
This book was also written for consumers of research and contains excellent explanatory material in statistics. Part II will be of special interest to readers of this text.

Kerlinger, Fred N. *Foundations of Behavioral Research.* New York: Holt, Rinehart and Winston, 1973.
A very intensive treatment of data analysis is contained in this text.

Reichard, Robert S. *The Numbers Game.* New York: McGraw-Hill 1972.

   Although written for an audience of business oriented readers, this text provides a thorough treatment of the uses and abuses of statistics. Another text by the same author entitled *The Figure Finaglers* deals with the same content, but in a more generalized research setting.

Ullmann, Neil R. *Statistics: An Applied Approach,* Lexington, Massachusetts: Xerox, 1972.

   This text assumes no prior knowledge of its readers and develops their understandings of statistics from general concepts to specific usages. Very readable.

Wheeler, Michael. *Lies, Damn Lies, and Statistics, The Manipulation of Public Opinion in America.* New York: Liveright, 1976.

   This is a thorough investigation of the workings of public opinion polls in America. It discusses their effects as well as the techniques involved; the politics of polling is discussed frankly.

Wright, R. L. D. *Understanding Statistics: An Informal Introduction for the Behavioral Sciences.* New York: Harcourt Brace Jovanovich, 1976.

   This text is similar in many respects to the Ullmann text listed above. It too stresses the concepts of statistics but with a highly visual and light-hearted approach. In addition, it is organized in such a way with self-tests and problems that it is nearly self-teaching.

Glossary of Symbols

This glossary contains symbols and abbreviations found in educational research reports. Each term represented by a symbol follows the presentation of the symbol itself. A further explanation of many of these terms may be had by referring to the body of the text through use of the index.

Symbols are used by researchers to present information in a concise way. Many of the symbols typically used are presented here, but other symbols we encounter are occasion-specific. For example, researchers often use letters, A, B, C and so on in order to refer to particular variables in their studies. Similarly, subscripts are used to distinguish between similar elements: for example pretest and posttest means may be presented as $\overline{X}_{pre}$ and $\overline{X}_{post}$ or as $\overline{X}_1$ and $\overline{X}_2$. The explanation of occasion-specific symbols is usually presented immediately before or after the presentation of the symbols themselves. A careful reading by the consumer will usually allow for a correct interpretation of the symbols.

$>$ — greater than

$<$ — less than

$\times$ — "by", as in 4 $\times$ 3, read "four by three"

% ile — percentile

σ — standard deviation

σ^2 — variance

α — alpha: level of significance

χ^2 — chi square

μ — population mean

' — adjusted (when used with MS or SS)

' — predicted (when used with X or Y or any letter symbolizing a variable)

ANACOVA — analysis of covariance

ANOVA — analysis of variance

b — between

d — difference

df — degrees of freedom

E — experimenter

f — frequency

F — a value resulting from a test of significance

$F_{.05}$ or $F_{.01}$ — value of F at the .05 or .01 level of significance

H — a value resulting from a Kruskal-Wallis analysis of variance

H — hypothesis

H_o — null hypothesis

m — mean

M — Mean

MANOVA — multivariate analysis of variance

Md — Mode

Mdn — Median

MS — mean square

N — number

n — number

ns — not significant

p — probability

r — correlation coefficient

$r_{1,2}$ — coefficient of correlation between variables 1 and 2

r_s — Spearman correlation coefficient

r^2 — cofficient of determination

R — multiple correlation coefficient

R — range

rho — Spearman correlation cofficient

s — standard deviation

s^2 — variance

S — subject

Ss — subjects

SS — sums of squares

sig. — significant

sigma — standard deviation

SD — standard deviation

t — a value resulting from a test of significance

$t_{.05}$ or $t_{.01}$ — value of t at the .05 or .01 level of significance

T — a value resulting from a Wilcoxon test of differences

T — a standard score

U — a value resulting from a Mann-Whitney test of significance

w — within

$\bar{x}$ — mean

$\overline{X}$ — mean

z — a standard score

Z — a standard score

Appendix B
Non-parametric Tests of Significance

Non-parametric statistical tests are encountered in the research literature usually when the type of data collected does not lend itself to analysis using the more typical parametric tests. Parametric tests assume that data are interval (continuous) and that they represent populations whose measurements on a given attribute are more or less normally distributed. It is further assumed that the variances of the groups of data are more or less the same. When these assumptions are not met, researchers will often use non-parametric procedures to analyze their data.

In the body of this text the most frequently encountered non-parametric test of differences, the chi-square test, was explained in some detail. In this section, six other tests encountered somewhat less frequently by consumers will be presented. In each of these tests, the data are analyzed, a statistic computed and a comparison is made between the computed statistic and the tabled values of that statistic. On the basis of that comparison a statement of the level of significance of the computed statistic is made. This is interpreted in exactly the same manner a level of significance is interpreted when it is derived from a parametric test.

Sign Test

The Sign Test is used with two correlated (dependent) sets of scores. The "sign" refers to a plus or minus sign used to determine gain or loss from one score to another, such as from pretest to posttest. The number of pluses and minuses are noted and analyzed, and the likelihood of the findings happening by chance are determined through the use of tabled critical values. This is one of the simplest tests of significance to compute and comprehend.

Wilcoxon Matched-Pairs Signed-Ranks Test

This test is similar to the Sign Test described above. It also is used with correlated data but is considered more powerful than the sign test because it considers the magnitude of the difference between each pair of scores as well as the direction of the difference. This test is comprised of an analysis of the difference between each pair of scores, a ranking of the differences and the computation of a value. The obtained T value is compared to tabled values of T to determine the level of significance assigned to the obtained T.

Median Test

This is another relatively simple test of differences between sets of scores, but unlike the Sign or Wilcoxon Tests, the median test is used for two (or more) sets of scores from *different* subjects. In essence, all scores are combined and a median from the combined distribution is found. Then the scores are separated into the two original distributions and a count is made for each distribution of how many scores are above and below the combined median. This has the effect of dividing the two distributions into four cells. Then a chi-square analysis is performed and interpreted as is usually done.

Mann-Whitney U

The *Mann-Whitney U* test like the median test described above, is applied to sets of scores from different subjects. The procedure begins with ranking the scores of each distribution and determining which group of scores generally ranks lower. This analysis yields a *U* statistic which may be compared to tabled values to determine significance.

Kruskal-Wallis One-way Analysis of Variance

When there are more than two groups to be analyzed for differences, the Kruskal-Wallis *H* statistic is useful. In this procedure all scores considered together are ranked; then the scores are divided into their original groupings and the rankings are added. After further manipulation of these data, an *H* statistic is derived and is compared to the critical values of chi-square to determine significance.

Friedman Two-way Analysis of Variance

This technique is used with three or more sets of data from the same subjects. The scores of each subject are ranked subject by subject and are analyzed to obtain a calculated value which is compared to tabled values of chi-square.

There are still other non-parametric tests in existence but their appearance in the research literature is so rare that they will not be mentioned here. The text suggested below may be inspected for further information.

Further Reading

Seigel, S. *Nonparametric Statistics.* New York: McGraw-Hill, 1956.
 This is the standard reference source for non-parametric statistics.

Appendix C

Multivariate Analyses

A variety of procedures are grouped under the heading of *multivariate analyses*. These procedures have three characteristics in common: they analyze several variables and many subjects at one time, they use correlational procedures and their computation is very complex. A complete and thorough understanding of these procedures requires an extensive background which most readers of this text will not possess. As consumers of research however, we may become acquainted with the techniques to the extent that we understand the procedures in principle and are aware of the uses-interpretations and abuses-misinterpretations when we encounter these procedures in the research literature we peruse.

Two major groups of multivariate procedures frequently encountered in research are *factor analysis* and *profile analysis*. Examination of table C.1 is helpful in showing the similarities and differences between them.

Table C.1 shows a *data matrix*. In this matrix there are fifteen subjects (1–15) represented on the vertical axis; there are ten variables (a–j) represented on the horizontal axis. The scores for each subject on all variables appear in the rows running left to right. The scores for each variable on all subjects appear in the columns running top to bottom. *Factor analysis* examines the relationship among the variables—it focuses on the columns and the interrelatedness of the data

Table C.1. Example of a Data Matrix

Subjects	a	b	c	d	e	f	g	h	i	j
1	14	23	17	9	6	21	2	4	18	27
2	10	15	14	38	8	25	15	4	33	62
3	50	25	20	33	9	28	14	2	32	37
4	42	24	18	22	6	24	9	14	40	53
5	38	22	17	25	5	15	7	12	12	48
6	37	33	8	18	4	52	17	4	11	39
7	16	7	14	35	14	19	3	10	12	60
8	29	19	6	18	10	16	20	11	15	38
9	24	12	3	17	8	28	18	14	37	35
10	47	25	18	19	7	33	12	14	36	45
11	42	30	15	10	15	37	15	8	28	52
12	19	31	10	15	12	42	9	7	23	29
13	12	14	11	12	14	60	14	3	32	37
14	38	16	7	18	9	33	10	12	38	51
15	17	8	9	20	10	54	10	13	29	48

in the columns; it is concerned with how the *variables* cluster. On the other hand, *profile analysis* examines the relationship among the subjects—it focuses on the rows and the interrelatedness of the data in the rows: it is concerned with how the *subjects* cluster. Both factor analysis and profile analysis can be performed on the same data and use similar techniques, but they represent procedures which seek to answer different questions.

Factor Analysis

In the understanding of any science, a knowledge of the relationships among variables is essential. In the social sciences, particularly psychology, the variables encountered are extremely complex and interrelated. It is no wonder then, that *factor analysis* was developed by psychologists in their attempt to understand the cognitive and affective components of human beings. Factor analysis is a procedure that developed in order to provide mathematical models for the explanation of theories concerning human behavior and abilities. It is exploratory and descriptive and as we shall see later, it is fraught with problems of interpretation.

Before describing the uses of factor analysis we need to understand the term *construct* (accent on the first syllable). A construct is a hypothetical, broad human attribute; examples are intelligence, self-concept, anxiety. It is hypothetical because it needs to be inferred from observable behaviors. For example, what is intelligence? One could argue circularly (as some do) that intelligence is the attribute measured by an intelligence test. This however is not very helpful in understanding intelligence. We could look at an intelligence test and see what is being measured. We might find that the test is composed of measures of vocabulary, computational ability, memory, and others. Each of these measures may be considered a minor variable which is a part of a superordinate variable we choose to call intelligence. If we were to devise our own intelligence test what might it be comprised of? We might ask, "What does an intelligent person do?" or "How would you know an intelligent person from an unintelligent person?" We might say that an intelligent person is a person who can cross a busy street without getting run over, compute rapidly without pencil and paper and anticipate the morals to each of Aesop's Fables. Each of these three abilities may be considered a variable which is a part of the construct intelligence. Thus a construct may be defined as a label given to a collection of variables which comprise it. A construct is said to be hypothetical because its existence can only be inferred by the presence of its constituent variables. Indeed, different sets of variables are often given the same label; inspection of the composition of different tests supposedly measuring intelligence will show this clearly.

Uses of Factor Analysis

The development of constructs is an attempt to satisfy the laws of parsimony needed in any science. In psychology especially, where the variables are many and complex, the reduction of a group of related variables to a single construct is a noteworthy and essential achievement. Factor analysis is a key procedure in this endeavor. It may be used to search for a construct in a group of potentially related variables, or identify and explain the variables in known constructs or develop tests to measure constructs.

Factor analytic studies are found most often in the field of personality. This is not surprising since the development of a subject's personality is a combination of a myriad of complex social and genetic variables. In order to understand what is involved in factor analysis, let us take a problem in personality from inception to conclusion, step by step.

228

Let us suppose that we want to explore the construct *extroversion*. We seek to determine its constituent variables and the relative effect each variable has on the construct. Our first step is to select the variables we believe might be a part of it. We ask ourselves, "How would we know an extrovert if we saw one?" Well, he or she would be friendly. Is that it, though? Are all friendly people extroverts? No, they are also talkative. And so first we develop a list of these specific attributes, friendliness, talkativeness and others, then we find or develop instruments to measure each, and finally we test a large sample of subjects with each instrument. Each test is a measure of a variable. The scores of each subject on each test comprise the raw data which will be organized into a data matrix and from which the factor analysis will proceed.

Our second step is to compute the correlations of each variable with each of the other variables. For ease of inspection, all the obtained correlation coefficients are presented in matrix form. Table C.2 shows a correlation matrix of the eight variables we have chosen* to use in our exploration of the extroversion construct. The correlation coefficients for each pair of variables are found in the rows and columns of the matrix. Variable 4, Lack of Nervousness for example, is found to correlate .67 with variable 3, Talkativeness. Variable 8, Egocentricity correlates .07 with variable 4, Lack of Nervousness and so on. Inspection of the coefficients in this matrix shows some substantial relationships among the variables as well as some negligible ones. This encourages us to go further in our analysis.

The third step is the *extraction* of the factors. By means of a computational procedure based upon the idea of partial correlation, the interrelationships among the variables are analyzed and it is determined how the variables cluster. Each cluster of variables is called a factor, and variables are clustered for as long as they share interrelatedness. Usually two or three factors will account for almost all the commonality in a group of eight variables. Table C.3 shows a matrix of extracted factors. The eight variables are listed in the left column from top to bottom; the three factors indicated by roman numerals are in the three remaining columns. The coefficients in the matrix show the correlation of each of the eight variables with each of the three factors. For example, variable 5, Inner Security, correlates with Factor I .60, with Factor II .30, and with Factor III .36. Each variable-factor correlation is called a *loading;* for example one speaks of variable No.

Table C.2. A Correlation Matrix of 8 Variables of Extroversion

Variables	1	2	3	4	5	6	7
1. Need for other people							
2. Friendliness	.63						
3. Talkativeness	.41	.45					
4. Lack of Nervousness	.30	.21	.67				
5. Lack of Fear	.57	.48	.41	.47			
6. Desire for Acceptability	.14	.59	.33	.12	.23		
7. Inner Security	.23	.73	.11	.73	.68	.15	
8. Egocentricity	.13	.22	.51	.07	.32	.28	.57

*Note the specific use of the word "chosen" in this context. As will be discussed later, this has an important effect on our interpretation of the completed factor analysis.

3, Need for Other People, having a loading of .41 on Factor I. These factor loadings show the extent to which each variable is related to a given factor. Variable 3 shows a moderate loading (.41) on Factor I, a substantial negative loading ($-.64$) on Factor II, and a small negative loading ($-.14$) on Factor III.

Further inspection of table C.3 shows the presence of many loadings in the 30s, 40s and higher. This would represent a considerable overlap among variables which is to be expected since the variables were chosen because they were thought to be related to the construct Extroversion. Our problem now is to manipulate the data in such a way as to differentiate the factors.

The fourth step is the *rotation* of the extracted factors. This rotation procedure manipulates the data in such a way as to maximize the loading of any one variable on one and only one factor. The effect of the rotation procedure is to make maximum distinction between the factors and show which variables contribute most heavily to the formation of which factors. Table C.4 shows a rotated factor matrix based on our eight variables of Extroversion. Note how the loadings on these rotated factors compare with the loadings on the unrotated factors in table C.3. For example, in the unrotated matrix, Variable 1, Friendliness was shown to have loadings of .47, $-.71$ and .03 on Factors I, II, and III respectively. The loadings of .47 and $-.71$ are substantial loadings. But on the rotated matrix, Variable 1 loads .70 on Factor I and merely .03 and .10 on Factors II and III. Thus the two substantial loadings on the unrotated factors are transformed to one substantial

Table C.3. An Unrotated Factor Matrix.

	Factors		
Variables	**I**	**II**	**III**
1. Friendliness	.47	$-.71$	.03
2. Lack of fear	.39	$-.62$	.10
3. Need for other people	.41	$-.64$	$-.14$
4. Lack of nervousness	.49	.31	.35
5. Inner Security	.60	.30	.36
6. Talkativeness	.45	.21	.47
7. Desire for Acceptability	.38	.25	$-.10$
8. Egocentricity	.54	.27	$-.23$

Table C.4. A Rotated Factor Matrix.

	Factors		
Variables	**I**	**II**	**III**
1. Friendliness	.70	.03	.10
2. Lack of fear	.73	$-.09$	$-.05$
3. Need for other people	.74	.13	.17
4. Lack of nervousness	.02	.65	.21
5. Inner Security	.05	.71	.28
6. Talkativeness	.10	.65	.18
7. Desire for acceptability	.01	.10	.45
8. Egocentricity	$-.04$	.23	.60

loading on the rotated factor. This makes an interpretation much easier. Also note in table C.4 how the rotation procedure has separated the factors. In the unrotated matrix, for example, Factor I showed loadings of the eight variables ranging from .38 to .60. But after being rotated as shown in table C.4, Factor I shows only three high loadings, .70, .73, .74 on variables one, two, and three respectively. Variables four through eight show negligible loadings on this factor. Similarly, the rotated Factor II shows three high loadings, .65, .71 and .65 and variables four, five and six; and low loadings from the remaining variables. Factor III shows two variables, seven and eight loading highly while the other variables do not. Thus the process of factor rotation shows us that Factor I is comprised mostly of Variables one, two and three; Factor II is comprised mostly of Variables four, five and six, and Factor III is comprised mostly of Variables seven and eight. We have effectively maximized the loadings to make more clear which variables go with which factors. Now the data are more useful to us in understanding Extroversion, and we have fulfilled our need for simplicity and parsimomy.

The fifth and final step in our analysis is the interpretation of the rotated factors. We need to examine each factor, identify the variables which load on it and then assign a name to it. The name for a given factor can be a combination of the names of the variables of which it is comprised, or the name could be a new label which would subsume the variables involved. In an example, Factor I which is loaded on Friendliness, Lack of Fear, and Need for Other People, might be named *Gregariousness*. Factor II which is loaded on Lack of Nervousness, Inner Security, and Talkativeness might be labelled *Confidence* and Factor III which is loaded on Desire for Acceptability and Egocentricity might be called *Ego-orientation*.

It is at this point, the interpretation of the analysis, that our project is complete. We set out to explore the construct Extroversion, and we found out that the eight variables we selected to describe it were indeed interrelated, and furthermore grouped themselves into three factors which we called Gregariousness, Confidence, and Ego-orientation. This may help us and others understand Extroversion. We accomplished this understanding by imposing a mathematical model on our data in an effort to explain it and reduce it. But mathematics is not reality but merely a language which seeks to describe reality. And there is more than one mathematical model which can be employed. Now we have to ask ourselves, "Is this what extroversion really is?" This is what we call it, but is this what it really is? Are the eight variables we started with the only ones that could be used or are there other variables which we did not use which would correlate even higher than the ones we did use? Will our description of the construct Extroversion hold up to the test of reality? Factor analysis alone cannot answer these questions. Continued addition of potentially useful variables must occur to satisfy our questions concerning the completeness of the variable list. And the construct must be tested against reality through the use of appropriate validation procedures. Factor analysis is the beginning of knowledge not a final result, and as such it requires some follow up analysis to be of value ultimately. Factor analysis explores and describes—it does not confirm.

Evaluating Factor Analysis Studies

As was indicated earlier, the computational procedures used in factor analysis are complex and difficult. It is easy for the consumer to get involved in or intimidated by the complexities of the analysis, and neglect to ask some very basic questions about the data themselves. Our first concern should be with the quality of the raw data—the scores of the subjects on the variables used in the analysis? Who were the subjects and under what conditions were the scores obtained?

Were the tests reliable and valid? Were the tests independent of one another? This is important to know because sometimes in personality measurement different tests share items in common; this has the effect of forcing correlations when in truth none may exist. Another concern we should have deals with the obtained correlations between the variables. Were the assumptions for using the correlational procedures met (e.g. linearity, distribution equivalence, etc.)? Were the coefficients sufficiently large to be useful? This is important because it is mathematically possible for two variables to have a very low correlation with one another, yet both have high loadings on a factor.

If we find that we can have reasonable confidence in the raw data and in the obtained correlations we still have a mammoth problem which is inherent in the entire procedure known as factor analysis. The problem may be introduced by suggesting that factor analysis should not be considered as *a procedure,* but rather as a generic name for *a number of similar procedures.* Factors are said to be *solved* when they are analyzed, but there are many possible solutions to a factor analysis, each solution depending upon the particular method of factor extraction and rotation employed. There are several ways of extracting factors: common are the centroid, principle axes and square root methods. And then there is no agreement on how many factors should be extracted. And finally there are several methods of rotating the factors: orthogonal and oblique methods with many possibilities in each category. We readers of factor analytic studies are left with the question of which choice did the researchers make and why did they make that particular choice. There is no agreement as to which is the "best" method or which procedures yield the "best" solution. The "best" method may be one in which the researchers have a preference or vested interest.

The "best" solution may be the one which explains the data in accordance with the researchers' biases. And to complicate matters further, all methods used are mathematically equivalent!

What this tells us is that a given correlation matrix may yield many different but mathematically equivalent solutions; each solution may be interpreted differently. A given solution may be more acceptable to one researcher than another, but it is purely judgmental that one method is preferable to another. This leaves the reader in a dilemma as to how much confidence to have in *any* factor analysis. And to make matters worse, there are not that many people with the time and interest who also have the expertise in factor analysis to challenge or reanalyze the results of the factor analytic studies found in the literature.

Yet, with all these problems factor analysis is a useful way of explaining and simplifying complex interrelationships. As consumers, we must understand its weaknesses, however, as well as appreciate its strengths.

Profile Analysis

In the previous section, we saw how factor analysis may be used to explore relationships among *variables* seeking to cluster them into groups of variables called factors. Profile analysis is a group of methods which seeks to explore relationships among the *subjects;* it seeks to cluster the subjects into groups which have certain characteristics in common. The uses of these techniques are found in psychiatry, psychology, counseling, personnel selection and other fields where typology and/or placement of subjects is a major concern. Profile analysis is the generic term for two methods of grouping people. One method is concerned with a problem in which a researcher has data on subjects and wants to know which subjects "stick together" on certain variables. Those which do stick together constitute a group. This technique is called *profile clustering.* On the other hand, if a researcher already knows which of the subjects are in which groups, then the concern is to be able to distinguish these known groups on the basis of their scores. This technique is called *discriminate analysis*. Both techniques use similar computational procedures and like factor analysis they suffer from problems in interpretation.

Profile Clustering

The profile clustering technique starts with subjects who have not been classified into groups. Then a variety of measurements are collected on these people and based upon the relationships among the measurements the subjects are grouped. For example, suppose researchers are interested in exploring the personality types found in a college freshman class. They first select the variables to be considered, such as extroversion, anxiety, emotional stability, friendliness, activity level, etc. Then the subjects are tested on each variable. With these data—the scores for each subject—the profile clustering proceeds. One of the two basic methods may be employed: a) a *distance* measure which considers the distance of one person's scores from another or b) a *factor analysis* of the subjects' sets of scores. The findings of either of these analyses would be a grouping of the students into, say, two groups: active/excited and passive/reflective. Often the findings are presented in graphic form.

Profile clustering is most useful in the development of classification schema or taxonomies. But like factor analysis the description of the findings is highly theoretical; it needs to be validated through use in the real world. For example, a profile clustering technique could be used for distinguishing between neurotic and psychotic patients on the basis of measurements taken on them. But when other people from outside the sample used in the analysis are tested, will they fit into the hypothetical groups? The assessment of validity is a necessary follow up to the original analysis. As suggested above adequate sampling is extremely important in profile clustering. Replication of a study with other samples is appropriate in order to bolster confidence in a profile clustering study. Also, the variables used in the analysis should be relevant, perhaps theoretically based, in order to be included in the analysis.

Discriminate Analysis

Discriminate analysis is the other side of the profile analysis coin. This technique is used when the sample is comprised of subjects already classified into groups. The problem for the researchers is to analyze the subjects' scores so that the groups may be easily distinguished from one another. For example, suppose researchers have identified good and poor readers in a sample and want to understand their differences on a set of relevant variables such as intelligence, self concept, verbal ability, etc. Data are collected from both groups on these variables and a special type of factor analysis is performed to derive a cluster of weighted variables called a *discriminant function*. This *discriminant function* is in essence a factor, the first discriminant function explains the most about the variables, and the second and third ones derived explain less and less.

There are two major uses of discriminant analysis. It may be used for placement. For example, if a reader's scores on the set of variables correspond to say, the characteristics of the poor readers, then he or she may be *placed* in that group. On the other hand, discriminate analysis may be used to *understand* the characteristics of the groups. *Placement* usage has many problems chief among which is the problem of overlap: does the discriminate function provide sufficient separation between the groups to allow placement with a measure of confidence. Perhaps the better use of discriminate analysis is the *understanding* of the relationship among the variables to the groups.

All the problems inherent in the interpretation of factor analysis discussed above apply to profile analysis: selection of variables, relationship with reality, characteristics of raw data, etc. As a result, these methods are not often encountered in the literature. This brief presentation will serve to alert the consumer of research to the existence of these methods and the care needed in utilizing the results.

Further Readings

Nunnaly, Jum C. *Psychometric Theory,* New York: McGraw Hill, 1967.

A deeper understanding of the theories underlying correlation, multivariate analysis, factor analysis and discriminate analysis will be found in Nunnally's text. The reading is not easy and requires some background in algebra but the explanatory comments are excellent. Chapters 4, 5, 9, 10 and 11 are most germane to the content of this section.

Harmon, Harry H. *Modern Factor Analysis*. Chicago: University of Chicago Press, 1976.

Horst, Paul. *Factor Analysis of Data Matrices*. New York: Holt, Rinehart Winston, 1965.

Mulaik, Stanley A. *The Foundations of Factor Analysis*. New York: McGraw-Hill, 1972.

The uses and abuses of factor analysis are presented in the first chapters of each of these texts. (The texts themselves in their entirety are meant for the most advanced students who have extensive backgrounds in mathematics). The first chapter of the Harmon text includes an interesting history of the technique and discusses its applications and limitations. Chapter one of the Horst text has a good non-mathematical introduction. It also discusses the role of data in science and presents the objectives and applications of the technique. The Mulaik text's first chapter has a nice introduction and an example.

Messick, Samuel and Jackson, Douglas, *Problems in Human Assessment*. New York: McGraw-Hill, 1967.

This book of readings contains two excellent articles: Eysenck, Hans J. "The Logical Basis of Factor Analysis." This has still another good explanation of factor analysis. Guilford, J. P. "When not to factor analyze." The author presents several *caveats* to research producers which are of interest to us as consumers.

Appendix D
Evaluating Educational Research

The focus on this text has been to develop a research consumer's ability to read educational research critically. This appendix attempts to draw all this information together to enable readers of reserach to evaluate systematically the research they encounter in the professional literature of their fields. Having so evaluated research, readers will be able to estimate the degree of confidence they can place in the research findings and thus use them intelligently.

It has been the point of view of this text that there is no one way of finding truth. The various methods of experimental and descriptive research, the variety of measurement devices which could be employed, the many possible analytical techniques available, all have their place in the research enterprise. Each procedure has its strong and weak points. A major issue of concern for consumers is whether a given research study used the best approach and procedures for the research question being investigated. This is a judgment that is made by the reader, but if the contents of this text have been understood, the judgment will be an informed one rather than an arbitrary one.

There are no universally accepted standards for evaluating research, indeed the state of the art is quite rudimentary. Most existing instruments are designed only for experimental research and consist of a check-list type format dealing with procedural matters such as sampling, control of extraneous variables, completeness of reporting, etc. These matters are analogous to the relationship between the reliability and validity of a test: reliability is a necessary but not sufficient condition for validity. This text takes the point of view that the procedural matters in a research study, important as they may be, must be judged in an overall framework of its validity. That is, the basic issues surrounding a study must be considered to be at least as important as the procedural issues, if not more so. The rating schema presented below was conceived in accordance with this view.

The Content of the Schema

The rating schema is organized into three levels: Level I is concerned with some basic overall issues in a research study. Level II deals with the research report itself—its organization and inclusiveness. Level III deals with the nitty gritty procedures involved in the study—what the researchers did.

It will be noted that a judgment concerning the importance or significance of a study is not included in this schema. This is a deliberate omission, made to reflect the realities of the research scene. The fact is that most consumers of research are not sufficiently knowledgeable about a given field to make a good judgment of this sort. And even to those who are knowledgeable, a given study may or may not seem important, depending upon the interests and biases of the individual consumer. For example, some studies are so narrow in scope or otherwise limited as to seem virtually useless. Yet in combination with other studies of similar scope they may be a genuine contribution to the literature. In another dimension, a study might appear to have no apparent application to anything, yet it could at some future time contribute to the development of a theory which itself would find application. Of course, a decision concerning the importance of a study may need to be made by a funding agency to determine if the money for funding a study is to be well spent. But for the purpose of most consumers who seek to determine the veracity of completed research, the question is best not considered.

Each question in each level of the schema is followed by a rating scale, and each level or part is given an overall rating based upon the ratings of the questions in it. You will note that the final rating of each of Levels I and III is the lowest rating given to any of its component questions. In its computation, the overall rating of the entire research study can be no higher than the lowest of ratings of individual questions in Levels I and III. Thus, if one question in Levels I or III is given a very low rating, the overall rating for the entire study will suffer accordingly. This may seem unduly harsh, but the fact is that all the components of a research enterprise must fit together. A chain can not be stronger than its weakest link. If a study is perfect in all respects but one, say, the sample was biased or an invalid test was employed, the one weakness has the effect of contaminating the entire study and potentially rendering its findings useless.

Remember that this schema is designed to evaluate a research study in terms of the veracity of its findings; in other words, can these results be believed? It is not meant necessarily to cast aspersions upon the researchers who may have done the best they could. A low return rate from a mailed questionnaire or the use of the only instrument available which unfortunately has unknown qualities—these are not necessarily to be blamed on the researchers. They should be given due credit for the effort if the best that could have been done was indeed done.

The Limitations of the Schema

This rating schema is not precise. No attempt has been made to weigh the various elements included according to their importance. Moreover, many ratings require judgments on the part of the raters, and these will be subject to the idiosyncracies of the individual raters. Also not all consumers, not even the most sophisticated ones, will have all the necessary background and information to rate each and every question presented. Accordingly, the best use of this schema is to focus the consumer's attention in a short, summary form on the various aspects of a research study which could influence the veracity of its findings. Each question should be answered as best it can with whatever information is available bearing in mind that in this life, truth may be approached and estimated but never unmistakably determined.

Rating Schema for Evaluating Educational Research

Instructions: Read the research report carefully and critically. Respond to each of the questions by circling a rating *Excellent, Good, Fair, Poor*. If the question is not applicable to the research study, circle *N/A*. If the information is not available, thus unknown, circle *U*. The final rating for the entire research study is an estimate of the confidence that can be had in the veracity of the research study's findings.

Level I—*Basic Issues*   *Rating*

1. How reasonable are the assumptions—
   explicit and implicit—upon which the
   study is based?   Excellent Good Fair Poor U N/A

2. How well does the research problem fit
   into a context of theory, practice, or other
   research?   Excellent Good Fair Poor U N/A

3. How consonant is the research strategy
   with the research problem?   Excellent Good Fair Poor U N/A

4. How qualified and unbiased is the re-
   searcher?   Excellent Good Fair Poor U N/A

5. In a formative evaluation, how knowl-
   edgeable and unbiased is the evaluator? Excellent Good Fair Poor U N/A

6. In a summative evaluation, how inde-
   pendent and unbiased is the evaluator?   Excellent Good Fair Poor U N/A

Enter here the *lowest* of these six ratings _____

Level I

Level II—*The Research Report*

1. How succinct and unambiguous is the
   statement of the research problem?   Excellent Good Fair Poor U N/A

2. How reasonable are the operational defi-
   nitions of the terms?   Excellent Good Fair Poor U N/A

3. How fully reported are the procedures
   employed in the study?   Excellent Good Fair Poor U N/A

4. How intelligible is the research report? Excellent Good Fair Poor U N/A

Enter here the *average* (median) of these four ratings _____

Level II

Level III—*The Procedures*   *Rating*

A. Design and Sampling

1. In an experimental study, how well did
   the design control threats to internal and
   external validity?

History	Excellent	Good	Fair	Poor	U	N/A
Maturation	Excellent	Good	Fair	Poor	U	N/A
Pretesting	Excellent	Good	Fair	Poor	U	N/A
Instrumentation	Excellent	Good	Fair	Poor	U	N/A
Regression	Excellent	Good	Fair	Poor	U	N/A
Selection	Excellent	Good	Fair	Poor	U	N/A
Mortality	Excellent	Good	Fair	Poor	U	N/A
Experimental Participation	Excellent	Good	Fair	Poor	U	N/A
Multiple Treatment Effect	Excellent	Good	Fair	Poor	U	N/A

2. In a longitudinal study, was there an implicit or an explicit selection bias?
   Excellent   Good   Fair   Poor   U   N/A

3. In a longitudinal study, was the initial
   sample sufficiently large and representative?
   Excellent   Good   Fair   Poor   U   N/A

4. In a cross sectional study, how well were
   the variables of history and selection considered?
   Excellent   Good   Fair   Poor   U   N/A

5. In a survey, was the sample sufficiently
   large and representative?
   Excellent   Good   Fair   Poor   U   N/A

6. In a survey, was the response rate sufficiently large to retain the qualities of the
   original sample?
   Excellent   Good   Fair   Poor   U   N/A

Enter here the *lowest* of these fourteen ratings   _____

Level III A

B. Instrumentation   *Rating*

1. Was the measurement instrument used the best way to obtain data relevant to the purposes of the study?   Excellent   Good   Fair   Poor   U   N/A

2. Are the assumptions upon which the measurement instrument is based reasonable?   Excellent   Good   Fair   Poor   U   N/A

3. Is the level of inference required in order to proceed from the data to the attribute sufficiently low to justify a description of the attribute?   Excellent   Good   Fair   Poor   U   N/A

4. If a measurement instrument is generally considered valid, is its use in this specific research study valid?   Excellent   Good   Fair   Poor   U   N/A

5. Is the measurement instrument appropriate for the specific subjects to whom it was applied?   Excellent   Good   Fair   Poor   U   N/A

6. Is the measurement instrument sufficiently sensitive to measure the attribute or a change in the attribute if a change indeed occurred?   Excellent   Good   Fair   Poor   U   N/A

7. Was the measurement instrument administered properly?   Excellent   Good   Fair   Poor   U   N/A

8. In a cross sectional study, how accurate were the data based on recollections?   Excellent   Good   Fair   Poor   U   N/A

9. In a survey, how unbiased was the measurement instrument?   Excellent   Good   Fair   Poor   U   N/A

10. In an evaluation, how appropriate, meaningful and varied were the types of data?   Excellent   Good   Fair   Poor   U   N/A

11. In a cross cultural study, did the researchers possess the special competencies to operate effectively in an unfamiliar culture?   Excellent   Good   Fair   Poor   U   N/A

Enter here the *lowest* of the 11 ratings   _____

Level III B

C. Analysis and Interpretation   *Rating*

1. How complete and appropriate is the description of the data?   Excellent Good Fair Poor U N/A

2. If inferences were made from a sample to a population, was the inference justified by a test of statistical significance?   Excellent Good Fair Poor U N/A

3. If frequencies are presented, were the obtained frequencies compared to the expected frequencies by a test of statistical significance?   Excellent Good Fair Poor U N/A

4. If a correlation coefficient(s) was presented was it tested for statistical significance?   Excellent Good Fair Poor U N/A

5. If the data were transformed from nominal to ordinal or interval, was the transformation and subsequent analysis reasonable and appropriate?   Excellent Good Fair Poor U N/A

6. In a cross cultural study, was the necessary data available and comparable?   Excellent Good Fair Poor U N/A

7. In a trend study, was an observed trend temporary or permanent?   Excellent Good Fair Poor U N/A

8. In a trend study, was the trend of the variable being studied independent of other significant variables?   Excellent Good Fair Poor U N/A

9. In a trend study, were the sets of data used truly comparable?   Excellent Good Fair Poor U N/A

10. In a casual comparative study, was the inference of causality (if any) reasonable?   Excellent Good Fair Poor U N/A

11. In a correlational study, was a statement of a causal relationship between the variables avoided?   Excellent Good Fair Poor U N/A

12. If a summary of data was presented, was the summary an accurate and complete representation of the data?   Excellent Good Fair Poor U N/A

Enter here the *lowest* of these 12 ratings _____

Level III C

Rating for the entire research study (Enter here the lowest of the four ratings: Level I, II, IIIA, IIIB, IIIC.) _____

Index